TOPICS IN MANAGERIAL ACCOUNTING

TOPICS IN MANAGERIAL ACCOUNTING

Second Edition

Edited by

L.S.ROSEN
York University

McGRAW-HILL RYERSON LIMITED

Toronto   Montreal   New York   London   Sydney
Johannesburg   Mexico   Panama   Düsseldorf   Singapore
São Paulo   Kuala Lumpur   New Delhi

TABLE OF CONTENTS

III.   CORE ACCOUNTING TECHNIQUES AND MANAGEMENT EVALUATIONS   139

VI.   SOME EXTENSIONS 369

QUESTIONS 401

PREFACE

This collection of readings is directed towards persons taking
their first or second course in management accounting at the
undergraduate or graduate level. Most of the main themes of the material
and reasons for selecting specific articles are explained in the intro-
ductions to each of the six sections of the book—especially to
Sections I, II and III.

The principal point of most of the articles is that management
accounting procedures ought to be tailored to the specific use which is
to be made of the information. This is such a common-sense theme;
yet, it is amazing how much classroom time and the variety of
examples that are required to get most people to appreciate reasons for
the theme. Probably the uphill battle is directly traceable to the
way financial accounting is traditionally taught, and accounting is
perceived. Somehow students enter courses with the belief that they will
come out knowing the *one,* universal way of accounting for management's needs. Most of the articles herein are thus selected to
counteract this unwarranted belief. Where possible, articles have been
selected which (a) provide illustrations of how accounting affects
decisions, and (b) show the relationship between specific decisions and
specific accounting techniques. Most of the introductory editorial
comment and exhibits are directed at these same objectives. Questions
about each reading probe relationships between accounting techniques
and management evaluations, as well as follow the usual approach
of forcing people to read portions of the article.

Editors of books of readings seem to be frequently asked to
justify existence of the book. The following additional observations
about this book are offered:

(a) Behavioral viewpoints are still not widely incorporated into
accounting textbooks; many class-tested behavioral topics are
presented herein.

(b) Practical and humorous examples often help persons to retain
concepts; a large percentage of the articles were selected with this
thought in mind.

(c) Controversial topics and recent developments may not appear
in textbooks, but are reprinted throughout this collection—especially
in Section II.

(d) Not all authors of textbooks can claim to be well-versed in all
topics they are expected to cover in their book; the writings of others
well-recognized for their expertise in a particular subject are thus worth
assigning to classes.

Successful use of a book of readings usually depends upon
whether the material is integrated with the principal textbook for a
course, and (unfortunately) upon whether questions on readings
are likely to appear on examinations. Exhibits III-1 and III-2 attempt

ix

to provide a cross-reference between articles and typical topics in management accounting courses. Sample questions about each article appear on pp. 401 to 412; and a response manual is available to instructors.

Many instructors and students gave me helpful comments about articles proposed for, or eventually used in, both this and the first edition. I am grateful to the following people for observations on portions of the material: T. Beechy; D. T. DeCoster; J. Dewhirst; T. Gilbert; B. M. Harnden; H. A. Kennedy; C. L. Mitchell; J. R. E. Parker; C. Schandl; M. J. Vertigan; J. Waterhouse; and anonymous reviewers for McGraw-Hill Book Company. Principal thanks must be reserved for the authors of articles and editors of journals who kindly gave me permission to reprint their material. R. J. Chambers deserves special mention for volunteering to amend his original articles specifically for readers of this book. Mrs. Pauline Geldart and Mrs. Dawn Amar cheerfully performed the secretarial tasks.

Comments from users will be appreciated.

York University   L. S. ROSEN
Toronto, Canada

Contributors*

R. L. Ackoff	University of Pennsylvania
R. N. Anthony	Harvard University
T. R. Archibald	University of Western Ontario
S. W. Becker	University of Chicago
A. Buckley	Consultant
E. H. Caplan	University of New Mexico
R. J. Chambers	University of Sydney
A. T. Demaree	*Fortune*
W. L. Ferrara	Pennsylvania State University
J. M. Fremgen	U. S. Naval Postgraduate School
M. H. Gilbert	Ernst & Ernst
H. R. Givens	Babson Institute
D. Green, Jr.	University of Chicago
H. C. Greer	Consultant
C. H. Griffin	University of Texas
J. C. Hayya	Pennsylvania State University
J. A. Higgins	Arthur Andersen & Co.
W. C. House	University of Arkansas
R. K. Jaedicke	Stanford University
W. S. Kallimanis	Boise Cascade Bags and Specialty Products
J. C. Lere	Illinois State University
C. J. Loomis	*Fortune*
R. K. Macleod	Lybrand, Ross Bros. & Montgomery
E. McKenna	Twickenham College of Technology
V. F. Ridgway	Colorado State University
A. A. Robichek	Stanford University
G. H. B. Ross	Touche, Ross & Co.
R. F. Vancil	Harvard University
W. J. Vatter	University of California, Berkeley
R. Villers	Consultant
M. Weiss	New York Institute of Technology
M. C. Wells	University of Sydney
T. H. Williams	University of Texas

* Noting the position of each at the time his article was written.

I
Introduction and Overview

A typical course in management accounting at an introductory/ intermediate level attempts to show how a management accounting system or technique can help managers make specific evaluations. Management may be required to make decisions about such matters as:

1. **Performance appraisal.** How efficient and effective was/is the actual performance of specific individuals when compared to some yardstick(s) of expected performance?

2. **Pricing.** How much should the company charge its customers for each product it manufactures, or service it performs? Is it necessary to provide additional services, such as low interest rate financing? (If the company is not a price leader, but is a follower, it does not have to face a pricing decision. Management's decision is an output one — do I produce or not at the current selling price?)

3. **Output.** What products should be manufactured or services performed, and at what levels of capacity? Should some components of a product be bought rather than manufactured?

4. **Financing.** How much money does the organization need at what date and for how long? Should funds be obtained from a bank, bondholders, stockholders, or from whom?

5. **Investment.** Which (generally, long-lived) assets should I sell, buy, or replace at what dates? In order to be more competitive, should some manual operations be mechanized? Which, of several competing assets, should be acquired?

6. **External reporting.** What accounting information is needed to furnish reports to owners and creditors as well as to government agencies?

1

7. **Income, manufacturing and other taxation.** How can various taxes be minimized while keeping within the spirit/letter of the law?

8. **Market area.** In which geographical areas is the company able to sell at a profit, given relatively known transportation costs?

9. **Record keeping.** How can the costs of bookkeeping (paying payables, recording receivables and cash entries, and so forth) be minimized while still maintaining adequate internal control in the system?

Management accounting techniques which are likely to be encountered in introductory/intermediate textbooks, and which may aid in the aforementioned evaluations, include: contribution margin analysis, cost-profit-volume analysis, budgeting, variable costing, return on investment, discounted cash flow analysis, standard costing, responsibility accounting, actual costing, full or absorption costing, process costing, job order costing, and many others.

Accounting information derived from applying the foregoing techniques should be combined with relevant data from many fields, such as economics, quantitative methods, psychology and sociology, in order to make sound decisions about applicable management evaluations. In some organizations the most important decisions may be pricing and performance evaluation while in others financing and record keeping could be the pressing problems. As several authors in this collection of readings state: the accounting system must be tailored to the specific, crucial problems of an organization. Crucial is used to denote those aspects of the organization which must be monitored continuously so as to help ensure survival and success.

In view of the number of techniques that could be claimed to be under the management accounting umbrella, large amounts of text space are required at the introductory/intermediate level simply to illustrate the mechanics of each technique. In what time and space remain, the author(s) of a text then attempt to stress the prime theme of showing what technique is best suited to which management evaluation, and under which conditions. A management accounting technique which appears successful for performance evaluation of one group of employees of a hospital may prove virtually useless in a repetitive manufacturing activity. Similarly, the management of one particular company may require several techniques to be built into its accounting system: three techniques for performance evaluation, two for pricing, one for external reporting, and so on.

Considerable learning effort must be placed on understanding which accounting techniques aid which management evaluations; otherwise, the course can easily become a mass of unrelated concepts. This book of readings attempts to bridge the potential comprehension gap between management evaluation and management accounting technique. The principle employed in this book is simply to have another one or two writers — other than the author(s) of the main textbook used in the course — explain relationships. Often a slightly different slant to a subject is all that may be required to trigger the vital first step towards comprehension.

Section I is a mixture of introduction and an overview which leans heavily towards the behavioral viewpoint — one not presented in much depth in some textbooks. The material may thus be read at various places throughout the course, with the behavioral pieces being especially worthy of thought after any lengthy technical section in the course on subjects such as standard cost variance analysis or process costing.

The first two articles are from the magazine *Fortune* and describe how parts of two large businesses have been managed in recent years. These descriptions should be particularly helpful to persons who may not have had much prior exposure to the environment of large businesses. A general reading only is prescribed early in an accounting course because technical business terms are abundant. At some later stage a group discussion of each case will aid integration of several accounting and business topics.

"RCA After the Bath" initially provides necessary background and then explains how a decision was made to invest heavily in manufacturing computers, how subsequent financial controls and accounting feedback on actual performance proved inadequate or was improperly interpreted, and how the decision was made — relying heavily on cash and profit projections — to abandon the venture (often called "taking a bath"). The tragedy helps to provide insight into the role accounting might play in an overall corporate information system, but particularly makes clear the need to tailor accounting techniques to management's needs. (" 'Speaking of the inadequacy of RCA's financial controls,' Donegan recalls, 'I hadn't seen what was happening. The group financial staff hadn't seen it. The corporate financial staff hadn't seen it. The outside accountants who were in our skivvies hadn't seen it. The trouble was they were all used to seeing a cash sales business'.")

"Harold Geneen's Moneymaking Machine Is Still Humming" makes many references to accounting while describing recent management procedures at International Telephone and Telegraph Corp. (ITT). Of particular interest are the explanations of possible relationships between accounting and stock market prices, the effect of accounting policies on net income, and the controllership relationships employed by I.T.T. ("Many analysts also believe that I.T.T.'s profit record is just too good to be true." " 'We simply don't manage earnings. I'll put it in blood if that'll help.' " ". . . I.T.T.'s unique controller set-up . . . has elements of a spy system. . . .") The case oozes with comments on how accounting may be used in business decisions, and how accounting must interact with the environment of business.

The next three articles set the stage for the assessment of specific management accounting techniques. In their different ways all the pieces address the prime theme of which factors should be reviewed in tailoring management accounting techniques to specific management evaluations. Anthony's "Framework for Analysis" distinguishes management control from strategic planning and technical control, and stresses the need for identifying when each of these three planning and control subsystems has sensible application. A very large portion of most introductory/intermediate management accounting courses tends to deal with the management control system. As Anthony states, mistakes occur when generalizations used in conjunction with either strategic planning or technical control are applied to management control. Buckley and McKenna, and Caplan, follow up on one of the possible broad mistakes which could be made — not giving sufficient attention to the human element in managerial control systems. This may often occur through treating a particular management accounting technique as a technical control device.

"Budgetary Control and Business Behaviour," originally pubished in England, reviews the writings of several organizational theorists and then sets out some practical suggestions for implementing budgetary control systems. Persons who have had some exposure to behavioral sciences should find the summaries particularly helpful, even though they may disagree, in places, with the coverage of the authors. The article is strong in providing a behavioral setting for management accounting and is not totally restricted to budgeting. Caplan expands upon the economic-man-versus-administrative-man theme raised early in Buckley and McKenna's work. Caplan wonders whether currently popular management accounting systems and various management accounting techniques are based on a realistic view of organizational behavior. Perhaps many of the techniques noted in management accounting textbooks have undesirable side effects, and thus hinder — not, on balance, help — management in important evaluations, such as performance appraisal.

1

RCA After the Bath

ALLAN T. DEMAREE*

> Things are looking up since Bob Sarnoff
> elected to take that epochal $490-million
> write-off, but there still are questions
> about his company's basic strategy.

RCA, a company that took one of the biggest losses in business history
last year, stands at a decisive turning point. So, for that matter, does
Robert W. Sarnoff, the man who runs it. In leading his company out of
computers, Sarnoff had to write off $490 million, but he averted a
financial crisis and got the company out of a business that had lost $90
million after taxes over five years. Now RCA is recovering, along with
the economy, and Sarnoff was able to report profits of $40 million in the
latest quarter — the first record quarter the company has had in three
years. But Sarnoff is still wrestling with some deeper problems about
RCA's basic strategy and "personality."

Justly famed as the pioneer of radio and television, RCA has traditionally concentrated its efforts in communications and electronics. Since
Sarnoff succeeded his father, the late Brigadier General David Sarnoff,
as chief executive in 1968, he has been building the company into what
can fairly be described as a conglomerate (though Sarnoff himself resists
the word). "The most trusted name in electronics," as RCA has billed
itself, remains heavily committed to its traditional businesses, but it
also rents cars, manages real estate, and makes carpets and TV dinners.
Physically, it is a company that little resembles what the General left
behind.

Beyond that, Sarnoff has been trying to change the company's
strategic outlook, its whole approach to doing business. Under the
General, no one doubted for a moment that RCA was a scientifically
oriented company; the needs of technological breakthroughs were the
basic source of earnings growth. Since he succeeded his father, Bob
Sarnoff has been trying to turn RCA into a market-oriented company.
Rather than rely on breakthroughs, Sarnoff wants a company that begins
by analyzing the needs of the market, draws on largely existing technology to produce what is needed, and then does a bang-up job of selling —

* Reprinted from the September 1972 issue of *Fortune* by special permission; © 1972
Time, Inc.

something that the General's RCA was rarely accused of doing. The change has meant a massive internal shift in power, away from the scientists and engineers and toward the marketers and product planners. It has torn at RCA's most cherished traditions and met embittered resistance from many old-timers. Sarnoff has so far encountered several setbacks and it is by no means certain that his efforts will ultimately achieve success.

One particular problem about his new strategic concept is that Sarnoff himself has not been entirely clear or consistent in implementing and talking about it. Even while trying to move the company away from his father's traditions, he has at times nurtured the mystique of high technology and sought to rival his father as a grand pioneer. And, unfortunately, the most conspicuous example of this "backsliding" was his single greatest failure — the venture in computers. It seems clear, in retrospect, that Sarnoff became entangled in computers largely because of a rather unfortunate analogy that he drew between them and color TV — the inevitable model of a business success at RCA and his father's crowning achievement.

A kind of parallel

Like color TV, computers had about them the glamour of high technology and big gambles; the investment was high and the payoff potentially large, though distant and uncertain. The analogy was defective in several ways; for one thing, RCA really had very little to contribute to computer technology. Still, even in defeat Sarnoff has linked his biggest decision in computers with the decision his father took in turning color TV into a triumph. "A hell of a lot of people disagreed with my father going ahead with color," he recalled recently. "It took a certain amount of courage and guts and he stayed with it. There is a kind of parallel in a way. It took courage to get out of computers."

Sarnoff's ambivalance about the company's strategy — his effort to break with the past and at the same time to emulate it — has until now produced such a poor financial record that it seems almost surprising that he has kept control of the company. The computer write-off reduced RCA's net worth by nearly a quarter, and last year's profits from continuing operations (i.e., the noncomputer businesses) came to little more than three-quarters of what they were before Sarnoff succeeded his father — $129 million, on sales of $3.5 billion. Directors of other large corporations have thrown out managers whose records were no worse than RCA's. (General Dynamics and International Paper are examples that come to mind.)

Yet Sarnoff has so far retained the support of his board of directors — save for a single dissident, Martin B. Seretean, who also happens to be an RCA executive and its biggest shareholder (he owns or controls 1,425,414 shares, versus Sarnoff's 79,338). "Bud" Seretean (pronounced Sair'-a-teen) acquired his stock and his seat on the board by selling

Coronet Industries, his carpet and home-furnishings company, to RCA last year. Like the General, Seretean is the son of immigrant parents, grew up in a modest New York neighborhood, and rose to the top by ability and hard work. As a boy, it happens, he blew the bugle (for $15 a month) at a summer camp sponsored by the Educational Alliance, a charity of which the General was himself a beneficiary, and later a benefactor.

Seretean makes no bones about being a stickler for performance. "If my operation doesn't cut the mustard," he has told the board, "then fire my ass outa here." Nor does he make bones about his conviction that Sarnoff hasn't cut the mustard. "I find it highly unusual that a management can write off $490 million and no one seems to question whether the same people ought to be running the company today," he says.

Seretean badgered Sarnoff to abandon the computer business several months before it was in fact abandoned. He has continued to criticize top management for maintaining a large, expensive corporate staff and for "failure to correct inferior performance" in several of the company's principal businesses — consumer electronics, N.B.C., and Hertz. The criticism has added impact because the earnings of Coronet, which Seretean still runs, have set records quarter after quarter, growing over 25 per cent so far this year.

But Seretean's shareholdings come to less than 2 per cent of RCA's outstanding stock, and the man himself has little leverage on the board. The directors, including the seven outsiders (out of seventeen), have been rather unreceptive to Seretean's views ("I have leprosy," he jokes) and they are inclined to give Sarnoff another chance. "The education of a chief executive is not always inexpensive," one outside director has observed philosophically.

Sarnoff himself has enough confidence in his own strength to talk of Seretean with considerable condescension. "Mr. Seretean is one of the finest rug merchants in the country," he says. "In a way, it's kind of exciting that in America you can do this kind of thing. But he is a relative newcomer to this company and I don't think that what he says or thinks is of great moment." Asked if he will fire Seretean, Sarnoff answers with a smile: "He reports to Mr. Griffiths (Edgar H. Griffiths, executive vice president) and Mr. Griffiths reports to Mr. Conrad (Anthony L. Conrad, president). I doubt that I would reach down that far."

Decisive and proud like his father, Sarnoff at fifty-four is also shy and sensitive by nature, with a quiet manner and a somewhat sardonic sense of humor. Cut from different cloth than the stereotypically single-minded businessman, Sarnoff thoroughly enjoys his leisure time and appreciates the arts. Twice married and twice divorced, he lives in an exquisitely furnished apartment overlooking the East River in Manhattan, where he is cared for by a Chinese couple and is the master of two shih tzu dogs. He dresses with elegance, owns a share in a restaurant in Venice, and surrounds himself with the paintings and sculpture of such modern artists as Max Bill, Alberto Giacometti, and his own close friend Enrico Donati.

"I was running things on my own"

As a young man, Sarnoff at first rejected the idea of a career in the company that his father built; his achievements would inevitably be credited to the General's influences, his failures measured against the General's success. But after Harvard, the Navy during World War II, and a brief stint with Cowles Publications, he took a job with RCA's broadcasting subsidiary, N.B.C. He began as a time salesman for network television when there barely was a network ("I was the expert on Howdy Doody," he says), moved through jobs in production and films, and was largely responsible for getting N.B.C. to produce *Victory at Sea*. Colleagues saw him as a sound if unsensational businessman who had developed an inner toughness about the endless behind-the-back allusions to his dependence on his father.

After eight years, when Bob was thirty-seven, the General named him president of N.B.C., an appointment that naturally gave him the "crown prince" label, and led to wisecracks about the swiftness of his rise. As head of N.B.C. for a decade, Sarnoff strove to establish his own autonomy. "One of my problems," he says, "was convincing people outside N.B.C. that I was running things on my own. I guess Tom Watson [Thomas Watson Jr. of I.B.M.] went through the same thing."

At times, Sarnoff's relations with his father were strained by personal disagreements. A former colleague remembers a time in the late Fifties when the two men communicated mainly through third parties. (Bob himself says that exaggerates the situation.) His brother Thomas, then and now an N.B.C. executive on the West Coast, disagreed with some of Bob's policies and carried his arguments directly to their father, which did little to improve family relations. Time gradually soothed the strains and Bob now refers to his father fondly as "the Gen." In 1966, when color TV was booming and the Sarnoff name was at its height, the General made his son president of RCA, and Bob succeeded his father as chief executive two years later.

At that moment, RCA was in trouble, but few people knew it. Extraordinary profits from television obscured basic weaknesses. RCA's traditional electronics and communication businesses were rapidly maturing. Profits from the sale of color TV sets were about to hit a peak and slide down a long slope. Sarnoff had to move RCA into new, faster-growing businesses and find a source of profits to replace color TV. He decided that the best prospects were acquisitions and computers.

Simultaneously, Sarnoff decided that there had been a fundamental shift in the electronics environment, and it was this more than anything that led him to undertake the drastic reshaping of RCA into a marketing company. Though the notion seemed heresy, he came to believe that the age of the big breakthrough in consumer electronics — the age in which the General had built RCA — had passed. "The physicists have discovered about all they are going to for consumer applications in the near future," says James Hillier, himself a renowned physicist who oversees RCA's laboratories in Princeton, New Jersey. Major inventions that filled obvious consumer desires, such as television, simply weren't in the cards anymore. Or, as one executive puts in in a marvelously mixed metaphor: "There is no genie in the bottle coming along on a great white charger down in Princeton."

If the chances of major inventions were in fact diminished, Sarnoff concluded, RCA could no longer count on maintaining a proprietary lead through technology. One company's product would be about as good as another's, and marketing would be critical to success. The change fit well with Sarnoff's own predilections. While his father doted on technology, he himself had a natural liking for advertising and design.

Up from mushrooms

Reshaping the company for this new role has been no simple task. Sarnoff installed a big headquarters staff to help him plan what markets to enter and what to produce. Seretean criticizes this staff on the grounds that it is expensive and unproductive, and that it interferes with the heads of operating divisions, who ought to be allowed to run their own businesses. Sarnoff redirected the efforts of the research laboratories, which were still thrashing about in efforts to make another breakthrough like color TV, and he shifted the emphasis from basic to applied research on specific products that fit his marketing goals. That effort appears to have been successful, after a period of low morale in which some scientists were making cracks about the labs being RCA's "mushroom factory" — where they were kept in the dark, fed a lot of manure, and finally canned.

Sarnoff painfully but properly reduced the autonomy of the divisions, which had operated as independent fiefdoms, and forced them to cooperate in a "systems approach" to developing products. He lopped off a dozen or so money-losing businesses, including 16-mm. projectors, electron microscopes, and marine radios (the first business RCA entered in 1919). Whereas the General had passed up chances to invest abroad, preferring to license his patents and know-how, Bob has tried to transform RCA into a multinational company. In four years he has increased the company's overseas investment by 72 per cent to $79 million, while RCA still receives some $65 million a year in revenues from licensing.

The internal resistance was intensified by Sarnoff's choice of people. In January, 1968, he recruited Chase Morsey Jr., a former director of marketing at Ford. Smooth-talking and persuasive, Morsey in turn recruited others from Ford, I.B.M., and elsewhere, and he soon became a sort of master planner and chief of the vastly expanded staff. He grew close to Sarnoff, and the old guard thought him altogether too powerful, too abrasive, a kind of "executive-suite Rasputin." Some newcomers had doubts about him, too. "Chase has a tendency to shoot from the hip," says William Acker, who came from I.B.M. to become No. 2 man in the computer division, "and once in a while he shoots himself in the foot."

Resentment of Morsey bubbled to the surface in bitter comments that exaggerated his foibles and his passion for golf. Once, when Morsey was absent from a meeting. Howard Letts, the long-time financial vice president, clasped his hands in an interlocking grip, addressed an imaginary ball, and said: "I guess Chase has some more important business having to do with green carpets."

Sarnoff blamed poor salesmanship for the drop in RCA's share of the color-television market, and he rather optimistically thought that more marketing pizazz and better styling would carry the day. Actually, the basic problem was deep-seated and was to some extent beyond Sarnoff's ability to deal with. In a sense, he was being made to pay for a decision of his father's. Back in the early 1960s the General, eager to report high profits (which in fact more than tripled between 1960 and 1967), invested less than he might have in further innovations in color, kept prices high, and in general made it easy for competitors to crowd into the market.

Bob Sarnoff's effort to beef up the company's styling and marketing of color, after he became the boss, turned out to be inadequate to the task. He shuffled around a lot of executives responsibile for color TV and, according to a former RCA man, "Morsey jumped in like a preborn expert." Sarnoff replaced the marketing vice president in consumer electronics at Indianapolis with Donald Dickson, whom Morsey had recruited from Warner-Lambert, where he had, among other things, run the chewing-gum division, American Chicle. Soon Morsey and Dickson were squabbling, and after fifteen months Dickson was sent back to New York. The head of the consumer-electronics business in Indianapolis was forced to resign and his boss in New York took early retirement.

Sarnoff has also built a $2-million design center in Indianapolis, and the consumer-electronics division has introduced some major improvements, such as solid-state sets for greater reliability and more generous warranties. But thus far, at least, the changes have not halted the erosion of RCA's share of the color market; the company now sells 23 per cent of domestically produced sets, versus 30 per cent when Sarnoff began making changes. "In a ship this size, you don't turn around overnight," Sarnoff says, "It takes a long time to make the changes and a long time for the changes to take effect."

Playing Ford to I.B.M.'s General Motors

It was to offset the declining profits in color TV that Sarnoff decided, in 1968, to make computers RCA's first priority. He set out to capture 10 per cent of the U.S. market and to be second only to I.B.M. Until then, RCA had drifted along in computers, ranking fifth or sixth in a field of eight, with a market share of 3 or 4 per cent; with his interest in high profits during the early 1960's, the General had also tried to run the computer business on the cheap. Sarnoff and Morsey thought that better marketing would prove to be the secret of success in computers, and they recruited L. Edwin Donegan Jr., who had been an I.B.M. divisional vice president, to take charge of computer sales. "It was apparent to me, from many conversations that we had," says Donegan, "that computers were to be to Bob Sarnoff what color TV was to his father. The guy who said it sounded reasonable was me."

Morsey sometimes used the analogy that RCA could play Ford to I.B.M.'s General Motors. But remarkably enough, neither he nor Sarnoff at that time calculated how much the strategy would cost or how long it would take to return a profit. For all of Sarnoff's stress on sophisticated business planning, the decision to plunge into computers had more than a touch of the General in it — gut feel and leap of faith were the decision's main ingredients.

A hard-working and likable Nebraskan, Donegan recruited some two dozen I.B.M. executives and tripled the sales force to more than 600. For a time, this rising investment seemed to work miracles. Despite a decline in the industry's sales, RCA's bookings climed 50 per cent in 1969 and 20 percent more in 1970, by which time the company had captured 7.5 per cent of the domestic market. Computers lost money, of course, but less than had been budgeted, and Donegan was promoted to head of the division.

Morsey, meanwhile, had hired Arthur D. Little Inc., the consultant, to develop a strategy for getting up to 10 per cent of the market. A major finding of the Little team was that, in order to capitalize on the next computer-buying cycle. RCA would have to deliver a line of new computers within a year after I.B.M. delivered its expected new series. Too far behind in design to develop a new computer that quickly, Donegan decided that RCA's new line would be its old line. That is, he would spruce up RCA's Spectra series, including some machines that had been returned by customers, equip them with larger memories and new skins (of a design and color scheme personally approved by Sarnoff). Reconditioning the Spectras would get two generations of use out of one generation of machines, and the body-shop operation would cost considerably less than if a computer were developed from scratch. Sarnoff enthusiastically approved the strategy and that marked the high point of Donegan's career.

Sarnoff, meanwhile, was buying up companies. All of the General's acquisitions — from Victor Talking Machine Co. in 1929 to Random House in 1966 — were designed to enhance RCA's powers in its traditional businesses. Bob's strategy was the polar opposite: to diversify into businesses that would grow faster than the traditional ones. He thought that moving more into service industries was a good idea, both because of their growth rate and because they were generally less cyclical and less capital-intensive than RCA's manufacturing operations. But he didn't insist on any particular rationale, so long as the businesses were profitable and well run.

Lazard Fréres, the investment banker, handled four major deals for RCA (for which it received fees totalling $1,925,000). André Meyer, the senior partner at Lazard and a long-time friend of the General, persuaded Bob to acquire Hertz in 1967; the General had earlier resisted the notion. When Meyer retired from the RCA board in 1969, the Lazard board member became Donald A. Petrie, an uncommon sort of investment banker whose strong convictions and caustic tongue were soon to give Sarnoff fits. Petrie worked on RCA's acquisition of three companies: F. M. Stamper (now the Banquet Foods subsidiary), one of the largest U.S. producers of TV dinners and other convenience foods; Cushman & Wakefield, a small, highly profitable real-estate management company that Sarnoff wanted largely to manage RCA's own widespread holdings; and Seretean's Coronet Industries.

Sarnoff paid $578 million in stock for the four companies, and he got his money's worth. In fact, according to RCA, the earnings per share of the acquired companies in 1967-71 averaged 97 per cent more than the earnings per share of RCA's other operations.* The strategy has increased RCA's revenues by more than $1 billion a year and reshaped the company in ways that no one could have imagined a decade ago.

"My job is on the line"

When Sarnoff was courting Coronet in October, 1970, he met Seretean and Petrie for dinner at the Oak Room of the Plaza Hotel in Manhattan. Seretean was concerned about the computer losses, but Sarnoff reassured him. He said that the business would break even the following year, and that by 1975 it would earn $50 million a year before taxes. "But what if it doesn't turn around?" Seretean asked. "Bud," Sarnoff replied, "my job is on the line." It was a remark that Seretean has not forgotten.

Not long after this dinner, Sarnoff's hopes for computers began to crumble. Because of the recession, computer users cut back excess capacity by returning machines to the manufacturers; and Donegan's "new" series simply didn't sell. RCA felt the impact more acutely than other companies because its liberal accounting and financial practices, which had lessened losses in good years, exposed it to greater losses in the downturn. For example, RCA had sold off computer leases at a discount to financial intermediaries, such as Transamerica. This increased RCA's income for the short run, but meant that the company had only a small base of lease customers providing the rental income needed to carry it through hard times.

Monthly reports to the board showed the computer business veering further and further off course. Early in 1971, Sarnoff told the board that the division's business plan, which had been due in January, would be delayed because of difficulty in estimating revenues. Petrie of Lazard was particularly worried. In person and by letter, he repeatedly pressed Sarnoff for explanations of what was going on; but month after month he was put off, and tensions between Petrie and Sarnoff grew. During this period Sarnoff suddenly encountered an unrelated and un-

---

*The calculation is performed by dividing the earnings of the four major acquired companies by the number of RCA shares paid for them and contrasting the results with the earnings of RCA's other operations divided by all the other shares.

suspected health problem. One evening in April, as he was undressing for bed, he passed out and collapsed on the floor. He was suffering from something called bundle-branch block, a condition in which the heartbeat slows to a point at which insufficient oxygen reaches the brain. Sarnoff had a pacemaker implanted and was back to conduct the annual meeting the next week.

What the financial staff didn't notice

In May, Petrie wrote to Morsey, listing a number of fundamental questions about the computer division that he wanted answered at the June board meeting, including questions about accounting techniques, depreciation policies, and financial controls. Petrie, who had gone to an I.B.M. executive training course in hopes of better understanding the computer business, was now coming to realize that RCA's central problem with computers was a financial one; it was, in fact, not dissimilar to the problems associated with other leasing businesses. As a veteran of both the Hertz and Avis organizations, Petrie felt qualified to speak up. But at the board meeting, Morsey still didn't have adequate answers; no one seemed to have them. In fact, Donegan, who had been promoted to head the computer group six months before, was himself only beginning to find out that RCA's liberal accounting policies tended to make the business seem healthier than it was.

Moreover, unlike I.B.M., RCA kept no detailed record on the status of each leased unit — a prerequisite for keeping abreast of the fortunes of a lease-based business. Speaking of the inadequacy of RCA's financial controls, Donegan recalls: "I hadn't seen what was happening. The group financial staff hadn't seen it. The corporate financial staff hadn't seen it. The outside accountants who were in our skivvies hadn't seen it. The trouble was they were all used to seeing a cash sales business."

The June board meeting *did* produce some information, however, and it was pretty shocking. Morsey finally presented the revised business plan, and it forecast a $37-million loss for 1971 — rather than the break-even year that Sarnoff had earlier predicted. Like earlier plans, it also forecast that the computer business needed outside financing of more than $500 million over the next five years.

Seretean erupted. He challenged RCA's assumption that I.B.M. would give up part of its market without cutting prices. Donegan and Morsey defended the assumption — "People thought G.M. would crush Ford," Morsey argued — but Seretean wasn't convinced. "I can think of two dozen things I would rather spend $500 million on," he concluded.

As it happens, Morsey was on especially shaky ground in defending his position because I.B.M., had *already* startled the rest of the computer industry by an unprecedented price cut. The cut mainly affected peripheral equipment, and the RCA executives had not yet had a chance to analyze its impact on their own company. The cut turned out to have a devastating effect, making it just about impossible for RCA to claim that it offered a price advantage to its customers.

On July 1, Morsey, with Sarnoff present, gave a special presentation on the computer business to Petrie and Stephen M. DuBrul Jr., a partner from Lehman Brothers, RCA's other investment banker. (DuBrul has since moved over to Lazard.) The presentation answered the questions that Petrie had been asking earlier. "I think I finally understand the computer business," Petrie told Sarnoff afterward. "My recommendation is that you get out right now because, in my professional opinion, you can't raise the half-billion dollars you will need to finance it." Sarnoff disagreed.

Just like the sunrise

The profits from many of RCA's other businesses, which had long helped to finance the computer venture, were now in decline. The recession was, of course, a major factor; but it is significant that RCA's biggest businesses were performing worse than their competitors.

Profits from consumer electronics had dropped 64 per cent in five years, while the profits of the company's principal competitors either declined less or rose. All the networks suffered from the loss of cigarette advertising, but N.B.C.'s profits were off considerably more than the broadcasting earnings of C.B.S. or A.B.C. While profits at Avis rose 23 per cent in 1971, Hertz profits dropped 38 per cent, because of what even RCA concedes was mismanagement. RCA's semiconductor business, small and rarely profitable, was ravaged by a general industry decline and lost some $24 million before taxes, twice what had been forecast.

During the first two weeks of September, a few high RCA officers contacted the other major computer manufacturers, except I.B.M. and Honeywell, to see whether they might be interested in buying the business *if* RCA decided to sell. There were no satisfactory offers. Meanwhile, RCA was losing more and more money. It was building a new computer headquarters in Marlboro, Massachusetts, which was costing $80,000 a day for construction, and it was transferring employees there at a cost that had reached almost $2 million. Donegan, who knew nothing of RCA's contracts with other manufacturers, began to suspect something strange was going on when he couldn't get Sarnoff's approval to respond to I.B.M.'s price cuts. A meeting of RCA's demoralized computer salesmen, scheduled to announce the company's response to I.B.M. in early September, was postponed. Sometime during this period, Sarnoff came to the conclusion that RCA had to abandon the business, even if no buyers materialized.

On September 16, he and four other officers gathered in his office. One of those present was Morsey, whom Sarnoff had recently made financial vice president and a member of the board. Now the guardian of the corporation purse, Morsey had made another estimate of computer losses, and he forecast that they would nearly double to $70 million, with no profits forecast until 1976. Those present all agreed with Sarnoff's decision to get out. Recalls President Anthony Conrad, who was intimately involved: "It was like the sun rising in the morning. Suddenly the path was pretty clear. . . . I've never seen a decision so osmotically come to pass."

Sarnoff now had to move quickly. Robert Werner, RCA's respected and powerful general counsel, told Sarnoff that since the management had reached a consensus, the company risked suits from customers and shareholders it it didn't put the question to the board immediately and then disclose its intentions to the public. For security reasons, when Sarnoff called an extraordinary board meeting for the next afternoon he refrained from telling many directors what the meeting would be about; they learned when they entered the room. They had no real choice but to vote yes or no — get out or stay in. If they delayed action, Werner advised, RCA would be legally required to announce that it was *considering* a decision to get out — a statement that would undermine RCA's credibility as a supplier and force it out of the business anyway.

The directors had little difficulty making up their minds once they heard the bad news, which Sarnoff let Morsey deliver. Morsey said that the computer division's five-year cash needs had escalated to $700 million and that the demands of other parts of the business would bring RCA's total requirement for outside financing to more than $1 billion. RCA was already carrying $996 million in debt (including debt that Hertz financed separately), and there was a distinct possibility RCA couldn't raise the additional $1 billion. It would have little trouble, Morsey said, if its profits grew at 10 per cent a year, but if they grew at only 7 per cent, or if a recession occurred at any time in the next five years, RCA could encounter "severe financing problems."

The meeting lasted two hours and twenty minutes. The vote to get out was unanimous. The most extensive debate concerned the wording of the press release that RCA would issue; Sarnoff proposed that the startling amount of the loss be omitted, but other directors argued that the amount be reported, and they prevailed. As the meeting broke, Petrie displayed his sense of humor. "Well, Bob," he asked, "aren't you going to say it's another RCA record?" Three months later, Petrie resigned from the board and from Lazard; he is now treasurer of the Democratic National Committee.

"Making a buck as fast as you can"

The decision has at least rid RCA of the specter of financial crisis; Sarnoff now sees no need for outside financing for several years. He hopes to get RCA earnings growing at a rate of at least 10 per cent a year and, in the near term, he has good prospects for doing so as the sales of TV sets and ad revenues at N.B.C. improve with the economy. Sarnoff has put new managers into the driver's seat at Hertz, and he says that the turnaround they are expecting will produce a record year in that business. Univac bought the computers that RCA had out on lease, for a down payment of $70 million, and Sarnoff expects the additional payments from Univac to exceed RCA's earlier estimates of $60 million. (The increased payments, if they materialize, would lower the amount of RCA's computer write-off, but they would not, under the company's accounting system, increase reported earnings.)

If Sarnoff keeps on the track of 10 per cent earnings growth, RCA will generate some $500 million internally, which it can invest in developing new businesses over the next five years. But the computer venture has left Sarnoff somewhat chastened, and a new spirit of caution pervades the company. "There is considerably less willingness to make massive investments that will pay out way off in the future," says James Johnson, a former I.B.M. vice president who succeeded Morsey as head of marketing. "Now the emphasis is on getting into new businesses for as little as possible and making a buck as fast as you can."

The biggest investments Sarnoff plans are in regulated communication businesses. He bought the Alaskan telephone system for $28 million last year and is committed to invest another $28 million in it over the next few years. Somewhat more venturesomely, he expects to ask the board to authorize the spending of $150 million on a domestic satellite-communication system, which the company could launch alone or, as is more likely, in partnership with others. In other businesses, where the risks are high (and the potential for profit great), RCA is placing what one executive calls "a lot of half-dollar bets." Translated, that means investments of $500,000 to $10 million or so — still a long way from the hundreds of millions that RCA sank into computers.

And now for the next color TV

Nevertheless, Sarnoff seems to keep feeling the tug to rival the General and to come up with "another color TV." When he is asked what that will be, now that his dreams for computers are shattered, Sarnoff answers: "The home information center." The term actually refers to the high-capacity coaxial cables that carry TV signals into many homes and to all the vaguely defined devices that Sarnoff sees attached to the cables' ends. In addition to transmission equipment, the devices might include machines to print newspapers in the home and keyboards that could be used to order merchandise after viewing it on a TV screen.

While the home information center has about it the aura of high technology, the differences between it and color TV are in fact considerable. Most important, the home information center involves neither a tremendous gamble nor a major breakthrough in technology. The know-how to produce most of the equipment is in hand, and large research investments are not needed. RCA already has the capability to manufacture, distribute, and service most of the consumer goods in question, and Sarnoff last year acquired a very small (but profitable) producer of two-way cable and other transmission equipment. The main barrier to having a home information center overnight is that it takes lots of time to lay cables and to work out the kinds of systems people will actually want. No one is very clear about the potential for profits or the size of the market; conceivably, the market could run to more than $1 billion in five years and three times that much in ten years.

RCA's next major consumer device will be a video recorder aimed at a market that has been estimated at $1 billion a year by 1980 (including hardware and software). The company's own version is called Selecta-Vision, a highly regarded machine that uses magnetic tape in a cartridge to record a TV program while you watch it — or even while you watch another program, or don't watch anything at all — and play it back later. It also will play recorded tapes, though these are expensive (some $35 per half-hour), and tapes than can be made at home with a camera that RCA will sell separately. RCA had earlier developed a video recorder that employed holography rather than magnetic tape; however, that system has proved too expensive for general consumer applications. (See "Stand By for the Cartridge TV Explosion," *Fortune,* June 1971.) Planned for introduction late next year, after an investment of about $8 million, the new SelectaVision recorder is tentatively priced at $700, considerably below systems that have been introduced by competitors.

Some forty RCA scientists at Princeton, and engineers in some of the company's divisions, are also working on a video recorder that would use a disc, hoping to develop a prototype by 1973. Since discs would cost much less than magnetic tapes, they could expand the demand for original programming, which might eventually range from Shakespearean theatre to golf lessons.

Sarnoff is also entering new industrial markets. RCA plans to set up and manage a private-line data-communication network connecting thirty-five U.S. cities, to supply internal corporate-communication systems to major companies. The service should make money, but RCA's main motive in supplying the system is to learn about its customers' data-communication needs, so that it can develop the required services and equipment.

A question about those future bets

Another intriguing development is a supermarket check-out system that uses computers and lasers to scan prices on packages and add up the bill, while it simultaneously updates information on inventories. By speeding the check-out process, RCA claims, the system can increase a store's volume by as much as 30 per cent; the Kroger chain has been delighted by the system's performance during a trial at one of its stores. RCA has invested some $10 million in the system and the company could begin selling it next year, in a potential market of $2 billion to $3 billion by 1980.

That these businesses have potential for profit is obvious, but RCA will, of course, have to stave off some tough competition. Likely competitors in video recorders include Sony, Philips, and others, and in the supermarket check-out business they include I.B.M. and N.C.R., with their crack sales forces and computer capabilities. The competition has outmuscled RCA before. The key question is one that Seretean raises by implication: Can a management that failed in computers, and has lagged behind its competitors in other major businesses, make better bets on the future than it has in the past?

2

Harold Geneen's Moneymaking Machine is Still Humming

CAROL J. LOOMIS*

> The question is whether the man widely
> regarded as the world's greatest business manager
> can go right on boosting I.T.T.'s earnings
> year after year, now that he's not so free
> to make acquisitions. The answer is that
> Geneen might do just that.

In the swirl of events last spring that made Dita Beard a household name, introduced the world to the shredding machine, and evoked a stupefying amount of editorial comment on the origins of an antitrust settlement between International Telephone & Telegraph Corp. and the Department of Justice, it sometimes seemed to be forgotten that the same settlement had dictated an entirely new business strategy for I.T.T. The company will never be the same. Its old strategy leaned heavily on acquisitions, which, in the wake of that settlement, the company is no longer completely free to make. The new strategy turns necessarily on internal growth. The change is obviously an enormous one for I.T.T., and it is made no less arresting by the fact that the company's redoubtable chairman and president, Harold Sydney Geneen, is now sixty-two and beseiged with questions about the future of its management.

The settlement, in case there is anyone who has not by now heard its terms, permitted I.T.T. to retain its largest subsidiary, Hartford Fire Insurance Co., but required it to divest itself of several other large units — Avis, Canteen, Levitt, and a portion of Grinnell — and to curtail major acquisitions in the U.S. The settlement is still under attack in the courts and it also shows signs of becoming one of the more popular Democratic campaign issues. Nevertheless, it is for the moment, and probably for the long term, setting the rules of the game.

Just how changed these rules are can be seen by contemplating the number of I.T.T. acquisitions during 1961-71. The total, incredibly, was around 250. They helped build I.T.T. into a mammoth company that

* Reprinted from the September 1972 issue of *Fortune* by special permission; © 1972 Time, Inc.

18

by last year had sales of $7.3 billion (enough to make it the ninth-largest U.S. industrial corporation) and an additionaal claim to $1.5 billion in revenues from nonconsolidated insurance and finance subsidiaries. Just about 75 per cent of those sales and revenues came from the acquired companies. Through it all, the company kept its attention fixedly on gains in earnings per share, achieving a standout record.

As sure as Christmas

The record was marred last year, it is true, by a bruising write-off of I.T.T.'s investment in Chile (mainly a telephone company), a charge that reduced profits for the year from $407 million to $337 million. But excluding both that extraordinary item and others reported in earlier years (all of which happened to be gains), I.T.T.'s earnings-per-share history under Geneen, who took over the company in 1959, now includes twelve straight years of increases. (The record also includes two years of increases before that, but these are never talked about at I.T.T. because they were "before Geneen.") These increases, furthermore, have been generally handsome, exceeding 10 per cent in all but three years of that period and averaging out to 11.3 per cent. This year, about as sure as Christmas, I.T.T. will report another increase, again exceeding 10 per cent.

But the main question, of course, is what the company can do in the future under that annoying new game plan devised for it by the Department of Justice. Among other things, the consent judgment that I.T.T. signed forbids it for ten years to acquire any U.S. company with more than $100 million in assets (that would, for example, rule out just about the entire *Fortune* 500 list). Nor can I.T.T. acquire during the decade any company with sales exceeding $25 million if it is considered, by certain definitions, to be a "leading company" in its industry. That still leaves I.T.T. with the option to acquire small U.S. companies, and it is doing so; in the nine months following the consent decree it acquired about twenty companies, most of them manufacturers, with an estimated total of $100 million in sales.

The company is also free, so far as the consent judgment is concerned, to acquire foreign companies of any size, and in that same nine months it took on about twelve with sales estimated to have exceeded $200 million, moving, in the process, into a brand-new industry, cosmetics and toiletries. ("Who knows?" says Geneen, sounding like a man who is not about to be bested by that consent decree. "We may even start to compete in the U.S. in that business.") But nationalistic currents set certain limits on foreign acquisitions, particularly those of any size. Though I.T.T. has acquired a number of companies in France, it has in the last few years failed at least twice to get French approval for proposed acquisitions, and has also been blocked in a major Belgian deal. "Nationalism," says Lyman C. Hamilton Jr., the company's treasurer, "is simply something we have to live with."

The name of the new game

Considering the various constraints, this year's acquisition rate, of around $400 million in sales, could turn out to resemble the pattern of the future. That $400 million is little more than 5 per cent of I.T.T.'s sales last year, whereas in the late 1960's acquisitions were annually adding anywhere from 20 to 35 per cent to I.T.T.'s sales base. There is no doubt, then, that the new game must be predominantly internal growth.

Geneen says unequivocally that I.T.T. can play that game. Besides, he adds, perhaps lapsing into a bit of rationalism, it would appear to him that the company no longer needs large acquisitions, that these have served their purpose, giving the company size, a strong profit base in the U.S. (which it lacked when Geneen took over), and entry into all sorts of industries that have prospered since I.T.T. got into them. Assuming a future in which the U.S. economy and the company's foreign markets grow, he would expect I.T.T. to grow much faster and, in fact, to go right on increasing its earnings indefinitely at a 10 per cent to 12 per cent annual rate. Harold Geneen, make no mistake, is a single-minded man.

It is of some help, in appraising Geneen's rosy thoughts about a world in which he is not making major acquisitions, to look back at just what effect I.T.T.'s acquisitions have had on its earnings per share up to now. That subject has been tough to attack in the past, mainly because not much earnings data has been available for the companies acquired, particularly after their disappearances into I.T.T. But in the last few years a voluminous body of information about I.T.T. has been collected in court records and government hearings, and from these sources it is now possible to pull some hard facts, to build some estimates upon them, and to come to a couple of conclusions.

One of these had to do with the effect that I.T.T.'s acquisitions, ranging from giant Hartford Fire (1971 revenues: $1.3 billion) to tiny items like Nancy Taylor Secretarial School of Chicago (under $50,000), had on earnings per share in the year they were acquired. Curiosity about that point has always focused on the conglomerates, some of which — Litton, before its recent miseries, was one example — were able to achieve instant earnings gains by swapping their own stocks, which commanded high prices in relation to earnings, for those of companies less favored by Wall Street. In other cases, the conglomerates no sooner took over a company than they changed its accounting practices, boosting its earnings in that way.

To Geneen's abiding distress, I.T.T.'s price-earnings ratio has always been relatively low, so the company has had very little opportunity to make really rich deals with its stock. On the other hand, it almost automatically switches the companies its acquires over to its own accounting policies — and these were described a few years ago by an accounting firm, making a study of I.T.T. for a company it was about to acquire, as 'liberal," defined as "tending to increase current reported earnings."

The upshot of all this is that I.T.T.'s acquisitions have helped its earnings in eight of the last eleven years (1961, 1963, and 1971 being the exceptions) but the help has usually been minor; in five of the eight years it involved 3 cents a share or less. Only in 1968, when I.T.T. was riding a relatively high p/e and bought a number of large companies, including Continental Baking and Rayonier, did acquisitions really juice up earnings, contributing 18 cents out of a total earnings gain of 31 cents. That happened to be a big year for accounting changes: Continental and Sheraton (acquired the year before) both went from accelerated depreciation to straight line, and Rayonier began to capitalize certain timber-carrying costs. Those changes, along with others that were made, accounted for 3 cents of the 18 cents and for another 4 cents besides.

A jewel in the collection

On balance, however, I.T.T. cannot be accused of having "bought" a lot of earnings over the years. That still leaves the possibility that its earnings-per-share growth has not been due so much to good management as to its ability to enter promising new fields. One way to examine that possibility is to look at the growth of I.T.T.'s acquired companies as compared to that of the businesses it already owned in 1960.

I.T.T. in that year made $30,600,000 on a business that was mainly based on telecommunication equipment, both its manufacture and its operation, and to a lesser extent based on the manufacture of consumer electronic goods in Europe and on defense contracting in the U.S. The operations of three I.T.T. South American telephone companies, in Brazil, Peru, and Chile, have since been nationalized. But the manufacture of telecommunication equipment has moved from being merely a good business to become an absolute jewel in I.T.T.'s collection, and the company's other 1960 businesses have also grown.

Putting a number to this growth and to that of the acquisitions is a complicated matter, involving decisions about such matters as the allocation of headquarters expenses (which have had a roaring growth rate, and are estimated to have amounted last year to $70 million) and the proper "base" year to use for the acquired companies. That is, should these companies be measured from the year *before* they were acquired (in which case "growth" is helped by I.T.T.'s accounting changes) or from the year of acquisition?

Fortune's procedure has been to estimate headquarters expenses and to allocate these in a manner that approximates a system used by I.T.T. for product lines, and to measure the growth of the acquired companies from the year of acquisition. By that method, the acquired companies (when weighted for their size and the length of time their growth has contributed to I.T.T.'s) are shown to have had a 12.5 per cent growth rate in profits. Rather amazingly, the 1960 companies, whose earnings in 1971 amounted to about $111 million, turn out to have grown at exactly the same rate.

The main point of this analysis, then, is that I.T.T. has shown an ability to make its operating divisions, both acquired and inherited, grow at impressive rates. Confidence about the company's ability to continue along this track is obviously implied in Geneen's optimistic view of the future. Also implied is at least a reasonable degree of satisfaction with the company's existing business mix, which must necessarily supply the growth from here on in, since it cannot be heavily supplemented by acquisitions.

"It looks good, but . . ."

It should be noted that stock-market investors do not share Geneen's optimism, just as they never seem to have quite trusted I.T.T. The company's stock sold off last year on news of the antitrust settlement, bounced back sharply, and then was clobbered this year, first by all those sordid revelations coming out of Washington, then by the news that the Federal judge in Connecticut who had approved the antitrust settlement was going to give the decision another look (which, in mid-August, he was still engaged in doing). A senior investment officer of a major bank said recently that some of his analysts had found in the Washington events a reason to turn sour on I.T.T. stock, the company's profit record notwithstanding. "They say, 'It looks good, but it doesn't smell good.'" Other analysts, however, dismiss those events as a passing problem, soon to be forgotten. "How many investors looking at General Electric today do you suppose ever stop to think they had guys who went to jail?" one analyst asked recently.

But even if this year's crisis does turn out to be only a passing problem, the odds would still not favor I.T.T. moving to a price that truly reflects its growth record. Since 1959 the company's earnings-per-share growth rate has been nearly triple that of Standard & Poor's 500 index; yet I.T.T. stock has for the most part sold at a price-earnings ratio only slightly higher than that of the S. & P. stocks, and in times of trouble has sold even lower. The present period would seem to qualify as a time of trouble: in mid-August, I.T.T. stock was selling around 54, or about fourteen times estimated 1972 earnings, while the S. & P. index stood at about seventeen times estimated 1972 earnings.

There are many possible explanations for the low repute of the stock. Institutions, which own more than 50 per cent of the stock, seem to worry about the "succession problem" — about how I.T.T. is to be managed when Geneen is not around to do it. Most individual investors probably do not find I.T.T. understandable. It is too big, too diversified, too complex; it is a conglomerate when these are out of style. Some analysts who have studied the company closely are intensely suspicious of its accounting. For example, they don't like I.T.T.'s habit of taking capital gains at the subsidiary level (say, at Sheraton or Levitt) and then treating these as regular income in the parent company's income statement. Many analysts also believe that I.T.T.'s profit record is just too good to be true. How, they ask, does a company so heavily engaged in cyclical businesses avoid the ups and downs in earnings that harass other cyclical companies?

Indeed, there seems to be almost no one on Wall Street, including those friendliest to I.T.T., who does not believe the company is "managing" or "smoothing" its earnings — i.e., manipulating in at least a minor way its revenues, costs, and reserves so as to keep earnings flowing evenly upward. This charge is of course familiar to I.T.T., whose managers insist that it is groundless — that the company's diversification, industrially and geographically, enables it to avoid cyclical dips. Herbert C. Knortz, the company's controller, tends to get a bit agitated at the charges of manipulation. "We simply don't manage earnings. I'll put it in blood if that'll help. What can I say? We do it right, we do it right, we do it right."

Whatever the reasons for I.T.T.'s low p/e, Geneen is extremely unhappy about it — to state the case mildly. And, from his point of view, it doubtless seems wrong that the architect of an outstanding growth record, a man universally acknowledged to be a master of management, an executive who has been compared to Alfred P. Sloan, doesn't get his due in the stock market. As an I.T.T. director says, "He simply thinks it isn't fair."

Geneen has tried hard to make the market see the error of its ways. Other chief executives, of course, have also attempted to promote their stocks, but Geneen, as one bank executive put the case recently, "is so . . . so . . . *overt.*" Geneen likes to hand out a list showing that, among nearly fifty companies with 1959 sales of more than $750 million, I.T.T. ranks second only to I.B.M. in per-share growth. He once spent a good part of a lunch telling a group of Morgan Guaranty executives that they were, in effect, stupid for not buying his stock when nearly every other bank in the country was. (Morgan later did become a buyer.) On another occasion, a subordinate told Geneen triumphantly, if a bit woozily, that he had just spent four hours drinking with analysts from a certain bank and that they had decided to buy 500,000 shares of I.T.T. stock. Back shot Geneen, "You should have kept drinking for eight hours. They would have bought a million shares."

I.T.T. is also known to have a low tolerance for criticism from Wall Street's analysts. On one occasion last year, the company protested heatedly when a major Wall Street brokerage firm looked ready to publish an adverse report on its stock. While other circumstances seem also to have entered in, the report did not appear. On the other hand, many analysts on Wall Street seem to have come to the conclusion that I.T.T. stock is good value at less than twenty times earnings. This summer a whole string of well-known research firms were recommending the stock — and still it was selling at fourteen times earnings.

Two shiny profit centers

The company now has a new hope about the stock: that once investors realize I.T.T. can grow without acquisitions, they will lose their mistrust of it as an investment. And with two main divisions of the company's business, Hartford Fire and telecommunication equipment, expected to furnish much of the growth, there is further hope that perhaps I.T.T. will no longer seem so incomprehensible to investors.

Last year Hartford and telecommunication equipment together

supplied the company with $176 million in profits, or about 43 per cent of I.T.T.'s total (before the Chilean write-off), and the two are expected by the company to increase earnings at least 15 per cent a year for some time into the future. Were they to achieve that growth rate this year, for example they would account for an increase of about $26 million in profits. If, meanwhile, I.T.T.'s other businesses, which last year earned $231 million, were to add merely $19 million in profits to their base — in other words, to grow at something like 8 per cent — the company as a whole would have achieved an 11 per cent growth rate, which, it will be recalled, is what I.T.T. executives get up in the mornings for. Since many of these other businesses should be benefiting from an improving U.S. economy, I.T.T. holds that the goal is certainly attainable.

Geneen changes his mind

It would have been hard to imagine a few years back that Hartford Fire would ever look like such a sweet proposition. The property and casualty insurance business was then considered a clinker, incapable of making money on its basic underwriting business. Geneen, for one, though he began moving I.T.T. into the life-insurance business in the mid-1960s, wanted no part of the casualty business, believing it to be unstable. The man who changed his mind was Felix G. Rohatyn, a director of I.T.T., a partner in Lazard Frères, and, of course, a headliner in this year's Senate hearings on Richard Kleindienst (a major question was whether Rohatyn had got Kleindienst to intervene on I.T.T.'s behalf with the Justice Department's Antitrust Division). Listening to Rohatyn, Geneen came to feel that casualty insurance was really two businesses: first, an underwriting business, which was indeed erratic, although in Geneen's opinion subject to some improvement; and second, an investment business, capable of producing a steady flow of profits from its stock and bond portfolio.

The subsequent steps by which I.T.T. and Hartford, the country's sixth-largest casualty company, came together and eventually merged have furnished the raw material for three sets of government hearings (two in Connecticut, one in Washington), a whole collection of lawsuits, and more newspaper stories than Hartford has policies. More newspaper stories are still likely to be written. Ralph Nader, whose home town of Winsted, Connecticut, is near enough to Hartford to have given him a special interest in this situation, continues to try in the courts to undo the merger. Meanwhile, the Securities and Exchange Commission appears still to be investigating the circumstances surrounding the 1969 disapproval of the merger by the Connecticut insurance commissioner, William R. Cotter (now a Congressman), and his subsequent change of mind.

Until Hartford is safely and irrevocably in the fold, there will be widespread unease at I.T.T., for it regards Hartford as a prize and perhaps even as, in one executive's words, "a gold mine." Geneen is described by another executive as "ecstatic" over Hartford, though

Geneen himself says that is an overstatement. "We view Hartford as the hub of our worldwide financial services and I am extremely impressed with their performance. But this is a regulated industry and things can happen. This business is something we're really going to have to work at."

The performance to which Geneen refers has come both from a general improvement in the casualty-insurance business and from Hartford's own efforts. Last year the industry had its best underwriting results since 1955, profiting from an improved ratesetting climate, from the apparent reluctance of policyholders to submit small claims, and from the absence of major catastrophes. Hartford, though it showed poorer underwriting results than most large casualty companies, nevertheless came up with its first underwriting profit since 1962. Meanwhile, its premium growth has for the last two years run at an average rate exceeding 18 per cent, far above both its old growth rates (average less than 10 per cent) and recent industry rates (12 per cent and under).

Harry V. Williams, chairman of Hartford, says his company has become more "venturesome" since merging with I.T.T. He also acknowledges a debt to I.T.T.'s famed business plans, which map out the growth of operating units for five years ahead and which Hartford incorporated into its own business nearly a year before its merger with I.T.T. was approved.

A friend in Hartford

At the rate Hartford is growing, it may in a few years lack the capital to support its premium growth, and I.T.T. would then expect to pump it up with additional capital. I.T.T. might not mind doing just that, for during the merger preliminaries the company was persistently assailed by critics who believed that it was I.T.T.'s intention to scavenge Hartford's wealth rather than aggressively to built its business. On the other hand, it should be mentioned that Hartford's wealth, in the form of a debt-free balance sheet, did a lot for I.T.T.'s debt ratio. Within months after the Hartford acquisition, the bond-rating services moved I.T.T. up from a Baa rating to A.

Hartford's portfolio wealth has also been finding its way into I.T.T.'s net income, though in a highly controversial way. For some time a number of companies, I.T.T. among them, have been attempting to persuade the accounting profession that insurance companies should be allowed in some systematic manner to take their unrealized portfolio gains into net income. The argument for doing so would be that these gains, just like other kinds of profits, add to the net worth of stockholders and therefore deserve recognition. I.T.T.'s position has received considerable support from accountants and analysts. But it has also received major, and so far successful, opposition.

In consequence, Hartford has simply been *realizing* capital gains for the last couple of years in amounts that it and I.T.T. say reflect Hartford's average returns on its stock portfolio over the last twenty years. Last year the gains taken amounted to about 6 per cent (pretax) of Hartford's average portfolio. The obvious disadvantage of this practice is that it requires the payment of capital-gains taxes. But that disadvantage is clearly outweighed in I.T.T.'s thinking by the advantage of getting those gains into earnings per share. Last year Hartford netted a total of $105 million, a fact that was prominenty recorded on I.T.T.'s income statement. The fact that $36 million of this amount came from capital gains was not recorded.

Hartford's unrealized capital gains amounted to about $270 million at the end of last year and, barring a major stock-market crash, should for years be available to supplement the steadily growing stream of interest and dividend income that rolls out of the company's portfolio. I.T.T.'s main problem, then, is to make sure that the "erratic" end of Hartford's business, underwriting, keeps contributing to total profits, or at least breaks even. Some insurance analysts believe that this could turn out to be quite a problem. They say that Hartford, in its pursuit of premium growth, has necessarily had to take on risks that may come back to haunt it and that could jeopardize the goal of a 15 per cent growth in earnings. A verdict on that one will have to wait.

Helping the Europeans catch up

I.T.T.'s telecommunications-equipment business has more predictable qualities. In Europe, where this business is centered, telephone operations are run by the national governments, which are supplied by a handful of big companies — I.T.T. being the leader in most countries, followed by Siemens of Germany and Ericsson of Sweden. Market shares are fairly stable and lead times on orders are long. I.T.T.'s companies are known by national names (e.g., Standard Elektrik Lorenz in Germany), are run by nationals, and normally accepted as good corporate citizens. (But it was big and disturbing news in Europe last spring when I.T.T. was revealed to have been conferring with the C.I.A. about the possibility of intervening in Chilean politics.)

The marvelous feature of the European telecommunication market, insofar as the suppliers are concerned, is its relative under-development. Most European countries have less than thirty telephones per hundred inhabitants; the U.S., in contrast, has fifty-eight per hundred. Europe has plainly decided to catch up, and a few years ago the demand for telephone equipment began to take off. I.T.T.'s tele-communication-equipment profits last year, amounting to $71 million, were twice what they were as recently as 1967; in 1971 alone they grew by 37 per cent.

Down the road, I.T.T. has hopes of becoming a supplier, out of its European plants, to the Soviet Union (telephones per 100 inhabitants: 4.5); I.T.T. already has an office in Moscow and later this year is scheduled to make a trade presentation there. The Soviet Union has indicated a preference for dealing with U.S. companies that have a broad range of products to sell, so that it can limit the number of suppliers. Few companies can outdo I.T.T. in that department.

Even the U.S. has suddenly begun to look like a promising telecommunication market to I.T.T. This summer in Honolulu I.T.T. won an important antitrust suit against General Telephone & Electronics, which was found by the court to have engaged in anticompetitive behavior by acquiring Hawaiian Telephone and then causing it to buy almost nothing but G.T.E. equipment. G.T.E. plans to appeal the decision, but at the moment I.T.T. believes its victory to have implications that may even call into question the Western Electric-A.T.&.T. supplier relationship. Ironically, if a substantial expansion of its domestic telecommunication business had been an alternative open to I.T.T. when Geneen took over, he might never have begun his acquisition program at all.

"We came into I.T.T. a good company"

Products and services aside, I.T.T.'s hope for future growth obviously rests on its management structure and techniques, which, despite such incredible goofs as the Washington shredding affair, nevertheless continue to appear of a very superior order. Among those who share that opinion, it turns out, are two businessmen who have had several years of exposure to this management environment and are now about to leave it: they are the chief executives of companies soon to be thrust out of I.T.T. by divestitures.

One of these men, Patrick L. O'Malley, chairman of Canteen Corp., made an unscheduled speech this year at I.T.T.'s annual meeting in May. His initial point was that he certainly thought Geneen deserved his $812,494 salary and bonus, if for no other reason than that he was forced annually to endure the endless irritations of the annual meeting. But O'Malley went on to make what was clearly a sincere tribute: "We came into I.T.T. a good company and we are going out of I.T.T. an excellent company. We have learned a tremendous amount about management." The force of this accolade was later somewhat reduced by a prospectus showing that Canteen has really not been one of I.T.T.'s stars. Cyclically vulnerable, Canteen has in the past three years just barely managed to hold its profits even at the $10-million level — doing that only by virtue of some 1970 accounting changes that added about $1 million to profits.

Any praise heaped upon I.T.T. by the other departing executive, Winston V. (Bud) Morrow Jr., president of Avis, has a special meaning, for Morrow came into I.T.T. organization reluctantly (when Lazard Fréres sold Avis to I.T.T. in 1965) and is leaving it almost gleefully. "When Geneen called to tell me we were to be divested," Morrow says, "I was able to control my disappointment manfully." During all his years at I.T.T., Morrow has fought to keep Avis as independent as possible. True, he filed the business plans and monthly management letters that I.T.T. requires, because there is no getting around those. But he did everything he could to keep the headquarters people off his neck, even going so far as to write especially long monthly letters in hopes that they would forestall questions. Most I.T.T. operating units pay headquarters an administrative fee, based on a percentage of sales; Avis for years paid nothing. Morrow has even avoided riding in I.T.T. planes, figuring that the less he was obligated to headquarters, the better.

Avis also managed to avoid I.T.T.'s unique controller setup, under which the chief financial officer in each operating unit, though charged with keeping his chief executive officer fully informed of his actions, reports directly to I.T.T.'s controller, Knortz — and looks to Knortz for raises and promotions. The setup was installed by Geneen in an effort to prevent unpleasant financial surprises. Nevertheless, it has elements of a spy system, and Morrow, for years, successfully resisted it. Then I.T.T. woke up to the fact that Morrow had put the system into place all through the Avis organization, i.e. he had the chief financial man in each division and country reporting directly to the Avis controller. After that, and with some amusement on both sides, Avis's controller began reporting to Knortz.

Morrow came around in a couple of other ways too. When Avis is finally split off (so far, I.T.T. has sold 23 per cent of its stock to the public), it will continue to have all those business plans and monthly management letters — shorter ones, perhaps, but still Avis will have them. Morrow will also have recollections of a couple of crucial chapters in Avis's relationship with I.T.T. One of these came when Avis decided it must make a costly, large-scale assault on the European market; I.T.T. encouraged the move and patiently absorbed the major losses that followed. The European market has since become one of Avis's great strengths and is a reason why the company's earnings have in the last two years grown at an average rate of nearly 30 per cent.

Some time later, when Avis wished to begin developing its computer rental and reservation system, called "Wizard," it proposed a plan that, Morrow now realizes, would have been a financial and technical disaster. I.T.T. would not buy the plan. "They were gun-shy of our claims," Morrow says, "and they were totally unimpressed by my feeling that this was going to be great for Avis's image. They were only interested in what it would mean in savings. The first thing you learn after you're acquired is that they didn't get rich by giving it away. We went through the drill and the justification for Wizard over and over for two years before we finally got an okay. I hated it at the time, but if they hadn't made us do that, if we had just plunged ahead, we would have been dead."

All in all, Morrow says, it has been "an interesting business-school course." He also sees it as having lasting effects. "If Geneen walked in here five years hence, he would be able to see that this had once been an I.T.T. company."

The letter Geneen used to write

That phrase, "five years hence," lands squarely on one of today's uncertainties about I.T.T.: the shape of its management in the next few years. Though looking and acting like a far younger man, Geneen will reach I.T.T.'s mandatory-retirement age of sixty-five in January, 1975. And what is to happen then?

To end any suspense about the matter, there seems to be almost no possibility that Geneen, if he continues to remain in good health, will step down at that point. He will not wish to, nor will I.T.T.'s directors be willing to view the mandatory-retirement rule as anything more than an irrelevancy to be brushed aside. Felix Rohatyn and Eugene R. Black, two key I.T.T. directors, both indicated recently that they would not consider invoking the rule in Geneen's case. In Rohatyn's words: "He can run any company that I'm a director of until he's ninety-two years old."

Nevertheless, the directors are forced to deal seriously with that other question that is usually couched in euphemistic terms: "Well, suppose that Mr. Geneen were to be hit by a truck tomorrow . . ." Geneen himself used to form one answer to this question by writing a letter every six months to Warren Lee Pierson, an I.T.T. director (now retired), stating his own opinions about who should succeed him. He does not write a letter anymore because, he explains, "I had a talk with the directors and I think they understand my feelings on this." His confidence on that subject may be unfounded. Black, for one, does not recall any such talk. Given a crisis, Black says. "We'd have a board meeting."

The logical contenders for Geneen's job, or for a No. 2 spot he sometimes hints he might create, are the three men who, with Geneen, form the Office of the President: Francis J. (Tim) Dunleavy, fifty-seven, Richard E. Bennett, fifty-two, and James V. Lester, fifty-three. All three came to I.T.T. from other industrial companies in the early 1960s and all began as executive assistants to Geneen, operating essentially as troubleshooters. Dunleavy is a genial, shrewd Irishman who has been Geneen's choice to chair a couple of board meetings that the boss missed. Bennett, an expert at cost cutting, is the most loquacious of the three. Lester both looks and talks a little bit like Geneen, and like him, has a considerable talent for financial matters.

These three men are today actively involved in the company's major decisions, which is a change from the days when Geneen would entrust these to no one else. Geneen takes more vacations these days and misses more meetings. But a certain snap goes out of the monthly management meetings when he steps out of them, and upon returning he may call for repeats of matters just discussed. "Instant replays," these moments are called.

Dunleavy, Bennett, and Lester are all obviously men of great experience and competence. But none seems the combination of extraordinary intelligence and enormous energy that is Geneen, and none seems capable of inspiring the kind of awe that focuses on him. One I.T.T. executive recently compared Geneen to General George Patton. Another quoted a favorite I.T.T. one-liner: "Is that G in Geneen pronounced as in God or as in Jesus?"

Geneen himself thinks that the countless meetings and reports to which the Office of the President is exposed have prepared its members for just about any manner of management responsibility. "This may be an unfortunate word," he recently said with a wink, "but it's as if they have been shredded and reprocessed." He goes on to imply that comparisons between himself and Alfred P. Sloan, the designer of General Motors' management system, may be both welcome and fitting. "I'm frankly a great admirer of General Motors. You know, G.M. is one of those companies in which some presidents have been better than others, but all have been good enough to keep the company moving."

"The best people to run companies are not the geniuses," he adds. "They're too difficult to get along with. The best people are well-rounded men with ambition." Would that describe himself? With a grin: "Oh, no. I'm a difficult person."

A difficult person for a difficult company — perhaps that is the way to describe the relationship that exists between Geneen and I.T.T. and to frame the problem that will appear when the relationship is ultimately dissolved. Geneen has made I.T.T. a monument in his own image, and there seems no way of knowing whether it is strong enough to be preserved by the next caretaker. Meanwhile, Geneen himself will be working to build the monument a little bit higher.

3

Framework for Analysis

ROBERT N. ANTHONY*

"Planning and control systems" is usually used as a generic term. However, this article points out that there are many different planning and control processes in business, and suggests a classification of them, which can serve as a framework for analysis.

Since dogs and humans are both mammals, some generalizations that apply to one species also apply to the other. It is for this reason that some new surgical techniques can be tested on dogs before being risked on humans. But dogs and humans differ, and, unless these differences are recognized, generalizations that are valid for one species may be erroneously applied to the other. For example, canine behavior can be largely explained in terms of conditioned reflexes, but human behavior is much more complicated. Similarly, some generalizations can be made about the whole planning and control process in a business; however, there actually are several quite different types of planning and control processes, and mistakes may be made if a generalization (principle, rule, technique) valid for one type is applied to the other.

The purpose of this article is to suggest a classification of the main topics or "species" that come within the broad term, Planning and Control Systems, and to suggest distinguishing characteristics of each. Hopefully, this will lead to a sorting out and sharpening of principles and techniques applicable to each species.

The particular classification chosen has been arrived at after careful analysis of how well various alternatives match statements made in the literature and, more important, what is found in practice. It is, however, tentative. Better schemes may well be developed, and we expose

* From *Management Services* (March-April 1964) , pp. 18-24. Reprinted by permission of the Editor.

This article is based on research done for the Division of Research at the Harvard Business School and financed by The Associates of the Harvard Business School. Both the professional and financial aspects of this support are gratefully acknowledged. For an expanded treatment of the subject see Robert N. Anthony, *Planning and Control Systems: A Framework for Analysis* (Boston: Harvard Business School, Division of Research, 1965).

this one primarily in the hope that discussion of it will lead to agreement on *some* scheme, not necessarily this.

In this article, we shall focus on a process labeled *management control*. We shall describe its main characteristics, and distinguish it from processes labeled *strategic planning* and *technical control*. (Two other processes, *financial accounting* and *information handling*, are also relevant, but space does not permit a discussion of them here.)

Obviously, we do not assert that these processes can be separated by sharply defined boundaries; one shades into another. Strategic planning sets the guidelines for management control, and management control sets the guidelines for technical control. The complete management function involves an integration of all these processes, and the processes are complementary.

We do assert that the processes are sufficiently distinct so that those who design and use planning and control systems will make expensive errors if they fail to take into account both the common characteristics of a process and the differences between processes. This article will deal with these similarities and differences and point out some of the errors that are made when they are not recognized.

MANAGEMENT CONTROL

Management control is the process of assuring that resources are obtained and used effectively and efficiently in the accomplishment of the organization's objectives.

Management control is a process carried on within the framework established by strategic planning. Objectives, facilities, organization, and financial factors are more or less accepted as "givens." Decisions about next year's budget, for example, are limited by policies and guidelines prescribed by top management. The management control process is intended to make possible the achievement of planned objectives as effectively and efficiently as possible within these "givens."

The purpose of a management control system is to encourage managers to take actions which are in the best interests of the company. For example, if the system is structured so that a certain course of action increases the reported profits of a division, and at the same time *lessens* the profits of the company as a whole, there is something wrong. Technically, this purpose can be described as *goal congruence*.

"TOTAL" SYSTEM NECESSARY

Psychological considerations are dominant in management control. Activities such as communicating, persuading, exhorting, inspiring, and criticizing are an important part of the process.

Ordnarily, a management control system is a *total* system in the sense that it embraces all aspects of the company's operation. It needs to be a total system because an important management function is to assure that all parts of the operation are in balance with one another, and, in order to examine balance, management needs information about each of the parts.

With rare exceptions, the management control system is built around a *financial* structure; that is, resources and outputs are expressed in monetary units. Money is the only common denominator by means of which the heterogeneous elements of output and resources (e.g., hours of labor; type of labor; quantity and quality of material; amount and kind of products produced) can be combined and compared. (Although the financial structure is usually the central focus, nonmonetary measures such as time, number of persons, and reject and spoilage rates are also important parts of the system.)

The management control process tends to be *rhythmic;* it follows a definite pattern and timetable, month after month and year after year. In budgetary control, which is an important part of the management control process, certain steps are taken in a prescribed sequence and at certain dates each year; the dissemination of guidelines, the preparation of original estimates, the transmission of these estimates up through the several echelons in the organization, the review of these estimates, final approval by top management, dissemination back through the organization, operation, reporting, and the appraisal of performance. The procedure to be followed at each step in this process, the dates when the steps are to be completed, and even the forms that are to be used can be, and often are, set forth in a manual.

INTERLOCKING SUBSYSTEMS

A management control system is, or should be, a *co-ordinated, integrated system:* that is, although data collected for one purpose may differ from those collected for another purpose, these data should be reconcilable with one another. In a sense, the management control system is a *single* system, but it is perhaps more accurate to think of it as a set of interlocking subsystems. In many organizations, for example, three types of cost information are needed for management control: (1) *costs by responsibility centers,* which are used for planning and controlling the activities of responsible supervisors; (2) *full program costs,* used for pricing and other operating decisions under normal circumstances; and (3) *direct program costs,* used for pricing and other operating decisions under special circumstances, such as when management wishes to utilize idle capacity. ("Program" is here used for any activity in which the organization engages. In industrial companies, programs consist of products or product lines, and "product costs" can be substituted in the above statements.)

Line managers are the focal points in management control. They are the persons whose judgments are incorporated in the approved plans, and they are the persons who must influence others and whose performance is measured. Staff people collect, summarize, and present information that is useful in the process, and they make calculations which translate management judgments into the format of the system. Such a staff may be large in numbers; indeed the control department is often the largest department in a company. However, the significant decisions are made by the line manager, not by the staff.

STRATEGIC PLANNING

Strategic planning is the process of deciding on changes in the objectives of the organization, in the resources that are to be used in attaining these objectives, and in the policies that are to govern the acquisition and use of these resources.

The word *strategy* is used here in its usual sense of deciding on how to combine and employ resources. Thus, strategic planning is a process having to do with the formulation of long-range, strategic, policy-type plans that change the character or direction of the organization. In an industrial company this includes planning that affects the objectives of the company; policies of all types (including policies as to management control and other processes); the acquisition and disposition of major facilities, divisions, or subsidiaries; the markets to be served and distribution channels for serving them; the organization structure (as distinguished from individual personnel actions); research and development of new product lines (as distinguished from modifications in existing products and product changes within existing lines); sources of new permanent capital; dividend policy; and so on. Strategic planning decisions affect the physical, financial, and organizational framework within which operations are carried on.

IRREGULAR IN NATURE

Briefly, here are some ways in which the strategic planning process differs from the management control process.

A strategic plan usually relates to some part of the organization, rather than to the totality; the concept of a master planner who constantly keeps all parts of the organization at some coordinated optimum is a nice concept but an unrealistic one. Life is too complicated for any human, or computer, to do this.

Strategic planning is essentially *irregular*. Problems, opportunities, and "bright ideas" do not arise according to some set timetable, and they have to be dealt with whenever they happen to be perceived. The appropriate analytical techniques depend on the nature of the problem being analyzed, and no overall approach (such as a mathematical model) has been developed that is of much help in analyzing all types of strategic problems. Indeed, an overemphasis on a systematic approach is quite likely to stifle the essential element of creativity. In strategic planning, management works now on one problem, now on another, according to the needs and opportunities of the moment.

The estimates used in strategic planning are intended to show the *expected* results of the plan. They are neutral and impersonal. By contrast, the management control process, and the data used in it, are intended to influence managers to take actions that will lead to *desired* results. Thus, in connection with management control, it is appropriate to discuss how "tight' an operating budget should be: Should the goals be set so high that only an outstanding manager can achieve them, or should they be set so that they are attainable by the average manager? At what level does frustration inhibit a manager's best efforts? Does an attainable budget lead to complacency? And so on. In strategic planning, the question to be asked about the figures is simply: Is this the most reasonable estimate that can be made?

Strategic planning relies heavily on *external information,* that is, on data collected from outside the company, such as market analyses, estimates of costs and other factors involved in building a plant in a new locality, technological developments, and so on. When data from the normal information system are used, they usually must be recast to fit the needs of the problem being analyzed. For example, the current operating costs of a plant that are collected for measuring performance and for making pricing and other operating decisions usually must be restructured before they are useful in deciding whether to close down the plant.

COMMUNICATIONS ARE LIMITED

Another characteristic of the relevant information is that much of it is imprecise. The strategic planner estimates what *will* happen, often over a rather long time period. These estimates are likely to have a high degree of uncertainty, and they must be treated accordingly.

In the management control process, the communication of objectives, policies, guidelines, decisions, and results throughout the organization is extremely important. In the strategic planning process, communication is much simpler and involves relatively few persons, indeed, the need for secrecy often requires that steps be taken to inhibit communication. (Wide communication of the *decisions* that result from strategic planning is obviously important, but this is part of the management control process.)

Strategic planning is essentially applied economics, whereas management control is essentially applied social psychology.

Both management control and strategic planning involve top management, but middle management (i.e., operating management) typically have a much more important role in management control than they have in strategic planning. Middle managers usually are not major participants in the strategic planning process and sometimes are not even aware of the fact that a plan is being considered. Many operating executives are by temperament not very good at strategic planning. Also, the pressures of current activities usually do not allow them to devote the necessary time to such work. Currently, there is a tendency in companies to set up separate staffs which gather the facts and make the analyses that provide the background material for strategic decisions.

Exhibit 1. Some Contrasts

	Strategic Planning	Management Control
Person primarily involved	Staff and top management	Line and top management
Number of persons	Small	Large
Mental activity	Creative; analytical	Administrative; persuasive
Variables	Complex; much judgment	Less complex
Time period	Tends to be long	Tends to be short
Periodicity	Irregular, no set schedule	Rhythmic; set timetable
Procedures	Unstructured; each problem different	Prescribed procedure, regularly followed
Focus	Tend to focus on one aspect at a time	All encompassing
Source of information	Relies more on external and future	Relies more on internal and historical
Product	Intangible; precedent setting	More tangible; action within precedent
Communication problem	Relatively simple	Crucial and difficult
Appraisal of soundness	Extremely difficult	Much less difficult

These and other differences between management control and strategic planning are summarized in Exhibit 1, above.

Strategic planning and management control activities tend to conflict with one another in some respects. The time that management spends in thinking about the future is taken from time that could otherwise be used in controlling current operations, so in this indirect way strategic planning can hurt current performance. And, of course, the reverse also is true.

More directly, many actions that are taken for long-run, strategic reasons make current profits smaller than they otherwise would be. Research and some advertising expenditures are obvious examples. The problem of striking the right balance between strategic and operating considerations is one of the central problems in the whole management process.

CONSEQUENCES OF CONFUSION

Following are statements illustrating some of the consequences of failing to make a distinction between strategic planning and management control.

"We should set up a long-range planning procedure and work out a systemized way of considering *all* our plans similar to the way we construct next year's budget." (A long-range plan shows the estimated consequences over the next several years of strategic decisions already taken. It is part of the management control process. Although it provides a useful background for considering strategic proposals, it is not strategic planning. Strategic proposals should be made whenever the opportunity or the need is perceived in a form that best presents the arguments.)

"The only relevant costs are incremental costs; pay no attention to fixed or sunk costs." (This is so in strategic planning, but operating managers are often motivated in the wrong direction if their decisions are based on incremental costs; for example, in intracompany transactions.)

"We may be selling Plant X some day. We should therefore set up the operating reports so that management will have at its fingertips the information it will need when it is deciding this question. For example, we should show inventory and fixed assets at their current market value." (Operating reports should be designed to assist in the management of current operations. Special compilations of data are needed for such major, nonroutine actions as selling a plant. Collection of such data routinely is both too expensive and likely to impede sound operating decisions.)

"Our ultimate goal is an all-purpose control system — integrated data processing — so that management will have all the data it needs for whatever problem it decides to tackle. We should collect data in elemental building blocks that can be combined in various ways to answer all conceivable questions." (This is an impossible goal. Each strategic proposal requires that the data be assembled in the way that best fits the requirements of that proposal. No one can foresee all the possibilities. The "building block" idea is sound with limits, but the limits are not so broad that all problems are encompassed.)

"All levels of management should participate in planning." (All levels of management should participate in the planning part of the management control process, but operating managers typically do not have the time, the inclination, or the analytical bent that is required for formulating strategic plans. Furthermore, such plans often must be kept highly secret.)

TECHNICAL CONTROL

Technical control is the process of assuring the efficient acquisition and use of resources, with respect to activities for which the optimum relationship between outputs and resources can be approximately determined.

The definition of technical control refers to outputs and resources. *Outputs* are the accomplishments of the organization, what it does, and *resources* are the inputs which the organization consumes. For a whole business, the outputs are the goods and services sold, which are measured by revenues earned, and the inputs are costs and expenses incurred. In rough terms, "outputs" equals "results," and "resources" equals "cost."

One of the important tasks in an organization is to seek the *optimum* relationship between outputs and resources. For some activities, this optimum relationship is fairly easy to establish: To manufacture a given part should require such-and-such labor, a certain sequence of machine operations, and so on. For other activities, there exists no "scientific" (even in the loose sense of this term) way of establishing the optimum relationship; for these activities, decisions as to what costs to incur depend on human judgment.

The term "managed costs" is a descriptive one for those types of resources for which an objective decision as to the optimum quantity to be employed cannot be made. An important management function is to make judgments as to the "right" amount of managed costs in a given set of circumstances. These are, by definition, subjective judgments.

Management control applies to the whole of an organization, and to any parts of the whole in which managed costs are significant. Technical control applies to those activities, and only to those activities, in which there are no significant elements of managed cost. Or more simply, in the management control process, management judgment is an important element; in the technical control process, the technique itself is dominant.

As an example of technical control, consider inventory control. If the demand for an item, the cost of storing it, its production cost and production time, and the loss involved in not filling an order are known or can be reasonably estimated, then the optimum inventory level and the optimum production schedule can both be calculated, and reasonable men will agree with the results of these calculations.

In other than exceptional circumstances, these calculations can determine the actions that should be taken. Management intervention is necessary only when these exceptional circumstances arise.

SOME AREAS CAN'T BE MEASURED

By contrast, consider the legal department of a company. No device can measure the quality, or even the quantity, of the legal service that constitutes the output of this department. No formula can show the amount of service that should be rendered nor the optimum amount of costs that should be incurred. Impressions as to the "right" amount of service, as to the "right" amount of cost, and as to whether the relationship between the service actually rendered and the cost actually incurred was "right" are strictly subjective. They are judgments made by management. If persons disagree on these judgments, there is no objective way of resolving the disagreement. Yet the legal department as a part of the whole organization must be controlled; the chief counsel must operate within the framework of policies prescribed by top management. The control exercised in this situation is management control.

Examples of activities that can be subjected to technical control are: automated plants, such as cement plants, oil refineries, and power generating stations; the direct operations of most manufacturing plants (but often not the overhead expense items); production scheduling;

inventory control; the "order-taking" type of selling activity; and order processing, premium billing, payroll accounting, check handling, and similar paperwork activities.

Examples of activities for which management control is necessary are: the total activities of most manufacturing plants, which include such "judgment" inputs as indirect labor, employee benefit and welfare programs, safety activities, training, and supervision; most advertising, sales promotion, pricing, selling (as distinguished from order taking) and similar marketing activities; most aspects of finance; most aspects of research, development, and design; the work of staff units of all types; and management activity itself.

The control appropriate for the whole of any unit which carries on both the technical and the management types of activities is management control. The control of the whole accounting department is management control even though technical control is appropriate for certain aspects of the work, such as posting and check writing.

Some people believe that the distinction between the two classes of activities described above is merely one of degree rather than of kind; they say that all we are doing is distinguishing between situations where control is "easy" and "difficult," respectively. We think the distinction is more fundamental than that, and hope this will be apparent from the following brief list of characteristics that distinguish managementt control from technical control.

Management control covers the whole of an organization. Each technical control procedure is restricted to a subunit, often a narrowly circumscribed activity.

Just as management control occurs within a set of policies derived from strategic planning, so technical control occurs within a set of well-defined procedures and rules that are derived from management control.

Control is more difficult in management control than in technical control because of the absence of a "scientific" standard with which actual performance can be compared. A good technical control system can provide a much higher degree of assurance that actions are proceeding as desired than can a management control system.

RULES CAN BE PROGRAMED

A technical control system is a *rational* system; that is, the action to be taken is decided by a set of logical rules. These rules may or may not cover all aspects of a given problem. Situations not covered by the rules are designated as "exceptions" and are resolved by human judgment. Other than these exceptions, the application of the rules is automatic. The rules can in principle be programed into a computer, and the choice between using a computer and using a human being depends primarily on the relative cost of each method.

In management control, psychological considerations are dominant. The management control system at most assists those who take action; it does not directly or by itself result in action without human intervention. By contrast, the end product of an inventory control system can be an order, or a decision to replenish a certain inventory item, and this order may be based entirely on calculations from formulas incorporated in the system. (The formulas were *devised* by human beings, but this is a management control process, not a technical control process.)

In a consideration of technical control, analogies with mechanical, electrical, and hydraulic systems are reasonable and useful, and such terms as feedback, network balancing, optimization, and so on, are relevant. It is perfectly appropriate, for example, to view a technical control system as analogous to a thermostat which turns the furnace on and off according to its perception of changes in temperature. These analogies do not work well as models for management control systems, however, because the success of management systems is highly dependent on their impact on people, and people are not like thermostats or furnaces; one can't light a fire under a human being simply by turning up a thermostat.

A management control system is ordinarily focused on a financial structure, whereas technical control data are often nonmonetary. They may be expressed in terms of man-hours, number of items, pounds of waste, and so on. Since each technical control procedure is designed for a limited area of application, it is feasible to use the basis of measurement that is most appropriate for that area.

APPROXIMATIONS MEET DATA NEEDS

Data in a technical control system are in real time and relate to individual events, whereas data in a management control system are often retrospective and summarize many separate events. Computer specialists who do not make such a distinction dream about a system that will display to the management the current status of every individual activity in the organization. Although this *could* be done, it *should not* be done; management doesn't want such detail. Management does not need to know the time at which lot No. 1007 was transferred from station 27 to station 28; rather, it needs to know only that the process is, or is not, proceeding as planned, and, if not, where the trouble lies.

Similarly, technical control uses exact data, whereas management control needs only approximations. Material is ordered and scheduled in specific quantities, employees are paid the exact amount due them, but data on management control reports need contain only two or three significant digits and are therefore rounded to thousands of dollars, to millions of dollars, or even (in the U.S. Government) to billions of dollars.

A technical control system requires a mathematical model of the operation. Although it may not always be expressed explicitly in mathematical notation, there is a decision rule which states that given certain values for parameters $a, b, \ldots n$, action X is to be taken. Models are not so important in management control. In a sense, a budget or a PERT network are models associated with the management control process, but they are not the essence of the process.

The formal management control *system* is only a part of the management control *process,* actually a relatively unimportant part. The system can help motivate the manager to make decisions that are in the best interests of the organization, and the system can provide information that aids the manager in making these decisions; but many other stimuli are involved in motivating the manager, and good information does not automatically produce good decisions. The success or failure of the management control process depends on the personal characteristics of the manager: his judgment, his knowledge, his ability to influence others.

TECHNIQUE IS ALL-IMPORTANT

In technical control, the system itself is a much more important part of the whole process. Except in fully automated operations, it is an exaggeration to say that the system *is* the process, but it is not much of an exaggeration. The technical control system ordinarily states what action should be taken; it makes the decisions. As with any operation, management vigilance is required to detect an unforeseen "foul-up" in the operation, or a change in the conditions on which the technique is predicated. And management will be seeking ways to improve the technique. In general, however, the degree of management involvement in technical control is small, whereas in management control it is large.

As new techniques are developed, there is a tendency for more and more activities to become susceptible to technical control. In the factory, the production schedule that was formerly set according to the foreman's intuition is now derived by linear programing. And, although not too long ago it was believed that technical control was appropriate only for factory operations, we now see models and formulas being used for certain marketing decisions, such as planning salesmen's calls and planning direct mail advertising. This shift probably will continue; it is a large part of what people have in mind when they say, "Management is being increasingly scientific."

Following are statements illustrating the consequences of failing to make a distinction between management control and technical control:

"Computers will make middle management obsolete." (Although computers can replace human beings in technical control, they are not a substitute for the human judgment that is an essential part of the management control process.)

"Business should develop a management control system like the SAGE and SAC control systems that work so well for the military." (The military systems mentioned are technical control systems. They are not related to the management control problem in the military, let alone that in business.)

"The way to improve the management control process is to

develop better management decision rules." (This implies that mathematics, rather than human beings, is the essence of management control.)

"Transfer prices should be calculated centrally." (This gives no recognition to negotiation and the exercise of judgment by divisional managers.)

"If you follow the planning and control techniques described in this book, your profits are a near predictable certainty." (This implies that the technique, rather than the quality of management, is the principal determinant of success.)

SUMMARY

We have described several subsystems that come under the general heading, "planning and control systems." Although related to one another, they have different purposes and different characteristics; different ways of thinking about each of them are therefore required. Generalizations about the whole area are, if valid, so vague as not to be useful. By contrast, useful generalizations, principles, and techniques can be developed for each of the subsystems. Mistakes are made when those valid for one subsystem are applied to another.

4

Budgetary Control and Business Behaviour

Mgt. Control

ADRIAN BUCKLEY and EUGENE McKENNA*

Nowadays most companies of any size employ some of the techniques of management accounting. Probably the most widely used is budgetary control.

The process of budgeting consists of planning, controlling, co-ordinating and motivating through money values, members, and departments within an organisation. In a nutshell, the budget is a plan — usually for one year ahead — in quantitative terms. The control follows by means of comparing actual performance against the performance standard and taking corrective action where necessary. The key features of budgetary control are as follows:

> The system is a yardstick for comparison. The planned performance is meant to be perceived by management as a target that should motivate managers towards achievement of the goal implied by the budget.
>
> The system transfers information in quantitative terms.
>
> It isolates problems by focusing upon variances.
>
> The identification of variances makes the system an early warning for management action.
>
> It should identify and highlight performance items as opposed to non-performance items (non-performance items include cause and effect outside the control of the company, e.g. a strike in a tyre supplier will affect Ford sales, but Ford cannot be said to be to blame).
>
> It is a tool of management, not a policing mechanism.
>
> It should be a formalised system culminating in management action.

The sinews of the budgeting process — and indeed of most other management control systems — are the influencing of management behaviour by setting agreed performance standards, the evaluation of results and feedback to management in anticipation of corrective action where necessary.

* From *Accounting and Business Research* (Spring 1972), pp 137-50. Reprinted by permission of the Editor.

Since most management controls are conceived and operated by accountants, it is relevant to question whether accountants in general are aware of the impact upon people of these control systems. For there is a body of research findings which is highly critical of accounting control procedures. But, at least in this country, the accounting literature appears only to have given marginal coverage[1] to this most important topic and the syllabuses and examination questions of all the bodies of accountants make little reference to behavioural science. This may be because, as Tricker[2] points out "the accountant is sometimes suspicious of the emphasis in management studies on people. People are difficult to quantify," but "the understanding of management planning and control systems hinges on an understanding of people. Organisational theory has a place in the accountant's background knowledge." However, the Association of Certified Accountants has recently announced a proposed new examination syllabus which includes a paper on Human Relations.

Control and Company Objectives

Most management control systems are assumed to operate as part of a series of devices designed to enable the company to achieve its corporate objective. Budgetary control is in addition a monitor of actual out-turns in the light of short-term estimates of performance. But given that management controls aim to help the achievement of the corporate objective, it is pertinent to ask what most meaningfully constitutes a corporate objective.

When accountants examine this problem they invariably think in terms of maximising profit. A study by Caplan[3] showed that 75 per cent of accountants viewed this as the key business objective, whilst of a sample of non-accounting general managers only 25 per cent saw this as the primary business objective.

The traditional economic theory of the firm explains the behaviour of "economic man" in pursuit of maximum profit. The theory views the entrepreneur as confronted with:

a demand function, in which the prices of the commodities he sells are given by the market;

a cost function, in which the prices of the factors of production which he purchases are given by the market;

a production function, which is essentially a statement of engineering technology.

---

1 See, for example, E. A. Lowe, "Budgetary Control — An Evaluation in a Wider Managerial Perspective", *Accountancy*, November 1970; T. W. McRae, "The Behavioural Critique of Accounting", *Accounting and Business Research*, No. 2, Spring 1971; I. Gibson, "Management by Objectives," *Management Accounting*, May 1970; R. I. Tricker, *The Accountant in Management*, Bastford, 1967.
2 R. I. Tricker, ibid.
3 Edwin H. Caplan, *Management Accounting and Behavioural Science*, Addison-Wesley, 1971.

In this situation the entrepreneur's behaviour is assumed to be predicted by his desire to maximise economic profits. This theory of business behaviour is based on the following set of assumptions:

complete knowledge of alternative courses of action;

unlimited cognitive capacity;

perfect knowledge of outcomes;

total rationality in decision choice.

The modern theory of financial management takes a view near to economic theory in suggesting that: "the operating objective for financial management is to maximise wealth or net present value"[4] of the owners.

But neither of these views is endorsed by research findings in this area, and it is doubtful whether the concept of profit maximisation is relevant to any but the most entrepreneurial of businesses.

Indeed most economists would view the economic theory of the firm as an abstraction which hardly simulates today's business world. Ideas of rationality and perfect knowledge are inconsistent with the realities of uncertainty and limited reasoning. There is also substantial opinion which questions the profit maximising desire of the firm. Some writers, having observed the development of the modern corporate entity, and the divorce of ownership and control, assert that managers, with minimal equity stakes in the company, are less motivated than the owner-manager.[5] Others[6] have suggested that economic survival may be the primary goal of a business. Alternatively, some firms[7] may appear to maximise sales provided that a satisfactory return on invested capital is earned.

This approach is well in line with the concept of "satisficing" developed by Herbert Simon[8] from his observations of the workings of administrative systems. Instead of economic man, Simon talks of "administrative man." Whilst economic man maximises — selecting the best course of action available — administrative man satisfies — that is, he selects a course of action which is satisfactory or good enough. In business terms, administrative man seeks adequate profit rather than maximum profit; a fair price rather than maximum price.

Another concept of the role of the company sets out somewhat

4 Ezra Solomon, *The Theory of Financial Management,* Columbia University Press, 1963.

5 For example, Thorstein Veblen, *Absentee Ownership,* Macmillan, 1923.

Adolf A. Berle and Gardner C. Means, *The Modern Corporation and Private Property,* Macmillan, 1932.

Robert A. Gordon, *Business Leadership in the Large Corporation,* The Brookings Institution, Washington, 1945.

Edith T. Penrose, *The Theory of the Growth of the Firm,* Oxford University Press, 1959.

6 K. W. Rothschild, "Price Theory and Oligopoly," *Economic Journal,* September 1947.

Peter F. Drucker, "Business Objectives and Survival Needs: Notes on a Discipline of Business Enterprise," *The Journal of Business,* April 1958.

7 William J. Baumol, *Business Behaviour, Value and Growth,* Macmillan, 1959.

8 Herbert A. Simon, *Administrative Behaviour,* Macmillan, 1960.

ideological goals, i.e., conducting[9] "the affairs of the corporation in such a way as to maintain an equitable and working balance amongst the claims of the various directly interested groups — stockholders, employees, customers and the public at large." How this compromise is achieved may vary from one firm to another, but the existence of a balance pre-supposes a conflict with profit maximisation which is solely a shareholder objective.

The interpretation of the firm's goals as the various interacting motives of the interested parties is endorsed by the research of Cyert and March,[10] who argue that "the goals of a business firm are a series of more or less independent constraints imposed on the organisation through a process of bargaining among potential coalition members and elaborated over time in response to short-run pressures. Goals arise in such a form because the firm is, in fact, a coalition of participants with disparate demands, changing foci of attention, and limited ability to attend to all organisational problems simultaneously." "In the long run, studies of the goals of a business firm must reflect the adaption of goals to changes in the coalition structure." This concept, the behavioural theory of the firm, implies that it is meaningless to talk of a single organisational goal. It is the participants who have personal objectives, and organisational goals can only mean the goals of the dominant members of the coalition.

A similar picture has been suggested in the theory of managerial capitalism.[11] "Top management, owning little or no equity in the firm, has three main motives: growth, because growth provides job satisfaction, job expansion, higher salaries, higher bonuses and prestige; continuity of employment, which means for the management team as a whole, avoidance of involuntary takeover; and reasonable treatment of share-holders and generally good relations with the financial world."[12]

Samuel Richardson Reid[13] has suggested that the concern of management for such factors as security, power, esteem, income and advancement within the firm may result in emphasis on growth of size rather than profit maximisation.

In summary, economic theory views the firm as an entrepreneur rather than as an organisation, and, assuming perfect knowledge of all market conditions, stresses profit maximisation. The behavioural theory, based on observations of how modern complex business enterprises function, sees a series of goals — the goals of the key individual members of the managerial coalition — as motivating decision making. As pointed out by Caplan,[14] "Most attempts to explain, predict, or motivate human

9 Frank Abrams quoted in E. S. Mason, 'The Apologetics of Managerialism, *Journal of Business,* January 1958.
10 Richard M. Cyert and James C. March, *A Behavioural Theory of the Firm,* Prentice-Hall, 1963.
11 Robin L. Marris, *The Economic Theory of Managerial Capitalism,* Macmillan, 1964.
12 Robin L. Marris, "Profitability and Growth in the Individual Firm," *Business Ratios,* Spring 1967.
13 Samuel Richardson Reid, *Mergers, Managers, and the Economy,* McGraw-Hill, 1968.
14 Edwin H. Caplan, *op. cit.*

behaviour on the basis of economic factors alone are likely to be notably unsuccessful."

The Roots of Management Control

The underlying rationale of most business control procedures is traceable to authoritative styles of management, although this leadership pattern is gradually being superseded by a more enlightened, democratic form which is inversely opposite to its nineteenth century forerunner. But it is questionable as to whether, in general, control procedures are changing in sympathy with more participative styles of management.

In this area Rensis Likert[15] distinguishes four styles of management. System 1, the exploitive authoritative type uses fears and threats, communication is downwards, superiors and subordinates are psychologically distant and almost all decisions are taken at the apex of the organisational pyramid. System 2, the benevolent authoritative style is where management uses rewards to encourage performance, upward communication flow is limited to what the boss wants to hear, subservience to superiors is widespread and, whilst most decisions are taken at the top, some delegation of decision-making exists. System 3, the consultative type, is where management uses rewards, communication may be two-way although upward communication is cautious and limited, by and large, to what the boss wants to hear; some involvement is sought from employees, and subordinates have a moderate amount of influence in some decisions. But again broad policy decisions are the preserve of top management only. System 4, the participative style, gives economic rewards and makes full use of group participation and involvement in fixing high performance goals and improving working methods. Communication flows downward, upward, with peers, and is accurate; subordinates and superiors are psychologically close and decision-making is widely done throughout the firm by group processes. Various personnel in the organisation chart overlap — they are members of more than one group — and thereby link members in the firm. The System 4 style of leadership is said to produce greater involvement for individuals, better labour/management relations and higher productivity.*

System 4 managers exercise "general rather than detailed supervision, and are more concerned with targets than methods. They allow maximum participation in decision-making. If higher performance is to be obtained, a supervisor must not only be employee-centred [as opposed to job-centred] but must also have high performance goals and be capable of exercising the decision-making processes to achieve them."[16]

15 Rensis Likert, *New Patterns of Management,* McGraw-Hill, 1961.
* But whilst this may generally be true, Fiedler's findings (Fred E. Fiedler, *A Theory of Leadership Effectiveness,* McGraw-Hill, 1967) suggest that styles of leadership other than System 4 can be perfectly effective. According to Fiedler, in any situation cognisance must be taken of the extent of job structuring, power vested in the leader, and the relationship between leader and group member.
16 D. S. Pugh, D. J. Hickson and C. R. Hinings, *Writers on Organisations,* Penguin, 1971.

Closely associated to Likert's concepts is Douglas McGregor's postulation of Theory X and Theory Y behaviour within organisations. Theory X behaviour, as observed in the traditional concept of administration suggests that:[17]

> "The average human being has an inherent dislike of work and will avoid it if he can."

> "Because of this human characteristic of dislike of work, most people must be coerced, controlled, directed, threatened with punishment to get them to put forth adequate effort toward the achievement of organisational objectives."

> "The average human being prefers to be directed, wishes to avoid responsibility, has relatively little ambition, wants security above all."

Because this philosophy of management behaviour became less prevalent in organisations which were moving towards industrial democracy, McGregor proposed alternative explanations for human behaviour in business — namely Theory Y. The assumptions behind Theory Y behaviour are.[18]

> "The expenditure of physical and mental effort in work is as natural as play or rest."

> "Man will exercise self-direction and self-control in the service of objectives to which he is committed."

> "The average human being learns, under proper conditions, not only to accept but to seek responsibility."

The corollaries of Theory Y are important. They are that many more people in the firm are able to contribute constructively towards the solution of problems; second, that the main reward in the work situation is the satisfaction of the individual's self-actualisation needs (see also our reference to Maslow, below); third, the potential of the average person in the organisation is not being fully tapped.

McGregor makes the point that whilst staff departments exist essentially to control the line (as is postulated by Theory X), conflict will exist between staff and line management. This conflict may be eliminated if the role of the staff specialist is perceived as being that of providing professional aid to all levels of management, i.e. a supportive relationship.

It should be noted than an investigation undertaken by Caplan[19] indicated that there were definite indications of cost accounting systems being based on the assumptions of the authoritative and Theory X models of behaviour. Thus, whilst management leadership styles have been evolving from System 1 through towards System 4, the management accounting system has not moved with the rest of the organisation.

---

17 Douglas McGregor, *The Human Side of Enterprise,* McGraw-Hill, 1960.
18 Douglas McGregor, ibid.
19 Edwin H. Caplan, *op. cit.*

For budgetary control purposes, Likert's findings suggest that the more participative the process of setting budgets, the more effective they are likely to be in terms of committing personal motivation towards their achievement. This view was confirmed by Coch and French[20] in a study of the effectiveness of participative versus non-participative budgets. Similarly Hofstede[21] tested the hypothesis that higher participation leads to higher budget motivation and found a positive correlation between these factors. In support of this, Bass and Leavitt[22] found that employees participating in setting standards performed better than those who did not.

But beware budget biasing and pseudo-participation. In connection with budget biasing — which is discussed in some depth later — managers may inflate costs or reduce revenue at the budget stage, thus making the budget standard more readily achievable; this is clearly easier to do in a participatory system. However, the problems inherent in this situation may be reduced[23] by an in-depth review during the process of developing the budget. In connection with pseudo-participation there can be no better example than the following, quoted from research findings by Chris Argyris.[24] "The typical controller's insistence on others' participation sounded good to us when we first heard it in our interviews. But after a few minutes of discussion, it began to look as if the word 'participation' had a rather strange meaning for the controller. One thing in particular happened in every interview which led us to believe that we were not thinking of the same thing. After the controller had told us that he insisted on participation he would then continue by describing his difficulty in getting the supervisors to speak freely. For example:

"We bring them in, we tell them that we want their frank opinion, but most of them just sit there and nod their heads. We know they're not coming out with exactly how they feel. I guess budgets scare them; some of them don't have too much education. . . . Then we request the line supervisor to sign the new budget, so he can't tell us he didn't accept it. We've found a signature helps an awful lot. If anything goes wrong, they can't come to us, as they often do, and complain. We just show them their signature and remind them they were shown exactly what the budget was made up of. . . .'

"Such statements seem to indicate that only 'pseudo-participation' is desired by the controller. True participation means that the people can be spontaneous and free in their discussion. Participation, in the

[20] L. Coch and J. R. P. French, "Overcoming Resistance to Change," *Human Relations,* Vol. 1, 1948.
[21] G. H. Hofstede, *The Game of Budget Control,* Tavistock Publications, 1968.
[22] B. M. Bass and H. J. L. Leavitt, "Some Experiments in Planning and Operating," *Management Science,* No. 4, 1963.
[23] M. Schiff and A. J. Lewin, "The Impact of People on Budgets," *The Accounting Review,* April, 1970.
[24] Chris Argyris, "Human Problems with Budgets," *Harvard Business Review,* Jan.-Feb., 1953.

real sense of the word, also involves a group decision which leads the group to accept or reject something new. Of course, organisations need to have their supervisors accept the new goals, not reject them; however if the supervisors do not really accept the new changes but only say they do, then trouble is inevitable. Such half-hearted acceptance makes it necessary for the person who initiated the budget or induced the change, not only to request signatures of the 'acceptors' so that they cannot later on deny they 'accepted', but to be always on the lookout and apply pressure constantly upon the 'acceptors' (through informal talks, meetings and, 'educational discussions of accounting') ."

Budget Motivation

The accountant generally perceives the budget as being a commitment, in quantitative terms, of future performance. As Robert Anthony[25] says "by agreeing to the budget estimates, the supervisor in effect says to management: 'I can and will operate my department in accordance with the plan described in the budget'." Hofstede[26] summarises this position by saying that "budgets and cost standards act as incentives for motivating the budgetees." However, this view is not necessarily universally accepted by authorities. Gordon Shillinglaw[27] says "what is not commonly understood is that the budget itself is not intended to act as a motivating force." But there is evidence that the budget can be a motivator. Is this generally true? Does motivation vary from tight budgets to loose budgets? What happens if the agreed budget becomes patently unachievable?

In examining the question of whether the budget is a stimulus or not, it is first necessary to look at some of the general concepts of motivation in business. For, as Hofstede[28] observes, "There is no reason to assume that the basic needs of the budgeted manager will be any different from the basic needs of other people."

The theories of three of the leading writers — Maslow, Herzberg and McClelland — on the subject are therefore summarised.

Maslow, Herzberg and McClelland

Maslow[29] conceives of the individual as striving to satisfy a hierarchy of basic needs represented in the pyramid in Exhibit I below.

The foot of the pyramid represents the most basic need and the individual strives to move upwards through the hierarchy towards the apex of self-actualisation. Maslow observes[30] that "man is a wanting

25 Robert N. Anthony, *Management Accounting*, Richard D. Irwin, 1964.
26 G. H. Hofstede, *op. cit.*
27 Gordon Shillinglaw, "Divisional Performance Review: An Extension of Budgetary Control," in C. P. Bonini *et al., Management Controls,* McGraw-Hill, 1964.
28 G. H. Hofstede, *op. cit.*
29 Abraham H. Maslow, *Motivation and Personality,* Harper and Row, 1954.
30 Abraham Maslow, ibid.

Exhibit I Maslow's Hierarchy of Basic Needs

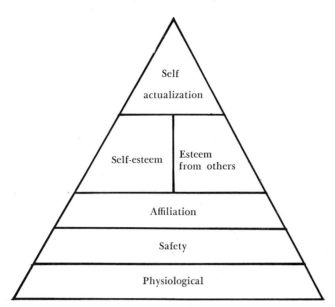

animal and rarely reaches a state of complete satisfaction except for a short time. As one desire is satisfied, another pops up to take its place." Thus only if the lower needs are satisfied will the higher needs appear. Physiological needs include food and rest. Safety needs include job security, a modestly comfortable and predictable routine and a desire for fair treatment and justice from supervisors in the job situation. Frustration of the safety needs lies at the root of resistance to change. Higher than safety needs come affiliation needs — social contacts, belonging to a group, love, etc. Maslow's next level is esteem, divided between self-esteem — the desire for achievement, competence, autonomy, strength, adequacy, mastery — and esteem from others — appreciation of performance, status, recognition. Desire for power also probably belongs in the esteem category. Self-actualisation, at the apex of Maslow's pyramid, implies fulfilling one's ultimate desires, or doing what one is truly fitted for.

Maslow's concept has been tested empirically* and is widely ac-

---

* For example D. T. Hall and K. E. Nougaim, "An Examination of Maslow's Need Hierarchy in an Organisation Setting," *Organisational Behaviour and Human Performance,* 1968, No. 3, find support for the hierarchy in a field study based on the success of management trainees over a five-year period in the American Telephone and Telegraph Co. R. Pellegrin and C. Coates, "Executives and Supervisors: contrasting definitions of career success," *Administrative Science Quarterly,* 1957, No. 1, observe that whilst executives tend to see success as career accomplishment, first line supervisors viewed success in terms of security and income. Similarly, L. Porter, "Job attitudes in Management," *Journal of Applied Psychology,* 1963, No. 4, found that top executives are more concerned with esteem and self actualisation than managers occupying lower levels in the organisation.

cepted, for example by McGregor,[31] and in terms of explaining actions seems intuitively appealing. How it affects budget motivation is discussed below.

The second motivational theorist looked at here is Fred Herzberg.[32] His concept is empirically based — although there are dissentient views[33] to his total concept — and is built on the principle that people are motivated towards what makes them feel good and away from what makes them feel bad. Herzberg's research identifies the following factors as producing good feelings in the work situation:

Achievement

Recognition

The work itself

Responsibility

Advancement

All of these are real motivators. By contrast Herzberg suggests that the following factors arouse bad feelings in the work situation:

Company policy and administration

Supervision

Salary

Interpersonal relations

Working conditions

These latter factors are clearly concerned with the work environment rather than the work itself. Herzberg calls these "hygiene factors," and they differ significantly from motivators inasmuch as they "can only prevent illness, but not bring about good health." In other words, lack of adequate "job hygiene" will cause dissatisfaction, but its presence will not, of itself, cause satisfaction; it is the motivators that do this. The absence of the motivators will not cause dissatisfaction, assuming the job hygiene factors are adequate, but there will be no positive motivation. Herzberg's findings are summarised in Exhibit II below.

As Herzberg[35] explains, referring to the diagrams, "the length of each box represents the frequency with which the factor appeared in the events presented. The width of the box indicates the period in which the good or bad job attitude lasted, in terms of a classification of short duration and long duration. A short duration of attitude change did not last longer than two weeks, while a long duration of attitude change may have

31 Douglas McGregor, *op. cit.*

32 F. Herzberg, *Work and the Nature of Man,* World Publishing Co., 1966.

33 See for example, J. R. Hinrichs and L. A. Mischkind, "Empirical and Theoretical Limits to the Two-Factor Hypothesis of Job Satisfaction," *Journal of Applied Psychology,* Vol. 51, No. 2, 1957; Paul F. Wernimont, "Intrinsic and Extrinsic Factors in Job Satisfaction," *Journal of Applied Psychology,* Vol. 50, No. 1, 1966; V. H. Vroom and N. R. F. Maier, "Industrial School of Psychology," *Annual Review of Psychology,* No. 12, 1961.

34 F. Herzberg, B. Mausner and B. Snyderman, *The Motivation to Work,* Wiley, 1959.

35 F. Herzberg, *op. cit.*

Exhibit II **Satisfiers and Dissatisfiers according to Herzberg**

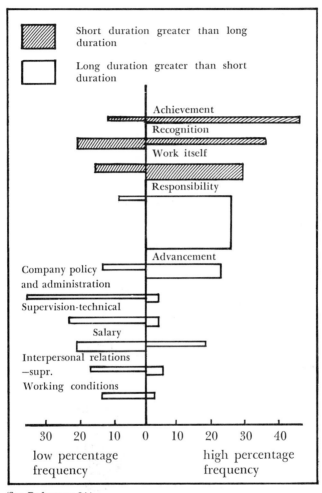

(See Reference 34.)

lasted for years." It will be noted that the length of the salary bar is such that it is both satisfier and dissatisfier. In fact, in the Herzberg experiment it was the most ambiguous of all of the factors highlighted, although the negative element tended to predominate.

It is axiomatic in Herzberg's approach that job satisfaction and job dissatisfaction are not opposites. The opposite of job satisfaction is not job dissatisfaction but no job satisfaction; the opposite of job satisfaction is lack of job dissatisfaction. The essence of Herzberg's message to business is that employee motivation is a function of challenging work in which responsibility can be assumed. Towards this end he prescribes various methods of "job enrichment."

As Hofstede[36] says, in setting Herzberg's motivation, i.e. hygiene factors in the context of Maslow's hierarchy of basic needs "although some of the hygiene factors, like salary, may be related to several basic needs (e.g., safety, affiliation, and esteem needs), the general tendency of the above list is that the motivators are related to needs considerably higher in the pyramid . . . than the hygiene factors." Hofstede goes on to point out that "in Western countries physiological needs are almost universally satisfied; safety needs, to a greater extent; on the other hand, the standard for satisfaction of, for example, achievement needs will be much higher in the case of some occupational groups, for example scientists, than for others, for example assembly line workers." We attempt below to put the Herzberg approach into the framework of budget motivation.

The third major contributor to motivation theory considered here is D. C. McClelland.[37] He suggests that two major needs can be discerned; these are:

- ☐ The need for achievement, which should be thought of as achievement identifiable with one's own efforts. In complex working organisations this is often very difficult.

- ☐ The need for power, which is not just limited to power over others, but includes also power over one's own liberty of action. Again, in work organisations a person's liberty of action obviously has to be constrained. Whilst constraints are necessary in the organisation, unnecessary ones convert motivation to frustration.

Building in Maslow's hierarchy implies that achievement and power become dominant drives when the physiological needs are satisfied.

In developing his concept of the "achievement motive," McClelland focuses upon the drive of people to be challenged and to be innovative, and he found that the drive for achievement varies in individuals according to their personality and cultural background. Classifying people as "high achievers" and "low achievers," he suggests that high achievers make more successful managers than low achievers. According to McClelland, high achievers relish responsibility and seek out problems which offer challenge; he tends to set himself standards that stretch him and he derives satisfaction from their achievement. The need for positive feedback as a barometer of his performance is important to the high

[36] G. H. Hofstede, *op. cit.*
[37] D. C. McClelland, *The Achieving Society*, The Free Press, New York, 1967; D. C. McClelland, J. W. Atkinson, R. A. Clark and E. L. Lowell, *The Achievement Motive*, Appleton-Century-Crofts, 1953.

achiever. But with targets set too low, no challenge exists and hence no satisfaction is derived from achievement; at the other extreme, standards set too high tend not to motivate because of the high risk of failure. The high achiever is generally less directly concerned with money than the low achiever — because satisfaction flows from accomplishment. However, money reward may have significance in terms of being seen to be held in esteem. To the high achiever the opportunity for personal satisfaction from successfully accomplishing tasks is of the essence. Clearly the need to identify the personal characteristics of the high achiever and the low achiever is essential, in the context of both the budget and general management, if the best is to be got out of people.

Maslow, Herzberg and McClelland in the Context of Budget Motivation

Having summarised each of the above experts' theses, it is necessary to place their findings within the overall framework of budget motivation. Maslow's motivational hypothesis would suggest the need to stress those factors near the apex of the hierarchy of basic needs. Hofstede[38] interprets this theory with reference to the budget as follows. "In the case of our budgeted managers, we can expect their . . . need fulfilment to be fairly high on the . . . pyramid. Therefore, attempts on budget motivation by building on the lower-level needs for these people will be likely to have either no effect, or possibly a negative one. Positive budget motivation will only be possible by trying to fulfil the higher needs; esteem from others, self-esteem, and possibly some kind of self-actualisation."

The implications of Herzberg's findings are evidently the need to stress, in the budget system, the presence of motivating factors and an adequate level of hygiene factors.

The relevance of McCelland's approach lies in the fact that the budgeted manager should seek challenge from the setting of budget standards.

But there are additional guidelines that can be gleaned from the rules of Maslow's and Herzberg's approaches to motivation. Rewards, in terms of salary increments, promotion, etc. are often based upon performance relative to budget — although this generally operates in parallel with superiors' interpretation of the level set in the budget. However, given Herzberg's findings that salary is generally either neutral or a dissatisfier — although Maslow's and McClelland's views of salary as fulfilling esteem desires must not be overlooked — it may be logical to sever the connection of budget performance and salary review. Ross[39] has shown that separating evaluation and control improves communication. This would tend to diminish feelings of injustice relative to budget performance. If salary and promotion are based, even in part, upon performance versus budget these injustice feelings may arise because of

[38] G. H. Hofstede, *op. cit.*
[39] I. C. Ross, "Role Specialisation in Supervision," *Doctoral Dissertation,* Columbia University, 1952.

the varying subjective standards which managers set for themselves in the budget situation. Examples of varying standards include new managers, or managers setting their first budget standards, who may desire to achieve their initial budget, and set standards accordingly; managers who have regularly achieved budget may set increasingly demanding targets; and managers who, because they have frequently failed to reach budget, set increasingly more difficult — even fantasy-budget standards. These behavioural patterns are considered further later in this paper.

In the budget situation, Maslow's affiliation needs may be met by budgetees tending to develop informal groups who will resist budget pressures exerted by the controller's department. This sort of occurrence most often happens in an authoritative management environment, or where the control system is of an authoritative type (see the discussion of Likert's work earlier in this paper). Argyris[40] observed this tendency in a study of employee behaviour in relation to budgets.

Maslow's esteem needs and Herzberg's recognition and achievement desires are relevant to the budget because managers obviously wish to succeed and be seen to succeed. Similarly Herzberg spotlights responsibility as one of the key motivators of managers — this suggests, for budgets, the need to stress participation in setting standards.

Other Motivational Theorists

Many other investigators have developed formulations to explain the behaviour of people and their business motivation.

Vroom[41] is one example. His basic model is as follows:

Motivation = f (Valence × Expectancy)
in which the concepts are defined as follows:

Motivation: the force to perform a certain act.

Valence: the orientation (preference of attainment above non-attainment) of a person towards a certain outcome of his act.

Expectancy: the degree to which a person believes a certain outcome of his act to be probable.

In the budget context the Vroom formula becomes:

Budget motivation =
  f[Valence of attaining budget
  × Perceived influence on results
  + Σ(Valences of other effects of actions
  × Expectancies of these other effects)].
  in which the concepts mean the following:

40 Chris Argyris, *The Impact of Budgets on People,* The Controllership Foundation, 1952.
Chris Argyris, "Human Problems with Budgets," *Harvard Business Review,* Jan.-Feb., 1953.
41 V. H. Vroom, *Work and Motivation,* John Wiley, 1964.

Budget motivation: the force to take actions necessary to attain the budget.

Valence of attaining budget: the preference of attaining the budget above not attaining it.

Perceived influence on results: expectancy of the effect of one's action on budget results.

Valences of other effects of action: the preferences for these other effects.

Expectancies of other effects: the degree to which the budgetee believes these other effects to be probable.

Becker and Green[42] present precepts not dissimilar to McClelland. They accept that the level of aspiration of employees is related to their performance and go on to show that the business firm may be highly influential in affecting levels of aspiration of employees. This, of course, would be confirmed by Herzberg.

Stedry[43] is also concerned with aspiration levels in budgeting. He set out to probe the impact of budget level on performance. He showed that aspiration level formation played a big part in actual performance, and that highest results were achieved by those with highest aspiration levels. Stedry's study affirmed the adage that budgets should be "attainable but not too tight." In a subsequent study with Kay,[44] Stedry looked at the effect of more than one aspiration level. Goals were set either at a normal level (achievable 50 per cent of the time) or a difficult level (achievable only 25 per cent of the time). The findings of the researchers are interesting. Difficult goals appear to lead either to very good or very bad performance in comparison with performance with normal goals. In the case of the good results it appeared that the formal goal had become an aspiration level. But where very bad performance followed the difficult goal, the budgetee evidently perceived his target as being impossible, he failed to set an aspiration level and began to show withdrawal symptoms. Thus where the difficult goal was seen as a challenge (as it tended to be with the "high achievers" and also with the younger participants), actual performance was better than target. But where the difficult goal was viewed as impossible, performance fell below even the normal goal.

With regard to aspiration levels, Child and Whiting[45] have determined that:

Success generally leads to a raising of the level of aspiration, and failure to a lowering.

[42] S. Becker and D. Green, "Budgeting and Employee Behaviour," *Journal of Business,* October, 1962.

[43] A. C. Stedry, *Budget Control and Cost Behavior,* Prentice-Hall, 1960.

[44] A. C. Stedry and E. Kay, *The Effects of Goal Difficulty on Performance: A Field Experiment,* Sloan School of Management, Massachusetts Institute of Technology, 1964.

[45] I. L. Child and J. W. M. Whiting, "Determinants of Level of Aspiration: Evidence from Everyday Life," in Brand (ed.) *The Study of Personality,* John Wiley, 1954.

The stronger the success, the greater is the probability of a rise in level of aspiration; the stronger the failure, the greater is the probability of a lowering.

Shifts in level of aspiration are in part a function of changes in the subject's confidence in his ability to attain goals.

Effects of failure on level of aspiration are more varied than those of success.

They also found some evidence to the effect that failure is more likely than success to lead to withdrawal in the form of avoidance of setting an aspiration level. We are sure that this is in line with many accountants' experience.

Hofstede's[46] research confirms many of the above findings. Defining aspiration level as that "level of future performance in a familiar task which an individual, knowing his level of past performance in that task explicity undertakes to reach," he tests the effect on out-turn of varying degrees of "tightness" in the budget. His findings are summarised in Exhibit III, which shows the level of expense on the vertical axis and

Exhibit III   Hofstede's Research Findings

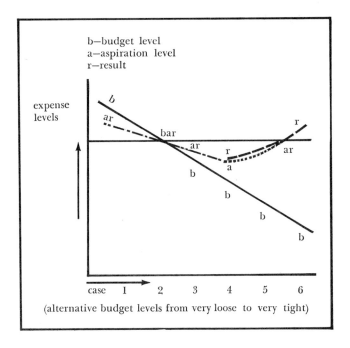

[46] G. H. Hofstede, *op. cit.*

the degree of "tightness" of the budget on the horizontal axis going from very loose on the left to very tight on the right.

It can be seen that as budgets become tighter the budgetee adapts his aspiration level to the budget level. In case three the actual results coincide with the aspiration level and although the budget has not been achieved, the actual results are better than normal. The budget in case four is much tighter, and although the employee was motivated and aspires to higher levels, his actual results fail to rise. After this point his aspiration and results fall because the budgetee no longer believes it possible to reach the budget level. In case six the budgetee looks upon the budget as being utterly impossible, and this creates negative motivation and performance deteriorates in sympathy.

The key findings of Hofstede's study are that performance improves when the following features are present in the budget process:

participation in the setting of the budget,

frequent communication about cost and budget variances with the boss,

knowing exactly which costs one is responsible for,

frequent group meetings of the boss with subordinates.

Obviously different managers and supervisors will have different aspiration levels. It may be that controllers can affect actual performance by ensuring that high achievers are set challenging targets. But there is a difference between the challenging target and the impossible. What is challenging to one manager may be impossible to another, and it is our contention that the controller must be sympathetic to the aspiration goals of his managers if he is to achieve full effectiveness.

Budget Biasing

As mentioned above, Child and Whiting showed that past budgeting performance affected aspiration levels. Lowe and Shaw[47] have also shown how past results *vis-a-vis* budget can influence the level at which future budgets are set. As would be anticipated, where budgetees "are allowed to take part in a bargaining type process for fixing their own budget standards they tend to bias information according to the way in which they perceive themselves to secure greatest personal benefit." Generally managers saw it in their personal interest to agree to lower rather than higher budget standards. Similarly Schiff and Lewin[48] observed a tendency for managers in a participatory budget environment to bias budget costs upwards and revenues downwards. As Lowe[49] points out, "The rational economic behaviour of individual managers will be moti-

[47] E. A. Lowe and R. W. Shaw, "An Analysis of Managerial Biasing: Evidence from a Company's Budgeting Process," *Journal of Management Studies,* October 1968; E. A. Lowe and R. W. Shaw, "The Accuracy of Short-Term Business Forecasting: An Analysis of a Firm's Sales Budgeting", *Journal of Industrial Economics,* Summer 1970.
[48] M. Schiff and A. Y. Lewin, *op. cit.*
[49] E. A. Lowe, *op. cit.*

vated by a desire to strike a balance between present security in retaining their job, and increasing future income. A manager in the budgeting process, may reason that a conservative forecast increases the likelihood of achieving a favourable budget performance in the coming budget period, and therefore his superior's approval *then,* but at the cost of possibly disappointing his superior *now* with the size of his present forecast. Where a manager has little or no good will left because of poor past budgeting performance he may well be tempted to make extravagantly high forecasts now in order to maintain his superior's present acceptance despite the possible dire consequences later. . . . In contrast the manager who has plenty of such good will stored up with his superior may well find it possible to temper his forecasts now with a view to obtaining more good will later." Sometimes genuine over- or under-estimation occurs. Here Lowe and Shaw[50] observed for level of sales budgeted that "when sales . . . are rising there is a tendency to underestimate and when falling there is a tendency to overestimate the level."

Budget Communication

The direction of flow of budgetary control information within an organisation may have critical repercussions for its efficiency. The situation in which information flows from the budget controller's department upwards first to more senior management — a characteristic of the authoritative control systems referred to above — is clearly in breach of the control principles of Likert's system 4 democratic style of management in which communication is downwards, upwards, and with peers, and is accurate.

In these circumstances the manager will, as McRae[51] observes, "tend to feed up the kind of information he thinks his superior likes; and this will probably be information which causes least stress and tension." As Argyris[52] says "playing it safe is a way to keep the road to advancement open."

Miles and Vergin[53] have appreciated the communications failure of traditional control systems and they have summarised their findings and precepts for a behaviourally sound control system as follows: "The principal flaw in the traditional theory of control according to the behavioural scientists, is the assumption that control is exercised downwards in the organisation — by superiors or subordinates charged with carrying out detailed organisational assignments. In the traditional control model, its critics argue, the organisation is pictured as essentially machine-like. Control procedures are designed to monitor the machine's performance along a number of dimensions and to despatch various reports to upper level officials. Management, in this model, stands at

50 E. A. Lowe and R. W. Shaw, *op. cit.* (1970).
51 T. W. McRae, *op. cit.*
52 Chris Argyris, *Integrating the Individual and the Organization,* John Wiley, 1964.
53 R. E. Miles and R. C. Vergin, "Behavioural Problems of Variance Controls," *California Management Review,* Spring 1966.

the 'control panel' alert to evidence of negative deviation from pre-established standards and procedures and ready to pull switches and twist dials to enforce compliance at any point at which such deviation may occur.

"The behaviouralists grant that management may gather information on discrepancies and attempt to restore conformance. But, they argue, it is the individual organisational member who actually exercises control — who accepts or rejects standards, who does or does not exercise care in the performance of his duties, or who accepts or resists efforts to change his behaviour to achieve some objective or goal.

"While behavioural scientists have generally not translated their criticism into detailed prescriptions for the design of control systems, it is possible to abstract from their statement some conditions which they feel must be present in the organisational environment and some requirements which they believe must be met by management control systems.

"Standards must be established in such a way that they are recognised as legitimate. This requires that the method of deriving standards must be understood by those affected, and that standards must reflect the actual capabilities of the organisational process for which they are established.

"The individual organisation member should feel that he has some voice or influence in the establishment of his own performance goals. Participation of those affected in the establishment of performance objectives helps establish legitimacy of these standards.

'Standards must be set in such a way that they convey 'freedom to fail.' The individual needs assurance that he will not be unfairly censured for an occasional mistake or for variations in performance which are outside his control.

"Feedback, recognised as essential in traditional control designs, must be expanded. Performance data must not only flow upward for analysis by higher echelons, but they must also be summarised and fed back to those directly involved in the process."

It has also been shown,[54] in support of the desirability of downwards communication, that knowledge of results influences favourably future performance.

On other aspects of communication, is the budget account free from criticism? In our opinion the answer is no. The marketing maxim that the seller should use the tone of voice and the words that the consumer understands applies no less in the context of a budgeting framework. The budget accountant should be aware that non-accountant managers prefer to look at management information in terms other than a matrix of figures.

As Robert Townsend says,[55] "Statements comparing budget to actual should be written not in the usual terms of higher (lower) but in

[54] N. R. F. Maier, *Psychology in Industry, A Psychological Approach to Industrial Problems*, George G. Harrap, 1955.
[55] Robert Townsend, *Up the Organization*, Michael Joseph, 1970.

plain English of better (or worse) than predicted by budget. This eliminates the mental gear changes between income items (where parens are bad) and expense items (where parens are good). This way reports can be understood faster." Becker[56] suggests that accountants should look to the coding and receiving processes of the individuals to whom information is transmitted. This view is endorsed by Bruns,[57] Dyckman[58] and Birnberg and Nath.[59] All refer to the tendency of non-accountants to look literally at the title of an accounting document — for example a profit and loss account — and perceive it as just that. But they fail to appreciate how differences may arise by virtue of accounting treatments of say stock valuation, depreciation, profit on long-term contracts, etc. Solving the questions raised by this "functional fixation" is outside the scope of this article, but all accountants must be aware of its existence if they are to provide line management with the full support that it expects from finance men.

The Budget System — Punitive or Supportive?

Both McGregor and Likert suggest that for the modern organisation to be wholly effective it is necessary that employees should see themselves as having supportive relationships to other employees. In this (perhaps utopian) situation, the boss gives support to the employee as he wants the employee to be effective. From this it can be deduced that control systems would have the role of helping to make the manager more effective — that is, they would support him. But it has been suggested by Chris Argyris[60] (see below) that the way in which accountants operate budgetary control systems is punitive rather than supportive.

Budgets and People

The major study of the effect of budgets on people — by Chris Argyris[61] — was undertaken some twenty years ago. Nonetheless, the findings are relevant now if, as for example Caplan[62] believes, cost accounting systems are still based on the assumptions of an authoritative model of behaviour. Argyris set out to examine the effects of budgets on people in organisations. He observed that budget staff viewed their role as essentially one of criticism. They perceived themselves as watchdogs looking for and

56 S. W. Becker, "Discussion of the Effect of Frequency of Feedback on Attitudes and Performance," Empirical Research in Accounting: Selected Studies, 1967, supplement to Vol. V of *Journal of Accounting Research,* University of Chicago, 1968.
57 William J. Bruns Jr, "Inventory Valuation and Management Decisions," *The Accounting Review,* April 1965.
58 Thomas R. Dyckman, "The Effects of Alternative Accounting Techniques on Certain Management Decisions," *Journal of Accounting Research,* Spring 1964.
59 Jacob G. Birnberg and Raghu Nath, "Implications of Behavioural Science for Management Accounting," *The Accounting Review,* July 1967.
60 Chris Argyris, *op. cit.* (1952).
61 Chris Argyris, ibid.
62 Edwin H. Caplan, *op. cit.*

reporting to top management deviations from plan. The budget staff looked upon the budget as being a means of applying pressure and offering a challenge to line employees. Line supervisors objected to the method of budgetary control in the organisation because:

It merely reported results without commenting on reasons for the results.

The accountants were considered inflexible.

The budget staff were always increasing pressure by increasing targets. This was resented because it implied that they (the line) lacked adequate interest in their job and would not be interested were it not for the budget.

The budgets were always set unrealistically high.

Supervisors suggested that these problems could be overcome if accountants saw the other person's point of view; and further realised that budgets were only opinions and were not final. Argyris reports an astounding degree of aggression against the budget department, which is perhaps not surprising given first that the budget system in Argyris' study appeared to be a policing mechanism, and second that "success for the budget supervision means failure for the factory supervisor."[63] Some of the supervisors' comments about accountants were indicative of a control system that was anything but supportive. "Most of them are warped and they have narrow ideas. "They don't know how to handle people."[64]

In the jargon of the "managerial grid," the average budget accountant is a truly 9,1 manager. What is meant by this is explained by a brief examination of Blake and Moulton's[65] thesis. Their initial assumption is that management should aim to foster environmental attitudes conducive to efficient performance, and in so doing they must stimulate creativity, innovation, experimentation and enthusiasm for the job. The managerial grid combines the two key elements of business behaviour, namely concern for production and concern for people. In this context "concern for" is associated with the management style of the executive. "Production" is not limited to factory manufacturing techniques, but may refer to any task of management — excluding the management of people, which falls into the other heading — for example research and development, level of sales, the logistics of depot locations, etc. Concern for people encompasses all aspects of human relations, personal motivation and interpersonal contact.

With these two concerns — for production and for people — on axes as shown in Exhibit IV, it is comparatively easy to summarise a manager's style in relation to the maximum possible of 9.

Thus 9,1 management, or "task management," focuses wholly upon production, and the manager in this category can generally be said

63 Chris Argyris, *op. cit.* (1953).
64 Chris Argyris, ibid.
65 Robert R. Blake and Jane S. Moulton, *The Managerial Grid,* Gulf Publishing, 1964.

Exhibit IV   The Managerial Grid

Concern for people									
9		Country club management— (1, 9)				Team Management— (9, 9)			
8		Production is incidental to lack of conflict and "good fellowship."				Production is from integration of task and human requirements.			
7						Dampened pendulum— (5, 5)			
6						(Middle-of-the-road) Push for production but don't go "all out." Give some, but not all. "Be fair but firm."			
5									
4									
3		Impoverished management— (1, 1)							
2		Effective production is unobtainable because people are lazy, apathetic and indifferent. Sound and mature relationships are difficult to achieve because, human nature being what it is, conflict is inevitable.				Task management— (9, 1) Men are a commodity, just like machines. A manager's responsibility is to plan, direct and control the work of those subordinate to him.			
1									
	1	2	3	4	5	6	7	8	9

Concern for production

(See Reference 66.)

to have acute problems in dealing with people, but to be exceptionally competent technically. The 9,1 management style is entirely geared to high level productivity — at least in the short term. Superiors make decisions, subordinates carry them out without question. But this system has inherent weaknesses because subordinates will be working in an environment where none of Herzberg's motivators are present — achievement, recognition, responsibility and advancement will probably be absent and the nature of the work will not stimulate. Such factors as company policy and administration, salary, interpersonal contacts and working conditions must therefore all be acceptable if industrial strife is to be avoided. Shop floor conditions in the motor industry are a good example of the 9,1 management style, and the fact that its record of industrial relations is punctuated with disputes is indicative of the shortcomings of the task management style. It is also possible that this style of leadership is a major contributor to the polarisation of superior and

66 Robert R. Blake and Jane S. Moulton, "The Managerial Grid," *Advanced Management Office Executive*, Vol. 1, No. 9, 1962.

subordinates, which results in the "Them" and "Us" thinking[67] which is at the root of so many industrial disputes.

By contrast the 1,9 style, or "country club management," emphasises people to the exclusion of their performance. People are encouraged and supported, but their mistakes are actually overlooked, because they are doing their best — the maxim of "togetherness" applies. Direct disagreement or criticism of one another must be avoided at all costs and hence production problems are not followed up. This style of management can easily evolve when competition is limited, for example, the mature oligopoly.

The ideal of the managerial grid is to move towards the 9,9 style, and Blake and Moulton advocate a phased organisational development programme with this as the goal.

On the evidence presented here, the budget accountant falls into the 9,1 category; it is hoped that this paper may help him to increase his concern for people and thereby move upwards in the managerial grid.

Conclusions

We now bring together our examination of available research findings into a series of guidelines which we would regard as being indicative of good budgeting practice, given the implications of behavioural science. They are:

> In terms of setting standards, maximum participation should be sought. As Robert Townsend[68] says "budgets must not be prepared on high and cast as pearls before swine. They must be prepared by the operating divisions. Since a division must believe in the budget as its own plan for operations, management cannot juggle figures just because it likes to. Any changes must be sold to the division or the whole process is a sham." But the need for an in-depth review of budgets prepared on a participatory basis is paramount.
>
> Information flow should be downwards, upwards and with peers; *not* just upwards.
>
> There should be frequent communication about cost and budget variances with the boss.
>
> Managers should know exactly which costs they are responsible for.
>
> There should be frequent group meetings of the boss with his subordinates.
>
> Performance is clearly of essence in giving salary and promotion rewards. But in making these assessments of how well managers have performed it may be wise to leave the budget outside the appraisal.

[67] Michael Shanks, *The Stagnant Society*, Pelican, 1961.
[68] Robert Townsend, *op. cit.*

Budget accountants should communicate in the language of the person with whom they are dealing.

Budget accountants should be prepared to be humble in explaining their presentations. They must remember that non-accountants may not appreciate how variations may arise through different stock valuation methods, different depreciation methods, etc. In other words the non-accountant literally believes the title of the document — for example profit and loss account — with which he is presented.

Everything should be done to make the budget — and indeed any control system — supportive rather than punitive; the aim should be towards self-control rather than a policing mechanism.

The budget should not be used to pressurise line management.

The budget accountant must be sensitive to the reactions of management and supervisors to his control mechanisms.

Focus should be on efficiency variances. Variances that arise purely from accounting treatment should be omitted.

Budgets which are attainable but not too tight are the best motivators.

It is also of essence that the budget accountant understand the ways in which managers play the game of budget control, for instance:

"Difficult" budget goals may lead either to very good or very bad results compared with budgets set at a "normal" level. The difficult budget may either be perceived by the high achiever, to whom it represents an aspiration level, as a challenge; or by the low achiever as impossible.

Managers like to achieve budget, since in so doing they fulfil esteem and achievement needs.

Success generally leads to a rising of the level of aspiration, and failure to a lowering.

The stronger the success, the greater the probability of a rise in level of aspiration; the stronger the failure, the greater is the probability of a lowering.

Shifts in level of aspiration are in part a function of changes in the subject's confidence in his ability to meet goals.

Effects of failure on level of aspiration are more varied than those of success.

Failure may lead to withdrawal in the form of avoidance of setting a level of aspiration. This withdrawal, if failure persists, may lead to a complete breakdown in communications, and to personal and industrial relations problems.

Managers may bias standards conservatively in order to ensure that they achieve budget, arguing that superiors' short-term disapproval at a conservative budget will be compensated by approval when their budget is more than achieved. This tendency to play it safe more frequently occurs in an authoritative organisation.

When a manager has a poor track record of budget performance he may be tempted to make extravagantly high forecasts in order to gain short-term approval, despite probable dire consequences later.

When sales levels are rising there is a tendency to underestimate sales out-turns; when falling, the tendency is towards overestimation.

What we have tried to do in this paper is to summarise some of the findings of behavioural science on the topic of the budget. Necessarily our approach has been brief and all of the theories and research work to which we have referred clearly say much more than we have reported here. However, we hope that we have made readers aware of some of the ways in which employees react to budgets. We further hope that we have shown that budgets are powerful behavioural tools and if their use is to result in consistently desirable results it is important that accountants in budget departments should be aware of their behavioural implications.

5

Behavioral Assumptions of Management Accounting

EDWIN H. CAPLAN*

Accounting has been closely associated with the development of the modern business organization. Thus, we might expect accountants to show a strong interest in recent contributions to organization theory which increase our understanding of the business firm and how it functions. An examination of accounting literature, however, suggests that (despite the steadily increasing flow of accounting articles and texts incorporating the words "management" and "decisions" in their titles) accountants have been relatively unconcerned with current research in organization theory. Although the past few years have witnessed the beginnings of an effort to bridge this gap, much still remains to be done.[1] This paper attempts to demonstrate that an understanding of behavioral theory is relevant to the development of management accounting theory and practice.

The discussion to be presented here may be summarized as follows:

1. The management accounting function is essentially a behavioral function and the nature and scope of management accounting systems is materially influenced by the view of human behavior which is held by the accountants who design and operate these systems.

2. It is possible to identify a "traditional" management accounting model of the firm and to associate with this model certain fundamental assumptions about human behavior. These assumptions are presented in Table 1.

3. It is also possible to postulate behavioral assumptions based on modern organization theory and to relate them to the objectives of management accounting. A tentative set of such assumptions appears in Table 2.

4. Research directed at testing the nature and validity of accounting assumptions with respect to human behavior in business organizations can be useful in evaluating and, perhaps, improving the effectiveness of management accounting systems.

* From *The Accounting Review* (July 1966) , pp. 496-509. Reprinted by permission of the Editor.
[1] See, for example: Robert T. Golembiewski, "Accountancy as a Function of Organization Theory," *The Accounting Review* (April 1964,) pp. 333-41; and John J. Willingham, "The Accounting Entity: A Conceptual Model," *The Accounting Review* (July 1964), pp. 543-52.

Table 1. Behavioral Assumptions of "Traditional" Management Accounting Model of the Firm

---

Assumptions with Respect to Organization Goals

A. The principal objective of business activity is profit maximization (economic theory).

B. This principal objective can be segmented into sub-goals to be distributed throughout the organization (principles of management).

C. Goals are additive — what is good for the parts of the business is also good for the whole (principles of management).

Assumptions with Respect to the Behavior of Participants

A. Organization participants are motivated primarily by economic forces (economic theory).

B. Work is essentially an unpleasant task which people will avoid whenever possible (economic theory).

C. Human beings are ordinarily inefficient and wasteful (scientific management).

Assumptions with Respect to the Behavior of Management

A. The role of the business manager is to maximize the profits of the firm (economic theory).

B. In order to perform this role, management must control the tendencies of employees to be lazy, wasteful, and inefficient (scientific management).

C. The essence of management control is authority. The ultimate authority of management stems from its ability to affect the economic reward structure (scientific management).

D. There must be a balance between the authority a person has and his responsibility for performance (principles of management).

Assumptions with Respect to the Role of Management Accounting

A. The primary function of management accounting is to aid management in the process of profit maximization (scientific management).

B. The accounting system is a "goal-allocation" device which permits management to select its operating objectives and to divide and distribute them throughout the firm, i.e., assign responsibilities for performance. This is commonly referred to as "planning" (principles of management).

C. The accounting system is a control device which permits management to identify and correct undesirable performance (scientific management).

D. There is sufficient certainty, rationality, and knowledge within the system to permit an accurate comparison of responsibility for performance and the ultimate benefits and costs of that performance (principles of management.)

E. The accounting system is "neutral" in its evaluations — personal bias is eliminated by the objectivity of the system (principles of management).

Table 2. Some Behavioral Assumptions from Modern Organization Theory

---

Assumptions with Respect to Organization Goals

A. Organizations are coalitions of individual participants. Strictly speaking, the organization itself, which is "mindless," cannot have goals — only the individuals can have goals.

B. Those objectives which are usually viewed as organizational goals are, in fact, the objectives of the dominant members of the coalition, subject to whatever constraints are imposed by the other participants and by the external environment of the organization.

C. Organization objectives tend to change in response to: (1) changes in the goals of the dominant participants; (2) changes in the relationships within the coalition; and (3) changes in the external environment of the organization.

D. In the modern complex business enterprise, there is no single universal organization goal such as profit maximization. To the extent that any truly overall objective might be identified, that objective is probably organization survival.

E. Facing a highly complex and uncertain world and equipped with only limited rationality, members of an organization tend to focus on "local" (i.e., individual and departmental) goals. These local goals are often in conflict with each other. In addition, there appears to be no valid basis for the assumption that they are homogeneous and thus additive — what is good for the parts of the organization is not necessarily good for the whole.

Assumptions with Respect to the Behavior of Participants

A. Human behavior within an organization is essentially an adaptive, problem-solving, decision-making process.

B. Organization participants are motivated by a wide variety of psychological, social, and economic needs and drives. The relative strength of these diverse needs differs between individuals and within the same individual over time.

C. The decision of an individual to join an organization, and the separate decision to contribute his productive efforts once a member, are based on the individual's perception of the extent to which such action will further the achievement of his personal goals.

D. The efficiency and effectiveness of human behavior and decision-making within organizations is constrained by: (1) the inability to concentrate on more than a few things at a time; (2) limited awareness of the environment; (3) limited knowledge of alternative courses of action and the consequences of such alternatives; (4) limited reasoning ability; and (5) incomplete and inconsistent preference systems. As a result of these limits on human rationality, individual and organizational behavior is usually directed at attempts to find satisfactory — rather than optimal — solutions.

Assumptions with Respect to the Behavior of Management

A. The primary role of the business manager is to maintain a favorable balance between (1) the contributions required from the participants and (2) the inducement (i.e., perceived need satisfactions) which must be offered to secure these contributions.

B. The management role is essentially a decision-making process subject to the limitations on human rationality and cognitive ability. The manager must made decisions himself and must effectively influence the decision premises of others so that their decisions will be favorable for the organization.

C. The essence of management control is the willingness of other participants to *accept* the authority of management. This willingness appears to be a non-stable function of the inducement-contribution balance.

D. Responsibility is assigned from "above" and authority is accepted from "below." It is, therefore, meaningless to speak of the balance between responsibility and authority as if both of these were "given" to the manager.

Assumptions with Respect to the Role of Accounting

A. The management accounting process is an information system whose major purposes are: (1) to provide the various levels of management with data which will facilitate the decision-making functions of planning and control; and (2) to serve as a communications medium within the organization.

B. The effective use of budgets and other accounting control techniques requires an understanding of the interaction between these techniques and the motivations and aspiration levels of the individuals to be controlled.

C. The objectivity of the management accounting process is largely a myth. Accountants have wide areas of discretion in the selection, processing, and reporting of data.

D. In performing their function within an organization, accountants can be expected to be influenced by their own personal and departmental goals in the same way as other participants are influenced.

MANAGEMENT ACCOUNTING AS A BEHAVIORAL PROCESS

The management of a business enterprise is faced with an environment—both internal and external to the firm — that is in a perpetual state of change. Not only is this environment constantly changing, but it is changing in many dimensions. These include physical changes (climate, availability of raw materials, etc.), technological changes (new products and processes, etc.), social changes (attitudes of employees, customers, competitors, etc.), and financial changes (asset composition, availability of funds, etc.).

An important characteristic of "good" management is the ability to evaluate past changes, to react to current changes, and to predict future changes. This is consistent with the view that management is essentially a decision-making process and the view that accounting is an information system which acts as an integral part of this decision-making process. It is inconceivable, however, that any workable information system could provide data relative to all, or even a substantial portion, of the changes occurring inside and outside of the organization. There are several reasons for this. Many changes—particularly those that occur in the external environment—are simply not available to the information system of the firm. These changes represent "external unknowns" in a world of uncertainty and limited knowledge. Further, a substantial number of changes that occur within the firm itself may not be perceived by the information system. Thus, there exist "internal" as well as "external" unknowns.

Even if accountants were aware of all the changes which are taking place—or if they could be made aware of them—they still would not be able to reflect them all within their information system. There must be a selection process, explicit or implicit, which permits the gathering and processing of only the most critical information and facilitates the screening out of all other data. In the first place, many items of information would cost more to gather and process than the value of the benefits they would provide. Also, an excessive flow of data would "clog" the system and prevent the timely and efficient passage and evaluation of more important information.[2] Therefore, only a certain, very limited, set of data (i.e., observations about changes) can be selected for admission into the system. The essential point to be noted here is that decisions regarding what information is the most critical, how it should be processed, and who should receive it are almost always made by accountants. In addition, they are often directly involved, as participants, in the management decision-making process itself.

In carrying out these activities, accountants utilize a frame of reference that is, in effect, their view of the nature of the firm and its participants. The operation of their system requires them to be constantly abstracting a selected flow of information from the complex real world and using this selected data as the variables in their "model" of the firm. It seems clear that accountants exercise choice in the design of their systems and the selection of data for admission into them. It also seems clear that the entire management accounting process can be viewed from the standpoint of attempting to influence the behavior of others. It follows, therefore, that they must perform these functions with certain expectations with respect to the reactions of others to what they do. In other words, their model of the firm must involve some set of explicit or implicit assumptions about human behavior in organizations.

THE "TRADITIONAL" VIEW OF BEHAVIOR

Once it has been demonstrated that the management accounting function does by necessity involve assumptions about behavior, the next task is to identify these assumptions. Our investigation is complicated by the fact that nowhere in the literature of accounting is there a formal statement

2 This is the "capacity problem" discussed by Anton. See Hector R. Anton, *Some Aspects of Measurement and Accounting*, Working Paper No. 84 (Berkeley, Calif.: Center for Research in Management Science, University of Calif., 1963).

of the behavioral assumptions of the management accounting model of the firm. It is necessary, therefore, to attempt to construct such a statement. We begin with the premise that present-day management accounting theory and practice is the product of three related conceptual forces, namely, individual engineering technology, classical organization theory, and the economic "theory of the firm." An examination of the literature of management accounting suggests that accountants may have avoided the necessity of developing a behavioral model of their own by borrowing a set of assumptions from these other areas. If this thesis is valid, an appropriate point to begin the search for such assumptions is by an examination of the assumptions of these related models. Since much of the engineering view appears to be incorporated in the classical organization theory model,[3] it can probably be eliminated from this analysis without significant loss. Further, it appears that classical organization theory and economics do not represent two completely different views of human behavior, but rather that they share essentially a single view.

The following paragraphs will attempt to demonstrate that—with the exception of the modern organization theory concepts of recent years —there has been a single view of human behavior in business organizations from the period of the industrial revolution to the present, and that management accounting has adopted this view without significant modification or serious question as to its validity.

The Economic Theory of the Firm

It has been suggested that, from the beginnings of recorded history, the traditional determinants of human behavior in organizations have been either custom or physical force.[4] As long as this was the case, there was no real need for an organization theory or economic theory to explain how and why human beings worked together cooperatively to accomplish common goals. However, the changing structure of society, which accompanied—and to an extent caused—the industrial revolution, destroyed much of the force of these traditional determinants of behavior. The new entrepreneurial class of the eighteenth century sought not only a social philosophy to rationalize its actions, it also sought practical solutions to the immediate problems of motivating, coordinating, and controlling the members of its organizations. The second of these needs resulted in the development of the classical organization theories which will be discussed in the following section. The first need, i.e., the quest for a rationalization, ultimately led to the incorporation of the economic theory of the firm into the logic of the industrial society.

The economic theory of the firm can be summarized as follows.

---

[3] One of the earliest, and perhaps the best, example of this consolidation can be found in the work of Taylor. See, Frederick W. Taylor, *Scientific Management* (New York: Harper & Brothers, 1911).

[4] Robert L. Heilbroner, *The Worldly Philosophers* (rev. ed.; New York: Simon and Schuster, 1961), pp. 7-8.

The entrepreneur is faced with a series of behavior alternatives. These alternatives are limited by the economic constraints of the market and the technological constraints of the production function. Within these constraints he will act in such a way as to maximize his economic profit. This behavior is facilitated by the personality characteristic of complete rationality and the information system characteristic of perfect knowledge. Finally, the individual so described is one who is entirely motivated by economic forces. A more subtle elaboration of this last point is the view that leisure has value and that a person will not work except in response to sufficient economic incentives. Thus, the classical economist specifically assumed that man was essentially "lazy" and preferred to minimize his work effort.[5]

Most modern economists would agree that the classical theory of the firm is based on several rather severe abstractions from the real world of business enterprise.[6] Nevertheless, despite these criticisms, there can be little doubt that it has had a substantial influence on the development of management philosophy and practice. The explanation of human behavior offered by economists—i.e., economic motivation and profit maximization—was incorporated into the patterns of thought of the merging industrial community where it not only became established in its own right but also provided the philosophical and psychological foundations of the scientific management movement.

Classical Organization Theory

At the turn of the century Frederick W. Taylor began a major investigation into the functioning of business organizations which became known as the scientific management movement. Taylor's approach combined the basic behavioral assumptions of the economic theory of the firm with the viewpoint of the engineer seeking the most effective utilization of the physical resources at his disposal. He was concerned with men primarily as "adjuncts to machines" and was interested in maximizing the productivity of the worker through increased efficiency and reduced costs. Implicit in this approach was the belief that if men who might otherwise be wasteful and inefficient could be instructed in methods of achieving increased productivity and, at the same time, provided with adequate economic incentives and proper working conditions, they could be motivated to adopt the improvements, and the organization would benefit accordingly.[7]

March and Simon have noted that the ideas of the scientific management movement are based predominantly on a model of human

[5] This assumption is the basis for the "backward-bending" labor supply curve found in the literature of economics.

[6] See, for example, Andreas G. Papandreou, "Some Basic Problems in the Theory of the Firm," *A Survey of Contemporary Economics,* ed. Bernard F. Haley (Homewood, Ill.: Richard D. Irwin, Inc., 1952), Vol. II, pp. 183-219.

[7] James G. March and Herbert A. Simon, *Organizations* (New York: John Wiley & Sons, Inc., 1958), pp. 12ff.

behavior which assumes that "organization members, and particularly employees, are primarily *passive instruments,* capable of performing work and accepting directions, but not initiating action or exerting influence in any significant way."[8]

The scientific management movement flourished and rapidly became an important part of the business enterprise scene; in fact, for many years it virtually dominated this scene. Furthermore, even a brief glance at current management literature and practices should satisfy the reader that most of Taylor's views are still widely accepted today. Newer theories of management may have supplemented but they have never entirely replaced the scientific management approach.

About 1920, a second major pattern of organization theory, usually referred to as "principles of management" or "administrative management theory," began to develop. This body of doctrine adopted what was essentially a departmentalized approach to the problem of management. Its primary objective was the efficient assignment of organization activities to individual jobs and the grouping of these jobs by departments in such a way as to minimize the total cost of carrying on the activities of the firm. Writers of this school concerned themselves largely with the development of "principles of management" dealing with such subjects as lines of authority and responsibility, specialization, span of control, and unity of command.[9] This administrative management theory appears to have had a substantial and continuing influence on management theory and practice.

The work of Taylor and his scientific management successors led them into detailed studies of factory costs and provided an important stimulus for the development of modern cost-and-management accounting. Administrative management theory further contributed to this development through its emphasis on control and departmental responsibility and accountability. Finally, all of this occurred within the overall setting provided by the economic theory of the firm. In summary, it seems clear that with respect to both its philosophy and techniques, much of contemporary management accounting is a product of, and is geared to, these classical theories. This is what is referred to here as the traditional management accounting model of the firm.

A Tentative Statement of the Behavioral Assumptions Underlying Present-Day Management Accounting

It should now be possible to draw together the several strands of the preceding discussion and attempt to postulate some of the fundamental behavioral assumptions that appear to underlie the traditional management accounting model. These assumptions were presented in Table 1, p. 69. The parenthetical notations note the major conceptual sources of the assumptions. In some cases, there appears to be a considerable

8 Ibid., p. 6.
9 Ibid., pp. 22ff.

overlapping of sources; however, since this is not crucial to the present investigation, the notations have been limited to the primary, or most significant, area.

SOME BEHAVIORAL CONCEPTS OF MODERN ORGANIZATION THEORY

The preceding paragraphs were concerned with an effort to identify a set of behavioral assumptions which could be associated with current theory and practice in management accounting. We will now attempt to develop an alternative set of behavioral assumptions for management accounting—one that is based on concepts from modern organization theory.

Of the several different modern organization theory approaches, the "decision-making model" of the firm has been selected for use here. The basis for this choice is the close relationship which appears to exist between the "decision-making model" and the "information-system" concept of management accounting discussed earlier. The decision-making approach to organization theory effectively began with the writings of Chester I. Barnard, particularly in *The Functions of the Executive,* and was further developed by Simon and others.[10] The model is primarily concerned with the organizational processes of communication and decision-making. While drawing heavily on sociology and psychology, it is distinguished from these organization theory approaches by its emphasis on the decision as the basic element of organization.

Organizations are viewed as cooperative efforts or coalitions entered into by individuals in order to achieve personal objectives which cannot be realized without such cooperation. These individuals are motivated to join the organization and contribute to the accomplishment of its objectives because they believe that in this way they can satisfy their personal goals. It is important to note that these personal goals include social and psychological, as well as economic, considerations. Thus, the survival and success of the organization depends on the maintenance of a favorable balance between the contributions required of each participant and the opportunities to satisfy personal goals which must be offered as inducements to secure effective participation.

It is common practice to speak of organization goals; however, to be completely precise, it is the participants who have goals. The organization itself is mindless and, therefore, can have no goals. In the sense that it is used here, the term organization goals is intended to mean the goals of the dominant members of the coalition, subject to those con-

10 Chester I. Barnard, *The Functions of the Executive* (Cambridge: Harvard University Press, 1938); Herbert A. Simon, *Administrative Behavior* (New York: John Wiley & Sons, Inc., 1947); March and Simon, *Organizations;* and Richard M. Cyert and James G. March, *A Behavioral Theory of the Firm* (Englewood Cliffs, N.J.: Prentice-Hall, Inc., 1963). The preceding works represent the principal theoretical sources for the decision-making model discussed here.

straints which are imposed by other participants and by the external environment. This view implies an organizational goal structure which is in a constant state of change as the environment and the balances and relationships among the participants change. Under such circumstances, it seems meaningless to talk of a single universal goal such as profit maximization. To the extent that any long-run overall objective might be identified, it appears that this objective would have to be stated in very broad and general terms such as the goal of organizational survival.

The decision-making process is usually described as a sequence of three steps: (1) the evoking of alternative courses of action; (2) a consideration of the consequences of the evoked alternatives; and (3) the assignment of values to the various consequences.[11]

It has been suggested that any behavioral theory of rational choice must consider certain limits on the decision maker.[12] These include his (1) limited knowledge with respect to all possible alternatives and consequences, (2) limited cognitive ability, (3) constantly changing value structure, and (4) tendency to "satisfice" rather than maximize. Rational behavior, therefore, consists of searching among limited alternatives for a reasonable solution under conditions in which the consequences of action are uncertain.

The behavioral concepts which flow from the decision-making model have a number of interesting implications. For example, authority is viewed as something which is accepted from "below" rather than imposed from "above."[13] In other words, there must be a *decision to accept* authority before such authority can become effective. Further, human activity is considered to be essentially a process of problem-solving and adaptive behavior—a process in which goals, perception, and abilities are all interrelated and all continually changing.

To summarize the decision-making model, the basic element of organization study is the decision. The objective of managerial decision-making is to secure and coordinate effectively the contributions of other participants. This is accomplished by influencing, to the extent possible, their perception of alternatives and consequences of choice and their value structures, so that the resulting decisions are consistent with the current objectives of the dominant members of the organization.

While the theorists of the "decision-making" school have paid substantial attention to behavioral concepts, the literature does not appear to contain a detailed and complete statement of their underlying behavioral assumptions. Accordingly, it becomes necessary, as it was with the traditional accounting model, to abstract and formulate a set of assumptions. The modern organization theory assumptions presented in Table 2 represent an attempt by the present writer to identify and extend the

11 March and Simon, p. 82.
12 Simon, pp. xxv-xxvi.
13 Douglas McGregor, *The Human Side of Enterprise* (New York: McGraw-Hill Book Co., Inc., 1960), pp. 158-60.

behavioral assumptions of the decision-making model in terms of the management accounting function.

BASIC CONFLICTS BETWEEN THE BEHAVIORAL ASSUMPTIONS OF TRADITIONAL MANAGEMENT ACCOUNTING AND MODERN ORGANIZATION THEORY

An examination of the two sets of behavioral assumptions developed above suggests a number of interesting questions. Answers to these questions, however, can only be found through extended empirical analysis. Thus, whatever value attaches to the foregoing discussion appears to relate to its possible contribution in providing a theoretical framework for future empirical research. This research might be designed to explore such questions as the following:

A. What behavioral model provides the most realistic view of human behavior in business organizations? (Accountants should, perhaps, be willing to accept the research findings of organization theorists regarding this question.)

B. Is it possible to draw any general conclusions about the view of behavior actually held by accountants (and managers) in practice?

C. What, if any, are the major differences in the behavioral assumptions of the views in A and B above?

D. What, if any, are the consequences for the organization and its participants of the differences in the behavioral assumptions of the views in A and B?

E. Is it possible to design management accounting systems which are based on a more realistic view of behavior, and would such systems produce better results than present systems?

Lacking empirical evidence, any attempt to investigate the implications of the differences between the two views of behavior discussed in this paper must be considered highly speculative. We might, however, examine briefly a few of the major differences in order to illustrate the nature of the problem. Let us assume for the moment that the decision-making model represents a more realistic view of human behavior than the traditional management accounting model. Let us further assume that the traditional model is a reasonably accurate summary of actual management accounting views in practice. Under these circumstances, what are some of the consequences for business organizations of the use of accounting systems based on the traditional management accounting model of behavior? The system of classification used in Tables 1 and 2 will also be adopted here. Thus, this analysis will concentrate on four major areas: organization goals, behavior of participants, behavior of management, and the role of accounting.

Assumptions with Respect to Organization Goals

In comparing these two sets of assumptions, the most immediately apparent difference concerns the relative simplicity and brevity of the traditional accounting assumptions as contrasted to those of the organization theory model. This should not be particularly surprising since such a difference seems to be consistent with the general philosophies of the two models. There can be little doubt that the view of human behavior associated with the scientific management movement and classical economics is much less complicated than the behavioral outlooks of modern organization theory. In fact, the principal conflict between modern and classical organization theories appears to rest precisely on this issue. Since traditional management accounting is closely related to the classical models, it seems reasonable to expect that it will also tend toward a relatively simple and uncomplicated view of behavior. For example, with respect to organization goals, the behavioral assumptions of the accounting model focus on a single universal objective of business activity. The organization theory assumptions, on the other hand, suggest a much broader and rather imprecise structure of goals.

The traditional management accounting view of organization goals, which appears to be directly related to the theory of the firm of classical economics, may be summarized as follows: The principal objective of business activity is the maximization of the economic profits of the enterprise; the total responsibility for the accomplishment of that objective can be divided into smaller portions and distributed to sub-units throughout the organization; the maximization by each sub-unit of its particular portion of the profit responsibility will result in maximization of the total profits of the enterprise.

The entire structure of traditional management accounting appears to be built around this concept of profit maximization and the related (but quite different) idea of cost minimization. Management accountants have, for the most part, limited the scope of their systems to the selection, processing, and reporting of data concerning certain economic events, the effects of which can be reduced—without too many complications—to monetary terms. This approach is justifiable only if the particular class of events under consideration can be viewed as *the* critical variables affecting the organization. Thus, accountants have been able to rationalize the importance of the data flowing through their systems by relating this data and its use directly to the assumed goal of profit maximization. However, the classical economic view of profits as the universal motivating force of business enterprises has come under substantial attack in recent years. This attack has been based on two general issues. First, questions have been raised concerning the adequacy of economic profits as the sole significant explanation for what takes place within an organization. Second, it has been suggested that limitations on the decision-making process result in behavior which is best described as satisficing rather than maximizing.

It should be particularly emphasized that the recognition of a more complex goal structure does not mean that economic profits can be ignored. Obviously, business firms cannot survive for any extended period of time without some minimum level of profits. Nevertheless, the attempt to summarize the entire goal structure of a complex business entity through the use of one index may result in an overly simplified and unrealistic view of the organization. In short, profits may represent a necessary but not a sufficient definition of the goal structure of business organizations.

The view of organization goals, suggested by the behavioral assumptions of the decision-making model, has two major aspects. First, those objectives which are commonly referred to as goals of the organization are, in fact, the goals of the dominant group of participants. Secondly, it is suggested that these goals are the result of the interaction of a set of constantly changing forces. Thus, the goal-structure of an organization is not only rather imperfectly defined at any given point in time, but it is also in a continual process of change throughout time. In order to identify any truly universal goal, it may be necessary, as suggested earlier, to generalize to the very broad—and perhaps meaningless—level of an objective such as organization survival.

In view of the complex nature of organization goals, it is possible that the profit maximization assumption unduly restricts the role of management accounting to providing a limited and inadequate range of data for decision making. It is as if the accountant were viewing the firm through a narrow aperture which permits him to observe only a thin "slice" of the total organization activity. In emphasizing this narrow view, traditional management accounting appears to ignore many of the complexities and interrelationships that make up the very substance of an organization. What is the practical implication of these observations? How would management accounting change if accountants did not concentrate exclusively on profit maximization? It is likely that this, in itself, would not involve immediate operational changes but rather a change in underlying philosophy. As this philosophy is modified, it should become apparent that a number of specific changes in procedures and systems are in order. Examples of such specific changes might be found in the departmental budgeting and accounting techniques discussed below.

The traditional accounting assumption with respect to the divisibility and additivity of the responsibility for the accomplishment of organization goals seems to warrant some additional comment. Research in organization theory has indicated that individual members of an organization tend to identify with their immediate group rather than with the organization itself. This tendency appears to encourage the development of strong sub-unit loyalties and a concentration on the goals of the sub-unit even when these goals are in conflict with the interests of the organization. The usual departmental budgeting and accounting techniques, by which management accountants endeavour to measure the success of the various sub-units within an organization in achieving certain goals, are based on the assumption that profit maximization or cost minimization at the departmental level will lead to a similar result for the firm as a whole. Thus, accounting reports tend to highlight supposed departmental efficiencies and inefficiences. Reports of this type seem to encourage departmental activities aimed at "making a good showing" regardless of the effect on the entire organization. It appears to be common for departments within an organization to be in a state of competition with each other for funds, recognition, authority, and so forth. Under such circumstances, it is not very likely that the cooperative efforts necessary to the efficient functioning of the organization as a whole will be furthered by an accounting system which emphasizes and, even fosters inter-departmental conflicts.

The tendency for intra-organizational conflict appears to be further compounded by some of the common management accounting techniques for the allocation and control of costs. For example, in some organizations with relatively rigid budgeting procedures, it appears to be a normal practice for departments to attempt deliberately to use up their entire budget for a given period in order to avoid a reduction in the budgets of succeeding periods. Another example is the emphasis often placed on the desirability of keeping costs below some predetermined amount. In such cases, it is likely that, even though a departmental expenditure would be extremely beneficial to an organization, it will not be undertaken if such action would cause the costs of that department to exceed the predetermined limit.

Assumptions with Respect to the Behavior of Participants

The view of the individual inherent in the behavioral assumptions associated with traditional management accounting is one which has been completely rejected by most of the behavioral scientists interested in modern organization theory. To what extent this traditional view is actually held by accountants in practice is a question which, as stated earlier, can only be answered by empirical investigation. Our own limited experience suggests that it is held by a sufficient number of management accountants to be considered at least a significant view within the profession.

It is possible that the failure of management accountants to consider the more complex motivating forces which organization theory recognizes in the individual contributes to the use of accounting systems and procedures which produce "side effects" in the form of a variety of unanticipated and undesired responses from participants. For example, many management accounting techniques intended to control costs, such as budgeting and standard costing, may virtually defeat themselves because they help to create feelings of confusion, frustration, suspicion and hostility. These techniques may not motivate effectively because they fail to consider the broad spectrum of needs and drives of the participants.[14]

Assumptions with Respect to the Behavior of Management

Modern organization theory encompasses a view of the management process which differs substantially from the "classical" view associated

---

14 For a discussion of the behavioral implications of budgets, see Andrew C. Stedry, *Budget Control and Cost Behavior* (Englewood Cliffs, N.J.: Prentice-Hall, Inc., 1960).

here with management accounting. It is interesting, however, that both models appear to take essentially the same position with respect to the basic purpose of managerial activity. This purpose relates to securing effective participation from the other members of the organization. One way of emphasizing the nature of the conflict between the two models in this regard is to examine the manner in which each attempts to accomplish this basic purpose.

According to the traditional accounting model, management must control the performance of others—the principal instrument of control being authority. This model assumes that participants must be continually prodded to perform and that this prodding is accomplished through the use of authority which is applied from above. Also, it places heavy reliance on the use of economic rewards and penalties as devices to implement authority and motivate effective participation.

The decision-making model, on the other hand, assumes that management must *influence* the behavior of others. Furthermore, this approach suggests that, unless individuals are willing to accept such influence, effective participation cannot be assured regardless of the extent of the formal (classical) authority available to management. Viewed in this sense, meaningful authority cannot be imposed on a participant; rather it must be accepted by him. Finally, the decision-making model assumes that the willingness of participants to accept authority and to make effective contributions to the organization depends not only on economic considerations but also to a substantial extent on social and psychological factors.

There seems to be a very close relationship between the behavioral assumption of traditional management accounting and those associated with the classical management view of the firm. This is evidenced not only in their historical development but also by the manner in which management and management accounting currently interact in the modern business organization. It appears reasonable to expect that the effect of this interaction is to strengthen a jointly shared philosophy with respect to human behavior and the role of management. Managers who tend toward the classical view of behavior are likely to find support from traditional accounting systems which provide the kinds of data that emphasize this view. This accounting emphasis in turn probably serves to focus the attention of management on issues and solutions which are consistent with the philosophy of the classical view. Thus, a "feedback loop" is established which appears to be an important factor in perpetuating this relatively narrow view of human behavior among both management and accountants.

Since the assumptions of the traditional accounting model are so close to classical organization theory and, in fact, appear to be a reasonably good description of the classical theory itself, it would be interesting to consider two questions. First, does the classical view of management provide an efficient solution to the problems of influencing behavior within an organization? Second, if the principal function of management accounting is to furnish relevant data for managerial decision making, should the accountant be concerned with providing the kinds of information that management actually wants or the kinds of information that management should want?

With respect to the first question, this paper has attempted to demonstrate that the classical view may not be an efficient approach in motivating organizationally desirable behavior. This premise appears to be supported by a substantial amount of theoretical and empirical research in modern organization theory. In terms of the present discussion, the important point is that traditional management accounting procedures and attitudes cannot be justified solely on the basis that they are consistent with other common management practices because serious questions have been raised regarding the desirability of many of these practices themselves.

In reference to the second question posed above, it can be argued that it is the task of management accounting to provide the information desired by management and to provide it in a manner which is consistent with existing management philosophy. In other words, it is not the responsibility of the accountant to attempt to change the viewpoint of management but only to function within the framework established by this viewpoint. The difficulty with this argument is that it treats accounting as something separate from management. This paper, on the other hand, assumes that management accounting is an integral part of management. The adoption of a more realistic model of behavior by accountants could place them in the position of leading rather than passively following the changes in management philosophy which are bound to occur as a result of the impact of modern organization theory. Thus, it might be hoped that the development of more sophisticated management accounting systems would encourage the evolution of a much more sophisticated management viewpoint in general.

Assumptions with Respect to the Role of Accounting

Modern economic organizations are, of course, highly complex entities. Business managers must continually operate under conditions of uncertainty and limited rationality. In addition, management accountants are subject to the same kinds of drives and needs as are other members of the organization. All of this suggests that management accounting systems could not, even under the best of circumstances, achieve the degree of certainty, neutrality, and objectivity that is often attributed to them. To the extent that management accounting fails to live up to its image in this regard, it can be anticipated that problems will arise for the organization. For one thing, organization members are often subject to evaluations based on information produced by the accounting system. These individuals are likely to be seriously confused and disturbed by a flow of seemingly precise and exact accounting data which they cannot really understand or explain, but which nevertheless implies that they are (or are not) performing their tasks properly. The better education of organization participants regarding the limitations of accounting data, while worthwhile in its own right, does not represent an adequate solution. A much more important step would be a clearer understanding of these limitations by accountants themselves.

Also, as members of the organizations which they serve, management accountants can be expected to seek such psychological and social objectives as security, prestige, and power. In some instances, they might also be expected—as suggested by the discussion of sub-unit goals—to view the success of the accounting department and the technical perfection of the accounting process as ends in themselves. Thus, it is possible that some management accountants tend to view their function as primarily one of criticizing the actions of others and of placing the responsibility for failures to achieve certin desired levels of performance. Where this tendency exists, it may be expected to have a significant effect on motivation and be a major source of difficulty within the organization.[15]

CONCLUSIONS

This paper has attempted to postulate a set of behavioral assumptions which could be associated with the theory and practice of "traditional" management accounting. The resulting set of fifteen assumptions represents an accounting adaptation of what might be termed the classical view of human behavior in business organizations. This view emphasizes such concepts as profit maximization, economic incentives, and the inherent laziness and inefficiency of organization participants. It is a model which is structured primarily in terms of the classical ideas of departmentalization, authority, responsibility and control. The accounting process which has emerged in response to the needs presented by this classical model appears to treat human behavior and goals essentially as given. Further, the generally accepted measure of "good" accounting seems to be one of relevance and usefulness in the maximization of the money profits of the enterprise.

In addition, we have examined a set of behavioral assumptions based on research in modern organization theory. It seems clear that a management accounting system structured around this second set of behavioral assumptions would differ in many respects from the accounting systems found in practice and described in the literature.

One should not infer that the traditional assumptions considered here are completely invalid. The very fact that they have endured for so long suggests that this is not the case. It should at least be recognized, however, that in many respects the extent of their validity may be subject to question. Also, it is not argued that all accountants limit themselves at all times to this traditional view. Rather, the two sets of behavioral as-

15 Chris Argyris, *The Impact of Budgets on People* (Ithaca, N.Y.; Prepared for the Controllership Foundation, Inc., at Cornell University, 1952).

sumptions discussed might be considered as extreme points on a scale of many possible views. The significance of the traditional point of view on such a scale appears to be twofold: (a) it is likely that the traditional model represents a view of behavior which is relatively common in practice; and (b) this view seems to underlie much of what is written and taught about accounting.

If the modern organization theory model does ultimately prove to be a more realistic view of human behavior in business organizations, there is little doubt that the scope of management accounting theory and practice will need to be expanded and broadened. In particular, accountants will have to develop an increased awareness and understanding of the complex social and psychological motivations and limitations of organization participants. What is urgently needed, and what we have had very little of in the past, is solid empirical research designed to measure the effectiveness with which management accounting systems do, in fact, perform their functions of motivating, explaining, and predicting human behavior.

II
Reporting Issues

The five readings in this section mainly focus on what are labelled external reporting (financial accounting) issues. Management accounting textbooks tend to use considerable space pointing out the deficiencies—for many management evaluations—of accounting techniques which have their roots in the constraints of financial accounting. Hence, it is wise to review the environment of financial accounting before proceeding to management accounting topics.

Deficiencies of individual financial accounting techniques for management evaluations occur because of major differences in the perceived roles, including traditions, of external and internal (management) accounting. Legal requirements and legal relationships between managers and owners of organizations have a significant impact on financial accounting "principles" (techniques). In contrast, management accounting has far less concern with legal requirements, other than taxation regulations. On a superficial cost-benefit basis, many small organizations feel that one basic accounting system is all that is required for both financial and managerial needs. Thus, compromises are introduced into management accounting systems to accommodate external reporting requirements; and, the accounting system then becomes farther and farther removed from the ideal of being tailored to specific, crucial needs of the organization's managers/owners.

The first two readings in this section identify some of the constraints within which external accounting presently operates, and note possible effects on the uses which can be made of resulting information. The remaining three articles discuss techniques which are potentially applicable to both financial and managerial accounting. An identification of the implicit assumptions underlying financial

accounting can be of immense help in grasping management accounting
course themes—especially that textbook space devoted to being critical
of particular accounting techniques which have grown out of
external reporting systems.

"A Shareholder's Perspective on External Accounting Reports"
looks at who prepares and who uses the output of financial
accounting. A critical flaw in the overall concept of external reporting
is identified: ". . . management controls the contents of the external
reports which are the major information source for shareholders
who want to evaluate management's performance and control their
actions." The author then states that such a flaw, although tempered
somewhat by government legislation and pronouncements of accounting
bodies, leads to a diversity of methods of recording and reporting
the same transaction and an emphasis on less relevant, more objective
data. Such a problem obviously need not exist in internal reporting.

"The Fine Print at Ampex" builds on the previous article
by briefly noting the role of the auditor in external reporting and the
criticism which both a company and its auditors can encounter
from the financial press. Specifically, *Forbes* concludes that the auditors
should have forced Ampex to give additional disclosure of loss
provisions in its general purpose report to outsiders. *Forbes* reasons
that with the additional information readers would have been alerted
to the pending "disaster." A step removed from criticism in a magazine
would be a lawsuit against the directors, officers and auditors of a
company for issuing misleading reports. All of these considerations play
an important role in the state of cautious progress which pervades
the field of external reporting. The message about trying to view
accounting reports through the eyes of users applies to management
accounting as well, but the matter of possible lawsuits is quite different.
(See, for example, "RCA After the Bath", p. 8).

"The Direct Costing Controversy—An Identification of Issues"
introduces the valuation base debate, which is continued in the
next two articles. (See Exhibit II-1, p. 91, and the accompanying
discussion.) The author states that direct or variable costing for
inventory valuation has become "one of the most prominent current
issues" and then observes that "the abandonment of the historical cost
basis would render direct costing just as obsolete as the alternative full
costing." Other worthwhile themes in the article include the importance
of income taxation in external accounting techniques, usefulness of
direct-versus-full costing reports in external decision-making, and
categorization of the nature of arguments underlying this costing
controversy.

"Elements of Price Variation Accounting" and "Continuously
Contemporary Accounting" address important accounting measurement
topics which often tend to be dismissed quickly in textbooks. One
reason for brief exposure in many textbooks is that, on the surface,

the material seems to be complex, and must be read carefully. Often, however, greater understanding of a subject is achieved by critically examining alternative approaches which have been proposed— a prime reason for the inclusion of these articles in this book. These two readings are from a six-part series which examines many facets of the measurement problem common to both financial and managerial accounting. The author, R. J. Chambers, is an advocate of the use of selling market prices (See Valuation (3)(b) and accompanying discussion in Exhibit II-1, p. 91), modified for price-level changes.

It is extremely important in reading Chambers' two pieces to observe that he attaches great significance to reporting a person's financial position (balance sheet) which shows *"both* the result of all past events affecting his asset holdings and his debts to others, *and* (forms) the basis of all reckoning about what he will do from that time forward." Conventional accounting reports seen in practice can claim the former point — that effects of past events are disclosed; however, they are generally not thought to be very strong inputs for making current investment decisions. In Chambers' view accounting reports should tell managers/owners what they have available in funds for switching into other assets—hence, current selling market prices become vital information.

If, for example, you know that the current selling price of your idle land is $500,000, you are in a position to compare the future return on investment you will obtain by holding onto the land, versus selling it and using the $500,000 proceeds to invest elsewhere. Accounting statements which report selling prices are clearly valuable in investment decisions because managers have to know the magnitude of the valuation—in this case $500,000. Historic cost of land is only by coincidence useful for such a decision. Historic cost would mislead those managers who have the prime task of scanning the marketplace for investment opportunities.

In summary, Chambers sees the supplying of a particular piece of information—selling prices of the organization's currently held assets and liabilities — as a prime role of accounting. Naturally, he is also interested in a particular method of income measurement— as described in the articles. He leaves to other managers the job of ascertaining future returns on investment from holding the present asset versus holding some other asset. When another asset will yield a higher return on investment—for instance, 10 per cent on the $500,000 proceeds of disposal, versus 9 per cent in price appreciation from holding on to the land—the land should be sold. Historic costs may not highlight the need to trade assets. Knowledge of selling prices may spur managers on to better decisions.

The extent to which selling market prices could be used effectively as a basis for external financial reporting is an interesting question. The first two articles in this section of the book indicate some of the

practical problems which would have to be faced in improving
financial reporting. Educating preparers and users of accounting
information is clearly another major difficulty to be overcome.

*   *   *   *   *

Exhibit II-1 (p. 91) presents an oversimplification of the possible
measurement or valuation bases which are or could be used in
accounting systems. The main choice, aside from the past, present and
future time horizon, is the buying-market versus selling-market viewpoint.
To choose a simple example, from the standpoint of a wholesale
distributor of eggs, the buying price would be the price paid to the
farmer (the usual source) and the selling price would be the price
charged to retailers such as supermarkets (the usual customer).
From the farmer's standpoint the selling market price would be that
sum paid by the wholesaler; the ascertainment of buying price presents
something of a challenge — unless the chicken happens to be an
entrepreneur—and management accounting techniques would have to
be utilized (cost of feed, depreciation on accommodation, and so
forth, would be assembled into a cost per egg).

The difference between buying-market and selling-market
prices can be considered in theory as total accounting gross profit to
that particular enterprise. The point of profit recognition in the
accounts is governed by various realization rules. If inventory is bought
at \$2.00 (buying price) and immediately "valued" at \$2.50 (selling
price, net of disposal costs), profit is recognized (realized) at the point of
purchase.* If the inventory is "valued" at \$2.00, profit* recognition
is delayed, perhaps until a sales contract is signed with an outsider,
or cash sales price is collected, or legal title passes, or whatever; when
goods are deemed to be "sold," accounts receivable becomes the
asset "valued" at selling market price.

Accounting profit recognition does not have to occur at one
particular point in time, but may be recorded in two or more
accounting periods. The commonly cited example would be long-term
construction contracts where accounting profit could be recorded
over several years on a percentage-of-completion basis. In Exhibit II-1
such a profit recognition method is labelled the "Value Added"
category and simply represents other possibilities than buying and
selling price valuations. Some government output and productivity
statistics tend to follow the "value added" approach on the assumption
that portions of profit are made at a variety of times, such as: when
raw materials are purchased, when goods are manufactured, when sales
contracts are signed, when cash sales price is collected, and when
warranty work is performed.

---

* The entire difference of 50 cents (\$2.50 — \$2.00) does not necessarily represent
profit or income, and depends upon the income and capital maintenance definition in
use. However, for simplicity, the 50 cents is regarded here as profit.

Exhibit II—1

Possible Accounting Measurement Yardsticks

Possible Prices / Time Horizon	(1) Buying Market Price (Sometimes referred to as entry or input price)	(2) Value-Added Methods	(3) Selling Market Price (Sometimes referred to as exit or output price)
(a) Past	— Commonly used in external reporting to price such assets as inventory, land, equipment and intangibles	— An example would be percentage-of-completion basis of income recognition	— An example of where this is currently used is when an asset was written down to net realizable value in a previous period
(b) Present	— Examples would be reproduction or replacement costs in the usual buying market		— Net realizable price in today's usual selling market — Chambers' Continuously Contemporary Accounting
(c) Future	— Discounted (future) cash costs (at buying price)		— Discounted (future) cash receipts (at selling price)

NOTE: The above prices could be measured in dollars of varying purchasing power or price-level restated to dollars of overall common purchasing power.

The currently popular version of historic cost accounting used in practice in merchandising businesses, and described in most conventional textbooks, draws from several categories in Exhibit II-1. For example, fixed assets such as land, buildings and machinery utilize valuation category 1 (a) (buying market, past). Long term investments written down to net realizable value in a previous period follow valuation category 3 (a). Short term accounts receivable are typically valued at 3 (b), whereas long term non-interest-bearing accounts may be discounted per 3 (c). In essence, practical accounting tends to utilize whatever seems to make current sense and disregards internal consistency in valuation, as would occur when only one of the categories was adopted.

Exhibit II-1 could be set in three dimensions to acknowledge a difficulty which arises from using the dollar as the one common denominator of accounting measurement. The third dimension would merely be a price-level restatement of each category in two-dimension Exhibit II-1. Price-level accounting is a measurement system which combines two yardsticks: dollars and constant purchasing power. Mechanically, a price-level restatement operates through altering the number of dollars in accounting reports to reflect any changes in what a dollar will buy. For example, suppose a country has had only one hundred dollars in circulation throughout the world, and suddenly decides to print and distribute free another ten dollars. All other factors being equal, accountants should then multiply their figures by 110/100 to reflect the change. That is, 10 per cent more of that country's dollars are needed to buy a cross-section of the same goods and services as existed when only one hundred dollars were in circulation.

Price-level restatements should be contrasted with other categories in Exhibit II-1. Whereas price-level accounting is primarily designed to recognize a country-wide phenomenon (commonly called general inflation/deflation) affecting purchasing power of a *dollar*, other categories refer to individual assets, liabilities, and (in some cases) equities. Thus, although price-levels may have risen 10 per cent, the replacement cost of one item, a color television, could have dropped 20 per cent.

It is not difficult to visualize, for most or all of the price bases in Exhibit II-1, where each is probably the best basis to use for a specific evaluation. Chambers has shown where current selling-market prices have use; past buying-market prices could easily be the cheapest basis to use when the accounting system is merely an invoice processing device; later articles will discuss discounted cash techniques; and so forth. The interesting, unresolved question, though, is whether *both* the preparer and the user can be educated to know when to use each valuation.

6

A Shareholder's Perspective on External Accounting Reports

T. ROSS ARCHIBALD*

Why the dissatisfaction with current external
accounting reports? Here are some suggestions
for improving them.

This article analyzes external accounting reports from the viewpoint of
company shareholders who attempt to use these reports to maintain
control of their assets which are being operated for their benefit by hired
managers.

It is proposed first to examine the nature and function of current
external accounting reports to determine the reasons for present dissatisfaction and then review some alternatives for improvement. On the basis
of this study, I argue that the bulk of the problems can be traced to a
single crucial flaw in the basic structure: despite the fact that external
accounting statements are meant to report on managerial operation of
owner resources, it is management that controls the content of these
reports. The major implications of this failing are identified and
analyzed, and then suggestions are made to rectify the error so that
external reports may serve their basic function of providing useful
economic data to facilitate investor decisions.

The Nature of External Accounting Reports

An examination of the history and development of external accounting
reports seems to support the contention that they can only be justified
in terms of their usefulness to the people who read them. A recent
definition of accounting emphasizes the needs of the users. The committee
which produced *A Statement of Basic Accounting Theory* defined accounting as "the process of identifying, measuring and communicating
economic information to permit informed judgements and decisions by
the users of the information".[1]

In light of this definition, external accounting reports are regarded

* From the *Canadian Chartered Accountant* (February 1971), pp. 105-10. Reprinted
by permission of the Editor. This article is based on a study supported by the
Associates Research Fund, School of Business Administration, University of Western
Ontario. The author gratefully acknowledges this assistance.
1 *A Statement of Basic Accounting Theory* (Evanston, Illinois: American Accounting
Association, 1967).

as reports to outsiders on the functioning of a particular entity within its environment. The most significant readers of these external reports are the owners of the company—the shareholders, both current and prospective. This is not to ignore the significance of creditors, tax authorities, regulatory bodies, trade unions, etc., but the remainder of this article rests on the basic assumption that the most important reader of financial statements is the shareholder.

It seems clear that external reports are the reports of management. The managers are reporting to the shareholders or owners economic data on the events that have transpired in the past period, say a year, between the particular entity and its environment. In effect the shareholders of public corporations have turned over their assets, the resources of the firm, to the managers who have the responsibility of operating these assets in the best interest of the shareholders. Thus a significant function of the external accounting reports in this current situation is to provide appropriate information to asset owners (shareholders) so that they may review and control the actions of the asset operators (managers).

There are three essential elements that must be present in any effective control system:

☐ First, one needs some performance criteria—some basic standard of achievement;

☐ Second, there must be some communication system which reports to the persons in control relevant information about the performance of the reporting unit with respect to the standards of performance (sometimes called feed-back);

☐ Third, there must be some mechanism to enable the persons in control to require the actors to change their behavior in order to meet the achievement standards.

When we consider external accounting reports with reference to these control system elements it seems obvious that financial statements must be classified as the second element—they are the major part of the communication system which provides relevant information to shareholders about the performance of their hired managers. Presumably, when performance is not up to par for a particular standard, then the owners can step in and demand better performance of the existing managers, or for that matter, change them. Although there is not a great deal of evidence about incidents where poor managers are in fact replaced, there are some documented examples. Perhaps the most visible manifestation of shareholder dissatisfaction with management performance is to be found in proxy contests. In these relatively rare situations the shareholders have become so dissatisfied with the firm's performance that they gather together and challenge the existing managers in an attempt to replace them. An empirical study which examined 40 proxy contests in the United States revealed "that contests are usually begun in firms which have relatively low rates of return".[2] Certainly we cannot

2 Richard, Duval and Douglas Austin, "Predicting the Results of Proxy Contests," *Journal of Finance* (September, 1965), p. 471.

conclude that significant departures from some normal notion of rate of return will automatically result in a proxy contest, but it is reasonable to assume that managers do regard external statements as reports on their performance and, consequently, they are motivated to make such reports appear as favourable as possible. Otherwise dissatisfied shareholders may depose them.

Management Control of External Reports–an Unsatisfactory Situation

Management is charged with the responsibility for the development and presentation of external accounting reports which are then rendered to shareholders in order to facilitate their decisions. I intend to argue strongly that this situation where management is in control, not only of the assets of the organization, but also of the system that reports their use or misuse of these assets is clearly unsatisfactory. Such a set of circumstances breeds ideal conditions for the usurpation of company resources. Worse still, it is impossible to institute an effective control system in these circumstances.

Herbert E. Miller commented on this problem: "To satisfy the requirements of objective and impartial reporting on the performance of management, financial statements must be as free as possible from the influence of management. It would be unnatural to expect a group of human beings to be completely unbiased in the assessment of its attainments and failures".[3] Perhaps the most succinct statement on the matter was made by Sidney Davidson when he said that "published financial statements are reports on management; they can be meaningful only if management is unable to control their contents."[4]

On the other side of the question, many managers feel that they must maintain control of the external reporting system. A good illustration of this position is to be found in the *Financial Post* article, "The Sad Story of How Steep Rock Divorced Its Auditors". The then Steep Rock president, Neil Edmonstone, is quoted as saying the following about his shareholders' auditor:

"When you get into these kinds of unhappy arguments, you're going to look for new associates. I firmly believe they were wrong in handling the matter the way they did. There was plenty of room for flexibility, but it wasn't used.

"Hell, we gave them geological reports to support our view, but they didn't choose to accept them. I think that puts them outside their field of competence."[5]

I feel I must emphasize that this section is not intended to be an indictment of management integrity. The essential argument is simply

3 Herbert Miller, "Audited Statements–Are They Really Management's?" *Journal of Accountancy*, (October 1964), pp. 43-46.
4 Sidney Davidson, "The Day of Reckoning — Managerial Analysis and Accounting Theory," *Journal of Accounting Research*, (Autumn, 1963), pp. 117-26.
5 Alexander Ross, "The Sad Story of How Steep Rock Divorced Its Auditors", *Financial Post*, (April 11, 1970), p. 7.

that, given human behaviour, the ground rules are set up improperly. Who could possibly be anxious to report unsatisfactory performance to his superiors? Since managers control the information system which reports on their own performance, it is perfectly natural that they obscure the failures and emphasize the successes. However, such circumstances are clearly inappropriate for the generation of useful external financial statements. Certainly no company president would let any division manager control the system that reported upon his actions in the division. External reports should be developed to communicate the best available economic information about the events that affect the entity within its environment to the people who really own the entity—in this case, the shareholders.

The Manifestation of This Flaw in Current Reporting Practices

An examination of the accounting literature reveals a dominant theme which suggests strongly that management will select and change accounting methods so as to create the statements they believe the owners want to see regardless of the underlying economic circumstances. In other words when operating results are something less than ideal, the managers who are in effective control of the external reporting system will manipulate accounting methods so as to convey the illusion of satisfactory performance.

A number of authors have commented on this general theme. Michael Schiff reviewed the financial statements of Chock Full O'Nuts Corp. to illustrate "the choice of accounting methods as a device available to managers attempting to make stockholders happy".[6] Schiff analyzed the judicious changes in accounting treatments that permitted management to "smooth the trend of per-share earnings in recent years", and concluded from this example that the application of generally accepted accounting principles facilitates the reporting of earnings per share in a constant or rising pattern to give the effect of "pseudo profit maximization".[7] An article by John Myers, "Depreciation Manipulation for Fun and Profits," dealt explicitly with the change from accelerated to straight-line depreciation.[8] Although Myers was careful not to impute motives to the 19 switch-back firms in his study, he stated his purpose in the following manner: "I merely show that the opportunity does exist to change (from accelerated to straight-line) for profit manipulative purposes if the motive exists."[9] Perhaps the clearest illustration of the problem comes from a manager, although second hand through Maurice Moonitz, "As one highly-placed executive told me, 'My objective is to

[6] Michael Schiff, "Accounting Tactics and the Theory of the Firm", *Journal of Accounting Research*, IV, No. 1. (Spring, 1966) , pp. 62-67.
[7] *Ibid.*, p. 66.
[8] John Myers, "Depreciation Manipulation for Fun and Profits", *Financial Analysts Journal*, (November-December, 1967), pp. 117-23.
[9] *Ibid.*, p. 119.

report the same earnings per share as last year, plus five cents, and I will attain that objective if the independent accountants let me'."[10]

The Role of the Auditor

The obvious question is: "What about the shareholder's auditor in this situation?" My hypothesis is that the auditor is just not sufficiently independent to overcome the power position of management.

The duties of the independent auditor are specified in such documents as the Canada Corporations Act and The Business Corporations Act, 1970, of Ontario. A review of the relevant passages reveals that the auditor is appointed by and reports to the shareholders. He stands between management and the shareholders and his duty is to comment on the propriety of the statements that management is passing on to the owners. I am not suggesting that the auditor is helpless and cannot aid in the communication of meaningful information to the shareholders, but he is restricted by law in the role he can play. His statutory duty is to make simple statements on two basic issues:

First, that in his opinion the financial statements present fairly the financial position of the company and the results of its operations. And second, that these statements have been prepared in accordance with generally accepted accounting principles and that these principles have been consistently applied. Note that the auditor is not empowered to state whether a different set of accounting principles would have yielded "better" reports in the sense of more meaningful and realistic statements. His duty is limited to an opinion as to whether the particular package of accounting principles used by the organization's management is consistent and generally acceptable and yields "fair" statements.

The true problem emerges when management decides to use an accounting principle which shows them in a better light than the accounting principle they are currently using, but the new principle is nonetheless generally accepted. Since it would seem that the auditor's major duty is to comment on the general acceptability of the principles and the "fairness" of the resulting statements, he is severely constrained when he starts arguing rationally that the new rule is somewhat less realistic. At this point it becomes abundantly clear that despite the fact the auditor is appointed by the shareholders, management writes the cheque. In any event, it would seem to be a true statement that a strong and determined management can generally get rid of any auditor if it so chooses. This simple fact leads to the belief that the auditor is not sufficiently independent to counterbalance the power position given to management over the form and content of the financial statements.

In light of the environment described above, managers who report upon their own performance and shareholders' auditors who are not

10 Maurice Moonitz, "Discussion Comments", *Research in Accounting Measurement.* Edited by Robert K. Jaedicke, Yuji Ijiri and Oswald Nielsen. (Evanston, Illinois: American Accounting Association, 1966), p. 121.

given sufficient legal authority to counterbalance management's power position, it is somewhat easier to understand some of the specific complaints about external reports. Given this analysis let us now examine the two major resulting problems in some detail.

Proliferation of Generally Accepted Accounting Principles

The first major complaint is the lack of inter-firm and inter-industry comparability, largely due to the proliferation of generally accepted accounting principles (GAAPs). Clearly it is to the advantage of every management to make an exhaustive search to find that accounting principle which places its report to shareholders in the best light. It would seem that all managements have a vested interest in maintaining as flexible a set of GAAPs as they possibly can.

Most of the arguments with respect to GAAPs seem, on the one side, to demand that they be narrowed so that only a very few if not a single principle is applicable for each particular account for all firms. On the other side, there is the suggestion that since economic circumstances differ, therefore the accounting principles we use to describe the economic circumstances must also differ. However, it is difficult to find many studies which support an alternative accounting principle on the basis of its superiority in describing the economic events.[11] But, if it is rare to find some sort of empirical documentation for the existence of different GAAPs, it is even a rarer circumstance to find a company management justifying the adoption of a particular GAAP on the basis of its superiority in reflecting economic reality.

In a study I made of 69 United States firms that switched from accelerated to straight-line depreciation, I generated some data which bear on this particular issue.[12] During interviews with a sub-sample of fifteen of these switch-back firms, I asked about the factors that induced the return to straight-line. A mere five firms commented on the nature of depreciation at all; and on analysis of these statements it turned out that only one of these five firms cited any evidence that was even consistent with the return to straight-line depreciation. Possibly it is even more revealing to know that two of these five replies concerning the nature of depreciation were the *only* comments relating to a better matching of cost and revenues that were made in all fifteen interviews.

Perhaps the late Charles Johnson would view these interview data as sufficient empirical evidence to support his classic barb: "But if you can imagine that in wrestling with the choice of depreciation methods the minds of those involved in the decision were ever troubled

---

11. An interesting exception to this rule is found in an article by Isaac Reynolds entitled, "Selecting the Proper Depreciation Method", *Accounting Review*, (April, 1961), pp. 239-248. In this study Reynolds describes the asset service flows which are consistent with the currently popular depreciation methods in order to show the service flow assumptions implicit in the selection of these methods.

12. Ross Archibald, "The Return to Straight-Line Depreciation", Unpublished Ph.D. dissertation, University of Chicago, 1969.

by the question of which approach resulted in the fairer presentation of performance, you have a more lively imagination than have I."[13]

Thus we are faced with a situation in which firm managers have an incentive to seek out and perpetuate a host of different GAAPs so that they can always present their reports in the best possible light. Given management control of the contents of external reports and the current legal structure which denies the auditor sufficient power and independence to counterbalance management, a narrowing of the available GAAPs seems highly unlikely.

A continuation of this situation is a serious problem indeed. The function of external reports is purely and simply to reflect the economic accomplishments of the reporting firms. Most sophisticated statement readers are aware that the measurements of income and wealth position for any period less than the life of the firm are certain to be arbitrary, but the penalty for imprecise measurement of economic performance is poor resource allocation in the economy. If, as many believe, financial statements do provide a large part of the most significant information for the decision makers who decide to put assets into one sector of the economy or another, there exists an imperative need for realistic accounting reports. Otherwise we are going to continue to face serious misallocations of the scarce resources available in our economy.

Objectivity and Subjectivity–Irrelevance and Relevance

Many writers have argued that the truly relevant economic information to be contained in external reports must be about the future. Ladd comments about financial accounting reports in his statement, ". . . information must be related to the present and to the future, not to the past. Once a decision has been made and resources committed, congratulation or recrimination—depending on the outcome of the act—are about the only possible courses of action."[14]

This brings us face to face with the other major problem that the accountants must face when they prepare external reports: the objectivity versus subjectivity dilemma. The auditors, enlisting the aid of the traditional accounting literature have insisted on objective verification in the form of a technical accounting definition of realization before a particular event is reflected in the books. Consequently, valuable property which sits in, say, the middle of downtown Toronto is reflected on the books at the price it cost a company sometime in 1895. This too is an unsatisfactory situation, but I would like to suggest that such strange logic exists in large part as a reaction to the powerful control that management has in the development of its statements. This insistence on

---

13 Charles Johnson, "Management's Role in External Accounting Measurements", *Research in Accounting Measurements.* Edited by Robert K. Jaedicke, Yuji Ijiri and Oswald Neilson. (Evanston, Illinois: American Accounting Association, 1966), p. 91.
14 Dwight Ladd, *Contemporary Corporate Accounting and the Public,* (Homewood, Illinois: R. D. Irwin, Inc., 1963), p. 15.

the objective evidence of a realized transaction is one of the few functioning weapons in the auditor's armoury.

Since it is the future that is most relevant, it seems only logical that external statements must be future orientated. In the words of Howard Ross: "What has happened in the past is water over the dam, of no direct interest to anyone except a historian".[15] Obviously one cannot completely ignore the events of the past. It may well be that the management who made the errors or brought about the successes of the past which are being reflected in the statements have not been punished or rewarded as they should be. One must look at past history in order to evaluate performance and mete out the appropriate rewards or punishments. However, the emphasis on the future as opposed to the past is essential because it is the things that are going to happen in the future that are of *most* interest to the current report readers.

In support of my argument that we should incorporate subjective evaluations about the future in external reports, it is worthwhile pointing to the growth in the usefulness of the information flow generated by the accounting system that some people refer to as internal or managerial accounting. Internal accountants are justifiably praised for the developments that have taken place over possibly the last fifty years and certainly the last twenty-five years. All of the powerful techniques and tools that seem to come from the most recent research are being incorporated into that type of management analysis. From simple capital budgeting models which use forecasted cash flows, to the most sophisticated operations research models, subjective evaluations of events are the prime ingredient in the generation of useful reports. It seems that in order to develop meaningful information which has economic relevance, you have to use subjective evaluation. Again, Howard Ross commented: "We will only produce better statements if we sanction and indeed encourage more valuations—a much greater judgmental element."[16]

A major contention of this article is that these economically relevant tools and the necessary subjective evaluations that lead to such good results for internal management must be applied to external accounting reports in order to make them useful and meaningful. It is difficult to defend a total reliance on objectivity. Certainly the notion of realization and objective verification of transactions is a valuable concept which imparts a great deal of credibility to the external reports based on them; but what immutable law confines us to the production of a single accounting report? There have been numerous suggestions about multiple accounting reports.[17] The system proposed by Charles Horngren, which retains the distinction of realization through the concept of an objective transaction but also recognizes such things as holding losses or gains on assets, might be incorporated into a second set of state-

[15] Howard Ross, "The Current Crisis in Financial Reporting", *Canadian Chartered Accountant*, (May, 1967), p. 385.
[16] *Ibid.*, p. 388.
[17] *A Statement of Basic Accounting Theory, op. cit.*

ments which come much closer to reflecting economic reality.[18] Certainly there are a host of arguments on both sides of the question but the critical issue seems to be this: there are a number of techniques and tools available that can turn external reports into useful documents. Accountants are really being derelict in their duty if they do not use all of the tools available in order to render an external report as close to economic reality as possible. This argument was also the main thrust of Sidney Davidson's article and it seems that this is a very fruitful direction for external reporting to take.[19] There is just no logical reason to deny the reader of external reports the same quality of information that has proven so useful to internal report readers for at least the last twenty-five years.

Towards a Solution

Any resolution of the problems inherent in current external reporting must be based on the proposition that somehow the power to control the contents of the reports on itself must be taken away from management. The most obvious solution is to create a buffer that will attenuate this overwhelming power of management and at least interpose someone or something between the people who are doers and managing the assets and the people who own the assets.

There are a number of potential mechanisms that could provide the necessary buffer. In a revision to The Business Corporation Act, 1970, of Ontario, there is provision for an audit committee of the Board of Directors.[20] This committee, which may be composed of not fewer than three directors of whom the majority shall not be officers in the company or an affiliate company, has the responsibility of reviewing the financial statements of the company. Since these directors are not otherwise associated in the operations of the organization, they may provide some measure of independent review on the actions of management. Furthermore, the auditor has the right and may be required to appear before any meeting of the audit committee and should be given the opportunity to be heard. Although this is definitely a step in the appropriate direction, we will have to wait and gather some experience with this new committee before being assured that it will function as a sufficient barrier in order to attenuate the tremendous power that the management can influence on the annual reports.

An alternative mechanism is being used in Sweden. Under the particular legal provisions shareholders owning a minimum of 10 per cent of the outstanding common stock can have their own shareholders' auditor appointed.[21] It would seem that such an independent outside

18 Charles Horngren, "How Should We Interpret the Realization Concept?", *Accounting Review*, (April, 1965), pp. 323-33.
19 Sidney Davidson, *"Day of Reckoning . . .", op. cit.*
20 *Interim Report of the Select Committee on Company Law*, (Toronto: Province of Ontario, 1967), p. 92.
21 Edwin C. Bomeli, "Management Reviews by Scandinavian Accountants," *Journal of Accountancy*, (July, 1964), p. 35.

auditor could readily discern and tease out those peculiarities in managements' accounting for itself and then bring out a report that gives a much clearer picture of management stewardship of the owners' assets.

Perhaps the ultimate means of attaining true auditor independence for our system of external reporting will be the introduction of Auditcare—government operation of the public accounting profession. One would certainly hope that a more imaginative restructuring of the roles of those parties involved in preparing the financial reports and those parties attesting to the integrity of the resulting statements would yield the information necessary to meaningful shareholder decisions.

The Most Important Reader

This article has been written from the viewpoint that the shareholder is the most important reader of external accounting reports. It has also been assumed that this class of reader needs relevant economic information about the functioning of the enterprise within its environment in order to evaluate management performance and to make the necessary investment judgments and decisions. Current external reporting was examined and judged unsatisfactory for these purposes. The key problem was then isolated. Specifically, management controls the contents of the external reports which are the major information source for shareholders who want to evaluate management's performance and control their actions. This critical flaw in the reporting structure was shown to lie at the base of the two major problems in external reporting, the proliferation of GAAPs and the emphasis on less relevant objective information as opposed to the more relevant subjective information. Finally, certain means of providing a necessary buffer to remove management from their position of control over external reports were considered.

The main aim of this article is to bring the reality of management control of external reports to the attention of interested parties and to consider the serious problems that result from this aberration. If there is some merit in the position that this critical structural flaw is a major cause of the current dissatisfaction with external accounting reports, explicit recognition of the truth should prove beneficial to all concerned. Then, at the very least, we can concentrate on eliminating the key problem rather than continue to waste time and effort on making the incomparable comparable and on communicating objective but irrelevant information to report readers who need relevant economic data with a clear future and subjective emphasis.

7

The Fine Print at Ampex[*]

A businessman friend of ours who can't seem to resist dabbling in speculative stocks stopped by the office the other day to tell us about his latest fling in the market. "Can't miss," he assured us.

Another lunch with that broker of his, we thought. We didn't suppose he had bothered to take a look at this company's accounting? "Oh, they're not cooking the books—not with a guy like *this* on their board!" our friend replied, pointing out the name of a well-known chief executive of a conservative blue-chip company.

Evidently he hadn't heard what had happened at Ampex last year, we observed. "Oh, Ampex," sneered our friend. "That's ancient history."

Rummaging through our filing cabinets, we found Ampex's annual report for the fiscal year ended in April 1972 and shoved it across the desk. Take a look at that board, we replied. See the name William Blackie? Until about mid-1972 he was chairman and chief executive of Caterpillar Tractor and an accountant by training to boot. He joined the Ampex board in 1969.

An honorable man from an honorable company, we pointed out, and yet no protection against one of the clear-cut corporate disasters of recent times. When Blackie joined the board, the stock was in the mid-40s; it is now bumping around 6. Stockholders' equity has shrunk from around $145 million to $45 million or so in 1972.

We went on to say that we weren't knocking Bill Blackie. The mess wasn't his fault. But his name didn't turn out to be much protection for the investor. Neither did that of the prestigious auditing firm, Touche Ross & Co.

We showed our friend Touche Ross's letter in the 1972 annual report. It was a long letter as these things go. What it did was to withdraw its certification of the previous year's annual report. And it refused to certify 1972 results, except in combination with restated 1971 results.

Touche Ross, in effect, had to admit that it had put its seal to obviously inadequate financial reporting for fiscal 1971. In commenting on Ampex's horrendous fiscal 1972 loss — nearly $90 million — Touche Ross confessed, in effect, that well . . . er — maybe all that money wasn't lost in that year. Maybe some of it had been lost in 1971.

"Okay," retorted our friend, "but could *you* have recognized it at the time?" We went straight back to the filing cabinet after our ungrateful friend had departed. *Were* there any signs in the fiscal 1971 Ampex

* Reprinted by permission of *FORBES* (April 1, 1973), pp. 45-46.

annual report that would have warned us of impending disaster? That things were far worse than the report showed?

First stop, the footnotes. Well, Ampex *had* made an accounting change all right. But not the type we would have expected. Instead of deferring certain engineering costs, they were now expensing them against current income. This was a conservative change; it had worsened the 1971 loss by $2.7 million. Retroactively, the change also lowered previously reported 1970 earnings by about $1 million, and 1969 retained earnings by another $1.7 million. If anything, we might have found such a change encouraging, we thought.

Then, in the president's letter, there was the revelation that Ampex had been capitalizing a small portion of its research and development, instead of expensing it all as everyone had assumed. But now they *were* expensing it *all*. Another switch to more conservative accounting.

For the life of us, we couldn't find a single red-flag warning signal in the 1971 report that things were about to get much, much worse for Ampex. Sure, there was a deficit, $12 million, as against 1970 earnings of $11.3 million. But the worst was over, according to the president's letter and the typically optimistic forecasts in the divisional commentaries. Fiscal 1972 would be a profitable year for Ampex, predicted then-chief executive William E. Roberts. "Our product lines have never been in a stronger competitive position," he wrote.

Okay, we said to ourselves, now let's see what Touche Ross made Ampex reveal when 1971 results were restated in the fiscal 1972 report. Aha! The report still showed a loss of $12 million for 1971, but this time expenses were more explicit. Three reserves, totaling $14.7 million, had been buried under operating expenses and selling and administrative expenses in the previous go-round—undoubtedly on the theory that each one, in itself, was "not material."

Aha! Now we had it. Knowledge of these reserves certainly would have been a "material" clue to the investor. That is, if they had been reported at the time, not just retroactively. But Touche Ross had failed to insist on their inclusion. The reserves would have told stockholders that Ampex management thought it would probably lose $4.6 million eliminating product lines and selling off divisions, another $4.3 million in "doubtful" accounts, merchandise returns and marketing allowances, and another $5.9 million in royalty payments to record companies that might not be covered by apparently disappointing revenue from Ampex's stereo-tape sales.

We asked ourselves: Are we just splitting hairs? We pondered a minute, and decided we weren't. Touche Ross, we thought, should have forced the company to break out these reserves. Had this happened, Touche Ross would have had two choices: 1) to give a clean opinion, implicitly endorsing the adequacy of the reserves, or 2) to give a qualified opinion, raising questions about those reserves. We wondered if Touche Ross had asked itself such questions as: Would Ampex be able to sell enough stereo tapes to meet its royalty payments to record companies?

Costs and expenses:

Cost of sales and operating expenses	253,472
Selling and administrative expenses	57,864
Interest expense	13,409

Costs and expenses (Note 1):

Cost of sales and operating expenses (Note 3)	243,181
Selling and administrative expenses (Note 3)	53,427
Provision for royalty guarantees in excess of unit royalties payable, including in 1972 the settlement of two principal royalty contracts and $6,650,000 for estimated future losses (Note 2)	5,883
Provision for uncollectible accounts (Note 4)	4,295
Provision for cost of discontinuance and disposal of divisions and product lines (Note 3)	4,550
Interest expense	13,409

Before and After. Hidden in the original 1971 Ampex annual report (above) were three key reserves later broken out in restated 1971 figures a year later.

How long did tapes of popular tunes hold their value? How soon would Ampex be able to find a buyer for the losing businesses? As things turned out, the reserves were grossly inadequate (tape inventory over a year old was written off completely in 1972), but Touche Ross had avoided having to make a judgment in 1971.

Psychologically speaking, the way the 1971 report was handled, the loss was reassuring, rather than threatening. It looked as if Ampex had really bitten the bullet. Maybe it was even playing at the "big bath" game. (The big bath is when management writes off everything it can in one brutal year, virtually assuring itself of a turnaround the following year.) In fact, the real bath was yet to come.

Were we being too hard on the auditors? We asked John Shank, a highly regarded professor of accounting at the Harvard Business School.

"As far as I'm concerned," Shank told us, "the original 1971 Ampex annual report is probably as gross a miscarriage of auditing procedure as you'll ever find. Granted, the amount in the reserves wasn't very large, but they presented important warning signals. At the least, the auditors should have qualified their opinion with a phrase like 'subject to the adequacy of the reserves'." This, in Shank's view, would have made it clear that the auditors couldn't evaluate whether the reserves were adequate. That would have been a red flag. Shank continued: "Specifically, what I think Touche Ross failed to do here was recognize that the situation was getting a lot more risky, and that they had to do a lot more investigating than usual. I mean things just don't go to hell this quickly—there had to have been a lot of signs floating around if the auditors had bothered to check."

How about Touche Ross? What did it have to say for itself at this point? At length, we located a Minneapolis-based Touche Ross senior partner named E. Palmer Tang, the man who conducted the 1972 Ampex audit. "I take issue with your statement that the reserves were inadequate in 1971," Tang insisted. The reason why those same reserves had to be increased by almost $47 million in 1972, he explained, was that Ampex's stereo-tape business fell out of bed, and Ampex elected to clean up all its royalty payments with one of the record companies. "The company we're auditing sets the policies, and we look at them to see if they're reasonable or not," he argued. "You look at the historical data, and you try to keep up with the economic changes in the industry, and for that matter in the whole economy."

Well, we thought, what else could Tang say? After all, Touche Ross was being sued because of its 1971 Ampex audit in a number of class actions—along with Ampex officers, ex-officers and directors.

But one thing still bothered us: Bill Blackie of Caterpillar. An accountant by training, he has long preached conservative accounting. We reached him at home in Peoria, Ill. "I believe in it more conservatively than ever now," Blackie replied in his Scotch burr. Why didn't he resign from the Ampex board when he saw what was going on, we asked? "I think that outside directors become most valuable when a company gets into trouble," said Blackie. "That's *not* the time to quit. But, you know, it would be indiscreet for me to talk further on this topic."

Part of Touche Ross's letter certifying Ampex's 1971 statements.

In our opinion, the consolidated financial statements referred to above present fairly the financial position of Ampex Corporation and Subsidiaries at May 1, 1971, and May 2, 1970, and the results of their operations and changes in financial position for the years then ended, in conformity with generally

so determined because of the effect on such estimates or changed circumstances during 1972. Therefore, we no longer express the opinion given in our report dated June 21, 1971, that the financial statements at and for the year ended May 1, 1971, present fairly the Company's financial position, results of operations and changes in financial position at that date and for that year. Further we do not express an opinion

Second Thoughts. In 1972 Touche Ross withdrew its letter (top) certifying Ampex's 1971 statements.

We could certainly appreciate Blackie's reluctance to talk. Just like the auditors, Blackie and the other outside directors were strangers to the record business. They, too, had relied on management's judgment —until it was too late. A few months after the 1971 annual report came out, however, they realized that something was wrong. Acting quickly, they realigned top management. Gone were President William E. Roberts and Executive Vice President John P. Buchan, along with over 40% of top management. They also called back Touche Ross for an intensive investigation, which led to the sharply qualified 1972 Touche Ross opinion.

Judgment, we said to ourselves as we put down the telephone. Management's judgment. Outside directors seldom have the time to become sufficiently familiar with operations to second-guess management. And, given today's accounting procedures, there seems to be little motivation for auditors to give qualified opinions. "Subject to" clauses in auditors' letters are now so infrequent that they cause quite a stir when they do appear. If the auditors force management to present an unduly pessimistic picture and results later improve, they risk losing a client. But isn't that a risk they are paid to take?

As usual it is the shareholder—the man with the least information with which to appraise management's judgment—who really suffers.

Is it any wonder individual investors are shunning the stock market these days?

8

The Direct Costing Controversy—
an Identification of Issues

JAMES M. FREMGEN*

Whatever one's view of direct costing may be, it is impossible to deny that it has become one of the most prominent current issues in the continuing discussion that surrounds the evolution of accounting theory and practice. Direct costing has been considered and reconsidered by both its advocates and its opponents from just about every conceivable point of view for more than a quarter of a century. Hence, it is appropriate at this time to review some of the arguments for and against the concept and to attempt to identify the principal issues in the controversy. My purpose here is to examine these issues critically and dispassionately — recognizing my own limitations as a partisan in the dispute. This presentation is in the nature of an interim report, with primary attention focussed upon the development and present status of direct costing but with some consideration of the prospects for the future also. My objective is to crystallize issues, not to resolve them. It is possible that, given the present status of the accountant's art, they are irresolvable.

Concern With External Reports Only

Direct costing has undoubtedly attained the status of an accepted technique of internal reporting to management. (This does not mean, of course, that it is used in all firms or even in a majority of them.) In the

* From *The Accounting Review* (January 1964), pp. 43-51. Reprinted by permission of the Editor.

The author gratefully acknowledges the comments and suggestions of his colleagues at the University of Notre Dame, and particularly those of James O. Horrigan and Ray M. Powell. He is also indebted to Charles T. Horngren and George H. Sorter of the University of Chicago for their stimulating discussions in this journal and in correspondence. All shortcomings in this paper, however, are entirely of the author's own contrivance.

area of external reports to stockholders, creditors, and other interested outside parties, however, the controversy is in full bloom. The discussion in this paper will be confined to the implications of direct costing in external reports. There are two reasons for this. First, as already indicated, it is in external reporting that the real controversy lies today. Second, the basic criterion guiding the selection of internal reporting practices is utility to management. What is useful to management is good management accounting. In external reporting, the criterion of utility is still present; but it is more difficult to define. The market for external reports is much broader than that for internal reports, and the needs and interests of the various users of the former are more diverse than those of a single firm's management. Thus, in practice, the criterion of utility as applied to external reports has come to be interpreted as general acceptance. As we all know, general acceptance is actually predicated upon quite a variety of premises, ranging from the matching concept to the Internal Revenue Code. Ideally, however, general acceptance ought to be based upon economic realities and logic. However subjective and tenuous this ideal may be, it is a worthy goal; and we should attempt to evaluate direct costing within a framework wherein economic facts and relationships are paramount.

Historical Cost Assumption

A second constraint within which the discussion must proceed is the current generally accepted practice of valuing inventories at historical cost, however measured. At a time when increasing attention is being given in the accounting literature to alternative bases of inventory valuation, this may appear to be an overly restrictive framework for discussion. But direct costing is a historical cost method. The abandonment of the historical cost basis would render direct costing just as obsolete as the alternative full costing.

A Note on Terminology

As a final note before beginning a critical examination of the issues, it is appropriate to consider the terminologies of the alternative costing methods. No matter how entrenched the term "direct costing" may be, it really is not suitable. The distinction at the heart of the method is that between variable and fixed costs, not between direct and indirect costs. The British term, "marginal costing," is not desirable either in view of the very specific meaning of the term "marginal cost" in microeconomic analysis. Particularly in view of the increasing popularity of the concept, general adoption of the term "variable costing" is highly desirable; and that term will be used consistently throughout the remainder of this paper.

On the other side of the controversy, the alternative concept is best described as "full costing" to indicate the inclusion in inventory of all production costs. "Absorption costing" is not really objectionable, but it is less descriptive. Finally, I have a very positive dislike for the term "conventional costing." This is not at all descriptive and makes about as much sense as it would to call the incumbent party the "conventional party" in American politics.

SOME EARLY ARGUMENTS IN THE CONTROVERSY

Most of the early arguments in the controversy over variable costing were discussed within the framework of internal reporting. They are, however, generally relevant to external reporting as well; and most of them have been extended to this area at one time or another. For present purposes, it will be sufficient to consider three of these early arguments on each side of the controversy.[1]

Early Arguments in Favor of Variable Costing

1. Variable costing involves the separate reporting of variable and fixed costs. The separation of variable and fixed costs has generally been conceded to be useful to management.[2] Whether it is equally useful to stockholders, creditors, and other outside parties is problematic. In any case, there is no reason why variable and fixed costs cannot be recorded and reported separately under full costing as well as variable costing. As a practical matter, they seldom are. Nevertheless, the separation of fixed and variable costs should be regarded as a benefit from variable costing in current practice and not as an inherent advantage.

2. Variable costing facilitates incremental profit analyses.[3] This alleged advantage of variable costing follows from the previous one, and the same counter-argument is applicable. There is no theoretical reason why the same information (i.e., variable profit) should not be available in full costing reports. Once again, too, there is the question as to whether such information is relevant to the users of external reports. We shall return to this question later in the paper.

3. Variable costing removes from income the effect of inventory changes.[4] This is one of the arguments most frequently advanced for variable costing. Under full costing in a period of declining sales, net income may not reflect the decline in sales volume because production volume has been maintained and a substantial portion of the fixed

---

[1] The discussion here is not intended to be exhaustive. Rather, it is designed to indicate the types of arguments raised for and against variable costing. These "early" arguments, incidentally, are by no means extinct; they continue to appear in the current literature. For a more complete discussion of these early pros and cons of variable costing, see *Current Application of Direct Costing,* NAA Research Report 37 (New York: National Association of Accountants, 1961) and "Direct Costing," *NACA Bulletin,* Vol. 34 (April 1953), Section 3.

[2] *Current Application of Direct Costing, op. cit.,* pp. 5-7.

[3] *Current Application of Direct Costing, op. cit.,* pp. 22-40, and "Direct Costing," *op. cit.,* p. 1127.

[4] *Current Application of Direct Costing, op. cit.,* pp. 81-4, and "Direct Costing," *op. cit.,* p. 1127.

production costs of the period has been deferred in inventory. Under variable costing, these fixed costs would be treated as current expenses, not chargeable to inventory. Thus, in variable costing, net income is more directly a function of sales volume than in full costing and is unaffected by production volume.

This particular argument is deficient in that it presumes there is something wrong with the volume of production as well as the volume of sales influencing income. In other words, underlying this contention is the more basic one that fixed production costs are not properly chargeable to the product. Thus, the argument concerning the impact of inventory changes on income is a corollary to the more fundamental argument as to whether fixed manufacturing costs are product costs or period costs. This question will be considered shortly.

Early Arguments Against Variable Costing

1. It is difficult in practice to separate variable and fixed costs.[5] This contention is, of course, valid from the viewpoint of practical application; but it is not a damning flaw of the variable costing concept. It is a problem of measurement, not of theory. To be sure, measurement problems are very real and very important ones; but they often can be solved. In view of current practices, apparently a substantial number of industrial firms believe that this particular measurement problem can be solved effectively.[6]

2. Variable costing tends to ignore or understate the importance of fixed costs. Probably the most familiar example of this argument is the contention that pricing decisions based upon variable costs may result in prices that fail to cover all costs.[7] This contention has always struck me as being particularly weak, however. To begin with, it seems to ignore the role of the market in price-setting decisions. Further it appears to presume that business managers are not very bright; and this hardly seems to be a valid generalization.

3. Variable costing understates inventory values.[8] This argument presumes the validity of the product cost treatment of fixed manufacturing costs. Considered in light of current practice, variable costing quite clearly understates inventory values. Current practice, of course, is subject to change and, in this particular connection, has come under heavy attack in recent years. Unless valid theoretical arguments can be raised in support of the product cost treatment, the inclusion of fixed

5 "Direct Costing," *op. cit.,* pp. 1127-8.

6 "Separating and Using Costs as Fixed and Variable," *NAA Bulletin,* Vol. 41 (June 1960), Section 3.

7 Adolph Matz, Othel J. Curry, and George W. Frank, *Cost Accounting,* 3rd Edition (Cincinnati: South-Western Publishing Company, 1962), pp. 798-9, and John J. W. Neuner, *Cost Accounting,* 6th Edition (Homewood: Richard D. Irwin, Inc., 1962), pp. 783-4. It should be noted that, while these writers discuss this argument, they do not necessarily accept it.

8 "Direct Costing," *op. cit.,* p. 1128.

costs in inventory is merely a practice—albeit one of long standing—based upon unsupported judgements.

Conclusions on Early Arguments

It may appear that I have endeavored to disparage all of these early arguments raised here; and, indeed, such was my intention. The objection to these arguments is not that they are necessarily invalid but that they are superficial. They fail to attack the basic premises underlying the variable costing and full costing techniques. Recently these basic premises have been exposed and subjected to careful scrutiny. The result has been a vigorous and stimulating controversy over the relative theoretic merits of full and variable costing.

INCOME MEASUREMENT: THE PERIOD/PRODUCT COST QUESTION

Probably the most fundamental point of controversy between variable and full costing is the question of whether fixed manufacturing costs are costs of the product produced or of the period in which they are incurred. Traditionally, accounting reports have treated them, substantially at least, as product costs. Variable costing would treat them wholly as period costs. Logically, treatment should follow from the nature of the costs; and there is a very clear dispute regarding the nature of fixed production costs.

The Period Cost Concept

The concept of a period cost, or capacity cost, has been explained by many writers. One good explanation of this concept was offered by Charles T. Horngren and George H. Sorter.

> Proponents of variable costing maintain that fixed factory overhead provides capacity to produce. Whether that capacity is used to the fullest extent or not used at all is usually irrelevant insofar as the expiration of fixed costs is concerned. . . . As the clock ticks, fixed costs expire, to be replenished by new bundles of fixed costs that will enable production to continue in succeeding periods.[9]

The period cost concept, in its essence, states that there are certain costs which, by their nature, expire with the passage of time, regardless of production activity. They are incurred for the benefit of operations during a given period of time. The benefit is unchanged by the actual level of operations, if any, during that period; and it expires at the end of the period in any event.

The period cost concept clearly conflicts with the traditional accounting view that costs attach to production. Paton and Littleton, for example, averred that all costs attach to goods or services sold and that

---

[9] Charles T. Horngren and George H. Sorter, " 'Direct' Costing for External Reporting," *The Accounting Review*, Vol. 36 (January 1961), p. 88.

"time periods are a convenience, a substitute"[10] for the product in the process of matching costs with revenues. To my knowledge, only one advocate of variable costing has taken specific issue with this traditional view of the time period. David Green, Jr., raised the question of the time period versus the product very pointedly.

> Again there is a suggestion of choice of orientation—to the product or to time interval. Why choose the product?
> In large part, the work of the accountants is related to the time interval. Indeed, the income statement becomes meaningful only when the time period is known.[11]

He went on to argue that it is the process of dividing the life of an enterprise into relatively short time periods, such as a year, that distinguishes the accountant from the historian.[12] Whether one agrees or disagrees with Green's conclusion regarding the product/time period question, his direct identification of the issue is a significant contribution to a clear understanding of the variable costing controversy.

The Product Cost Concept

Two of the most vigorous proponents of the product cost concept in the recent literature have been William L. Ferrara and Philip E. Fess.[13] Basically, they have argued that all manufacturing costs are costs of the product and that there is no such thing as a manufacturing cost of the period. Ferrara, writing alone, contended that, logically, all so-called fixed production costs should be amortized by a unit-of-output method, which would make them variable costs.[14] Time period amortization is acceptable only as a practical convenience, the need for which derives from uncertainty as to future operations. Writing jointly, Fess and Ferrara supported a value-added approach to revenue recognition but accepted the deferral of revenue recognition to the point of sale on

---

10 W. A. Paton and A. C. Littleton, *An Introduction to Corporate Accounting Standards* (Urbana: American Accounting Association, 1949), p. 15.
11 David Green, Jr., "A Moral to the Direct-Costing Controversy?" *The Journal of Business,* Vol. 33 (July 1960), p. 221.
12 *Ibid.*
13 See, for examples, William L. Ferrara, "Idle Capacity as a Loss — Fact or Fiction," *The Accounting Review,* Vol. 35 (July 1960), pp. 490-96; Ferrara, "The Importance of Idle Capacity Costs — A Rejoinder," *ibid.,* Vol. 36 (July 1961), pp. 422-24; Philip E. Fess, "The Theory of Manufacturing Costs," *ibid.,* Vol. 36 (July 1961), pp. 446-53; and Fess and Ferrara, "The Period Cost Concept for Income Measurement—Can It Be Defended?" *ibid.,* Vol. 36 (October 1961), pp. 598-602.
14 Ferrara, "Idle Capacity as a Loss—Fact or Fiction," *op. cit.,* p. 490. I believe there is a need for much more study of the nature of fixed costs. Many costs are fixed by definition — notably depreciation. Unit-of-output depreciation, as contrasted with the more commonly used time-based methods, renders depreciation a variable cost (as recommended by Ferrara). If there is an important distinction between fixed and variable costs — and variable costing most certainly presumes there is — it is disquieting to observe that so significant a cost item as depreciation may be either variable or fixed, depending upon a managerial decision between equally acceptable alternative accounting procedures.

grounds that measurement is more objective at that point. The deferral of revenue recognition, they contended, must then be parallel by the deferral of all production costs, regardless of their behavior with respect to changes in volume.[15]

At another time, when I was not attempting to be dispassionate in my point of view, I took what might be regarded as the extreme position in support of the product cost concept. I contended that

> . . . in theory, there is no such thing as a true period cost. All costs incurred by a firm, including non-manufacturing costs, are costs of the product. For the product of a firm is not merely a physical commodity from a production line; it is a bundle of economic utilities, which include time and place as well as form. Thus, in theory, distribution and administrative costs are just as much costs of the product as are factory costs. The product is not complete until it is in a form and place and at a time desired by the customer; and this product completion involves distribution just as essentially as it does manufacturing.[16]

This position might be restated as follows: An enterprise is not interested in capacity as such but in production and the consequent revenue. Capacity is merely a means to production and should be regarded as part of the cost thereof in the same way as materials and labor. To quote Fess, ". . . a plant is not purchased for the sake of owning masonry but for the services it will provide."[17]

According to the product cost approach, fixed costs are assigned to the product rather than to the period because it is the product that generates revenue. The time period is viewed as a passive factor, purely incidental to the operations of the firm. Revenue derives from the sale of the product (or, at least, is ordinarily recognized when the sale takes place), no matter when that sale occurs; and *all* production costs are matched with the revenue in the period of sale.

ASSET MEASUREMENT: THE NATURE OF SERVICE-POTENTIAL

Fundamental to any decision as to what constitutes the value of an inventory is a definition of the concept of an asset. The familiar definition of the Committee on Accounting Concepts and Standards of the American Accounting Association is that assets are "aggregates of service-potentials available for or beneficial to expected operations."[18] Recently Robert T. Sprouse and Maurice Moonitz asserted that "assets represent expected

---

[15] Fess and Ferrara, *op. cit.,* p. 600.

[16] James M. Fremgen, "Variable Costing for External Reporting — A Reconsideration," *The Accounting Review,* Vol. 37 (January 1962), p. 78.

[17] Fess, *op. cit.,* p. 448.

[18] *Accounting and Reporting Standards for Corporate Financial Statements and Preceding Statements and Supplements* (Columbus: American Accounting Association, 1957), p. 4.

future economic benefits."[19] These definitions may be taken as essentially identical. This concept of service-potential, or future benefit, has played an important role in the controversy over variable costing.

Cost Obviation Concept of Service-potential

One interpretation of the service-potential notion has been that assets have service-potential to the extent that they avert the necessity for incurring costs in the future. Robert B. Wetnight contended that variable costing meets the test of future benefit better than full costing.

> If this test of future benefit is applied to the two methods of costing under discussion, it can be seen that direct costing most closely fits the requirements. In the first place, there is a future benefit from the incurrence of variable costs. These costs will not need to be incurred in a future period. However, in the case of the fixed costs, no future benefit exists, since these costs will be incurred during the future period, no matter what the level of operations.[20]

David Green coined the term "cost obviation" and posited the concept as the basis for the measurement of all assets excepting financial claims, such as cash and receivables. He suggested that the measurement of an asset is the costs that will be obviated in the future as a result of cost incurrence in the past. And he pointed out that the past incurrence of fixed production costs does not avoid the reincurrence of the same costs in the future.[21]

The most expansive discussions of the cost obviation notion have been by Horngren and Sorter. In their first article on the subject, they offered it as support for variable costing. They stated there that

> . . . a cost has service potential, in the traditional accounting sense, if its incurrence now will result in future cost avoidance in the ordinary course of business . . .
>
> Expressed another way, if the total future costs of an enterprise will be decreased because of the presence of a given cost, that cost is relevant to the future and is an asset; if not, that cost is irrelevant and is expired.[22]

This position might be restated as follows: The production of goods for inventory in one period enables a firm to realize some revenue in a subsequent period without reincurring the variable costs of producing that inventory. But the availability of inventory completed in one period does not forestall the incurrence of any fixed costs in a subsequent period.

19 Robert T. Sprouse and Maurice Moonitz, *A Tentative Set of Broad Accounting Principles for Business Enterprises,* Accounting Research Study No. 3 (New York: American Institute of Certified Public Accountants, 1962), p. 20.
20 Robert B. Wetnight, "Direct Costing Passes the 'Future Benefit' Test," *NAA Bulletin,* Vol. 39 (August 1958), p. 84.
21 Green, *op. cit.,* p. 223.
22 Horngren and Sorter, *op. cit.,* p. 86.

Hence, the variable costs are relevant to future periods, but the fixed costs are not.

In a second article, Horngren and Sorter pursued the cost obviation concept further and refined it somewhat. To begin with, they made it clear that they would include opportunity costs within the scope of cost obviation. Specifically, the loss of future revenues is a cost to be avoided.[23] More significantly, they sought to disassociate their position from variable costing. They propounded a theory of "relevant costing" in which only such costs as will obviate future costs or lost revenues are relevant and, hence, properly chargeable to inventory. Under this theory, fixed production costs might be relevant under certain conditions. Specifically, fixed costs would be included in inventory when future sales demand would exceed existing productive capacity, when future sales would be lost forever because of a shortage of inventory, or when variable manufacturing costs are expected to rise in the future.[24] One practical problem apparent in relevant costing is the burden placed upon the accountant (or someone) of determining whether a given inventory is actually necessary to meet future needs or whether it is excessive. (Note that, if inventories were generally viewed as necessary at their existing levels in order to avoid losing future orders, the practical effect of relevant costing would be equivalent to that of full costing.) Horngren and Sorter have recognized this problem, and they concede that relevant costing would be more difficult to apply than either full or strict variable costing. Nevertheless, they believe their position is conceptually sound.

There is, to be sure, a distinction between variable costing and relevant costing as described above. There are also certain similarities between them which admit of their being considered jointly in contrast to full costing. Specifically, both variable and relevant costing accept the possible treatment of fixed manufacturing costs as costs of the period rather than of the product. Variable costing goes one step further and insists upon such treatment in all instances. In correspondence, Horngren and Sorter have argued that any linking of relevant costing to variable costing misses the fundamental point of their theory, namely, that it is future oriented. It is not concerned with the time-period expiration of fixed costs but with future benefits. It would seem, however, that, while one may wish to emphasize that only variable costs are inventoried because only they will obviate future costs, he must also recognize the concomitant expensing of fixed costs in the period of incurrence. The latter fact may not be viewed simply as a secondary side effect; it must be justified in itself if relevant costing is to stand. This is not to say that relevant costing cannot stand, of course. If one accepts the cost obviation approach to asset valuation, then the time-period expiration of fixed costs as called for in relevant costing is correct. In other words, the

---

[23] George H. Sorter and Charles T. Horngren, "Asset Recognition and Economic Attributes—The Relevant Costing Approach," *The Accounting Review,* Vol. 37 (July 1962) p. 394.
[24] *Ibid.,* p. 399.

future orientation of relevant costing may not and need not overlook the resultant current expensing of fixed costs. Both implications of the method are consistent with its basic premise.

Revenue Production Concept of Service-potential

The cost obviation interpretation of service-potential is relatively recent. Others have interpreted the service-potential of an asset to mean its capacity to contribute to the production of revenue in the future.[25] This revenue production approach distinguishes between unexpired and expired costs, respectively, according to whether their incurrence will or will not contribute to the realization of revenue in the future. Under this theory, any cost essential to the production of a product that may reasonably be expected to be sold (and thus generate revenue) is a cost of obtaining such revenue, and should be deferred in inventory so that it may be matched with the revenue in the determination of income for the period of sale.

Conclusions on Alternative Interpretations of Service-potential

At the risk of oversimplification, I believe it is correct to say that the cost obviation concept of service-potential necessarily presumes the validity of the period cost treatment of fixed costs. Similarly, the revenue production concept as outlined above is inextricably linked with the product cost position. These are the conflicting points of view, and there is no supreme principle of accounting upon which we can call to resolve the conflict. Both positions are internally consistent. Any selection between the two must be primarily intuitive. Inasmuch as intuition is not a standardized commodity, it is probable that the fate of variable costing and/or relevant costing in external reports will be determined ultimately on grounds of utility.[26]

INVENTORY COSTING AND DECISION-MAKING

The basic justification for the preparation of financial reports at all is that they are useful to someone. Logically, therefore, the standards of financial reporting should be designed to further this objective of usefulness. While variable costing has been generally conceded to be useful in

[25] See, for example, Fremgen, *op. cit.*, p. 77. One member of the Committee on Accounting Concepts and Standards that drafted the 1957 American Accounting Association statement has indicated to me that, at the time that statement was prepared, he understood service-potential to mean revenue production, especially in the case of inventories.

[26] In 1953 a research study by the National Association of Accountants concluded that the costing method to be employed in profit measurement should be selected on the basis of utility. However, it stated further that each company must decide for itself in this matter. (See "Direct Costing," *op. cit.*, p. 1119.) I cannot agree that this extremely important aspect of utility in external reports may be left to the discretion of the individual firm.

reports to management, is it useful also in reports to stockholders, creditors, and other outside parties? Green[27] and Horngren and Sorter[28] believe that it is. I am not prepared to answer this question at this time. Frankly, I have no information that would suggest a preference on the parts of the users of external financial reports for either full costing or variable costing. However, it is relevant to consider the distinctions between variable and full costing reports. The principal distinctive features of the variable costing income statement are (1) that it shows directly relationships between costs and volume and (2) that it makes net income a function of sales volume to the exclusion of production volume. With regard to the first feature, we must remember that management has some degree of control over costs and/or volume. Normally the users of external reports have none. The latter group's decisions are on a different plane.[29] The question then is this: On that plane, are cost-volume relationships as significant as they are to management? With respect to the second feature of the variable costing income statement, this is either misleading or correct depending upon whether production volume should or should not influence income. Again we face the product/period cost question.

This discussion suggests that whether variable costing ever achieves general acceptance will depend primarily upon whether it comes to be regarded generally as useful in external reports (and, to be realistic, upon its acceptance for federal income tax reports also). Thus, it is important that we investigate the relative utilities of variable and full costing in external reports to the extent that these can be ascertained.

THE FUTURE OF VARIABLE COSTING

After a quarter of a century of development, variable costing is being considered more and more frequently as an acceptable technique of inventory measurement in external as well as internal financial reports. If variable costing is accepted, it may be taken either as an alternative to or as a replacement for full costing. Certainly, there would be nothing unique about two different methods of measuring one quantity being acceptable in accounting practice—particularly where inventories are concerned. Nevertheless, I feel that the conceptual differences between variable and full costing are so great that their concurrent general acceptance would not be in the best interests of financial statement readers or of the accounting profession. Financial statements are, after all, media of communication; and it is difficult to see how communication can be effective where two fundamentally conflicting methods of reporting the same information are considered equally correct.

[27] Green, *op. cit.*, p. 222.
[28] Horngren and Sorter, " 'Direct' Costing for External Reporting," *op. cit.*, p. 91.
[29] Fremgen, *op. cit.*, p. 80.

Inventory Valuation at Net Realizable Value

As a final note, it is possible that the controversy over variable costing may be discarded in lieu of being resolved. Some attention is being given in the current accounting literature to the proposal that inventories be valued at net realizable values.[30] If this were to become the generally accepted practice, both variable and full costing would be irrelevant and both might be laid to indeterminate graves. In light of the history of the development of accounting principles, however, and in view of the general tenor of the reactions from accounting practitioners to Sprouse and Moonitz's recommendation of net realizable value in inventory,[31] it is reasonable to anticipate that any change so basic as the abandonment of the historical cost basis will not come about quickly. Hence, it is probable that the direct costing controversy will be with us for some time yet and that the issues considered here will have to be faced. Whether the controversy will ever be resolved — let alone what the resolution will be — is an unanswerable question at the present.

[30] Sprouse and Moonitz, *op. cit.*, pp. 27-30.
[31] "Comments on 'A Tentative Set of Broad Accounting Principles for Business Enterprises'" *The Journal of Accountancy,* Vol. 115 (April 1963), pp. 36-48.

9

Elements of Price Variation Accounting

R. J. CHAMBERS*

There has been a great deal of discussion about what accounting produces and what it should produce, and what accounting rules should be adopted to cope with the changes in prices and in the purchasing power of money which are our common experience. The kinds of circumstance dealt with in many expositions are limited; and often the case illustrations used are quite complex—so complex that we are not quite sure which facets of the problem have been covered by any given proposal.

It is here proposed to tackle the problem in the opposite way. We shall take a series of cases of the very simplest kind and develop conclusions from them which can be applied in the more complex cases of experience. We shall not pass over the most trivial cases; it often occurs that the solutions of problems are passed by when we pass by their simplest occurrences.

There are a few common ideas which we shall need to use. The first is the idea of a financial state. This is the position of a person or a business at a point of time in respect of money or money's worth. The financial state or position of a person is *both* the result of all past events affecting his asset holdings and his debts to others, *and* the basis of all reckoning about what he will do from that time forward. The discovery of that state is therefore an important element in forming judgements about the past and in forming plans about the future.

Financial state can be discovered at any time by listing the assets of a person or firm and assigning to them their present market prices, and by listing liabilities to others and assigning to them the amounts then owed. It can also be ascertained by a continuous accounting process which incorporates cumulatively the financial effects of all events as they occur. Such a record needs to be cross-checked from time to time by the method of direct discovery mentioned above; for it is quite possible that the recording system may fail to pick up all the events having effects on financial state, from such causes as inadvertence, unintentional error, deliberate error, and outright misappropriation.

Financial state, as we have described it, is essentially what is meant by "state of affairs" and financial position. It may have been and

* From *The Accountant* (February 26, 1970), pp. 299-303. Reprinted by permission of the author and editor.

may still be interpreted otherwise. But if shareholders and investors generally are not informed of the state from time to time, as we have described it, they will be unaware of the magnitudes of the rights and interests which they buy, hold, and sell.

Given the financial states at two points of time, it is possible to deduce the change (other than by new contributions or withdrawals) in the rights of persons or companies in their assets. This may be called the net profit of the concern for the intervening period. It is not possible to derive net profit without reference to two such states. The recording of cash receipts and payments is only part of the process of deriving the change in state. Income calculation requires also that the change in stocks on hand, the change in plant and similar assets (depreciation) and other similar effects, be brought into account.

With these preliminaries in mind we shall now examine a series of possible circumstances and events relating to A—who may be a person or any kind of business firm.

Case 1

No transactions, no changes in prices; cash holdings only
Suppose A has $100 in cash at January 1st, 19x1, and that he keeps it till the end of the year. And suppose that there has been no change in the prices of any goods during that year. At the end of the year he could buy exactly the same collection of goods as he could have bought for $100 at the beginning of the year. Financially, that is, in respect of his power to buy other things, he is exactly as well off at the end as at the beginning of the year.

Case 2

No transactions, a rise in the level of all prices; cash holdings only
Suppose A has $100 in cash at January 1st, 19x1, and that he keeps it till the end of the year. And suppose that for some reason the prices of all goods rose by 10 per cent during the year. This could be due, for example, to an increase in the supply of money relatively to the supply of goods, such as gives rise to inflation. At the end of the year, A could not buy the same collection of goods as he could have bought at the beginning of the year, no matter what that collection might be. Although he holds dollars, just as he held dollars at the beginning, they mean less to him in terms of what he could buy with them.

We will use the sign $ to signify that the monetary unit we are referring to is always a dollar. But we must distinguish dollars at different times if we are to make reference to what can be bought with $1. We will call the dollars at the beginning of the year $\$_0$ and dollars at the end of the year $\$_1$. Then, in this case, $\$_1 110 = \$_0 100$ in terms of what A can buy. But at the end of the year A and everyone else have only $\$_1$. As A has only $\$_1 100$, he is worse off than he was at the beginning of the year by $\$_1 10$. We could also say he was worse off by $\$_0 9.1$, since $\$_0 9.1 =$

$_1$10. But this would be meaningless at the end of the year, for nobody would have any $_0$ and no prices would be quoted in $_0$.

Case 3

No transactions, a fall in the level of all prices; cash holdings only
Suppose everything was as in Case 2 but at the end of the year all prices were lower by 10 per cent. In this case only $_1$90 would suffice to buy the same goods as could have been bought for $_0$100 at the beginning of the year. But as A still has $_1$100 he is $_1$10 better off, in terms of what he could buy, than at the beginning of the year.

Case 4

No transactions, no changes in prices, goods holdings only
In this and the next two cases we assume A holds goods only. We could suppose A held any good or goods, but certainly not some of *all* the goods available. We will take for simplicity a piece of land, and we will suppose that the selling price of that piece of land at the beginning of the year was $100. In the present case, no changes in prices, A could get $100 for the land at the end of the year and with it he could buy exactly the same collection of goods as he could have bought at the beginning of the year. He is as well off at the end as at the beginning of the year.

Case 5

No transactions, all prices rise but one; goods holdings only
Suppose as in Case 2 that during the year all prices rose by 10 per cent, except the price of the land which A held through the year. This is the first case in which we recognize a common phenomenon, namely, that all prices do not rise or fall together or at the same rate. In this case, A could only get $_1$100 for the land at the end of the year, and in terms of what he could buy with it he is $_1$10 worse off than he was at the beginning of the year.

We could also state a slightly more interesting case:

Case 5a

All prices rise but not at the same rate. Suppose that at the end of the year A could sell the land for $_1$105. As $_0$100=$_1$110, he would be only $_1$5 worse off, in terms of what he could buy, at the end of the year. And if he could sell the land for $_1$115 all other things being the same, he would be $_1$5 *better off* than he was at the beginning of the year.

Case 6

No transactions, all prices fall but one; goods holdings only
As Case 3 is the contrary case, so to speak, of Case 2, so Case 6 is the contrary case to Case 5. If all other prices fall by 10 per cent and the

price of A's land remains at $100 (that is $\$_1 100$) he will be $\$_1 10$ better off at the end of the year. We could also state a variant case which could have been covered in Case 5A:

Case 6a

One price rises, all others fall. If all prices fell by 10 per cent but A could get $\$_1 105$ for his land at the end of the year he would be better off by $\$_1 15$ in terms of what he could buy.

Case 7

No transactions; debt and cash holdings
Suppose that on January 1st, 19x1, A borrowed $100 from B and held that sum through the year. At the end of the year he would owe B $100 still and could pay him back with the $100 he then held, no matter whether the prices of any or all other goods had risen or fallen in the year. This is a common feature of all contracts involving the payment of fixed sums of money. Contracts could, of course, be drawn so that other sums than the amounts loaned are repayable by borrowers; but the usual case is of the kind above mentioned.

If the prices of all other goods had risen in the year, both A and B would be able to buy less with the $100 than could have been bought at the beginning of the year. And if the prices of all goods had fallen, both A and B would be able to buy more. But if A pays B back at the end of the year A is neither better off nor worse off than at the beginning —he has $0 at both dates. This illustrates the perfect hedge against the risk of changes in the prices of things, a perfect hedge being a device by which the hedger neither gains nor loses from the events he hedges against.

It was not necessary to use the symbols $\$_0$ and $\$_1$ in the case given; but it would be useful to keep in mind that, for the settlement of any debt $\$_1 100$ will satisfy the loan $\$_0 100$ at the beginning of the year. The symbols are necessary in demonstrations of all other cases.

Case 8

No transactions; debt and cash and goods holdings
Suppose that on January 1st, 19x1, A borrowed $\$_0 100$ from B and immediately bought a good N with $\$_0 60$, keeping that good and the remaining $\$_0 40$ in cash till the end of the year. And suppose that the general level of prices rose in the year by 10 per cent, and that at the end of the year the selling price of N was $\$_1 75$. The general level of prices is a notion we did not use in Case 2 and subsequently; we supposed that all prices rose by 10 per cent. We could then say $\$_0 100 = \$_1 110$. But we can say exactly the same thing about the relationship between the symbols $\$_0$ and $\$_1$ if the general level of prices rose by 10 per cent; that is, if some prices rose more and some less—an idea we introduced in Case 5.

We can set up A's position at January 1st, 19x1 thus:

Cash	$\$_0 40$	Loan payable to B	$\$_0 100$
Good N	$\$_0 60$		
	$\$_0 100$		$\$_0 100$

and his position at December 31st, 19x1 thus:

Cash	$\$_1 40$	Loan payable to B	$\$_1 100$
Good N	$\$_1 75$	Gain	$\$_1 15$
	$\$_1 115$		$\$_1 115$

Here is a case in which, if A sells the good N and pays off B he will be $\$_1 15$ better off. He has hedged perfectly against the change in the general level of prices, and he has been able to gain the whole of the numerical increase in the price of the good N. Notice, however, that the gain is $\$_1 15$; not $\$_0 15$. If, on the other hand, the price of the good N had been $\$_1 45$ at the end of the year, and all other things had been the same, A would have been worse off by $\$_1 15$; he would have to find $\$_1 15$ elsewhere to pay off B.

Case 9

No transactions; equity and debt; cash holdings only
We are seldom able to borrow the whole of a sum we wish to have on hand to use at our discretion (the kind of circumstance we considered in Case 8). We are expected to have some assets of our own. In fact, in Cases 1–6 it was assumed, without stating it explicitly, that the entire equity in or ownership of the cash and goods referred to ran to A. We will make this explicit henceforward.

Suppose A had $\$_0 100$ at January 1st, 19x1 of which $\$_0 50$ was his own and $\$_0 50$ was a loan from B. Suppose the general level of prices rose by 10 per cent during the year.

We can set up A's position at January 1st, 19x1 thus:

Cash	$\$_0 100$	B's equity	$\$_0 50$
		A's equity	$\$_0 50$
	$\$_0 100$		$\$_0 100$

and his position at December 31st, 19x1 thus:

Cash	$\$_1 100$	B's equity	$\$_1 50$
		A's equity	$\$_1 50$
	$\$_1 100$		$\$_1 100$

The numbers are all the same, and they balance. But A is not as well off as he was at the beginning of the year. Because $\$_0 100 = \$_1 110$, $\$_0 50 = \$_1 55$. But he only has $\$_1 50$. He is worse off by $\$_1 5$; but only by $\$_1 5$ because his borrowing of $\$_0 50$ served as a hedge against half the effect of the rise in the general level of prices on the $100 holding of cash. The result can be contrasted with that of Case 2, where in the absence of borrowing A was $\$_1 10$ worse off.

We could state A's equity at December 31st, 19x1 rather more explicitly. We could say that the amount of his *original* equity was $\$_1 55$ and the amount of his loss in the year was $\$_1 5$; making his equity $\$_1 50$ at the end of the year.

Case 10

No transactions; equity and debt; cash and goods holdings
Suppose, as in Case 8, that at January 1st, 19x1, A had assets: cash $\$_0 40$ and good $N\$_0 60$; and that, as in Case 9, these assets were financed as to $\$_0 50$ by A and as to $\$_0 50$ by a loan from B. And suppose, as in Case 8, that the general level of prices rose by 10 per cent in the year, and the selling price of the good N was $\$_1 75$ at the end of the year.

We can set up A's position at January 1st, 19x1 thus:

Cash	$\$_0 40$		B's equity	$\$_0 50$
Good N	$\$_0 60$		A's equity	$\$_0 50$
	$\$_0 100$			$\$_0 100$

and his position at December 31st, thus:

Cash	$\$_1 40$		B's equity	$\$_1 50$
Good N	$\$_1 75$		A's equity	$\$_1 65$
	$\$_1 115$			$\$_1 115$

Notice that A's equity is 15 units greater at the end of the year than at the beginning; this is as it was in Case 8. But in this case A is not better off by $\$_1 15$ at the end than he was at the beginning in spite of the rise of 15 units in the price of the good N. Since $\$_0 100 = \$_1 110$, his opening equity is equal to $\$_1 55$; he is therefore better off by $\$_1 10$ only. But if he had not borrowed he would have been better off by $\$_1 5$ only, since his opening equity, $\$_0 100$ in that case, would have been equal to $\$_1 110$.

We could state A's equity at December 31st, 19x1 explicitly as in Case 9. It could be represented as original equity $\$_1 55$ plus gain in the year $\$_1 10$.

Notice that, although in Case 9 A borrowed the same amount, $\$_0 50$, he did not make the same gain in that case as in Case 10. The amount of the gain in the year depends on what A does with the proceeds of the loan. In Case 9 the amount borrowed hedged half of the effect of the rise in the general level of prices on the cash holding. This can be said because all A held was cash. But in Case 10 it is not possible to attribute the hedging effect to either of the assets separately; the assets are a pool of common money's worth, supplied partly by A and partly by B. In this simple case, we could say that the change in A's equity arose as follows:

		At Jan. 1st		Equivalent in $\$_1$	Actual at Dec. 31st	Gain Col. 3—Col. 2
Equities (Cr)	B	$\$_0 50$	=	$\$_1 55$	$\$_1 50$	$+\$_1 5$
	A	$\$_0 50$	=	$\$_1 55$	$\$_1 65$	$= +\$_1 10$
Assets (Dr)	Cash	$\$_0 40$	=	$\$_1 44$	$\$_1 40$	$-\$_1 4$
	N	$\$_0 60$	=	$\$_1 66$	$\$_1 75$	$+\$_1 9$

A's gain thus arose from two different directions: the change in the general level of prices, which affects all monetary balances (the loan from B and the cash held) ; and the change in the non-monetary asset balance relative to the change in the general level of prices. This analysis will help us to solve the more complicated case where there are transactions.

It will also be clear that we can treat all monetary balances as a net figure for the purpose of calculating the gain or loss. The amount of cash held was $\$_0 40$; the amount owed to B was $\$_0 50$; we can describe this as net monetary assets of $-\$_0 10$, and obtain the same result. We can for the same reason treat amounts owing to A as part of the net monetary balances; the result would be the same if, instead of $\$_0 40$ in cash, A began the year with $\$_0 10$ in cash and a debt receivable of $\$_0 30$, and finished the year with $\$_1 30$ in cash and a debt receivable of $\$_1 10$. We will use this to simplify the demonstration in the next case.

Case 11

Transactions; equity and debt; holdings of cash, receivables and goods
We have now reached the common case of commercial experience. If there are transactions, there can be changes during the year in every kind of asset and equity balance; and there could be changes in the prices of any goods bought or sold and of goods held. It may seem that this is a very complex set of affairs to account for, particularly when the previous cases dealt with very few changes. But those cases have provided all the means of finding the result without great difficulty.

Suppose A's position at January 1st, 19x1 were as follows:

Cash	$\$_0 10$	A's equity	$\$_0 100$
Debtors	$\$_0 30$		
Goods N	$\$_0 60$		
	$\overline{\$_0 100}$		$\overline{\$_0 100}$

And suppose A bought and sold goods, borrowed $50 from B, received payment for some goods but not for others; so that A's position at December 31st, was as follows:

Cash	$\$_1 30$	B's equity	$\$_1 50$
Debtors	$\$_1 40$	A's equity	$\$_1 115$
Goods N	$\$_1 95$		
	$\overline{\$_1 165}$		$\overline{\$_1 165}$

And suppose the general level of prices rose by 10 per cent during the year.

We can find out very simply whether A is better or worse off in terms of his capacity to buy goods in general. For as $\$_0 100 = \$_1 110$, and A's equity at the end of the year was $\$_1 115$, he is better off by $\$_1 5$.

Notice that it does not matter when A borrowed from B, or when the goods were bought and sold, or when the debtors paid or ran into debt, during the year. The net result, or net profit, is perfectly correctly calculated from the figures given, whatever those dates were.

Suppose we were also given the following account of transactions:

	$	$
Sales proceeds		150
Less Opening goods at selling prices	60	
Purchases	170	
	230	
Less Closing goods at selling price	95	
		135
Increment to A's equity		$15

If the general level of prices had moved steadily upwards during the year, these amounts of money would all be of mixed purchasing power. Hence we have used no subscripts with the $ sign. It may not seem as though these amounts could be added up to give any sensible total. But we do know that if A began the year with $_0 100$ he would have to have $_1 110$ at the end of the year to be just as well off as he was at the beginning, simply because $_0 100 = _1 110$. The above calculated increment, whatever its amount, runs to A's equity account.

We can deduce the profit of the year by deducting the number of units necessary to make the opening number of dollars in that account equal to the closing number of dollars which have the same general purchasing power. We will call this number a capital maintenance adjustment. We debit the above income account with $10 and credit A's equity account with the same sum. At December 31st A's equity accounts will then be:

A's equity, January 1st	$_1 110$
Profit of the year	$_1 5$
	$_1 115$

Prices of Assets

One feature of the above demonstrations may have passed unnoticed. When dealing with goods holdings we referred throughout to the resale prices of the goods on hand at the end of a period. This may not have been noticed because it is such an ordinary and commonsense thing to think of when we are considering how well off we are from time to time, or what we can afford to buy at any time. Now that it has been mentioned it will be obvious that the terms in which we described the different cases and financial states and results, could not be used with reference to the balance sheets and profit and loss accounts commonly produced.

The common accounting practice is to introduce purchased goods into the accounts at the prices paid for them and to use those prices for any transfers subsequently made to other accounts, including finally the charges in respect of them in trading and profit and loss accounts. However, one of the functions of accounting is to derive the result of doing business in a period. The result of any operation is the difference between what is put in and what is taken out. In simple cases this is obvious. If A buys oranges for 2 cents each and sells them for 3 cents each the result is 1 cent each. But if A buys a case of oranges he does not reckon the result except by reference to the whole set of separate sales. Similarly if, instead of thinking in terms of single transactions because they are numerous and different, we must think in terms of the events of a whole period, the result for a period is the difference between what is put into the period and what is taken out of the period.

With what, then, does a firm go into any period? With the amount of its net assets, i.e., the difference between the amounts of its assets and its liabilities. But at what prices the assets? If A bought goods for $5 and at the end of the year the selling price was $4, the common practice would be to show the stock at the end of the year at $4. It would be said in defence of this that the loss has occurred by the end of the year, and should be taken into account in that year. However, if A's selling price for the goods at the end of the year were $7, there would be some objections to showing the closing stock at this price; the common tendency would be to show the stock at $5, its cost. But if the selling price is used when it is below cost, why cannot the selling price be used when it is above cost? No additional line of argument, no additional rule or principle, can do away with the inconsistency in the practices mentioned. If in one case the loss is deemed to fall in the year in which the resale price fell below cost, in the other case the gain should be deemed to fall in the year in which the resale price was above cost.

Again, if we are to determine the result for the year, it does not seem correct—and it is certainly inconsistent—to use the selling price in determining some part of the year's output (namely, the revenue from sales) and the cost price in determining another part of the year's output (namely, the unsold goods which are part of the following year's inputs).

It may be argued against this that until the goods have been sold we cannot take account of selling prices. But when we have to treat the business of firms period by period, we invoke quite a different rule than the rule which we use in simple isolated transactions. That rule is the accrual rule. We use it to justify the charging of expenses at the end of a year before we have paid out the cash; and for bringing into account depreciation before we have disposed of durable assets. We often do not know the exact amounts of these charges, but we find no difficulty in entering some amount for them year by year. There is, in principle, no difference between these cases and bringing into account the resale prices of goods on hand; even if those prices are only approximations, they are no worse than other approximations commonly made. If this were done, both revenues and expenses would be dealt with consistently—both by the accrual rule.

If we ever have to work out our personal financial affairs we go about it in exactly this way. We would not find out what we paid for the things we own—ask any holder of worthless stock: he will not think he is as well off as when he bought it. We all reckon, when we have seriously to reckon, in terms of the selling prices of what we own. Those prices represent our command over money and hence over other things. They are essential elements of our financial position.

10

Continuously Contemporary Accounting

R. J. CHAMBERS*

The "varieties" of accounting commonly used or proposed are all based on one or two reasonable or plausible grounds. Historical cost accounting is held to give an account of what has been done with the funds which became available to a firm or its managers. Price level adjusted accounting, it is claimed, takes account of the necessity, if money sums are to be added, of expressing all those sums in units of similar purchasing power. Replacement price accounting, it is claimed, takes account of current prices and of the desirability of calculating income by reference to the maintenance of capital in some sense. Present (or discounted) value accounting, it is said, is forward-looking and for that reason is closely related to decision-making.

These claims, as we said, are all plausible. But if we accept them *all* as plausible, then none of the above varieties of accounting meets all the criteria. Historical cost accounting, for example, entails the addition of sums of money paid or received at different times when the purchasing power of the dollar was not the same. Replacement price accounting does not give stewardship accounts in the same sense as historical cost accounting; neither does present value accounting. The reader may make other such contrasts.

It would be valuable to have a variety of accounting which is both backward-looking and forward-looking; which yields a basis both for judgements of stewardship (and generally of past performance), and for judgements about future prospects; which avoids, or somehow copes with, the problems both of changing prices and changes in the purchasing power of money; which represents results and financial position in a way which is fair to all readers of financial statements. We claim that a variety of accounting which we have called continuously contemporary accounting meets all these requirements as far as they can be met.

FEATURES OF THE SYSTEM

Monetary Accounts

Over a very large range of accounting entries this system is no different from conventional accounting. All transactions of which at least one-half

* From *The Accountant* (April 30, 1970), pp. 643-47. Reprinted by permission of the author and editor.

of the double entry relates to cash, amounts payable or amounts receivable, will be recorded initially in the same way. This covers all usual transactions between the firm as such and the outside world. All operations on cash accounts, debtors' accounts and creditors' accounts (long- or short-term) will be exactly the same as they are now. The propriety of this will be obvious, for in relation to outsiders the firm is bound to the monetary amounts, payable or receivable, for which it has contracted. Whether prices or price-levels subsequently go up or down, the money amount of a debt or claim is fixed in the ordinary course of events.

Inventories

For inventory or goods accounts the initial entries will be the prices paid. These entries will be the "other" halves of entries in cash-book or creditors' accounts. Now, whenever the price of a good or service used by a firm rises or falls, its management must do its reckoning in terms of the new price. It must do so whether rises in selling prices, switches in factor inputs, changes in product composition or any other possibility is being considered. And it must do so because it cannot know how soon its competitors will respond to the same change in input prices which it has experienced. If a firm's management must do its reckoning in this way, its accounts should contain figures which are appropriate to this reckoning. To bring about this effect, the recorded unit price of any goods on hand will be changed whenever a change occurs in the purchase price. The value of the balance of the goods account will be increased if the unit price has risen; there will be a corresponding credit to a price variation account. Downward movements in prices will give rise to similar but opposite kinds of entries.

The entries may be illustrated. Suppose the balance of a certain material in stock consists of 100 units at $2 each, and that the firm buys another 50 units at $2.10 each. The value of the 100 units in stock will be raised to $2.10 per unit. The balance of the materials account will be 150 units at $2.10 per unit. And the credit to the price variation account will be $10 (100 units at 10 cents each). Notice that all units of stock are then at the same price, an actual current price; and that this is more sensible than carrying the materials at two different prices when they are the same materials.

At the end of the year we want to know how the firm stands financially in relation to the rest of the community. How a firm stands is given by the equivalent in money of what it holds, that is, the selling prices of its assets separately. We must therefore find the selling prices of its stock of goods. For those goods which can be sold the firm already has a price list. Some may be unsaleable, particularly some work in progress; but for any goods for which a market price can be found, that price will be the present money equivalent per unit. A schedule of all goods on hand giving their resale prices in their present condition will be compiled. If the sum of these prices exceeds the total book value of the stock at current purchase prices (see previous paragraph) the excess will be credited to the price variation account, and the amount shown in the schedule at resale prices will be shown as the amount of the assets. If the book value exceeds the amount of the resale price schedule, the latter will still be shown as the amount of the assets, but the price variation account will be debited the difference.

Profit and Loss Account

During the year the goods account will have been credited with the current recorded cost of the goods sold; the profit and loss account will have been debited like amounts. The profit and loss account will have been credited the amounts charged to customers or the cash received from sales. The balances of the price variation account or accounts will also be brought into the profit and loss account. The balance of the account at this stage we will simply call "increment."

One other thing will have been happening during the year. The purchasing power of the dollar will have been changing. We cannot take account of this from day to day, or even monthly. And as daily business is done in terms of prices as they are quoted, it is not necessary to take account of changes in purchasing power very often. But at the end of the year account should be taken of it. Otherwise we may suppose that the firm has become better off, in terms of what can be bought generally, than in fact it has become.

We can make allowance for the change in purchasing power very easily, provided that the opening and closing prices used in valuing assets (other than monetary assets) are prices ruling at opening and closing dates. Suppose a general price index stood at 100 on January 1st (t_0) and 110 on December 31st (t_1). Every dollar $(\$_0)$ represented in the balance sheet at January 1st is equal in purchasing power to 1.10 of the dollars used in the balance sheet at December 31st. Using the notation we introduced in the previous article, $\$_0 1 = \$_1 1.10$. The profit of a year is the amount by which the firm is better off at the end than it was at the beginning of the year. But we cannot discover this if the opening and closing amounts of the owners' equity are expressed in dollars of different purchasing power. Suppose we express the opening equity in dollars of the closing date; that is to say, we add, to the original number, 10 per cent of it in the present case. Deducting the amount of this 10 per cent from the balance of the profit and loss account (the increment) so far calculated, we will obtain the net income in $\$_1$. And crediting the same amount to a capital maintenance adjustment, which will be part of the owners' equity accounts, we will have an amount for owners' equity, expressed in $\$_1$, which is equal in purchasing power to the original owners' equity expressed in $\$_0$. The balance of net income and all other balances in the balance sheet will be in $\$_1$, and it is therefore quite proper to add, subtract or calculate ratios or percentages for any of them.

SYMBOLIC DEMONSTRATION

We may represent the system symbolically as follows:

Let $\$_0$ and $\$_1$ represent dollars of the purchasing power of the dollar at the dates t_0 and t_1 respectively, the opening and closing dates of an accounting period.

Let $\$_0 M_0$ and $\$_1 M_1$ represent the amounts of the net monetary assets of the firm at the two dates. Net monetary assets are cash balances and accounts receivable, net of accounts payable. M_0 and M_1 are two different numbers in the usual case.

Let $\$_0 N_0$ and $\$_1 N_1$ represent the amounts of the non-monetary assets at the two dates. They are the sums of the resale prices of all assets other than monetary assets.

Let $\$_0 R_0$ and $\$_1 R_1$ be the amounts of the owners' or shareholders' equity in the net assets of the firm at the two dates.

Now, the balance sheets of the firm at the two dates may be shown thus:

at t_0, $\$_0 M_0 + \$_0 N_0 = \$_0 R_0$
at t_1, $\$_1 M_1 \times \$_1 N_1 = \$_1 R_1$

The amounts on the left-hand sides of these equations are derived by actually checking the quantities of assets and liabilities, and using the resale prices of non-monetary assets. They are factual statements at the dates to which they relate. We want to find what the profit of the year is.

Let p be the proportionate change in the general level of prices during the year, expressed as a decimal fraction (such as .10, where the price index has risen by 10 per cent).

We may then write $\$_0 1 = \$_1 (1+p)$.

At the end of the year the only dollars in circulation and the only dollars in which prices are then expressed are $\$_1$. We can write the balance sheet at t_0 in terms of $\$_1$ by using the relationship $\$_0 1 = \$_1 (1+p)$, thus:

at t_0, $\$_1 M_0 (1+p) + \$_1 N_0 (1+p) = \$_1 R_0 (1+p)$
And as we have said above
at t_1, $\$_1 M_1 + \$_1 N_1 - \$_1 R_1$

These two equations are all in terms of $\$_1$. We can therefore subtract the right-hand sides, at t_0 from t_1, to obtain the net profit, thus:

Net profit $= \$_1 R_1 - \$_1 R_0 (1+p)$
$= \$_1 (R_1 - R_0 - R_0 p)$

And we can represent the owners' equity at t_1 thus:

Opening balance	R_0 } i.e.,	
Capital maintenance adjustment	$R_0 p$ } $\$_1 R_0 (1+p)$	
Profit of the year	$\$_1 (R_1 - R_0 - R_0 p)$	
Total closing owners' equity	$\$_1 R_1$	

Now what should happen if we accumulate entries of transactions

in the books of account during a year, if we incorporate the price variations in the manner described earlier and if changes in the purchasing
power of the $ are occurring slowly during the year? We cannot keep
track of $s with a whole series of different purchasing powers. We keep
the daily records only in terms of numbers of $s regardless of their pur-
chasing power. We could keep the whole year's records in the same way
as they are now kept, if we wished, provided only that the opening and
closing balances were correct in terms both of quantities and the unit
prices then prevailing. But in this case the account balances would not
be continuously consistent with current prices during the year. We
mention the possibility, however, simply to show that if we know the
kinds of figures we need at the year's end, and if we obtain them from
observations independently of the book balances (correcting the book
balances where necessary), no major change need be made in day-to-day
book-keeping. The *critical differences* between this system and traditional
accounting are the unit selling prices used at balance dates and the
simple calculation of the capital maintenance adjustment.

DURABLES AND DEPRECIATION

We have spoken of "goods" throughout, making no reference to durable
goods such as plant which depreciates. In essence, depreciation is just
another kind of price variation. If the resale price of a machine falls in a
period through its use and obsolescence, the amount of the fall is the
depreciation. It seems to some people that this is a curious idea of
depreciation; especially to those who think depreciation occurs in some
regular fashion such as may be represented by a straight line or a curve.
But depreciation does not occur in regular fashion; the most obvious
evidence is the frequency with which "book" surpluses or deficits occur on
the sale of plant, and the frequency with which assets survive long after
the asset has been written off according to a "regular" pattern. Some
may object, on the other hand, on the ground that prices are not available for all assets in all conditions. But there are many more sources of
information on second-hand prices than those people imagine. And if a
good is not saleable, it has no present financial characteristic, even though
it is expected to assist in the earning of future income.

There may be some difficulties in respect of some assets. But if the
system meets many of the tests which an accounting system is required
to meet, we do have a clear idea of the *kinds* of figures which it must
yield. Accountants may then quite properly use their judgements in
approximating resale prices from other price information. To attempt
to do what yields a useful and usable result is far better than producing,
by routine, figures which are nothing like what is useful and usable.

SOME OBJECTIONS ANSWERED

Some object to the system on the ground that, to use current resale prices
in respect of durable assets, implies that it is intended to sell them. Of

course it does not. A shareholder can look at the buyer's quotation for his shares day after day without any intention of selling them on a particular day. He simply wants to know how his investment stands. A car owner or home owner may do likewise for the same reason. If any of these persons concludes at some time that he will be better off by taking the price offered and doing something else with it, he will do so then. But watching one's position, like watching the financial position of a firm, is preparing oneself for what one might do when better opportunities arise. No other kind of information is equally serviceable for this purpose.

Others may object on the ground that the mere discovery of a resale price does not guarantee that that price will be obtained if the good is sold at the time. It is not the intention of the system to predict with a high degree of accuracy what would be obtained if any good were sold. The intended function of the balance sheet is to provide an indication of the current financial relationship of the firm with the rest of the world. Quoted prices, or the best approximations to them, are used because they are the prices which indicate the extent of the firm's claims against all other goods and services. Resale prices are not the opinions of the firm or its officers alone, as many figures in traditional balance sheets are admitted to be. They are prices or approximations to prices which others in the community are prepared to pay or are currently paying.

This quality of the system is particularly important as far as outsiders are concerned. If the management of a firm, or its accountant, reports in its financial statements what is thought, inside the firm, to be the values of its assets, there can be no assurance that the resulting statements of position and results fairly represent the firm's real situation. Insiders may be pessimistic or optimistic; in either case the reported figures may diverge materially from the judgements which outsiders would make of their components. Because traditional accounting is not firmly tied to currently quoted prices, there are many cases in which glowing impressions have been given of failing companies, and modest impressions have been given of companies which really control far greater asset values than those reported. This puts outsiders at the mercy of insiders, unless outsiders have the money, time, patience and ingenuity to find out the facts for themselves.

EXAMPLE

We may now give a slightly more complex example of the method used in Case 11 of the previous article, for that case gave an example of continuously contemporary accounting. The full details of the positions and transactions of a firm are given in tabular form in the work sheet below. The key letters in the "Transactions and events" column are given to aid the tracing of the double entries. It is assumed that in the year the index of changes in the general level of prices rose by 10 per cent.

The cash, debtors and creditors balances and movements need no

Work Sheet for year ended December 31st, 19x1

	At January 1st, 19x1		Transactions and events		At December 31st, 19x1	
	Dr	Cr	Dr	Cr	Dr	Cr
Assets						
Cash	20		390D	230E / 55G	125	
Debtors	40		400A	390D	50	
Goods	120		250B / 30C	260F	140	
Plant	80			20H	60	
Land	40		10J		50	
Equities						
Creditors		50	230E	250B		70
Owners:						
paid in		150				150
capital maintenance adjustment		30		18K		48
undistributed profit		70		7L		77
profit of year				80M		80
Profit and Loss Account						
Sales				400A		
Cost of goods sold (adjusted to cost at time of sale)			260F			
Price variation adjustment:						
goods				30C		
plant (depreciation)			20H			
land				10J		
Running expenses			55G			
Capital maintenance adjustment:						
on opening balance			18K			
on undistributed profit			7L			
Net profit			80M			
	$300	$300	$1,750	$1,750	$425	$425

explanation; they are obtained in the same way as under present forms of accounting.

The goods, plant and land will have been valued at resale prices at January 1st, 19x1. The balances of goods, plant and land at December 31st, 19x1 will have been obtained in the same way — by evidence of possession and quantity and by the use of resale prices. The price variation adjustment for goods (C) will be the sum of adjustments made during the year, as goods held were repriced consequent upon price movements, and of adjustments at the end of the year for variations between book and actual quantities and repricing at resale prices. The cost of goods sold (F) is the adjusted cost at the time of sale; that is the original price paid plus any variations due to changes in the particular prices of the goods between purchase and selling dates. Running expenses (G) are net cash outlays for all annual costs of operation. The price variation adjustments for plant (H) and land (J) are obtained by inference from opening and closing values.

The opening balance of the capital maintenance adjustment is the accumulated adjustment, for changes in the general level of prices (or the purchasing power of money), in respect of the amount paid in by owners some time previously. The sum ($180) of the amount paid in and the capital maintenance adjustment is the equivalent in purchasing power at January 1st, 19x1 of the amounts previously paid in. The adjustment (K) of $18 during the year is to take account of the rise of 10 per cent in the general level of prices during 19x1, in respect of this opening balance of $180. There is a similar adjustment (L) in respect of the opening balance of undistributed profit. Both adjustments are necessary because the total amount of the opening net owners' equity (or net assets) is subject to the fall in the purchasing power of money in the year.

Although, in the formal demonstration, we identified the different $s by different subscripts, there is no need to complicate the accounts in this way. At the end of the year, as we have said, all the sums expressed in $s are in $s of the then prevailing purchasing power. No one can possibly interpret them at the time in any other way. And the devices we have used have the effect of representing them in $s of the same kind. A profit and loss account and balance sheet can easily be drawn up from the work sheet.

APPRAISAL

We will appraise the system by reference to the points mentioned at the beginning of this article and held to be the grounds for adopting one or other of the methods mentioned in the first paragraph.

First, the accounts contain the original entries of transactions exactly as they occurred. The final financial summaries do not contain the unmodified results of manipulating those entries; for the events of the year will have necessitated modification of many of them. But the accounting system does contain them, and they may be checked in their original form in the course of any audit of the accounts. Auditors are able to give assurance that no unauthorized or improper usage of the firm's funds has occurred, to give a warrant of good stewardship in that sense. Historical cost accounting is justified on all these grounds. The proposed system satisfies them.

Second, price level adjusted accounting is justified on the grounds that it avoids the addition of quantities of unlike $s, and that it takes account of the effects on income of changes in the purchasing power of money. The proposed system also satisfies both of these specifications. In the course of deriving the final figures there are additions and subtractions of different $s. But the overall corrections, the price variation adjustments and the capital maintenance adjustment, and the use of current prices at the close of the year, have the effect of making the final statements into statements in homogeneous dollars.

Third, price level adjusted accounting does not give final statements in terms of current prices; for original prices are merely corrected by an overall price index. The use of current prices is one of the advantages claimed for replacement price accounting. The system proposed also uses current prices — in making the price variation adjustments and in deriving the financial position at the year's end by reference to current prices. Though the proposed system uses different current prices (selling prices) from those of the replacement price proposal, it does use current prices.

Fourth, present (discounted) value accounting is said to be necessary for forward-looking estimation. But it presupposes that the reported present values are reliable. The system here proposed requires no such assumption, on the ground that no future estimates are free of the biases and guesswork of those who make them. The system goes as far as it is possible to go, by seeking to give the best indication that can be given of the actual state of a firm as it faces the future at each reporting date. It therefore meets the principle that the information be useful for forward-looking estimation, without committing readers of financial statements to the optimistic or pessimistic outlook, as the case may be, of managers or accountants of firms.

In meeting all these tests in its own special way, the system has other important practical consequences. One can proceed to analyse the financial statements of a firm at any date without committing the solecism of relating figures in unlike dollars. The figures in the balance sheet and the net income figure are all in $s of the closing date. If all firms used the same system, as they would if it were generally adopted, inter-firm comparisons of ratios and relationships would be realistic and mathematically valid. They are not under present accounting. Inter-period comparisons of ratios would also be valid; for although successive financial statements are in different $s, the ratios of any particular year are pure numbers or percentages and are thus comparable with like numbers or percentages of other years. Above all, the figures would be readily interpretable because they are all in reasonably up-to-date purchasing power units, year by year.

CONCLUSION

We have sketched only briefly the reasons for, and the characteristics of, the system. Continuously contemporary accounting meets most, if not all, of the requirements of users and the general tests of logic and mathematical propriety, whereas other proposals meet few of them. The number of criteria met by any system is a test used in appraising all kinds of product and device. On this ground, the system proposed has marked superiority over all others.

Author's Note:

A first approximation to the method of accounting here suggested was developed in *Accounting, Evaluation and Economic Behavior* (1966). The author has since found it possible to dispose with some features of the earlier proposals which gave rise to criticism of inconsistency. The particular method of dealing with the price variation adjustments illustrated in this paper is only one of a number of possible methods. The method illustrated involves fewer departures from the conventional process of accounting during any period than some other methods. But strictly, to be continuously contemporary at all times, all asset balances should be adjusted continuously to the resale price basis.

However this and other variants of the general proposal would all yield the same net income and balance sheet figures.

III

Core Accounting Techniques and Management Evaluations

The Introduction to Section I listed several management evaluations which are necessary in various organizations, and listed also several management accounting techniques which might aid in specific evaluations. It was observed that a prime objective of most introductory/ intermediate management accounting courses is to show which accounting technique aids which management evaluations under which conditions.

Exhibit III-1, "Tailoring Accounting Techniques to Management Evaluations", (pp. 143-145) attempts in a somewhat rough manner to indicate relationships between techniques and evaluations. Any chart of this nature must be interpreted with care because simplifying assumptions abound and terminology is condensed. However, the exhibit can be useful until the point where a learner develops a comfortable comprehension of the boundaries of management accounting thought. General guidance as to the meaning of the various management evaluations (such as pricing, or output) is provided in the Introduction to Section I. The terminology employed in the chart is not universally acknowledged by even those authors whose work is reprinted herein. Management evaluations are interrelated; hence some accounting techniques (such as cost-volume-profit analysis) are listed opposite several evaluations. For convenience, references to articles are listed opposite techniques and related evaluations.

Manufacturing organizations require systems which accumulate factory costs and thereby enable the company to cost partially and fully completed products ("value" work in process and finished goods inventories). When inventory quantities have been costed, income statements and balance sheets can be prepared and the organization can meet its obligation for external reporting and income taxation. Exhibit III-2, "Inventory Costing Systems", (p. 147) sets out some of the many methods which may be employed in order to cost inventories of work in process and finished goods, as well as to ascertain cost of goods sold.

One point must be kept firmly in mind while studying Exhibits III-1 and III-2. A complex organization which encounters many or all of the management evaluations shown in Exhibit III-1 would likely utilize one comprehensive management accounting system. Costs, revenues, assets, liabilities, and equities would be accumulated in many, many detailed account categories or cells. When the need for information to aid in specific evaluations arises, only those few expenses and revenues which have relevance to the problem would be retrieved from their storage cells and assembled in an accounting report. The data in some storage cells could be used dozens of times, whereas other cost/revenue, asset/liability categories may be seldom used. The number of cells and the basis of categorization would depend on what that company wished to stress — information for pricing and performance evaluation, or whatever. In contrast, some smaller organizations not subject to as many environmental changes could elect to prepare a few reports which would then be used — perhaps foolishly — for all their decisions. Ideally, the design of systems should occur after cost-benefit analysis.

"Management Misinformation Systems" elaborates on this problem of the design of information systems. With the aid of a variety of interesting illustrations the author identifies five common errors made in designing systems, and then outlines a possible design procedure to avoid such errors.

"The Chop Suey Caper" was written in response to a financial accounting debate as to whether so-called conglomerate corporations should report separate net profits and net assets for each of their divisions. Nevertheless, much of the article amusingly discusses a recurring headache for preparers and users of accounting information — relevance of cost and revenue *allocations* for specific decisions. For example, depreciation expense on a factory building could be split among several departments in order to arrive at a full cost of each class of inventory, for subsequent use in external reporting. However, does such an allocation procedure make sense if the accounting data is needed for some other purpose such as to aid in short-term pricing decisions or performance appraisal? In many cases the answer would be "No!" because the subdivided figures are not relevant for the particular decision. In other cases, the answer might be "No!" because any allocation process would be too arbitrary and would muddy the issue under consideration. The author, Greer, looks at these problems in an illustration that may be long remembered.

"Matrix Theory and Cost Allocation" acknowledges that accountants make cost allocations in compiling information to aid in some management evaluations, and then illustrates how the procedure can be simplified by employing matrix concepts. Although this and similar articles were written over a decade ago, the approach has not been illustrated in most widely used management accounting textbooks. Nevertheless, the use of mathematics in compiling management accounting information is increasing, and time may be saved by searching recent accounting literature for mathematical shortcuts to mechanical problems.

"The Fable of the Accountant and the President," the source of which is unfortunately unknown, provides a quick overview of income effects of direct (or variable) costing. Exhibit III-1 and Article 8 also explain direct versus full costing and show where they may have use for particular management evaluations.

"Cost Concepts for Control" and "Tailor-making Cost Data for Specific Uses" are directed at the prime theme of most introductory/intermediate management accounting courses. The former is mainly concerned with performance evaluations and in a very readable style examines the role of motivation. ("We are convinced . . . that approaching the control problem in terms of human motivation . . . is much more fruitful than . . . any . . . mechanical approach." ". . . there probably are some who will, in one way or another, obtain too much no matter how tight the control system is." ". . . to some people the very attempt to describe costs in terms of human reactions smacks of trickery. . . . I think this feeling arises from the implicit assumption that there must be some objective way of defining cost, and . . . this simply is not so.") The latter article illustrates the relationships between several accounting techniques and management evaluations. ("What I have tried to do is to make it clear that the use to be made of cost data governs their content and that cost data must be tested for relevance before they can be relied upon in management decision-making.")

The process of preparing budgets can be very beneficial simply because it forces thought about the future, and, in particular, requires an identification of interrelationships affecting an organization. In essence, budgets can be excellent vehicles for coordination. Yet, as Buckley and McKenna and some of the authors in Section IV observe, so-called "fixed" budgets may have undesirable side effects for performance evaluation of specific managers. Specifically, fixed budgets contain information which can be used in a punitive manner. Types of flexible budgets (prepared after activity has occurred) have been devised to overcome weaknesses of fixed budgets for performance evaluation purposes. However, fixed budgets still possess weaknesses for output, pricing, financing and investment decisions because they are often based solely on "most likely" levels of future activity. "Toward Probabilistic Profit Budgets" illustrates three approaches to the preparation of probabilistic budgets, all of which incorporate additional information which may aid in management evaluations.

"An Application of Curvilinear Break-even Analysis" provides a simple mathematical illustration of maximum profit computation when non linear expense and revenue functions exist. As the author observes, the illustration helps some people understand the concept of derivatives and obtain greater appreciation of applications of break-even analysis.

"Profit Centers, Transfer Prices and Mysticism" take a critical look at management control of decentralized companies. The article drew a response from K. W. Lemke in *Abacus* (December 1970) and a reply from Wells in *Abacus* (June 1971). The next article, by Vancil, also examines the profit center concept. In several senses this type of debate is a classic example of confusion as to the role of specific accounting techniques in various management evaluations. Wells clearly notes that some form of transfer pricing is required for external reporting and income taxation and that these purposes can require different data from others — such as performance appraisal.

*   *   *

Exhibit III-1 (pp. 143-145), "Tailoring Accounting Techniques to Management Evaluations," should be viewed as a device to assist in tentatively integrating one's thoughts. To the beginner the Exhibit may seem overwhelming; to the journeyman it is likely to be acceptable but not exciting. The purpose of Exhibit III-1 is to encourage persons to prepare their own overview charts after studying the articles in this book, reading a textbook and analyzing cases.

Columns B and C in Exhibit III-1 attempt to divide management accounting techniques into two broad categories. Column C lists techniques which tend towards being "ideals." They may be of interest to large organizations which wish to spend money on a good, comprehensive accounting system to aid them in a host of evaluations. Often the techniques in Column C are refinements designed to pinpoint the nature of a problem or give specific recommendations. In contrast, Column B is concerned with relatively cruder devices which give a general indication that a problem exists or that a particularly broad path should be followed. For example, a dentist could quickly examine your teeth with hand instruments and give advice that further steps should be taken (Column B approach). The dentist could also thoroughly check your teeth with the aid of five or six X-rays (Column C approach) and give more concrete advice. In some cases X-rays would not be necessary because the problem and solution might be obvious; similarly; there are likely to be circumstances when costly accounting procedures need not be followed. Small companies might often base their accounting system on Column B techniques; and, when a special need arose, they would have their accountants tabulate information from invoices and other source documents — and not directly from ledgers and regular reports.

Exhibit III – 1

Tailoring Accounting Techniques to Management Evaluations

A. Management Evaluation or Decision	Management Accounting Technique		D. Reading References in this Book	
	B. Overall, Broad or Crude Procedure	C. Specific or Refined Procedure	Article Number	Author(s)
1. Performance Appraisal (primarily of individual managers)	• Accounting return on investment • Fixed budgets	• Responsibility accounting • Flexible budgets, and variance analysis • Human resources accounting • Some variances from standard cost (e.g., a price variance may be the responsibility of a particular purchasing clerk)	3 4 5 15 16 19 All of Section IV	Anthony Buckley and McKenna Caplan Anthony Vatter Wells
2. Pricing of Products and Services (i.e., setting of selling prices)	• Direct or variable costing • Master budgeting; profit budgets • Break-even analysis and cost-volume-profit analysis (in multi-product companies) • Full inventory cost plus profit (see Exhibit III – 2)	• Contribution margin analysis • Break-even analysis and cost-volume-profit analysis (in a single product division or company) • Program costs/budgets	8 14 18 27 28 30 31 32	Fremgen (Fable) Givens Lere Kallimanis Greer Jaedicke and Robichek Macleod

Exhibit III – 1 – continued

| A. Management Evaluation or Decision | Management Accounting Technique | | D. Reading References in This Book | |
	B. Overall, Broad or Crude Procedure	C. Specific or Refined Procedure	Article Number	Author(s)
3. Output (quantities and qualities of products and services, including types of components of manufactured goods, i.e., make components vs. buy)	• Accounting return on investment • Break-even analysis and cost-volume-profit analysis (in multi-product companies) • Social cost/benefit comparisons • Direct or variable costing • Some fixed budgets	• Contribution margin analysis • Break-even analysis and cost-volume-profit analysis (in a single product division or company) • Incremental/differential cost and revenue comparisons • Program costs/budgets • Volume or capacity variance analysis between actual and standard costs	8 10 11 12 13 14 16 17 18 19 27 28 31 32 33	Fremgen Chambers Ackoff Greer Williams and Griffin (Fable) Vatter Ferrara and Hayya Givens Wells Lere Kallimanis Jaedicke and Robichek Macleod Ross
4. Financing Requirements (number of dollars required for what length of time and from which sources)	• Profit budgets • Accrual basis "funds" statement	• Cash budgets • Cost of capital computations	1 28 30	Demaree Kallimanis Greer
5. Investment and Disinvestment (i.e., asset levels; men/machine trade-offs)	• Accounting return on investment • Profit budgets • Pay back measures of cash return on investment	• Discounted cash flow capital budgeting techniques • Risk analysis; use of objective or subjective probabilities • Sensitivity analysis	1 2 5 9 10 16	Demaree Loomis Caplan Chambers Chambers Vatter

	• Break-even and cost-volume-profit analysis conducted on a macro basis	• Contribution margin analysis • Break-even and cost-volume-profit analysis conducted on a micro level • Post audit of previous capital expenditures	17 19 28 29 31	Ferrara and Hayya Wells Kallimanis House Jaedicke and Robichek
6. External Reporting (to stockholders, general creditors, and the public)	• Historic reports assembled on a macro basis • See Exhibit III – 2	• Profit projections (forecasts) • Product line or segment reports where units are divisible • See Exhibit III – 2	2 All of Section II 12 19 33	Loomis Greer Wells Ross
7. Income Taxation (including other government legislation requiring information)	• Often closely related to external reporting; but some major differences exist		8 19 30	Fremgen Wells Greer
8. Market or Distribution Area (sell in which cities, towns?)	• Profit budgets	• Contribution margin analysis • Incremental cost/revenue comparisons	16 28 30	Vatter Kallimanis Greer
9. Record Keeping (processing of cash, receivables, payables, and other invoices)	• Single entry records	• Accrual bases of accounting, with internal controls included. See Exhibit III – 2	1 2	Demaree Loomis

Any categorization such as that between Columns B and C
(or between types of evaluations) is arbitrary. A caution is therefore in
order. A technique listed as an overall one in Exhibit III-1
(Column B) could be a specific one (Column C) for some companies
under particular conditions. A cash-and-carry grocery store, for
instance, might need little more than a cash register and a few
single entry records for all its needs.

Column D lists all the articles which even briefly discuss an
accounting technique having bearing on the management evaluation
shown in Column A. Persons desiring a quick indication of the
content of specific articles should refer to the questions assigned about
the article, as well as to introductory remarks on the first page of
some readings and editorial remarks at the beginning of each section
of the book.

Exhibit III-2, "Inventory Costing Systems", lists several alternative
techniques and costing choices which are available to "manufacturing"
companies for the purpose of attaching a cost to goods manufactured.
(Work in process and finished goods inventory, and cost of goods
sold.) The principal message which this Exhibit is designed to convey is:

> A choice must be made from *each*
> of Columns 1, 2 and 3 in order
> to have a complete inventory
> costing system.

The exhibit also shows which concepts are alternatives and which
are entirely different parts of the system.

For example, a simple system to aid in the costing of inventories
so that a balance sheet, income statement, and so forth, can be
prepared for *external reporting purposes,* Exhibit III-1, Management
Evaluation 6, — with information for other decisions not being
desired — would likely consist of (1A; 2A; 3A) or (1B; 2A; 3A).
Such systems merely collect actual costs and do not separate fixed from
variable manufacturing overhead. Thus, in many companies — but
not all — these systems would require less bookkeeping than some of
the other choices. The accounting cost would be tailored to the
anticipated use to be made of the system.

In contrast, a company which desires its accounting system to
aid in performance evaluation, pricing, output, external reporting
and possibly other evaluations would likely employ a (1A; 2D; 3B) or
(1B; 2D; 3B) combination. Such combinations are thus far more
than the minimum needs to arrive at a cost of manufactured inventories;
the extra accounting cost is incurred because it is expected to be
less than benefits.

Three additional points deserve stress:

1. The inventory cost will likely differ widely, depending
upon which combination is chosen. A (1A; 2A; 3A) selection, for
instance, includes both fixed and variable manufacturing overhead
at actual cost; whereas, a (1A; 2D; 3B) choice includes only

Exhibit III – 2

Inventory Costing Systems

1. Basic Accounting Procedure	2. Actual vs. Predetermined vs. Standard Costs (Which cost should be used for each cost element?)	3. Include vs. Exclude Fixed Manufacturing Overhead?
A. Process Costing Approach	A. Actual Direct Material / Actual Direct Labour / Actual Manufacturing Overhead	A. Full or Absorption Costing (includes the fixed portion of manufacturing overhead)
	B. Actual Direct Material / Actual Direct Labour / Predetermined Manufacturing Overhead	
B. Job Order Costing Approach	C. Actual Direct Material / Predetermined Direct Labour and Manufacturing Overhead	B. Direct or Variable Costing (does *not* include the fixed portion of manufacturing overhead)
	D. Standard Direct Material, Direct Labour, and Manufacturing Overhead	

variable manufacturing overhead at standard cost in per unit inventory costs. Income figures for a period will thus differ, depending upon which combination is selected. In sum, the combination would be selected after looking at the needs of the company in the long term.

2. Columns 1 and 2 do not list all of the alternatives which exist. The terms "process costing" and "job order" are likely explained at length in your principal textbook. They are just two of several ways of arranging accounts and averaging costs. The terms "actual," "predetermined" and "standard" are also explained in your textbook. Component 2C may not be explained and has been included in the exhibit to indicate that other choices exist. An automobile repair shop might employ a (1A; 2C; 3A) combination to aid in costing and pricing each car brought in for repairs. They may choose such a system because they need information quickly — so as to collect their cash before they turn over the car to the customer. The 2C portion of the system shows that parts (spark plugs, oil, points) used to repair the car would be accounted for differently from labor and overhead which may be on the basis of so many dollars per hour spent by the mechanic. Profit mark-up could be added individually to the parts as well as mechanic's labor and overhead cost to arrive at billing price. One company might employ several different systems, depending upon its needs for information. The used car division of the same company may, for example, select a (1B; 2A; 3A) combination to assist its managers in deciding whether some makes of automobile are not worth refurbishing and selling.

3. Predetermined and standard costs are not used only in "manufacturing" companies, but may be employed in sales and office staff control, and so on.

Like Exhibit III-1, Exhibit III-2 can appear overwhelming at first. However, many persons who have used it in conjunction with textbooks, articles and cases from the beginning of courses have found that the initial struggle with the exhibit was worth the effort.

11

Management Misinformation Systems

RUSSELL L. ACKOFF*

Five assumptions commonly made by designers of management information systems are identified. It is argued that these are not justified in many (if not most) cases and hence lead to major deficiencies in the resulting systems. These assumptions are: (1) the critical deficiency under which most managers operate is the lack of relevant information, (2) the manager needs the information he wants, (3) if a manager has the information he needs his decision-making will improve, (4) better communication between managers improves organizational performance, and (5) a manager does not have to understand how his information system works, only how to use it. To overcome these assumptions and the deficiencies which result from them, a management information system should be imbedded in a management control system. A procedure for designing such a system is proposed and an example is given of the type of control system which it produces.

The growing preoccupation of operation researchers and management scientists with Management Information Systems (MIS's) is apparent. In fact, for some the design of such systems has almost become synonymous with operations research or management science. Enthusiasm for such systems is understandable: it involves the researcher in a romantic relationship with the most glamorous instrument of our time, the computer. Such enthusiasm is understandable but, nevertheless, some of the excesses to which it has led are not excusable.

Contrary to the impression produced by the growing literature,

* From *Management Science*, Vol. 14, No. 4 (December 1967). Reprinted by permission of The Institute of Management Sciences.

few computerized management information systems have been put into operation. Of those I've seen that have been implemented, most have not matched expectations and some have been outright failures. I believe that these near- and far-misses could have been avoided if certain false (and usually implicit) assumptions on which many systems have been erected had not been made.

There seem to be five common and erroneous assumptions underlying the design of most MIS's, each of which I will consider. After doing so I will outline an MIS design procedure which avoids these assumptions.

GIVE THEM MORE

Most MIS's are designed on the assumption that the critical deficiency under which most managers operate is the *lack of relevant information*. I do not deny that most managers lack a good deal of information that they should have, but I do deny that this is the most important informational deficiency from which they suffer. It seems to me that they suffer more from an *over-abundance of irrelevant information*.

This is not a play on words. The consequences of changing the emphasis of an MIS from supplying relevant information to eliminating irrelevant information is considerable. If one is preoccupied with supplying relevant information, attention is almost exclusively given to the generation, storage, and retrieval of information: hence emphasis is placed on constructing data banks, coding, indexing, updating files, access languages, and so on. The ideal which has emerged from this orientation is an infinite pool of data into which a manager can reach to pull out any information he wants. If, on the other hand, one sees the manager's information problem primarily, but not exclusively, as one that arises out of an overabundance of irrelevant information, most of which was not asked for, then the two most important functions of an information system become *filtration* (or evaluation) and *condensation*. The literature on MIS's seldom refers to these functions let alone considers how to carry them out.

My experience indicates that most managers receive much more data (if not information) than they can possibly absorb even if they spend all of their time trying to do so. Hence they already suffer from an information overload. They must spend a great deal of time separating the relevant from the irrelevant and searching for the kernels in the relevant documents. For example, I have found that I receive an average of forty-three hours of unsolicited reading material each week. The solicited material is usually half again this amount.

I have seen a daily stock status report that consists of approximately six hundred pages of computer print-out. The report is circulated daily across managers' desks. I've also seen requests for major capital expenditures that come in book size, several of which are distributed to managers each week. It is not uncommon for many managers to

receive an average of one journal a day or more. One could go on and
on.

Unless the information overload to which managers are subjected
is reduced, any additional information made available by an MIS cannot
be expected to be used effectively.

Even relevant documents have too much repetition. Most documents can be considerably condensed without loss of content. My point
here is best made, perhaps, by describing briefly an experiment that a
few of my colleagues and I conducted on the OR literature several years
ago. By using a panel of well-known experts we identified four OR
articles that all members of the panel considered to be "above average,"
and four articles that were considered to be "below average." The authors
of the eight articles were asked to prepare "objective" examinations
(duration thirty minutes) plus answers for graduate students who were
to be assigned the articles for reading. (The authors were not informed
about the experiment.) Then several experienced writers were asked to
reduce each article to two-thirds and one-third of its original length
only by eliminating words. They also prepared a brief abstract of each
article. Those who did the condensing did not see the examinations to
be given to the students.

A group of graduate students who had not previously read the
articles were then selected. Each one was given four articles randomly
selected, each of which was in one of its four versions: 100 per cent, 67
per cent, 33 per cent, or abstract. Each version of each article was read
by two students. All were given the same examinations. The average
scores on the examinations were then compared.

For the above-average articles there was no significant difference
between average test scores for the 100 per cent, 67 per cent, and 33 per
cent versions, but there was a significant decrease in average test scores
for those who had read only the abstract. For the below-average articles
there was no difference in average test scores among those who had read
the 100 per cent, 67 per cent, and 33 per cent versions, but there was a
significant *increase* in average test scores of those who had read only
the abstract.

The sample used was obviously too small for general conclusions
but the results strongly indicate the extent to which even good writing
can be condensed without loss of information. I refrain from drawing
the obvious conclusion about bad writing.

It seems clear that condensation as well as filtration, performed
mechanically or otherwise, should be an essential part of an MIS, and
that such a system should be capable of handling much, if not all, of the
unsolicited as well as solicited information that a manager receives.

THE MANAGER NEEDS THE INFORMATION THAT HE WANTS

Most MIS designers "determine" what information is needed by asking
managers what information they would like to have. This is based

on the assumption that managers know what information they need, and want it.

For a manager to know what information he needs he must be aware of each type of decision he should make (as well as does) and he must have an adequate model of each. These conditions are seldom satisfied. Most managers have some conception of at least some of the types of decisions they must make. Their conceptions, however, are likely to be deficient in a very critical way, a way that follows from an important principle of scientific economy: the less we understand a phenomenon, the more variables we require to explain it. Hence, the manager who does not understand the phenomenon he controls plays it "safe" and, with respect to information, wants "everything." The MIS designer, who has even less understanding of the relevant phenomenon than the manager, tries to provide even more than everything. He thereby increases what is already an overload of irrelevant information.

For example, market researchers in a major oil company once asked their marketing managers what variables they thought were relevant in estimating the sales volume of future service stations. Almost seventy variables were identified. The market researchers then added about half again this many variables, performed a large multiple linear regression analysis of sales of existing stations against these variables, and found about thirty-five to be statistically significant. A forecasting equation was based on this analysis. An OR team subsequently constructed a model based on only one of these variables, traffic flow, which predicted sales better than the thirty-five-variable regression equation. The team went on to *explain* sales at service stations in terms of the customers' perception of the amount of time lost by stopping for service. The relevance of all but a few of the variables used by the market researchers could be explained by their effect on such perception.

The moral is simple: one cannot specify what information is required for decision-making until an explanatory model of the decision process and the system involved has been constructed and tested. Information systems are subsystems of control systems. They cannot be designed adequately without taking control in account. Furthermore, whatever else regression analyses can yield, they cannot yield understanding and explanation of phenomena. They describe and, at best, predict.

GIVE A MANAGER THE INFORMATION HE NEEDS AND HIS DECISION-MAKING WILL IMPROVE

It is frequently assumed that if a manager is provided with the information he needs, he will then have no problem in using it effectively. The history of OR stands to the contrary. For example, give most managers an initial tableau of a typical "real" mathematical programming, sequencing, or network problem and see how close they come to an optimal solution. If their experience and judgment have any value they may not do badly, but they will seldom do very well. In most management problems there are too many possibilities to expect experience, judgment, or intuition to provide good guesses, even with perfect information.

Furthermore, when several probabilities are involved in a problem the unguided mind of even a manager has difficulty in aggregating them in a valid way. We all know many simple problems in probability in which untutored intuition usually does very badly (e.g., what are the correct odds that two of twenty-five people selected at random will have their birthdays on the same day of the year?). For example, very few of the results obtained by queuing theory, when arrivals and service are probabilistic, are obvious to managers; nor are the results of risk analysis where the managers' own subjective estimates of probabilities are used.

The moral: it is necessary to determine how well managers can use needed information. When, because of the complexity of the decision process, they can't use it well, they should be provided with either decision rules or performance feed-back so that they can identify and learn from their mistakes. More on this point later.

MORE COMMUNICATION MEANS BETTER PERFORMANCE

One characteristic of most MIS's which I have seen is that they provide managers with better current information about what other managers and their departments and divisions are doing. Underlying this provision is the belief that better interdepartmental communication enables managers to coordinate their decisions more effectively and hence improves the organization's overall performance. Not only is this not necessarily so, but it seldom is so. One would hardly expect two competing companies to become more cooperative because the information each acquires about the other is improved. This analogy is not as far-fetched as one might at first suppose. For example, consider the following very much simplified version of a situation I once ran into. The simplification of the case does not affect any of its essential characteristics.

A department store has two "line" operations: buying and selling. Each function is performed by a separate department. The Purchasing Department primarily controls one variable: how much of each item is bought. The Merchandising Department controls the price at which it is sold. Typically, the measure of performance applied to the Purchasing Department was the turnover rate of inventory. The measure applied to the Merchandising Department was gross sales; this department sought to maximize the number of items sold, times their price.

Now by examining a single item let us consider what happens in this system. The merchandising manager, using his knowledge of competition and consumption, set a price which he judged would maximize gross sales. In doing so he utilized price-demand curves for each type of item. For each price the curves show the expected sales and values on an upper and lower confidence band as well. (See Figure 1.) When instructing the Purchasing Department how many items to make avail-

Figure 1. Price-demand curve

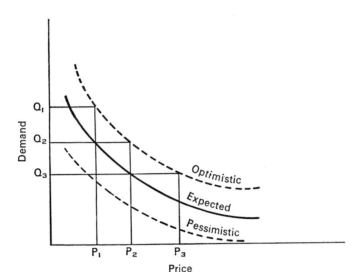

able, the merchandising manager quite naturally used the value on the upper confidence curve. This minimized the chances of his running short which, if it occurred, would hurt his performance. It also maximized the chances of being over-stocked but this was not his concern, only the purchasing manager's. Say, therefore, that the merchandising manager initially selected price P_1 and requested that amount Q_1 be made available by the Purchasing Department.

In this company the purchasing manager also had access to the price-demand curves. He knew the merchandising manager always ordered optimistically. Therefore, using the same curve he read over from Q_1 to the upper limit and down to the expected value from which he obtained Q_2, the quantity he actually intended to make available. He did not intend to pay for the merchandising manager's optimism. If merchandising ran out of stock, it was not his worry. Now the merchandising manager was informed about what the purchasing manager had done, so he adjusted his price to P_2. The purchasing manager in turn was told that the merchandising manager had made this readjustment, so he planned to make only Q_3 available. If this process — made possible only by perfect communication between departments — had been allowed to continue, nothing would have been bought and nothing would have been sold. This outcome was avoided by prohibiting communication between the two departments and forcing each to guess what the other was doing.

I have obviously caricatured the situation in order to make the point clear: when organizational units have inappropriate measures of performance which put them in conflict with each other, as is often the case, communication between them may hurt organizational performance, not help it. Organizational structure and performance measurement must be taken into account before opening the flood gates and permitting the free flow of information between parts of the organization. (A more rigorous discussion of organizational structure and the relationship of communication to it can be found in Reference 1, page 159.)

A MANAGER DOES NOT HAVE TO UNDERSTAND HOW AN INFORMATION SYSTEM WORKS, ONLY HOW TO USE IT

Most MIS designers seek to make their systems as innocuous and unobtrusive as possible to managers lest they become frightened. The designers try to provide managers with very easy access to the system and assure them that they need to know nothing more about it. The designers usually succeed in keeping managers ignorant in this regard. This leaves managers unable to evaluate the MIS as a whole. It often makes them afraid to even try to do so lest they display their ignorance publicly. In failing to evaluate their MIS, managers delegate much of the control of the organization to the system's designers and operators who may have many virtues, but managerial competence is seldom among them.

Let me cite a case in point. A Chairman of the Board of a medium-size company asked for help on the following problem. One of his larger (decentralized) divisions had installed a computerized production-inventory control and manufacturing-manager information system about a year earlier. It had acquired about $2,000,000 worth of equipment to do so. The Board Chairman had just received a request from the Division for permission to replace the original equipment with newly announced equipment which would cost several times the original amount. An extensive "justification" for so doing was provided with the request. The Chairman wanted to know whether the request was really justified. He admitted to complete incompetence in this connection.

A meeting was arranged at the Division at which I was subjected to an extended and detailed briefing. The system was large but relatively simple. At the heart of it was a reorder point for each item and a maximum allowable stock level. Reorder quantities took lead-time as well as the allowable maximum into account. The computer kept track of stock, ordered items when required and generated numerous reports on both the state of the system it controlled and its own "actions."

When the briefing was over I was asked if I had any questions. I did. First I asked if, when the system had been installed, there had been many parts whose stock level exceeded the maximum amount possible under the new system. I was told there were many. I asked for a list of about thirty and for some graph paper. Both were provided. With the help of the system designer and volumes of old daily reports I began to plot the stock level of the first listed item over time. When this item reached the maximum "allowable" stock level it had been reordered. The system designer was surprised and said that by sheer "luck" I had found one of the few errors made by the system. Continued plotting showed that because of repeated premature reordering the item had never gone much below the maximum stock level. Clearly the program was confusing the maximum allowable stock level and the reorder point. This turned out to be the case in more than half of the items on the list.

Next I asked if they had many paired parts, ones that were only used with each other; for example, matched nuts and bolts. They had many. A list was produced and we began checking the previous day's withdrawals. For more than half of the pairs the differences in the numbers recorded as withdrawn were very large. No explanation was provided.

Before the day was out it was possible to show by some quick and dirty calculations that the new computerized system was costing the company almost $150,000 per month more than the hand system which it had replaced, most of this in excess inventories.

The recommendation was that the system be redesigned as quickly as possible and that the new equipment not be authorized for the time being.

The questions asked of the system had been obvious and simple ones. Managers should have been able to ask them but — and this is the point — they felt themselves incompetent to do so. They would not have allowed a hand-operated system to get so far out of their control.

No MIS should ever be installed unless the managers for whom it is intended are trained to evaluate and hence control it rather than be controlled by it.

A SUGGESTED PROCEDURE FOR DESIGNING AN MIS

The erroneous assumptions I have tried to reveal in the preceding discussion can, I believe, be avoided by an appropriate design procedure. One is briefly outlined here.

1. Analysis of the Decision System

Each (or at least each important) type of managerial decision required by the organization under study should be identified and the relationships between them should be determined and flow-charted. Note that this is *not* necessarily the same thing as determining what decisions *are* made. For example, in one company I found that make-or-buy decisions concerning parts were made only at the time when a part was introduced into stock and was never subsequently reviewed. For some items this decision had gone unreviewed for as many as twenty years. Obviously, such decisions should be made more often; in some cases, every time an order is placed in order to take account of current shop loading, underused shifts, delivery times from suppliers, and so on.

Decision-flow analyses are usually self-justifying. They often reveal important decisions that are being made by default (e.g., the make-buy decision referred to above), and they disclose interdependent decisions that are being made independently. Decision-flow charts frequently suggest changes in managerial responsibility, organizational structure, and measure of performance which can correct the types of deficiencies cited.

Decision analyses can be conducted with varying degrees of detail, that is, they may be anywhere from coarse- to fine-grained. How much detail one should become involved with depends on the amount of time and resources that are available for the analysis. Although practical considerations frequently restrict initial analyses to a particular organizational function, it is preferable to perform a coarse analysis of all of an organization's managerial functions rather than a fine analysis of one or a subset of functions. It is easier to introduce finer information into an integrated information system than it is to combine fine subsystems into one integrated system.

2. An Analysis of Information Requirements

Managerial decisions can be classified into three types:

(a) Decisions for which adequate models are available or can be constructed and from which optimal (or near optimal) solutions can be derived. In such cases the decision process itself should be incorporated into the information system thereby converting it (at least partially) to a control system. A decision model identifies what information is required and hence what information is relevant.

(b) Decisions for which adequate models can be constructed but from which optimal solutions cannot be extracted. Here some kind of heuristic or search procedure should be provided even if it consists of no more than computerized trial and error. A simulation of the model will, as a minimum, permit comparison of proposed alternative solutions. Here too the model specifies what information is required.

(c) Decisions for which adequate models cannot be constructed. Research is required here to determine what information is relevant. If decision-making cannot be delayed for the completion of such research or the decision's effect is not large enough to justify the cost of research, then judgment must be used to "guess" what information is relevant. It may be possible to make explicit the implicit model used by the decision-maker and treat it as a model of type (b).

In each of these three types of situation it is necessary to provide feedback by comparing actual decision outcomes with those predicted by the model or decision-maker. Each decision that is made, along with its predicted outcome, should be an essential input to a management control system. I shall return to this point below.

3. Aggregation of Decisions

Decisions with the same or largely overlapping informational requirements should be grouped together as a single manager's task. This will reduce the information a manager requires to do his job and is likely to increase his understanding of it. This may require a reorganization of the system. Even if such a reorganization cannot be implemented completely what can be done is likely to improve performance significantly and reduce the information loaded on managers.

4. Design of Information Processing

Now the procedure for collecting, storing, retrieving, and treating information can be designed. Since there is a voluminous literature on this subject I shall leave it at this except for one point. Such a system must not only be able to answer questions addressed to it; it should also be able to answer questions that have not been asked by reporting any deviations from expectations. An extensive exception-reporting system is required.

5. Design of Control of the Control System

It must be assumed that the system that is being designed will be deficient in many and significant ways. Therefore it is necessary to identify the ways in which it may be deficient, to design procedures for detecting its deficiencies, and for correcting the system so as to remove or reduce them. Hence the system should be designed to be flexible and adaptive. This is little more than a platitude, but it has a not-so-obvious implication. No completely computerized system can be as flexible and adaptive as can a man-machine system. This is illustrated by a concluding example of a system that is being developed and is partially in operation. (See Figure 2.)

The company involved has its market divided into approximately two hundred marketing areas. A model for each has been constructed as is "in" the computer. On the basis of competitive intelligence supplied to the service marketing manager by marketing researchers and information specialists he and his staff make policy decisions for each area each month. Their tentative decisions are fed into the computer which yields a forecast of expected performance. Changes are made until the expectations match what is desired. In this way they arrive at "final" decisions. At the end of the month the computer compares the actual performance of each area with what was predicted. If a deviation exceeds what could be expected by chance, the company's OR Group then seeks the reason for the deviation, performing as much research as is required to find it. If the cause is found to be permanent the computerized model is adjusted appropriately. The result is an adaptive man-machine system whose precision and generality is continuously increasing with use.

Finally it should be noted that in carrying out the design steps enumerated above, three groups should collaborate: information systems specialists, operations researchers, *and managers*. The participation of managers in the design of a system that is to serve them, assures their ability to evaluate its performance by comparing its output with what was predicted. Managers who are not willing to invest some of their time in this process are not likely to use a management control system well, and their system, in turn, is likely to abuse them.

Figure 2. Simplified Diagram of a Market-Area Control System

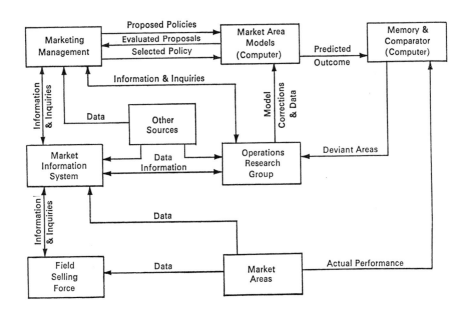

Reference

1. Sengupta, S.S., and Ackoff, R. L., "Systems Theory from an Operations Research Point of View," *IEEE Transactions on Systems Science and Cybernetics,* Vol. 1 (Nov. 1965), pp. 9-13.

12

The Chop Suey Caper

HOWARD C. GREER*

> This fable was written to demonstrate the
> elusiveness of the concept of divisional net
> profits. The article has been edited, with
> permission, to delete some references to specific
> divisional net profit measurement difficulties.
> Readers may thus concentrate on the message the
> author also conveys about the usefulness of
> cost allocation for some types of management
> decisions.

At the door to the supermarket my shopping cart collided with another. Its chauffeur proved to be Hal Hobbs, a neighbor and long-time business acquaintance. On recognizing me, he beamed.

"Aha!"he exclaimed cheerily. "Most appropriate! I need a chain-store expert, I meet one at the chain store."

"This is a gag?" I inquired, suspiciously. "I'm no expert on chain stores, or much of anything else, for that matter."

Hal looked offended. "You wrote a book," he protested.

"Forty years ago!" I reminded him. "And not a very good one."

"Yeah, but you were in the meat business for years . . . ran a big packing company, had a chain of food stores as an appendage. . . ."

"An experience I'd like to forget," I interrupted hastily. "Results of that food-chain venture hardly qualify me as an expert. . . ."

Hal was undaunted. He grinned. "Okay, so you know the wrong answers; maybe you can help me find the right ones." He gestured to a nearby bench. "Come on, sit down a minute. I need some advice."

I sighed, followed him slowly. Hal is worse than the Ancient Mariner, and I saw that I was in for it. We sat down. "What do you care about chain stores?" I demanded. "You're a banker."

"Bankers get mixed up in every kind of business," he assured me. "Right now, I've got a little chain of stores around my neck." He looked grieved.

"Lucky you!" I commiserated. "Which one?"

"Call themselves Mack's Markets. Ever hear of 'em?"

* From *The Journal of Accountancy* (April 1968) , pp. 27-34. Reprinted by permission of the author and editor. Copyright 1968 by the American Institute of Certified Public Accountants, Inc.

"They got a store in Danville?" I queried doubtfully. "Think I've seen it."

"Yup," he responded. "That one, and four others — Concord, Pittsburg, Antioch and Brentwood. Small operation; annual volume around $5 million. . . ."

"Annual profit around nothin'," I guessed shrewdly, "or you wouldn't be worried."

"Just about nothin'," he confirmed glumly. "They barely broke even last year, and it frets the stockholders."

"Of whom you're one?" I hazarded. "Or did you make 'em a loan?"

"Neither," he responded. "But almost as bad — there's some of the stock in one of our trusts, and the beneficiary is unhappy about it."

"Sell it," I advised promptly, but he shook his head, said it wasn't that easy.

I didn't ask him to explain; I knew he would, regardless.

"It's like this," he went on, pleased to have a captive audience. "Old man Mack, now dead, had this food store in Antioch, where the warehouse and office are still located. Not a bad little operation: he lived over the store, did most of the work himself, made a fair living out of it — you know how it is." I nodded understandingly.

"Getting older, he began worrying about what would happen to the business if he died. One-man show, might fold if he weren't around. Figured a little chain of stores like his would have a better chance of survival than one standing alone. Talked to couple of other store-owners similarly situated — and it wound up with their putting three units together, with Mack's as the nucleus. Later they took in a fourth — the one in Danville — eventually opened a new one — the so-called Eastside store in East Pittsburg — made it five altogether."

"Either too many or not enough," I commented sagely. He shrugged.

"Anyhow, in due course Mack died, like he thought he would. Left his stock in the enterprise in trust with our bank, benefit of his widow. Didn't leave much else, so she needs the income it should provide."

"And it doesn't provide any; she can't understand why, and you're in the grease."

He nodded gloomily. "Hell of it is," he added, "I can't understand why either."

I chuckled grimly. "This is where I came in," I told him. "Let me guess. Taken individually, each of the stores makes some money; taken collectively, they show up with no profit. That about the way it goes?"

"Right!" he confirmed, slapping my shoulder, "I knew you were the expert."

"My diagnoses are infallible," I assured him. "I don't even have to see the patient. Only thing I'm short on is effective remedies." But he ignored that latter remark.

"Look," he said, squinting thoughtfully. "Would you go over the figures with me some day when you're not too busy — wise me up a little on how to interpret them? I'm no accountant, you know —."

I'm a sucker for such appeals; told him sure, any time; wound up with a promise to join him for an afternoon session with some of the company officials, couple days later. Smart off and you get involved; it's just that easy.

Hal was back in his customary good spirits when I presented myself at his office, around noon on the appointed day. He bounced out of his chair, grabbed my arm and propelled me toward the door.

"Let's go to lunch, huh?" he boomed cheerfully. "Like Chinese food? Place nearby has the best in town. Want you to try it." I could have told him that a hamburger and milk would suit me better, but he gave me no chance to express a preference.

"Try the chop suey," he insisted, when we were seated in the restaurant, amid some pseudo-oriental decor and a pervasive odor of soy sauce. "It's real good."

I tried the chop suey. It *was* real good. I'd have preferred a hamburger.

"We'll drive out to Antioch," Hal told me blandly after lunch in his best take-charge manner. "That's their head office. Sam Stone, the general manager, is away, but Fred Fain, the treasurer, is the man I want you to meet; he puts the figures together. And he has rounded up the five store managers. Some of them are former owners of the individual stores. Each of them has his own interpretation of the results, and I want you to hear them." He chuckled maliciously. "Then you can tell me who's right, and I'll know where the trouble lies." That he expected to stump me, the expert, was all too plain.

Now, I'll tell it just like it went, altering only the names (to protect the innocent) and the figures (which have been freely rounded to simplify the presentation). You'll get the essentials of the picture just as I did, and you can expert your own way to a conclusion.

We assembled in a bare little conference room, in the combined warehouse and office over the Antioch store, where the cheerful clang of the cash registers from the floor below happily punctuated the debate. Hal introduced me to the treasurer, Fred Fain, and the five store managers, whom we can call Art Ash (Antioch), Bill Budd (Brentwood), Cap Clay (Concord), Dan Dow (Danville) and Ed Eck, (East Pittsburg). The store managers regarded me dourly; they had evidently encountered experts before.

"Okay, Fred," Hal instructed. "We want to look at those two statements you made up. First pass around copies of the company's income account for last year, the way you made it up for the directors; we'll go over that; then later you can give them the analysis you put together for me, on the basis of the store managers' interpretations."

Fain dutifully passed out copies of his statement, which (appropriately amended to emphasize the salient features) looked about as shown in Exhibit A.

Exhibit A
Mack's Markets, Inc.

Income Statement—Year 1967
(amts. in Ms—000 omitted)

Store Unit	Sales Revenue	Product Cost	Gross Margin	Store Expense	Profit Contribution
A	$1,400	$1,120	$ 280	$140	$140
B	1,200	960	240	130	110
C	1,000	800	200	120	80
D	800	640	160	110	50
E	600	480	120	100	20
All	$5,000	$4,000	$1,000	$600	$400

Overhead Expense		
Warehouse and Delivery	$250	
General Office	150	
Total		$400
Operating Result		
Gain (Loss)		—

Hobbs gave me a moment to digest the figures (the others, I judged, had seen them before).

"See, like I told you," he grumbled. "Gross, $5 million; net, zero. All the stores show a profit, taken individually; the bunch of them show no profit, taken collectively. All they earn at the local level is eaten up by the warehouse and general office expense."

"Do away with the warehouse and general office," I suggested.

"That's the way it used to be," Art Ash put in plaintively. "Old man Mack and I ran this little old store, right here in this one building, with no frills or trimmings — made a little money every year, got along okay." Ash looked aggrieved.

"Yeah, but you were the one came to see me in Brentwood," Bill Budd reminded him, "and told me some mass purchasing power would cut our merchandise costs enough to cover any general overhead a chain might run up." Budd looked aggrieved, too.

"Hold it," I interrupted, lifting an admonitory palm. "Don't take my suggestion seriously till we dig into this a little further. First, let me read off these figures, and see if we're agreed on what they indicate. Follow me through the analysis, and stop me if I get anything wrong."

They all picked up Fain's tabulation, and I continued.

"Your stores do varying amounts of business, as is to be expected, considering location, established patronage, competition and other factors. You all earn a gross margin of around 20 per cent on your sales revenue. Your store operating expenses diminish with diminished volume, but not proportionally, which is also to be expected. Your store profit thus dwindles from 10 per cent in Store A down to just over 3 per cent in Store E. . . ."

"We're just getting started," Ed Eck protested. "Give us a little time."

"I'm not criticizing," I told them. "I'm just reading the figures; the explanation can come later. Point is, the average store profit is only 8 per cent on sales, the general overhead runs 8 per cent on sales, and that leaves you collectively nowhere."

That went unchallenged. Hobbs cleared his throat.

"My idea," he put in, "was we should try to find out which units, if any, are returning less than their fair share of general overhead, so we'll know where our trouble lies."

I grinned cynically. "All you have to do then, is agree on how much overhead each store should absorb. That should be easy."

"You think so?" Hal queried morosely. "Okay, Fred, show him the figures."

The treasurer passed around another sheet, with a flock of numbers on it which looked about like those presented in Exhibit B (page 165).

"Let me explain," Fain cautioned us, "that these aren't any of them net profit figures for which I'm prepared to take any responsibility. I have simply broken down the results the way each of the store managers thought it should be done, then racked them all up on this one page so they can be easily compared." He paused. The men were all diligently studying the tabulation.

"You'll observe," Fain went on, "that the store profit figures are identical in all the cases; only the overhead distribution differs. For each manager, there is a pair of columns (four for Dow) expressing his views on a fair allocation of overhead among the stores, with the resultant net profit contribution of each, thus calculated.

"There wasn't room for 'em all in parallel across an $8\frac{1}{2}$-inch sheet, so you'll find Ash, Budd and Clay in the upper half of the page, Dow and Eck in the lower half." He turned to me, with a sardonic grin. "If I had known we were going to have an expert with us, I'd have provided space for him, too, after listening to our ideas, he could quick give us the right answer, and we'd have it on file for future reference."

"Skip me, pal." I urged him, "Let them talk, and I'll just listen."

Hobbs took command. "Okay, Art, you're first on the list; you tell us how you see it." Ash grumbled that a guy whose name began with A was always first on every list, but in this case he didn't mind.

"Very simple," he said, spreading his palms. "We got $400,000 general overhead, and five stores; that's $80,000 a piece. A store is a store is a store; we all benefit alike from being affiliated; we should each bear an equal share of our joint burden. That way," he consulted his figures, "looks like Antioch and Brentwood make some money. Concord breaks even, and the other two stores, being newer and smaller, run a loss that eats up the profits." He leaned back, complacently.

"Well, that's one man's opinion," Hobbs observed cheerfully. "Bill Budd, here, seems to have a different one."

Exhibit B
Mack's Markets, Inc.

Alternative Computations of Net Profit for Each Store Unit
(amts. in Ms—000 omitted)

Store Unit	Store Profit	Ash Version Ovhd.	Net	Budd Version Ovhd.	Net	Clay Version Ovhd.	Net
A	$140	$ 80	$60	$112	$28	$170	$ (30)
B	110	80	30	96	14	110	—
C	80	80	—	80	—	60	20
D	50	80	(30)	64	(14)	50	—
E	20	80	(60)	48	(28)	10	10
All	$400	$400	—	$400	—	$400	—

Store Unit	Store Profit	W&D	Dow Version G.O.	Comb.	Net	Eck Version Ovhd.	Net
A	$140	$ 90	$ 42	$132	$ 8	$150	$ (10)
B	110	75	36	111	(1)	110	—
C	80	50	30	80	—	80	—
D	50	15	24	39	11	50	—
E	20	20	18	38	(18)	10	10
All	$400	$250	$150	$400	—	$400	—

Overhead Allocation Bases

Ash — Uniform flat charge to each store
Budd — Charge proportionate to sales volume
Clay — Incremental cost, with rental adjustment reflected in overhead distribution
Dow — Measured service charge for warehouse and delivery; sales volume for general office
Eck — Historical expense increases for store units added

"Not too different," Budd countered, with a judicial air. "The general facilities benefit all of us — presumably — and we should all bear a liberal share of the burden. It might be more realistic, though, to recognize differences in store size in spreading the overhead cost. The larger stores do impose more burden on the central office and warehouse, perhaps somewhat in proportion to their relative volume." He glanced around, soliciting concurrence.

"In my analysis," he pointed out, "I've assigned the overhead expense on that basis, Stores A and B still show in the black, and Stores D and E in the red, but the differences are less than in Art's figures."

"Okay, Bill," Dan Dow interjected in some impatience. "You recognize the principle, but you don't apply it correctly. The individual stores should be charged with central facility expenses in proportion to their individual usage of those facilities. That may be, but isn't necessarily, in proportion to their volume."

He addressed himself to Hobbs, enlisting his support.

"Like in Danville," he went on, "we don't make too much use of the central warehouse or require many deliveries from it. We're in a different area; we can pick up a lot of our fresh produce locally, and do; we're right on the route followed by trucks from warehouses of grocery manufacturers in Hayward and San Leandro — they go right by our door and can drop off our consignments, without their going out to Antioch and back. . . ."

Ash, Budd and Fain all wanted to interrupt him, but he waved them down.

"Let me finish, will you?" he demanded. "We don't object to carrying our share of general office expense, but we see no justice in tagging us with maintenance of storage facilities we hardly use, and operation of trucks that come down to Danville only once a week. Charge us with warehouse and delivery expense in proportion to our call on those services, and you come up with figures that show our store is the most profitable one in the bunch!" He sat back grinning.

They all wanted to talk. Fain managed to get the floor.

"Look, Dan," he protested. "Maybe you do get direct delivery on a lot of your stuff, but it's the big jag of product that goes to the warehouse that secures a quantity discount on your purchases which you wouldn't otherwise get. Your expense might be less, but your margin would be less, too. . . ."

Dow grumbled something about taking his chances on that, but Budd didn't let him finish.

"Maybe you only get one delivery a week from the warehouse, but look how far it is to Danville. Take truck cost per mile, and divide it into the small tonnage you receive, and your supposed saving will vanish."

"Truck delivers Pittsburg and Concord on its way down to Danville," Dow pointed out. "The additional cost of the run to Danville is nominal. . . ."

Eck wanted to say something on that subject, but Clay cut him off.

"If you're going to figure it that way," he observed sardonically, "Antioch store shouldn't be charged any delivery expense at all. Store is right here in the warehouse; Art's stock clerk needs anything, he comes up to the second floor with a hand truck, helps himself, takes it down in the elevator. Stuff never sees a delivery truck. How come you didn't include that saving in your figure, Art?"

"I probably should have," Ash conceded. "Especially since my store expense is inflated by the cost of getting the stuff out of the warehouse. Every time my stock boy goes upstairs, he takes a half-hour off for a smoke in the washroom, and another half-hour leaning over that jill in the low-cut blouse that keeps Fred's stock records for him. . . ."

"There's another point," Fain interposed patiently. "Fact that the warehouse is close to one of the stores is a *warehouse-and-delivery* expense saving, not a *store* expense saving. If we move the warehouse somewhere else, like we've been talking about, it would change the delivery pattern. Should we then consider the savings attributable to individual store location?"

"Depends on where you put the warehouse," Dan Dow rejoined promptly. "Locate it back of my store in Danville, and we'll lick the pants off all the rest of you."

"Let me talk a minute, will you?" Ed Eck interjected plaintively. "To my mind you're going at this all wrong. My store is new and still small, and all such apportionments of overhead expense are bound to make it look bad. No chain would ever start a new store if its results were to be judged that way."

"How do you think they should be judged?" Hobbs asked him.

"By how much the added unit contributes in direct store profit, and how much *increase* there is in general expense with one more unit in the chain." When Fain growled, "Who knows?" Eck retorted firmly, "I do," and pointed to the figures under his name.

"I went back and dug up the expenses you could reasonably consider related to warehouse, delivery and general office functions, and calculated the approximate annual amounts by which they increased as each new unit was added to the chain. For Antioch alone they were $150,000; when Brentwood came in they went up $110,000; Concord added $80,000, Danville $50,000. . . ."

"And Eastside only $10,000," Ash hooted derisively. "So actually your little operation is the only one makes any profit at all!"

"Results for the whole chain were $10,000 better with my store included than they would have been without it," Eck insisted stubbornly. "When we started, you didn't add a foot of warehouse space, or an hour of delivery time (truck always took a full day for the Concord delivery, now drops off for us on the way and still gets done in a day's time). You've got maybe one more clerk in the general office, and that's the whole damn overhead related to the Eastside store."

"Where'd you get your figures?" Fain demanded suspiciously. "Not from me."

"Hell, man, they're mostly in the annual reports," Eck retorted, impatiently. Then he grinned. "Besides, I got a girl friend works in your accounting department. . . . She helped me with them a little." Fain scowled.

"Well, Ed had a point," Hobbs agreed, pacifically. "In fact, everyone seems to have a point, except Cap Clay here." He slapped the Concord manager's knee. "Cap don't say nothin', but he must know somethin'." He ran his eye over the sheet of figures once more. "Funny thing, Cap," he went on. "There's only one point on which all your colleagues are agreed — namely, no matter how you slice it, Concord comes up with no profit. You confirm that?"

Clay bestirred himself, laid aside the pipe he'd been smoking and sat forward in his chair, his expression one of tolerant amusement.

"You know what these rascals have done to me?" he inquired.

"They have stolen out of the Concord results the single most important profit-contributing element in the whole damn operation, and let the other stores get the benefit in their showing."

"How'd they do that?" Hobbs asked him.

"By adjusting the store rental charges from *actual amounts paid* to the *theoretical* rental value of the premises, as calculated by some real-estate appraisal outfit." I glanced at Fain for confirmation; he looked resentful.

"You see," Clay went on, "store chains are only ostensibly in the food business; what they're actually in is the real estate business. Their success, if any, lies chiefly in the management's astuteness in selecting up-and-coming store locations, getting into them at just the right time, at an economical rental, so they can capitalize on a surge of business when it develops."

The others were restive, but no one challenged him.

"I got started with the Concord store, on my own, years ago when Concord was just a little village. I got a long-term lease, with renewal options, at a very favorable figure, and our results naturally benefited accordingly."

"That was all reflected in the stock you got when you came into the combine," Fain reminded him.

"Sure it was," Clay agreed. "But you then threw all the properties into a realty company and let them charge each store the rent your expert figured it should pay, based on current conditions."

"Realty company merely breaks even," Fain insisted.

"Sure, but since Concord has grown a lot, my location now figures to be worth a lot more money, so you charge me more rent. In Antioch, on the other hand, where the building is old and the location deteriorating you use the gain from my — ahem — foresight — to offset the effect of old man Mack's poor judgment in taking a long-term lease on this building at a high rental." He snorted. "Actually, I'm paying about $20,000 a year of rent that ought to be charged to Art Ash, or to the warehouse. Correct for that, and apply Ed's theory on incremental expense, and you'll easily establish which store makes the most profit." Clay picked up his pipe, leaned back, and relapsed into triumphant silence.

Hobbs turned to me with an expression compounded of amusement and frustration. "See how it goes?" he inquired helplessly. "You got any ideas?"

"Come on, expert," Ash needled me. "You give us the answer, huh?"

"Well," I told him, with what I hoped was a placatory smile, "if all we're talking about is how to apportion overhead expenses, to get some measurement of each store's profit contribution, I've got a method that's just as good as any suggested so far, and probably just as defensible."

I ran my eyes over the group. "Okay, let's have it," Fain urged.

"Compute each store's percentage of total store profit, then distribute the overhead on those percentages. Like an income tax, sort of. Ability to pay. You know."

There was a moment's silence, while one or two pencils were busy.

"That way," Dow blurted finally, "no store would show a profit, or a loss."

"Right you are," I confirmed heartily. "And I'll take that for an answer as readily as any of the others."

"Hmm!" Fain volunteered, after a moment's silence. "I think you're on my side. I tell them it's pointless to make *any* distribution of the general overhead —."

"Not pointless, perhaps, but a bit dangerous. These several allocations all bring out factors of significance, but if you publish the results for individual stores, calculated on any basis, someone is bound to get a wrong impression, maybe jump to a wrong conclusion."

"My expert!" Hobbs groaned. "All he tells us is we've all got the wrong answer. . . ."

"Not the wrong answer, the wrong question," I interrupted.

"Which is?"

"How to make money in a chain of stores," I retorted promptly. "And the answer doesn't lie in juggling overhead distributions."

They all wanted to talk, but Hobbs said he'd heard enough, and anyway it was time for a drink, and he and I would stop for one on the way home. The meeting broke up. Everyone but Fain seemed glad to have me leave.

Hal, however, hadn't abandoned his argument. When we were seated a few minutes later, in a plushy cocktail lounge he had selected for us, he resumed the attack.

"Let's get back to business," he insisted briskly, when the drinks were before us. "You're an expert, and I put a simple question: in a chain of stores, how do you determine which ones are profitable and which aren't? Are you telling me there isn't any answer?"

"Not any *one* answer," I responded, "that reflects all aspects and all points of view. On a store-by-store basis each one of these units makes a profit contribution; collectively, these contributions aren't big enough to carry the general overhead. How much each store *should* contribute can be debated endlessly, but the debate isn't likely to improve your profit."

"You cost men are supposed to know how to allocate costs," he complained.

"We do," I assured him. "We know a lot of ways, and each one serves *some* purpose, but not *every* purpose. You've had a classic case presented this afternoon, with the usual contrasting alternatives — flat charge per unit vs. a sales-dollar percentage, assumed service availability vs. measured service usage, average overall cost vs. observed incremental expense, actual rentals paid vs. imputed rental value. They're all valid concepts, and each has some limited usefulness. But trying to evaluate the enterprise on a unit-by-unit basis won't lead you to a helpful conclusion. You can't judge the whole just by its parts."

"Why not?" he demanded. "That's all it is, just a bunch of parts —."

"Far from it," I countered quickly. "The fact of the *composite* is normally — and probably in this case — more important than facts about the *constituent elements*." When he still looked dissatisfied, I fished for an analogy.

"Look," I urged. "A multi-unit business — any multi-unit business — is like that chop suey we had for lunch. Its success lies in a judicious blending of diverse elements.

"When you savor chop suey, you don't try to tell yourself what share of your pleasure derives from the tidbits of pork, the bean sprouts, the water chestnuts, the soy sauce, and other items you fortunately can't even identify. You wouldn't particularly enjoy any one of those items if you were to consume it individually. It's because Lee Fong, out in the kitchen, knows how to *mix* them that you get a tasty meal."

I paused, took a pull at my drink. "Ditto the chain store business," I added, sagely, "or, for that matter, almost any other."

Hobbs was shaking his head. "You've got to have good component elements, or the mixture won't be any good."

"True enough," I agreed. "All I'm saying is you shouldn't let your evaluation of the *mixture* lead you into mis-evaluation of its *individual elements*." I emptied my glass. "Like with your food stores," I added, pressing the point home. "You may have units that are individually okay, just combined in the wrong mix."

We discussed this aspect for a while, but Hobbs couldn't get his mind off the overhead expense distribution problem.

"I shouldn't argue with an expert," he said finally, "but it still seems to me that accountants should be able to develop a scientific formula, taking into account all the factors you've mentioned. . . ."

"Oh, sure!" I agreed, as patiently as I could. "You can be scientific as hell, and some companies try to be. My point is: it just doesn't do you any good."

When he kept on looking unconvinced, I continued.

"Let me give you a prize example, taken from the railroad business, with which I have had a longtime connection." Hal interrupted me to order another round of drinks, then let me resume.

"Long years ago," I told him, "the Interstate Commerce Commission prescribed an accounting formula for determining the respective results of the carriers' freight and passenger operations. It is an excellent formula, both scientific and sensible; it would be hard to find a ground for criticizing it.

"Now this same formula has been applied by *every* passenger-carrying railroad, in *every* year, for at least a quarter century, and the results have been incorporated annually in its big ICC Form A report, with copies freely available to anyone interested. That should be authoritative enough, don't you think?" Hobbs nodded agreement.

"So what happens? In the two decades during which I have actively followed the matter, I doubt that a month has gone by without some public discussion of whether certain passenger trains lose money and, if they do, how much. Usually it's in connection with a hearing on a railroad petition to discontinue one or more trains, sometimes in a freight-rate controversy.

"Does the argument proceed on the basis of the ICC reports? Indeed not. Witnesses by the score get up and challenge the validity of the figures, and their views are sympathetically reported in the public press. Newsmen comment that the railroads "claim" they lose money on passenger service, the phrase clearly employed in disparagement of the rail spokesmen's credibility —."

"In spite of all that," Hal objected, "isn't the SEC now proposing that the results of all these new "conglomerate" corporations be reported on a divisional basis? So we can all find out which part of their business is producing how much profit, and so on?"

"Right you are," I confirmed gloomily. "It has been suggested that the Accounting Principles Board of the American Institute of CPAs (the practitioners' association) should come up with a recommendation on how such reporting should be done. I don't envy them the job!"

"Don't you believe investors should have the protection of complete information on how their funds are being administered?"

"Ah, nuts!" I exclaimed inelegantly. "Granted your premise, I'll contend that anything investors are told about divisional results in a complex enterprise is quite as likely to mislead as to educate them. Outsiders can't possibly comprehend the nuances of corporate policy, or the exigencies of managerial decisions—. Even boards of directors have trouble with questions like that —."

"Might discourage conglomerate formation," my friend murmured.

I snorted. "If it would, I could almost be for the idea, regardless of its patent philosophical defects. But look at the problem realistically. What can you do about divisional reporting for a conglomerate?" I ticked off the points on my fingers.

"One: You can prescribe a detailed and rigid formula for analyzing the results, applying it to *every* enterprise, in *every* accounting period, regardless of the nature of the business or its changing circumstances and component elements. All that will get you is a rash of criticism and a spate of controversy over the propriety of the accounting determinations and their validity in their application to the instant case. Result will be an obfuscation that the average investor will find it impossible to penetrate." I took a breath.

"Two: You can let each company establish its own pattern, altering it from year to year as management deems appropriate. Result, of course, will be complete noncomparability in reports of different companies, and from year to year in reports of the same company — and who'll be able to learn much from that?"

Hobbs was still dubious. "It's this general overhead allocation that's bugging you?" he inquired. "They could establish a basis —."

"Look," I demanded once more. "How you going to distribute a holding company president's salary over results of an insurance business, an airline, a meat packing enterprise and a machinery manufacturer? And what will you do with research and development expense when you don't know what your research will uncover, or which unit may benefit? And who should be charged how much for corporate image-adornment expense?" . . .

Hobbs, I could sense, was in somewhat the mood of the little boy who halted his father's discursive response to a casual question by saying: "Well, thanks, but I didn't really want to know that much about it." I could see him telling himself that it would be a long time before he again invited a dissertation from an accounting expert.

In any case, I hope he doesn't call on me again soon. I'm not all that fond of chop suey.

13

Matrix Theory
and Cost Allocation

THOMAS H. WILLIAMS and CHARLES H. GRIFFIN*

Much of the accounting data used in management control and administrative decision-making is a product of antecedent processes of cost allocation and expense distribution. Both of these operations assume the validity of cost divisibility and recombination. Existing practices of accountants in allocating costs and expenses to relevant production orders, products, processes and/or departments would appear to confirm the general acceptability of such an assumption. Effective cost control depends upon an identification of costs with responsibility centers, and the calculation of unit costs is especially important in measuring product or process profitability. In these and other types of analyses, the property of cost and expense analysis and synthesis is a uniquely useful accounting attribute.

In the analysis of costs, an important first problem which confronts the accountant is the measurement of benefits to be derived from the cost or expense elements which are not clearly identifiable with specific departments or cost centers. The reliability of successive allocations necessarily rests upon this first, basic determination. Once the interdepartmental relationships, or associations, are established quantitatively, there remains a second problem of arithmetically distributing costs in the previously established allocation ratios. The complexity of the latter problem increases geometrically with the increase in number of mutually related departments. In respect to reciprocally related accounting elements, matrix theory may be usefully applied both in aid of calculational simplicity and in promoting a clearer understanding of the basic structure of the interrelated elements.

Reciprocal Relationships

The problem of cost distribution is but a particular instance of the more general problem of reciprocal relationships. Consequently, by first examining the nature of the more general problem, and the several solution techniques which are available, it may be possible to establish a broader basis for the solution of a variety of similarly structured accounting problems.

* From *The Accounting Review* (July 1964), pp. 671-78. Reprinted by permission of the American Accounting Association.

The nature of reciprocal relationships may be illustrated by examining the details of calculating an employee profit-sharing bonus. Assuming that an allowable bonus is computed as a percentage of net profit after income taxes, and is also deductible in determining the tax liability, an interdependency relationship clearly exists. Determination of the income tax obligation is dependent upon the amount awarded as a bonus; concurrently the bonus is also evaluated in terms of the income tax liability. These variables may be expressed symbolically in the following equations:

$$B = \alpha(P - T)$$
$$T = \gamma(P - B)$$
$$P = \text{parameter}$$

where B=bonus, P=net profit before bonus *and* income tax, T=income tax, and α and γ are the bonus percentage and the income tax rate respectively. Although the mutual dependence of bonus and tax variables may be expressed in numerous ways, and algebraic formulation as given above is perhaps the most precise expression of such a reciprocal association.

A similar dependency structure is evident in many other accounting problems. For example, in the preparation of consolidated financial statements involving bilateral stockholdings, the investment elimination requires an analysis similar to that indicated above. Reciprocal distributions are also required where there are several mutually related service departments. In such mutual dependencies, there exists the same type of algebraic structure as illustrated previously. While accountants have traditionally dealt with such problems on an isolated individual basis — and with the use of familiar mathematical techniques — significantly they have often failed to recognize that each is essentially a specific instance of a more *general* problem to which a *general* mathematical system may often apply. The previous tax-bonus formulation is used again following to illustrate a general mathematical theory appropriately descriptive of reciprocal relationships. Thereafter, this theory will be applied to a more complex, yet frequently recurring, practical problem of cost allocation.

Solution Techniques

Two basic mathematical methods are frequently employed to solve problems involving interdependency elements. One is a variate on a trial and error procedure, viz., the successive iteration method; the other is the traditional solution form for systems of simultaneous linear equations.

In applying the successive iteration method, a correct problem solution proceeds from a progression of successive estimates. Each value estimate makes use of a previous estimate until solution values stabilize. For example, assuming that α (the bonus percentage) $= 10\%$, γ (the tax rate) $= 50\%$ and P (the profit before bonus and tax) $=\$100,000$, the order of solution is given following:

STEP	BONUS	TAX
1	$10,000	$45,000
2	5,500	47,250
3	5,275	47,362.50
4	5,263.75	47,368.13
5	5,263.19	47,368.41
6	5,263.16	47,368.42
7	5,263.16	47,368.42

The first approximation of bonus is based upon a zero tax amount; thereafter tax and bonus values are calculated sequentially, appropriate recognition being given to the previous calculation. Reference to the previous schedule discloses that the values stabilize with a bonus of $5,263.16 and a tax obligation of $47,368.42.

Using the same data, the problem may be more formally expressed as a system of algebraic equations, simplified as follows:

$$B = .10(P - T)$$
$$T = .50(P - B)$$
$$P = \$100,000$$
$$(1)\quad B = .10[100,000 - (50,000 - .50B)]$$
$$= \$5,263.16$$
$$T = .50(100,000 - 5,263.16)$$
$$= \$47,368.42$$

Significantly these values confirm the amounts previously established by the successive iteration method. Where an equation system is relatively simple, i.e., the system consists of a small number of variables and equations, the algebraic solution is perhaps the most efficient solution form. However, where there exist many variables, the successive iteration method is usually a more convenient algorithm. Most accountants are familiar with both of these solution techniques.

There exists, however, a more fundamental mathematical schema— matrix algebra — which will accommodate larger and more complex systems of equations involving many variables. In point of fact, the solution of simultaneous equations is based upon principles implicit in the theory of matrices.

The Matrix Structure

A matrix is a rectangular array of elements — numbers, functions, etc. — which can be used to examine problems involving *relations* between these elements. Although operations such as addition and multiplication can be performed on matrices, the matrix is not evaluated quantitatively. A matrix A may be represented

$$(2)\qquad A = \begin{bmatrix} a_{11} & a_{12} & \cdots & a_{1n} \\ a_{21} & a_{22} & \cdots & a_{2n} \\ \cdot & \cdot & \cdots & \cdot \\ a_{m1} & a_{m2} & \cdots & a_{mn} \end{bmatrix}$$

In the above expression, the first subscript for a given element indicates the *row* in which it appears and the second subscript denotes the *column*. Such a matrix with m rows and n columns is normally referred to as an $m \times n$ *matrix*, or a matrix of *order* (m, n).

One of the most important applications of matrix algebra relates to the study of systems of simultaneous linear equations. Consider the system of three linear equations in P, T and B given earlier, viz.,

$$\begin{aligned} B \;-\; .10P \;+\; .10T &= 0 \\ (3)\quad .50B \;-\; .50P \;+\quad T &= 0 \\ P \qquad\qquad &= 100{,}000 \end{aligned}$$

The 3×3 *matrix of coefficients* assumes the form

$$(4)\qquad \begin{bmatrix} 1 & -.10 & .10 \\ .50 & -.50 & 1 \\ 0 & 1 & 0 \end{bmatrix}$$

An ordering of coefficients of the equation system is a first condition to an application of the general solution technique for linear equations.

Once the elements are ordered, it is then appropriate to refer to *operations* on the matrix. For example, a matrix *sum* may be formed by adding corresponding elements of matrices of the same order; also it is appropriate to multiply a given matrix by a scalar or by another matrix. In scalar multiplication, each element of the matrix is multiplied by a real number. Where one matrix is to be multiplied by a second matrix, however, multiplication is possible only where the matrices are conformable for multiplication, i.e., where the number of columns in the first matrix is equal to the number of rows in the second. Given a 2×3 matrix A and the 3×2 matrix B, the matrix product AB, a 2×2 matrix, is given following:[1]

$$(5)\quad AB = \begin{bmatrix} a_{11} & a_{12} & a_{13} \\ a_{21} & a_{22} & a_{23} \end{bmatrix} \begin{bmatrix} b_{11} & b_{12} \\ b_{21} & b_{22} \\ b_{31} & b_{32} \end{bmatrix}$$

$$= \begin{bmatrix} a_{11}\,b_{11} + a_{12}\,b_{21} + a_{13}\,b_{31} & a_{11}\,b_{12} + a_{12}\,b_{22} + a_{13}\,b_{32} \\ a_{21}\,b_{11} + a_{22}\,b_{21} + a_{23}\,b_{31} & a_{21}\,b_{12} + a_{22}\,b_{22} + a_{23}\,b_{32} \end{bmatrix}$$

A facile use of this multiplicative process is especially important in the solution of systems of linear equations.

A knowledge of other matrix operations is also important in order to describe more completely the general technique for the solution of a system of linear equations; however, these few elementary matrix operations enable one to preview the ultimate objective, viz., to develop an economical and efficient method of handling cost allocation problems.

---

[1] Substituting integers for the symbols for each element of the two matrices, a matrix product is given below.

$$AB = \begin{bmatrix} 0 & 2 & 3 \\ 1 & -2 & 0 \end{bmatrix} \begin{bmatrix} -1 & 0 \\ 4 & -3 \\ 1 & 2 \end{bmatrix} = \begin{bmatrix} 11 & 0 \\ -9 & 6 \end{bmatrix}$$

Consider the following general system of linear equations:

$$
(6) \quad
\begin{cases}
a_{11}x_1 + \ldots + a_{1n}x_n = b_1 \\
\phantom{a_{11}x_1} \cdots \cdots \cdots \\
a_{m1}x_1 + \ldots + a_{mn}x_n = b_m,
\end{cases}
$$

where m may not be equal to n, i.e., the number of equations are unequal to the number of unknowns. Using matrix notation, such a system may be written:

$$
(7) \quad
\begin{bmatrix}
a_{11} & \cdots & a_{1n} \\
\vdots & & \vdots \\
a_{m1} & \cdots & a_{mn}
\end{bmatrix}
\begin{bmatrix}
x_1 \\
\vdots \\
x_n
\end{bmatrix}
=
\begin{bmatrix}
b_1 \\
\vdots \\
b_m
\end{bmatrix}
$$

This formulation parallels the system presented in (6), and may be verified by performing the indicated multiplication. If the coefficient matrix is denoted A, the vector of unknowns X, and the vector of constants B, the equation may be further abbreviated

$$(8) \qquad AX = B.$$

If values are determined for $x_1, x_2, \ldots, x_n$ which satisfy (7), these values also satisfy the linear equations in (6), and conversely. A determination of these values thus is equivalent to a solution of the set of equations.

Determination of an Inverse—The Essence of the Problem

The solution of equation (8) may be compared to the solution of an equation with one unknown variable. The solution of

$$(9) \qquad ax = b,$$

can be expressed as

$$(10) \qquad x = b/a.$$

Equation (9) was solved by multiplying both sides of the equation by $1/a$, frequently written a^{-1}. Using the matrix inverse notation, equation (8) may be rewritten

$$(11) \qquad X = A^{-1}B.$$

In the event that the coefficient matrix remains constant, the solutions for $x_1, \ldots, x_n$ can be easily evaluated merely by a simple matrix multiplication operation, once the initial calculation of A^{-1} has been made.[2] It is this property of the matrix solution technique that makes it especially useful to accountants in simplifying problems involving reciprocal relations.

The matrix notation easily accommodates both simple and complex systems of equations. For the relatively simple tax-bonus illustration

2 Various procedures exist for the systematic calculation of the inverse, depending upon the complexity of the problem. For problems involving relatively few variables, several manual computation techniques can be found in Franz E. Hohn, *Elementary Matrix Algebra*, The Macmillan Co., New York, 1950; for more complex problems, standard computer programs for the determination of a matrix inverse are available.

used earlier, the equation system (3) may be easily cast in the following matrix form:

$$(12) \quad \begin{bmatrix} 1 & -.10 & .10 \\ .50 & -.50 & 1 \\ 0 & 1 & 0 \end{bmatrix} \begin{bmatrix} B \\ P \\ T \end{bmatrix} = \begin{bmatrix} 0 \\ 0 \\ 100,000 \end{bmatrix}$$

The equivalence of this formulation and that given by equation system (3) can be verified by performing the indicated matrix multiplication.

Equation (12) may be expressed in matrix inverse form as follows:

$$(13) \quad \begin{bmatrix} B \\ P \\ T \end{bmatrix} = \begin{bmatrix} 1 & -.10 & .10 \\ .50 & -.50 & 1 \\ 0 & 1 & 0 \end{bmatrix}^{-1} \begin{bmatrix} 0 \\ 0 \\ 100,000 \end{bmatrix}$$

Determination of values for B, P, and T reduces to a problem of computing the inverse of the coefficient matrix and subsequently performing a simple matrix multiplication. In this instance, the following solution is derived.[3]

$$(14) \quad \begin{bmatrix} B \\ P \\ T \end{bmatrix} = \begin{bmatrix} 1.052631578 & -.105263157 & .052631579 \\ 0 & 0 & 1 \\ -.52631578 & 1.05263157 & .47368421 \end{bmatrix} \begin{bmatrix} 0 \\ 0 \\ 100,000 \end{bmatrix}$$

$$= \begin{bmatrix} 5,263.16 \\ 100,000.00 \\ 47,368.42 \end{bmatrix}$$

The Cost Allocation Model

The previous example illustrates, for a simple equation system, the use of the matrix notation in solving an elementary problem involving reciprocal relationships. The application to more complex systems is identical, although the arithmetic involvements are necessarily somewhat more tedious. The following problem in cost allocation for a manufacturer with five service departments and three producing departments is a case in point.

Assume that, after primary distributions have been made — and before reciprocal distributions are begun — the following account balances obtain:

Manufacturing Department A	$120,000
Manufacturing Department B	200,000
Manufacturing Department C	80,000
Service Department X_1	8,000
Service Department X_2	12,000
Service Department X_3	6,000
Service Department X_4	11,000
Service Department X_5	13,000

[3] The technique of synthetic elimination was used to calculate the inverse. See Franz E. Hohn, *op. cit.,* pp. 73-74.

The measure of interdependency of the various departments in respect to distributing service department expenses is given following:

Service Department X_1:

To Manufacturing Department *A*	25%
To Manufacturing Department *B*	25%
To Manufacturing Department *C*	25%
To Service Department X_3	10%
To Service Department X_4	5%
To Service Department X_5	10%

Service Department X_2:

To Manufacturing Department *A*	80%
To Service Department X_3	10%
To Service Department X_5	10%

Service Department X_3:

To Manufacturing Department *A*	20%
To Manufacturing Department *B*	30%
To Manufacturing Department *C*	20%
To Service Department X_1	5%
To Service Department X_2	10%
To Service Department X_4	10%
To Service Department X_5	5%

Service Department X_4:

To Manufacturing Department *B*	40%
To Manufacturing Department *C*	40%
To Service Department X_1	10%
To Service Department X_2	5%
To Service Department X_3	5%

Service Department X_5:

To Manufacturing Department *A*	10%
To Manufacturing Department *B*	5%
To Manufacturing Department *C*	5%
To Service Department X_1	20%
To Service Department X_2	20%
To Service Department X_3	20%
To Service Department X_4	20%

Accountants have traditionally solved this type of problem by the *successive iteration* method. Once the service department expenses have been successively distributed, the balance increments added by the reciprocal relationships are then distributed. The process is repeated until account balances stabilize. However, as noted earlier, these relationships can be expressed more precisely as a system of simultaneous equations and solved by methods of matrix algebra. If the *total* service department costs *after* reciprocal distribution are denoted $X_1, \ldots, X_5$, the relationship between service departments can be represented

$$
\begin{aligned}
X_1 &= 8{,}000 + .05X_3 + .10X_4 + .20X_5 \\
X_2 &= 12{,}000 + .10X_3 + .05X_4 + .20X_5 \\
(15)\quad X_3 &= 6{,}000 + .10X_1 + .10X_2 + .05X_4 + .20X_5 \\
X_4 &= 11{,}000 + .05X_1 + .10X_3 + .20X_5 \\
X_5 &= 13{,}000 + .10X_1 + .10X_2 + .05X_3
\end{aligned}
$$

Rearranging the equations to preserve vertical symmetry among the variables, the equation system is

$$
\begin{aligned}
X_1 \quad\quad\quad - .05X_3 - .10X_4 - .20X_5 &= 8{,}000 \\
X_2 - .10X_3 - .05X_4 - .20X_5 &= 12{,}000 \\
(16)\quad -.10X_1 - .10X_2 + X_3 - .05X_4 - .20X_5 &= 6{,}000 \\
-.05X_1 \quad\quad - .10X_3 + X_4 - .20X_5 &= 11{,}000 \\
-.10X_1 - .10X_2 - .05X_3 \quad\quad + X_5 &= 13{,}000
\end{aligned}
$$

From the above, the matrix of coefficients is easily determined to be:

$$
(17)\quad
\begin{bmatrix}
1. & 0 & -.05 & -.10 & -.20 \\
0 & 1. & -.10 & -.05 & -.20 \\
-.10 & -.10 & 1. & -.05 & -.20 \\
-.05 & 0 & -.10 & 1. & -.20 \\
-.10 & -.10 & -.05 & 0 & 1.
\end{bmatrix}
\begin{bmatrix}
X_1 \\ X_2 \\ X_3 \\ X_5 \\ X_4
\end{bmatrix}
=
\begin{bmatrix}
8{,}000 \\ 12{,}000 \\ 6{,}000 \\ 11{,}000 \\ 13{,}000
\end{bmatrix}
$$

The desired objective is, as before, a determination of appropriate values for $x_1, \ldots, x_5$, and it is now clear that the problem reduces to a calculation of the inverse of the coefficient matrix, i.e., if the coefficient matrix is denoted A, the vector of unknowns X, and the vector of constants B, the solution is of the form

$$(18)\qquad X = A^{-1}B.$$

The inverse of A is determined to be:[4]

$$
(19)\quad V^{-1} =
\begin{bmatrix}
1.0385469 & .0330747 & .0787780 & .1094473 & .2519694 \\
.0408924 & 1.0377815 & .1247000 & .0622133 & .2531175 \\
.1353058 & .1316976 & 1.0409525 & .0721631 & .2760238 \\
.0883998 & .0375576 & .1225132 & 1.0168434 & .2530628 \\
.1147092 & .1136705 & .0723954 & .0207742 & 1.0643098
\end{bmatrix}
$$

Once the inverse is determined, the problem is essentially an exercise in matrix multiplication.

A summary of the allocated costs is shown in Table I. Since X_1, $\ldots, X_5$ are defined as total costs *after* distributions, the upper half of the table can be prepared merely by multiplying the values of these variables

---

4 The technique of synthetic elimination can again be used to determine the inverse.

$$(20) \quad \begin{bmatrix} X_1 \\ X_2 \\ X_3 \\ X_4 \\ X_5 \end{bmatrix} = \begin{bmatrix} 1.0385469 & .0330747 & .0787780 & .1094473 & .2519694 \\ .0408924 & 1.0377815 & .1247000 & .0622133 & .2531175 \\ .1353058 & .1316976 & 1.0409525 & .0721631 & .2760238 \\ .0883998 & .0375576 & .1225132 & 1.0168434 & .2530628 \\ .1147092 & .1136705 & .0723954 & .0207742 & 1.0643098 \end{bmatrix}$$

$$\begin{bmatrix} 8,000 \\ 12,000 \\ 6,000 \\ 11,000 \\ 13,000 \end{bmatrix} = \begin{bmatrix} 13,657.46 \\ 17,503.59 \\ 13,290.64 \\ 16,368.06 \\ 16,780.64 \end{bmatrix}$$

by the predetermined distribution percentages. Values for the lower half of the table (cost transfers out) can be easily derived from the accumulations in the upper half. The completed summary of cost allocations indicates the flow of costs both in and out of relevant departments. The accounting function is especially sensitive to these data both in respect to traditional record-keeping and in appraising the effectiveness of cost management.

The "permanency" of the inverse is a particularly useful property. Once it is determined, the cost allocation problem remains essentially one of matrix multiplication so long as the distribution percentages remain invariate. Often these ratios continue unchanged for relatively long periods of time, and in consequence the method assures important accounting simplification. Although the previous illustration was limited to multivariate cost distribution, parallel accounting treatment would be accorded the traditional preparation of consolidated financial statements where intercorporate reciprocal stockholdings exist. In the latter case present solution methods are unusually cumbersome where the number of mutually related companies is large or the involvement of stockholdings complex.

COMPUTER APPLICATIONS

The previous illustrations have emphasized the non-mechanical solution of complex problems involving reciprocal relationships by the use of matrix algebra. As the number of departments, or variables, increases, this method of manual calculation becomes increasingly difficult. In such instances resort may be had to electronic computers in calculating the matrix inverse. For most computer installations, standard library routines (programs) are available for calculating the inverse and/or solving simultaneously systems of linear equations. In problems of cost allocation involving large numbers of departments, only one computer-based determination of the matrix inverse is required so long as the distribution ratios remain invariate. In each allocation the solution derives from a multiplication (vector) of initial cost values. The IBM 1620 — using a standard library program — determines the inverse of a given 5×5 matrix in approximately one minute (including input-output time). Where the

Table I
Summary of Cost Allocations

	Dept A	Dept B	Dept C	Dept X_1	Dept X_2	Dept X_3	Dept X_4	Dept X_5	Total
Total Cost Before Distribution	$120,000	$200,000	$80,000	$8,000	$12,000	$6,000	$11,000	$13,000	$450,000
Cost Transfers from:									
Dept X_1	3,415	3,414	3,414			1,366	683	1,366	13,658
Dept X_2	14,003					1,750		1,750	17,503
Dept X_3	2,658	3,986	2,658	665	1,329		1,329	665	13,290
Dept X_4		6,548	6,547	1,637	818	818			16,368
Dept X_5	1,679	839	839	3,356	3,356	3,356	3,356		16,781
	141,755	214,787	93,458	13,658	17,503	13,290	16,368	16,781	527,600
Cost Transfers to:									
Dept A				3,415	14,003	2,658		1,679	21,755
Dept B				3,414		3,986	6,548	839	14,787
Dept C				3,414		2,658	6,547	839	13,458
Dept X_1						665	1,637	3,356	5,658
Dept X_2						1,329	818	3,356	5,503
Dept X_3				1,366	1,750		818	3,356	7,290
Dept X_4				683		1,329		3,356	5,368
Dept X_5				1,366	1,750	665			3,781
				13,658	17,503	13,290	16,368	16,781	77,600
Total Cost After Distribution	$141,755	$214,787	$93,458	-0-	-0-	-0-	-0-	-0-	$450,000

matrix to be inverted is 30×30 calculation time approximates five minutes.[5] Accountants have been especially sensitive to the advantages of this compression in calculation time.

The National City Bank of New York announced recently that it had developed, in conjunction with the International Business

---

[5] As is evident in the previous illustration, the size of the matrix to be inverted is unaffected by departments (generally manufacturing) which have no reciprocal distributions. These departments are incorporated into the final solution when the summary of cost allocations is prepared.

Machines Corporation, an approach to [the distribution of over-head costs] which reduced actual computation time from 1000 man-hours to $9\frac{1}{2}$ minutes.

In one steel company, . . . 51 overhead departments, or cost centers, make about 600 interdepartmental charges, and the monthly distribution [of these charges] required formerly about 300 man-hours. This was reduced to 35 minutes on an electronic calculator — in this case a smaller machine than the one on which the [above] bank problem was calculated.[6]

Other impressive evidences of economies in accounting calculation time might be cited; these are but a small sample of the time consequence of computerized accounting. The cost allocation problem is but a single illustration of a catalog of similar problems to which the accountant may usefully apply matrix notation.

New Applications

Apart from its value in simplifying the difficulty and shortening the time span of many accounting operations, the matrix concept has also been appropriately applied in developing a number of *theoretical* formulations. The Leontief input-output model used in economic theory relies upon the matrix formulation to explain the interrelationships between relevant variables. This model has also been used in accounting analysis and was recently appraised in the following terms:

The input-output system provides a method whereby management can predict changes in the level of the balance sheet accounts which arise from some level of operations, analyze the impact on the accounting system and level of accounts brought about by changes in operating levels and conditions. The framework, common to all firms, also provides a uniform procedure for aggre-gating firm data and thus is a method of consistently establishing an inter-firm analysis for an industry or an inter-industry analysis for the economy.[7]

Professor Richard Mattessich also foresees special usefulness of the matrix notation in the creation of an abstract generalization model for accounting theory.

There are strong indications that the matrix formulation of accountancy facilitates not only the classifying analysis of flows, but also the explanation *why* such flows occur. The combination of accounting equations with production functions by means of matrix concepts has been successfully initiated in input-output accounting and might find further application and extension (to

[6] Grandjean G. Jewett, "The Distribution of Overhead with Electronic Computers," *The Journal of Accountancy*, June, 1954, p. 698.
[7] Allen B. Richards, "Input-Output Accounting for Business," *The Accounting Review*, July 1960, p. 436.

liquidity preference and investment functions, and so on) in other kinds of accounting systems.[8]

To the extent that matrix formulations of accounting analysis contribute to more rigorous and logical models of accounting theory, additional support is adduced for such methods. Surely this use provides an appropriate complement to the more practical benefits immediately available to the accounting practitioner.

[8] Richard Mattessich, "Towards A General and Axiomatic Foundation of Accountancy," *Accounting Research,* October, 1957, p. 348.

14

The Fable of the Accountant and the President*

ACT I:

Once upon a time a company was operating at a loss. Although its plant had a normal capacity of 30,000 widgets, it was selling only 10,000 a year, and its operating figures looked like this:

Price per unit	$ 1.00
Total fixed cost	$ 6,000.
Fixed manufacturing cost per unit	$ .60
Variable cost per unit	$ .65
Total unit cost	$ 1.25
Total manufacturing cost	$12,500.
Cost of closing inventory	$ 0.
Cost of goods sold	$12,500.
Sales revenue	$10,000.
Operating loss	$ 2,500.

ACT II:

Then one day a bearded stranger came to the board of directors and said "Make me president, pay me half of any operating income I produce, and I'll make you all millionaires."

"Done," they said.

So the bearded stranger set the factory running at full capacity making 30,000 widgets a year. His figures looked like this:

"Pay me," said the bearded stranger. "But we're going broke," said the directors.

"Oh!" said the stranger. "You can read the income figures, can't you? You have never been more profitable!"

Total fixed cost	$ 6,000.
Fixed manufacturing cost per unit	$ .20
Variable unit cost	$ .65
Total unit cost	$ .85
Total manufacturing cost	$25,500.
Cost of closing inventory	$17,000.
Cost of goods sold	$ 8,500.
Sales revenue	$10,000.
Operating income	$ 1,500.

* Source unknown.

Be careful of compensation plans + manipulation of figures

185

ACT III:

But just as everything seemed lost, an accountant in gleaming eye shade charged into the room. "Hold," he cried. "I have just changed to the system called VARIABLE COSTING. We charge only variable manufacturing costs to inventory. So now the figures look like this:

Variable cost per unit	$ .65
Cost of manufacturing 30,000 units	$19,500.
Cost of closing inventory	$13,000.
Variable cost of goods sold	$ 6,500.
Sales revenue	$10,000.
Contribution margin (here's where the trick comes in; we'll explain later)	$ 3,500.
Total fixed costs	$ 6,000.
Operating loss	$ 2,500.

So the bearded stranger was foiled and the directors are back looking for a way to earn income — and to sell off the inventory the stranger left them with.

15

Cost Concepts for Control

ROBERT N. ANTHONY*

The framework your Cost Concepts Committee used to state concepts relating to control is somewhat unconventional, and some background about our deliberations may help to explain why we finally decided on this framework. Initially, we attacked the problem by examining various types of cost constructions that are used for control purposes, in an attempt to find criteria for determining which of these was, in some sense, the "best." We had lots of possibilities: actual costs, basis standard costs, normal capacity costs, current budgeted costs, ideal standard costs, short-run standard costs, direct costs, attainable costs, systems that prorated all overhead, systems that prorated no overhead, and many more. In the course of our long discussions, one committee member would explain and uphold a technique that he had seen used effectively in some company, and another member would counter with a description of a completely different system that he had observed being used with apparently equal effectiveness in another situation. Although we tried very hard to do so, however, we could find no objective way of generalizing on which type of cost system was "best" for control purposes.

We eventually concluded that an attempt to find objective means of differentiating among the various control systems in current use was not feasible and that our failure to find such criteria indicated that we probably were not approaching the problem properly. The plain fact is that competent managements use a variety of cost constructions for control purposes, and each may find merit in its own system. It is also true that a system that works well in one company may not work at all in another company; even though the two companies have substantially similar control environments. It therefore became apparent that any attempt to define concepts in terms that implied that one of these systems was inherently good and all others inherently poor, or less good, was bound to be fruitless.

This conclusion led us to attack the problem in quite a different manner. We asked ourselves: "What does the control process actually

* From *The Accounting Review* (April 1957), pp. 229-34. Reprinted by permission of the Editor.

  This paper was one of three presented by members of the Committee on Cost Concepts and Standards at the annual meeting of the American Accounting Association, Seattle, August 31, 1956. It relates to the "Tentative Statement of Cost Concepts Underlying Reports for Management Purposes" published in the April 1956 issue of *The Accounting Review*.

consist of?" Most authorities agree that control, in the sense in which it is used in business management, has to do with the attempts of one person to direct or influence the actions of other persons. This personal, human element in the process came to be the focus of our thinking.

Although the management control process is often compared with mechanical or electrical control devices, such as the thermostat, such an analogy is apt to be quite misleading. A thermostat reacts to stimuli in a definite, predictable fashion. When the temperature goes down to a certain point, the furnace is turned on; when the temperature rises to a certain point, the furnace is shut off. Human beings, on the other hand, do not behave so predictably; human reactions to a stimulus are much more complicated, and human control systems cannot be so easily or so precisely designed as mechanical or electrical ones. If, for example, my wife tells me the room is too warm, my reaction may be (and after years of training, usually is) to open a window or to take some other steps to cool it; but, occasionally, I may procrastinate and do nothing, or I may even argue that the room is not too warm anyway.

Thermostats do not argue, they do not procrastinate, they do not resent being told what to do, they do not do what they think is best. In short, they are not human.

A management control system, which does involve human beings — indeed, whose only purpose is to influence the action of human beings — is therefore fundamentally different from mechanical or electrical controls. It follows that our attempt to examine a system in terms of its mechanics — the methods of setting standards, of prorating overhead, and so on — was bound to fail because it missed the main point entirely. And as soon as we considered the management control process as something that basically involved people and the reactions of people, it became evident that there were some useful things that could be said about the role of cost information in this process.

We ended up by grouping the control concepts under three headings, closely related to human reactions and stated in terms of the purposes for which cost information is used in the control process. These are: (1) to communicate information about approved plans, (2) to motivate people, and (3) to report performance.

COMMUNICATION

With respect to the communication of plans, we had in mind primarily the approved budget, which is the end result of the planning process discussed in another section of the Tentative Statement of Cost Concepts. The approved budget is a communication device in that it tells each unit of the organization something about what management expects it to do during the budget period and also shows the unit how its work fits in with the overall activity of the organization. In addition to the budget, plans and objectives are also communicated by cost standards.

Any means of human communication inevitably raises the problem of semantics. We are all increasingly aware of the fact that the recipient of a communication rarely, if ever, understands precisely what the author intended to say. This is as true with cost information as it is with any other language, and we therefore call attention in our report to the necessity of obtaining common agreement and understanding throughout the organization as to the precise meaning of the budget figures and cost standards used in that company.

MOTIVATION

Our second heading, costs as a motivating device, relates to what is, perhaps, the most important purpose of all; but it is also the most difficult one to state in writing. Let me try an example in an attempt to show how cost constructions can motivate people, that is, how they can influence the actions that people take. I choose, because it concerns all of us who are teachers, the prosaic matter of controlling the costs of mimeographing or other duplicating work. Visualize a school in which the administration recognizes the necessity for having its faculty generate a certain amount of mimeographing work but which recognizes also that funds available for this and other purposes are not limitless. How can control be exercised over the amount of funds spent for mimeographing and the manner in which the work is done? Of the many ways of solving this problem, I shall mention only enough to indicate how the cost system can help, in various ways, to motivate the people involved.

One possibility is to have no formal control at all. This is a common practice. When a school chooses to follow it, it presumably relies on custom, informal conversations, or perhaps even warnings of one kind or another, to keep the cost of duplicating work from becoming exorbitantly high. The fact that schools that follow this practice do not use costs as a control device in this area illustrates the point that cost control is by no means the only possible type of control.

Another possibility is to set up a budget for each department or other organizational unit in the school. Perhaps there will be an item in this budget for duplicating work, or alternatively the budget may specify an overall amount for the total needs of the department, of which duplicating work is but one element. These two types of budgets can motivate the department head quite differently. The first tells him that he is permitted to incur a certain amount of cost for duplicating work, considered by itself; the second tells him that he has certain funds with which to run his department, and it is up to him to decide whether his needs for duplicating work are more important than other possible ways of spending his departmental funds.

Now let us go a step further. How shall we define the "cost" of duplicating work? Shall we charge the department head with the labor cost of the girl in his own department (or a girl in some other department whose services he may borrow) who cuts the stencils? If we do, we remove any incentive for him to use his own or borrowed help, and we shall therefore expect that he will normally send the work to the central duplicating staff, rather than ask his own people to do it. Shall we charge him for the cost of this central staff? If we do not, there is no reason why he should not use it, whether his need is justified or not, and we therefore encourage thoughtless use of its facilities. If we do charge him, we may encourage him to go outside the school for his duplicating work if he can find an outside party who will do it at a lower cost. Perhaps this is what we want him to do. On the other hand, we may prefer that he have the work done inside. If so, maybe we should charge him only for the direct cost of the central staff, which will set up a differential against outside work.

I could introduce many other ramifications, but I hope I have said enough to demonstrate that to the extent that cost constructions are involved in this problem, the decision as to what type of cost should be used is arrived at, not by trying to find the true, objective cost of duplicating — if there is such a thing — but rather by using cost constructions that are calculated to motivate the department head to act as the administration wishes him to act.

The foregoing situation may be somewhat trivial. To show that similar considerations are involved in a factory problem, let us look briefly at the problem of the control of maintenance and repair costs. The maintenance function is that of keeping the buildings and equipment in good operating condition. This is partly the responsibility of the maintenance department, which incurs costs when it makes repairs or does other maintenance work, and it is partly the responsibility of the operating department foremen, who can influence the amount of required maintenance work by the care they give to their equipment.

There are at least a dozen ways in which the costs of the maintenance department can be charged to the several operating departments, and each gives a different "message" to the foremen as to how they should view their responsibility for maintenance. Here are a few of the possibilities and the implications that are likely to be conveyed by each.

Method No. 1: Do not charge any maintenance costs to the operating departments

Message: The operating foreman has no responsibility for maintenance costs. He requests the maintenance department to do the work that he thinks should be done, and the maintenance department has the responsibility for doing it. The maintenance department is implicitly responsible for the condition of the equipment.

Method No. 2: Prorate total maintenance costs to the operating departments on the basis of the number of direct labor hours incurred in each department

Message: Maintenance costs in total are expected to vary proportionately with plant activity. However, the foreman of each department has no direct responsibility for maintenance work, and the maintenance department, as in the first method, has full responsibility. The operating foreman is told his "fair share" of total maintenance costs incurred.

Method No. 3: Charge departments for each job they have done at a prescribed amount for each type of job

Message: The foreman is responsible for situations that create the need for maintenance work, such as machine breakdowns. The maintenance department is responsible for the cost of doing a given maintenance job. The foreman therefore need not be concerned with the efficiency with which the maintenance men work since he will be charged a prescribed amount for each job no matter how much is actually spent in doing the job.

Method No. 4: Charge each department for maintenance work at a prescribed hourly rate for each hour that a maintenance man works in the department

Message: The foreman is responsible both for situations that create the need for maintenance work and for the time taken by the maintenance people to do the work. Presumably, he has some control over the work of the maintenance men. He may, in some situations, even be authorized to hire outside maintenance people if he believes that they will do the work less expensively than the rates charged by the maintenance department.

None of the above methods is necessarily better than the others. Depending on what management wishes to accomplish, any one of these methods, or other methods not listed, or some combination of them, may be best for a given company. The problem is to decide what direction the motivation should take and then to select a method that influences the foremen to act in this manner.

In essence, the Committee concluded that the method of constructing costs for control purposes is governed by management policy, that the costs system should be designed to help carry out that policy, and that rigid mechanical rules are therefore not applicable.

So far, I have discussed only the basic idea of motivation. Our statement of cost concepts ideally should go considerably beyond this basic idea and list specific points that can be used as guides in constructing costs used for control purposes.

Frankly, we have made only a small beginning in this direction. We do emphasize the necessity for relating costs to personal responsibility, which is the "responsibility center" or "activity center" concept that has been written about extensively in recent years. We attempt to be fairly specific about what, as a practical matter, is meant by personal responsibility since there are few, if any, cost elements that are completely and solely the responsibility of a single person. But we do not feel sure enough of our ground to make very many generalizations in this area. The topic is one which is of great concern to people in practice, but it is also one on which, for some reason, not much has yet been written. We therefore simply cannot find many points that are sufficiently well substantiated to warrant including them in the Tentative Statement. This is one of the areas in which our statement is indeed extremely tentative, and with the passage of time, I think many specific and useful points can be added to this section of the statement.

Before leaving this subject, I want to mention briefly two other points that trouble some with whom we have discussed this section of the Tentative Statement.

One is the fact that, people being the way they are, not everyone is motivated identically by the same stimulus. That this is so is undeniable. Nevertheless, there must be some common patterns of human behavior that apply to large numbers of people. To go back to the example of the faculty members and the duplicating work, there undoubtedly are some faculty members who will not order too much duplicating work no matter how much leeway they are given, and there probably are some who will, in one way or another, obtain too much no matter how tight the control system is. But these groups must constitute only a minority, for if most people were in the first group, controls would be unnecessary; and if most were in the second group, controls would be impossible.

The second point is that to some people the very attempt to describe costs in terms of human relations smacks of trickery, of attempting to fool people. I think this feeling arises from the implicit assumption that there must be some objective way of defining cost, and as we emphasize in the introductory section of the Tentative Statement, this simply is not so. Perhaps it is sufficient to say here that any attempt to use costs to trick or mislead the organization is likely to be self-defeating, in that it will motivate people in quite a different direction from what is intended.

REPORTING

We come now to the third area, costs as a basis for reporting and appraising performance. In this area, we first must face a familiar paradox, which can be stated as follows: Cost reports describe what has already happened; therefore they cannot be used to control events, since no one can alter or undo what has already been done; therefore, a control report cannot really control anything.

One explanation of this apparent paradox is obvious, namely, that cost reports provide the basis for actions such as praise, criticism, or suggestions for change, all designed to improve *future* performance. We think, in addition, there is another, more subtle way in which cost reports influence performance, and indeed influence the very performance being reported on. Advance knowledge of the fact that a report on performance is going to be prepared can be an important stimulus to good performance on the part of the person being judged. I think this is well illustrated by our process of grading students, for it is doubtful that we would willingly undertake the grading drudgery unless we believed that the fact that students knew they were eventually going to be graded had in some way influenced the work they did during the year.

In the Tentative Statement, we list some concepts that are relevant to the reporting area, including methods of constructing and using standard costs, the idea of management by exception, the important point that control systems are likely to be ineffective unless the people involved believe that the standards are reasonable and equitable, the use of return on investment as an overall yardstick of performance, and so on. I think these are adequately stated in the report, and I will therefore not elaborate on them here.

CONCLUSION

This, then, was our approach to enumerating and defining the concepts relevant to costs for control. Our framework was the *purpose* for which costs are used. In such a framework, we recognized that human reactions and motivations were dominant considerations. Our problem thereupon became not strictly an accounting problem, such as the construction of a set of financial statements, nor an accounting-economics problem, such as that discussed in the planning section of the Tentative Statement. Rather, it was a problem involving both accounting and psychology, the study that deals with human reactions.

Your committee is not made up of psychologists; in fact, its members are somewhat skeptical of some of the psychological patter. We are convinced, however, that approaching the control problem in terms of human motivation — subjective though this approach is, and different though it may seem from the customary language of debit and credit — is much more fruitful than an attempt to define "true" costs, or to say whether ideal standards are better than normal standards, or any other mechanical approach.

The usefulness of such an approach becomes apparent when the concepts are applied to a practical control problem. Without such an approach, one can easily become immersed in pointless arguments on such matters as whether rent should be allocated on the basis of square footage or cubic footage. There is no sound way of settling such disputes. With the notion of motivation, the problem comes into clear focus: What cost constructions are most likely to induce people to take the action that management desires? Answering this question in a specific situation is difficult, and very little in the way of guides towards a specific answer will be found in our statement. But, at least, we think the concepts suggested here describe what the accountant is trying to do.

And as time goes on, we expect that out of experience, and discussions like the one we have today, more specific statements will evolve, so that eventually principles will be developed in the control area comparable with those developed over the years in the financial accounting area.

16

Tailor-making Cost Data for Specific Uses

WILLIAM J. VATTER*

Costs and cost data are important — not only to accountants who record and report such data, but also to a large number of other people. The greatest number of those interested in cost data are the people who share in some fashion in the task of management. As should be the case with any product or service, the demands of those people who use the results of cost analysis and cost accounting must and will be served. Just as soon as cost accounting is found inadequate for the needs it is supposed to meet, just as soon as cost accounting does not provide the data which management must have, cost accounting will either change to meet those needs or it will be replaced with something else.

The significance of cost data with regard to various problems of accounting, management and economic policy is a vitally interesting subject. It is a subject which deserves more attention from cost accountants everywhere. There is, however, a great deal of confusion and misunderstanding as to just how cost data are related to managerial and other decisions. To avoid this confusion and misunderstanding, it is essential to recognize that cost data must be treated differently when they are to be used for different purposes.

TWO HUMAN FAILINGS CLOUD THE SITUATION

It is a natural human trait to seek simple answers to our problems. One is often impressed with the confidence that people have in simple solutions. We are constantly seeking the one factor that will serve as the answer to a whole group of puzzles. We search for the key log in the jam, the straw that broke the camel's back — the philosopher's stone! Not that there is anything wrong with the simple answer if it really fits the problem. The trouble is that, in our zeal to get the one true and simple answer, we frequently overlook the real nature of the problem.

Worse, when we are faced with a complex problem that demands more careful analysis than we are willing to give, we get "practical" about it — that is, we assume away some of the issues, simply because

* From *N.A.(C.)A. Bulletin,* 1954 Conference Proceedings. Copyright 1954 by the National Association of Accountants. Reprinted by permission of the National Association of Accountants.

we do not know how to deal with them, or because we are unwilling to take the trouble to learn what we ought to know. The world, and each of our respective businesses, is so full of problems that it is not uncommon to find those problems solved by the most convenient means — which is to ignore them! We want simple answers and we get simple answers, even if they must be made simple by ignoring the questions!

A second natural human trait is the tendency to revere mathematics. A quantitative answer is somehow more appealing and more convincing than a nonnumerical one. Numbers convey a kind of meaning which is less likely to be misunderstood, because everybody has learned to count in the same way. However, we often go too far in our dependence upon the objectivity of numbers. We impute to numerical calculations a reality and a dependability which they may not in fact have. The fact is that numerical data can be manipulated in many ways, all of which are entirely correct arithmetically and many of which may be valid for certain circumstances. Sometimes, however, there may be little validity in the calculations, because they do not apply to the situation. Yet it is surprising how often people will believe that a given calculation is correct, merely because it is arithmetically consistent — it can be checked against the rules of arithmetic.

I have no real quarrel with the emphasis on figures to deal with complex managerial problems. Indeed, I have a healthy respect for those who tackle the problems of the real world which I avoid by my being a college professor. I do not wish to suggest that management should operate by guesswork or intuition or that the patterns of cost analysis developed by accountants and applied by you to the problems of business should be scrapped. I merely wish to point out that sometimes the ground rules may be more important to playing a game than is the method of keeping score. Even in keeping score, it is reasonably helpful to know what game is being played!

I am certain that the two human traits I have mentioned, the search for the simple answer and the reverence for mathematics, can cause a lot of trouble for cost accountants. Cost figures may actually be misleading if they are computed to fit one purpose and used for another purpose. The validity and results of a business decision may often be traced to the way in which costs were marshalled in tackling the problem.

FIGURES ON THE FAMILY CAR

The methods of assembling and applying cost information to the solution of business problems depend upon the specific purpose or use to be made of the figures. Data which may have one meaning under one set of circumstances will have an entirely different meaning under other conditions. Let me illustrate this by a very simple and common case, the family car. The data are those which could have come from your personal records — if you are accountant enough to keep such records, which I am not! The questions I shall ask are those which have actually been asked in recent months by my own family. I am fairly sure that these same questions have arisen in your own case. The data are as follows:

Annual Cost of Operating the Family Car

Fuel (720 gallons at 29 cents)	$208.80
Lubricating oil and additives	30.00
Chassis lubrications	16.50
Inspections and maintenance	35.00
Washing and polishing	28.50
Licenses, city and state	26.50
Garage rent (less portion applicable to storing furniture, etc.)	126.06
Public liability & property damage insurance (net after dividend)	67.80
Depreciation $2,500 − $900 ÷ 4 =	400.00
Personal property taxes (Valuation $200)	8.00
Total	**$947.16**

Per mile, for 10,800 miles, 8.77 cents

These figures presumably answer the question of how much it costs to drive a car per year. However, the only reason for wanting to know that is to be able to make a better decision with regard to some proposed action. The question of whether one can "afford" a car is too vague and meaningless to warrant much discussion here. I can assure you (from my own experience in selling cars) that the reasons for automobile ownership are far removed from any questions of economy or cost, in the great majority of cases.

Suppose the car is now in service and the question is raised to whether it should be used in preference to other transportation for a business trip of, say, 1,000 miles. Looking at the items in the cost schedule, it appears that the cost of fuel, lubrication, and perhaps some of inspection and maintenance, are relevant to the decision. These are costs that would be increased if we drove the car the extra distance, whereas washing and polishing, licenses, garage rent, insurance, depreciation, and property taxes would be irrelevant to the decision because they would be the same in total, whether or not the proposed trip is made. If (as some folks do) we trade cars often enough so that we do not purchase tires, it could well be argued that nothing should be shown for this item, since it is covered by depreciation. But, if we do not trade often enough to be able to overlook tire replacements, these should be about one-fourth cent per mile. Thus we have a per mile estimate of roughly three cents a mile as out of pocket cost to be considered in this situation. However, there probably should be something added to cover the extra *collision* risk (which presumably we are carrying without an insurance contract) and there may be other items, such as extra meals, bridge tolls, overnight lodging, etc., to take into account. Evidently what it costs to drive a car depends upon what you intend doing with it.

Some of you may say, "That's easy — it is the variable costs that are important anyway. Fixed costs are the ones to ignore!" Do not be too sure about that, either. If the question is asked as to whether or not the family should operate two cars instead of one, so that the use of the car by one person does not leave the rest marooned, the answer is to be found in a quite different way.

The variable costs, those which increase in total with the number of miles driven, are, in this case, quite irrelevant, unless the two cars in question have very different operating characteristics. These will be the same for either car for any given number of miles. If the total mileage for two cars is more than for one, then the variable costs are relevant, but only for the additional mileage. The fixed costs are really the important ones for this question. To acquire a second car will double the washing and polishing, the licenses, garage rent, insurance, depreciation, and perhaps more than double the personal property taxes. Worse yet, there should also be added the investment aspect of the transaction. Whether or not interest is a cost, it must certainly be taken into account when a decision involves tying up funds for such a purpose. Small wonder that the second car is often a smaller and less expensive vehicle. My own is a jalopy in the strict sense of that term!

All of this may raise another question — whether it is really wise to own a car in the first place. There are other means of transport — livery, taxicab, and car rental services would insist that at least there is something to be said for their side of the case. How could we use the figures given to establish an answer to this kind of question?

If we should give up automobile ownership, the costs shown in the schedule would be saved, except for the item of depreciation. This is ordinarily computed on the difference between original cost and ultimate trade-in value at the end of the intended service-life. In this case, the figures are a new cost of $2,500 three years ago, an expected trade-in at the end of four years at $900. The difference of $1,600 is spread over four years. Will this $400 per year be saved by disposing of the car? The car in question actually has a present market value of $800. If it is used for another year, it will bring only $600. The relevant depreciation for this purpose is only $200 for the next year, regardless of the other figures. But we should also include interest on the $800 present market value. If we had no car, the money could be put to work. What it would earn is what we lose by keeping the car.

There are perhaps other cost items that should be included. What about the dry-cleaning bills arising from walking three blocks in the rain to get the car from a parking space, while taxicabs roll past the door of the theatre? Or how about the suit that was ruined changing a tire just after leaving a friend's home at 12.30? Indeed, there are costs that do make a difference and there are computations other than the ones shown in the schedule. My illustration may seem biased against car ownership, but that is because I have not mentioned other, perhaps more important, factors than those included in the costs. My wife and I have two cars and I am sure we could not get along without both of them. She will not let me use hers, and I am too lazy to walk, even to the drugstore!

The question of whether or not one can really afford to operate a car may have strange implications. One member of our faculty (not an accountant nor in the business school) once asked what could be done about the very high cost of operating his car, which he figured at some sixteen cents per mile. The reply given him (by one who was something of a practical joker) was, "You don't drive the car enough for it to be efficient — hire a boy to drive it around the block for several hours each Saturday. That will get your cost down." I am sorry to report that the professor was stopped from this endeavor only by vigorous persuasion on the part of a more kindly colleague!

BUSINESS NEEDS WHICH CALL FOR TAILOR-MADE COSTS

Directing our attention more specifically to the subject of costs for special purposes in business situations, the first question to be raised is, "What is the nature of these different situations in which costs should be tailor-made?" I think the broad classification involved here is a four-fold one:

1. Measuring income.

2. Control of cost incurrence.

3. Overall planning.

4. Decision-making in specific situations.

MEASURING INCOME

In terms of financial reporting — that phase of accounting directed toward informing the employees, investors and the public of the financial activities and results of operations — the prime function of cost data is to measure the expense flow. The trouble encountered in this field is the fact that cost data are related to income in many different ways.

First, there are two or more basic approaches to the problem with respect to how price-fluctuations should affect income. Much has been said and done about this. We have had proposed various types of "lifo," related methods, and index numbers. Some still hold the view that good old "fifo" or "average" cost is to be desired. Many of you, I suspect, prefer standard cost pricing for inventories, with variances carried into the operating statement for the year. Some prefer to prorate some, or even all, standard cost variances to achieve a more conventional cost calculation for inventories and factory costs of goods sold. To prorate variances, however, is to me even more than a compromise. It is an admission that conventional accounting for purposes of measuring income is different from the meeting of managerial needs by the collection of cost-variance data.

What is true of prices can be true of other things, not only in terms of compromise methods but in the pattern of conflicting objectives.

The whole concept of matching costs with revenues can be viewed in at least two ways. When production fluctuates from month to month in order to keep in step with market demand, there is a problem as to how fixed costs shall be dealt with in the computation of inventories (i.e., as to how costs shall be assigned against a fluctuating revenue). Usually, this problem is solved by some pattern of normalization, an allocation of fixed costs levelling the otherwise awkwardly fluctuating inventory costs which would become high when production is low and low when production is high.

Along with this, comes a closely related problem as to what is meant by the "normal" output level. In standard cost theory, idle capacity cost is regarded as the cost of subnormal activity. Thus, costs of manufacturing may include costs that are not costs of product. There are costs of not producing, as well as costs of production.

In any event, the figures now to be presented are simple only because I have made them so. If this were a year-end statement, the proration of unabsorbed burden (or indirect costs) and/or the reallocation of variance would yield the results shown, only if all the possible patterns of accounting were to be realigned to the notion of total average annual cost. This is, of course, impossible, not only because cost accountants differ in their attitudes toward the handling of variances and underabsorptions, but also because the ordinary situation is too complex to permit such prorations on any but the simplest bases. Generally, as I suggested earlier, we solve complex problems by being practical. We force our problems to be simple.

In this instance, if we assign four-fifths of the manufacturing cost against the revenue for this period in the example given, the net income is conventionally established at $35,000. However, this calculation satisfies only those of us who are concerned about matching cost dollars with revenue dollars, all costs assumed to "rank abreast!" The statement appears below.

How to show fixed costs

Measuring Income

Sales 80,000 units at $5		$400,000
Manufacturing costs (100,000 units)		
Direct costs	$200,000	
Variable indirect	150,000	
Fixed indirect	50,000	
Total	$400,000	
Less inventory (1/5)	80,000	320,000
Gross margin		$ 80,000
Selling costs	$ 30,000	
General administration	15,000	45,000
Net operating margin (before income tax)		$ 35,000

There are some who think that the matching process is a matching of revenues for a period with costs assigned to that period. On this basis, fixed costs have no relevance whatever to products or to inventories. They should be "expended" in that period when they appear as costs of being in business. Thus, the inventory would be one-fifth of variable costs only, or $10,000 less, and the net margin would be only $25,000. This view really arises from recognition of managerial aspects of accounting. Whether "direct" or variable costing is right or wrong is a matter of purposes and situations. My only point here is to make it clear that, even for purposes of measuring income, there are different kinds of costs and different ways of handling cost data.

COST CONTROL

The second broad purpose that cost data are made to serve is the managerial objective of placing responsibility for the incurrence of cost. This phase of cost-analysis is not the same thing as the computation of unit cost for products and services. One of the major tasks of accounting, from the managerial viewpoint, is the tracing of costs to the making of decisions. If decisions which are made can be identified with their cost, good decisions can be distinguished from bad ones; we may not only learn from our mistakes but we may find those mistakes through analysis of costs associated with decisions.

For control purposes, bases of distribution, methods of cost reapportionment, and allocations by means of burden or indirect cost rates, are all likely to be irrelevant and useless. Worthy and estimable as such cost calculations may be for other needs, they simply do not apply, for the most part, to cost control in the sense we use the term. What is essential to cost control is "activity accounting" (to borrow a phrase from Eric Kohler). Costs must be related to the things being done, and this is largely a matter of setting costs against decisions.

To attempt cost control only by the use of unit costs seems to me to overlook the prime purpose of control, which is to see that the various levels of decisions that have to be made in a business are harmonious. The salesman who merely sells as much as he can of everything, the machine tool hand who merely minimizes scrap losses, the engineer who designs the most durable mechanism — may each be working against, rather than for, the satisfactory and profitable performance of the enterprise functions. The organization and planning devices that are used to specialize managerial and other skills are and should be supplemented by functional, departmental, and operational-activity classifications of cost. The classifications should follow the levels of responsibility. Costs over which a factory manager or superintendent has jurisdiction should be charged at that level. Those that are associated with other levels of authority or delegated functions should be so charged. Thus, it is doubtful whether, from this viewpoint, machinery depreciation, building maintenance, and a number of other costs should even appear at the level of a manufacturing department foreman, or an operating cost center in the product-costing sense of that term.

Yet, in the patterns of cost incurrence that are associated with given activities, care must be taken to remove the effect of variables which have no direct connection with the activity being costed. An illustration is afforded by the first of the two tables next shown. Changes in cost as here portrayed would seem to show this year's operations less efficient and more costly than last year's. This is true, but it is irrelevant if the price shifts are beyond the control of the department head. A more careful comparison, making allowances to be sure that price changes do not affect the comparability of data, yields a quite different result. The two sets of figures appear below:

Cost Control and Price Shifts

	This Year	Last Year
Direct labor	$28,000	$24,000
Direct materials	50,000	36,000
Indirect labor	10,000	8,000
Supplies	6,000	4,000
Power	2,800	3,000
Totals	$96,800	$75,000

Last Year Adjusted to Current Costs

	This Year	Last Year
Direct labor (up 20%)	$28,000	$28,800
Direct materials (up 40%)	50,000	50,400
Indirect labor (up 20%)	10,000	9,600
Supplies (up 40%)	6,000	5,600
Power	2,800	3,000
Totals	$96,800	$97,400

This kind of difficulty may, of course, be met by other means. But if real control is to be had by fixing responsibility for decisions, the irrelevant variables must be ruled out. This same kind of analysis requires adjustment of costs when standard conditions obtain with respect to equipment, materials or men. Proper adjustments are not always obvious or easy to make, but they must be made if the objective of cost control is to be attained.

OVERALL PLANNING

Much of what has been said about cost control applies equally well to the planning of costs. The attempt to forecast what costs should be and then to make them behave the way they should is the nearest business administration has ever come to a scientific or logical pattern. The attempt to forecast results and then to test these forecasts in experience is the pattern of scientific advance. Startling discoveries may arise when the reasons for failure are sought. Research — at the level of pure theory, or in the more mundane realms of product testing and development — can teach us much about management. It is important that the forecasts be sound and that proven hypotheses be employed, but every hypothesis has its limits. When I was a student in college chemistry, water was simply H_2O. Now, they tell me, there are nine kinds of water, each with properties and a formula of its own.

This same kind of thing is true of costs and cost behavior. Economists and cost accountants have never understood each other in this area, partly because they do not understand themselves. Let me illustrate. Every cost is a variable cost, and every cost is also a fixed cost over some range. The only difference is the size of the step. In theory, every plant can be expanded. Therefore, fixed costs may jump as we move from a high level of activity to a larger plant or a new set up of machinery, or another layout. We are frequently plagued by costs which jump at certain crucial points. These semifixed costs are merely smaller editions of the broad-scale fixed costs. Even so-called variable costs have their own little step-patterns. Raw materials and direct labor are acquired and applied in units that are least theoretically unreducible. One more unit of such costs (however small) is a step in the cost pattern.

There are several other observations which need to be made about costs for planning. One is that costs always look different in different circumstances. Increases in volume will always elicit more prompt expansion of staff than will be found feasible in terms of contraction, for the same amount of reduction in volume. Part of this is because of uncertainty and the desire to maintain continuity of operations. But part of it is the human desire to cling to what is, since we know not what should be!

Another observation is that costs need better classification than they are ordinarily given, and more study should be allotted to the problem of cost behavior. We should not wait for statisticians and economists to do such work for us. I have been much amused to see accountants striving desperately to perfect a formula to forecast travel costs as a percentage of sales, when it is clear that the factors governing the costs are not sales dollars or tonnage. Even more disturbing is the fact that, once a formula is set, the cost never falls below that formula. Strong pressure may keep it from rising, but it will not go any lower than we have said it should be!

Still one other point may be made on the planning aspect of costs. Rate of activity is often (and I think wrongly) taken as output or capacity or some related concept. Costs for planning and control purposes are related to decisions. Decisions have to do with inputs, not outputs. It would be better to talk and think about break-even charts, budgets, and other planning devices in terms of the input factors which must be controlled, rather than the output bases on which we can write up our post-mortems!

DECISION-MAKING: THE SPECIAL ORDER, CHOICE OF OUTPUT LEVEL

There is a great variety of cost situations in which the question of relevance must be asked again and again. It must be checked and re-checked, for cost data have a way of remaining mute and unchanged under differing conditions. The right cost for one purpose may be the misleading cost for another. A few illustrations may serve to point up these problems. I shall touch only briefly on each of the illustrations. Still, and even though these illustrations are not exhaustive, I think they will serve to present the general areas of importance, and the essential cost data, that are relevant to some specific decisions.

The data presented below this paragraph are directed to the question of whether or not a special order should be accepted. This order is special in that it is entirely unrelated to any other existing plans or commitments of the firm. The question in this case is whether or not the firm should accept an order for 1,000 units of this product at a price of $5 per unit. The figures follow:

The Special Order

Revenue (20,000 units)		$140,000
Factory costs (20,000 units)		
Variable	$92,000	
Fixed	18,000	110,000
Gross Margin		$30,000
Selling cost variable	$ 20,000	
Administration, fixed	16,000	36,000
Loss		$ 6,000

It will be seen that the total factory costs applicable to 20,000 units is $110,000, which is $5.50 per unit. The offer seems unattractive, until it is recognized that acceptance of the order will leave fixed costs un-affected. Thus, the relevant factory cost is $92,000 variable costs, or $4.60 per unit. Each additional unit produced will increase factory cost by $4.60. Thus, the acceptance of this order will tend to reduce a present loss by adding $5,000 to revenue and only $4,600 to factory costs. However, the selling costs are also variable. We have been assuming tacitly that they were fixed or, at least, would not be increased by the acceptance of the order under consideration. However, these selling costs might include packing, shipping or handling charges that would be increased if this order is accepted. The answer must be found by establishing which costs may be expected to increase if the order is taken and by how much. Only by such an approach can an intelligent decision be made.

Another question is choice of a level of output. The figures below show data regarding a loss-product. The selling price is set by competition and the market at $4.50. As can be seen there is no hope of making a profit, since the average unit cost is, even for the highest output level, $5.51. However, the question here concerns the level at which the loss will be least. These are the data:

Level of Output — Price Given

	Rate of Production and Sale			
	10,000	11,000	12,000	13,000
Factory cost, variable	$37,000	$40,800	$44,600	$48,400
Factory cost, fixed	9,000	9,000	9,000	9,000
Selling cost, variable	6,000	6,600	7,400	8,200
Administration, fixed	6,000	6,000	6,000	6,000
	$58,000	$62,400	$67,000	$71,600
Average unit cost	$5.80	$5.67+	$5.58+	$5.51−
Average variable unit cost	$4.30	$4.31	$4.33	$4.35

The answer seems obvious. The unit cost is least at the 13,000 unit level. This should be the point of lowest loss. But these total average unit figures are not relevant and the decision suggested by the falling average unit costs is wrong. For, if we analyze the *changes* in cost associated with the *changes* in output (differential cost), it will be seen that, to produce 11,000 units, involves costs of $62,400. This, compared with the cost of producing 10,000 units ($58,000), shows a differential of $4,400, or $4.40 per unit. With a price of $4.50, the deficit is reduced by $100 if the rate of operations is raised to 11,000 units. However, when we compare the cost at 11,000 units with that for 12,000 units, the differential is $4,600 or $4.60 per unit. There is a disadvantage of 10¢ per unit or $100 in the move from 11,000 to 12,000 units. A similar situation is found in the differential cost between 12,000 and 13,000 units. Hence, the firm will minimize its loss by expanding to 11,000 units, but not beyond.

It should be noted that total average unit cost is irrelevant for this purpose. It should also be pointed out that even average-*variable*-per-unit cost does not reflect the cost situation properly. There is no safe way to approach the cost angles of special orders or output variations except to consider variable costs only, and then at the indicated levels. Indeed, it is possible to go further than this. In any situation involving price or output variations, the only relevant costs are those variable changes associated with the proposed changes.

DECISION-MAKING: MAKE OR BUY, SELL OR PROCESS FURTHER

A frequently raised question, and one that deserves attention, is whether to make or buy an item. The illustrative data are given below:

Unit Cost of Part 17-432		Unit Costs Relevant to Make or Buy Decision	
Direct labor (current cost)............	$ 7.00		
Direct materials (current cost)....	8.00	Direct labor..................................	$ 7.00
Variable indirect cost...................	4.00	Direct materials............................	8.00
Fixed indirect cost.......................	3.00	Variable indirect cost....................	3.50
	$22.00	Total..	$18.50

Quotation is $20 each.

We see the costs of producing a certain part which can be purchased for $20 per unit. First, it should be noted that the earlier comments about currentness of costs are applicable here, as elsewhere. The data given seem to indicate that the item in question should be purchased, since the cost of production is $2 more than the quotation. However, the data as shown are misleading. If only the variable costs are considered (since the fixed costs will be the same whether we make or buy the item) the relevant costs are only $19 per unit.

But there is another angle. It is important that only escapable or avoidable costs should be recognized in a calculation such as this. It has been suggested that variable costs do not always behave as expected. Sometimes, they do not fall when activity is reduced. Hence, a more relevant figure may be had by including in the tabulation only those costs which could be saved if the part were not manufactured, in this case $3.50 variable cost per unit. If it were possible to reduce fixed costs by the decision to purchase this part, that portion of the fixed cost which could be saved by purchase is a relevant cost of continuing to produce the item. As for the situation here described, the decision should be to make this part.

The problem to be approached in the question of sales versus further processing is typical of many industrial situations. The alternative often exists of selling a given item at a given stage of completion or of processing it further to sell at a higher price. For instance, pork may be cured, smoked, canned, etc. Metals may be fabricated to different degrees. Other products may be delivered to the market in various forms. Management must decide for the particular firm how far processing will be carried toward the completely finished state. What costs apply to such decisions and how are they to be dealt with?

The data below refer to operations on two products which are produced jointly. The question raised is whether Product B should be sold as such or processed further to make Product C. The figures involved are:

Costs of carrying on the joint process $36,000
Output of A, 10,000 lbs., price $3.00 per lb., sales value $30,000
Output of B, 10,000 lbs., price $1.50 per lb., sales value $15,000
10,000 lbs. of Product B + $16,000 additional processing will yield 8,000 lbs. of Product C, unit price $4.

The question immediately arises as to the cost of Product B. This can be established conventionally in at least two ways. If the joint costs are divided on the basis of weight, the cost of 10,000 lbs. of Product B is $18,000. This, added to the cost of further processing gives a total cost of Product C as $34,000. Since the sale of the latter will bring only $32,000, it does not appear advantageous to carry on the additional processing. However, if the joint costs are divided on the basis of sales value, the cost of Product B is only $12,000 (one-third of $36,000) and the total cost of producing Product C is $28,000, which would indicate a margin of $4,000 to be gained by the additional processing.

Obviously, something is amiss here. The cost allocations give entirely inconsistent results. One or both of them must be wrong. There is no way to establish the correctness of either of these methods of cost allocation. The really important thing to see is that cost allocation between Products A and B is, for the purpose at hand, irrelevant. The way to approach the problem is to take the price of Product B and the revenue to be had from its sale as the cost of putting it into further processing. For that is precisely what is given up when Product B is subjected to further processing. The alternative or displacement cost is the relevant cost in this situation. The calculations would then be:

Displacement cost of putting Product B into further processing $15,000
Additional costs of carrying on the production of Product C 16,000
    Total cost of Product C $31,000
    Revenue from sale of Product C ($8,000 × $4) $32,000
      Advantage in further processing .... $ 1,000

The validity of this approach may be established by comparison of the total costs and revenues for each of the alternative actions:

Sell Product B Without Further Processing		Additional Processing – Sell Product C, Instead of Product B	
Sales of Product A......................	$30,000	Sales of Product A......................	$30,000
Sales of Product B.....................	15,000	Sales of Product C......................	32,000
Total revenue.................	$45,000	Total revenue..................	$62,000
Costs before splitoff...................	$36,000	Costs before splitoff..................	$36,000
		Additional processing.................	16,000
Total costs.......................	$36,000	Total costs........................	$52,000
Net margin.....................	$ 9,000	Net margin.....................	$10,000

The reader may perhaps feel that this situation has been forced by the use of a joint product illustration. This is not the case. The same approach would be indicated if Product A did not exist. The data relevant to the question of further processing must include the revenue foregone by not selling the output at the earlier stage of operations. The costs up to that point — unless they can be altered by the decision to process further — are irrelevant and should be ignored.

It is also worth noting that the joint cost situation is a great deal more common than it is ordinarily supposed to be. Most firms, for one reason or another, have joint costs of producing the various products. For example, to which product should the costs of personnel management be charged? The answer is really that personnel management costs apply to all products in a joint cost sense. Many service department costs are joint costs in this same way. In fact, it is really an unusual situation which does not reflect some elements of the joint cost problem. What has been said earlier in this discussion about the costs of not producing, the costs of being in business, the costs of inefficiency, etc., are cases in point.

The real problem of cost accounting from this viewpoint is not so much the working out of "bases for distributing" joint costs but of establishing when and how much cost is relevant to a given question.

DECISION-MAKING: SELECTION, REPLACEMENT
OF EQUIPMENT

Enough has already been said to cast some doubt on the too-ready acceptance of unit costs as a means of making managerial choices. However, one other area should be explored. Below are shown the data concerning two pieces of equipment which can be employed to carry on a specified operation, with outputs as stated:

Annual Costs

	Machine A 80,000 units	Machine B 100,000 units
Direct labor	$ 6,400	$ 7,000
Direct materials	8,000	9,000
Variable indirect	4,000	6,000
Fixed indirect	2,400	3,000
	$20,800	$25,000
	26¢ each	25¢ each

The unit cost comparison on the basis of the data is favorable to the larger machine. This advantage *might* apply to other levels of output but it might not. The relative proportions of fixed and variable costs have an important effect on the responsiveness of unit costs to shifting volume, and it is a dubious calculation which does not take this into account. If the data are set up for the operation of Machine B at a level of 80,000 units, we could have:

Direct labor	$ 5,800
Direct materials	7,500
Variable indirect	4,900
Fixed indirect	3,000
Total	$21,200 per unit 26.5¢

The reason for the higher cost at 80,000 volume is not merely the presence of fixed costs. It has been suggested that variable costs may or may not be proportionate to volume of output, or even to the level of input. To make judgments of the sort here under discussion, it is necessary to know something more about cost behavior than the simple dichotomy of variable and fixed costs.

Further, it should be noted that investment is reflected in these figures only by depreciation charges. This is inadequate if the amount of investment is substantial. Whether or not accountants believe that interest is a cost of manufacture is not really important in this situation. What is important is that the relative investment must be measured in making the decision between these machines. Needless to say, the situation should be studied with full recognition of income tax effects and with some regard for those risks of obsolescence, supercession and inadequacy that are not considered in the usual accounting depreciation charge. That is, there should be a careful judgment as to the capital recovery situation in regard to the rate of technical progress and possible market shifts. Cost figures need to be tailored to fit such a situation, so that they reflect, as best they can, the factors that are relevant to the decision.

To make even more clear that the cost data employed for management purposes must be fitted to the use to be made of them, consider the question of replacement. To make matters more concise, let us assume that ine company already owns five machines of Type A considered above. The question is raised as to whether these should be replaced by four Type B machines. This situation is purposely constructed to remove the cost fluctuation at varying volume. It is assumed that 400,000 unit capacity is needed now and in the future. Since Machine B is obviously superior to Machine A on a cost comparison basis, why not replace these machines?

The usual pattern of reluctance to replace centers around the unabsorbed book value of the old machines. But this is irrelevant for, whether or not the old machines are replaced — and regardless of their book value — the write-off is whatever it is. It is of *no* consequence, except as a tax saving.

One real confusion in the data lies in the fact that the cost attributed to the old machines (now in service) includes depreciation, which is also irrelevant since it is not a part of the data for decision. If the cost of an A-type machine is $10,000 and the use-life for depreciation is 10 years, then, for five machines now in service, there has been included in cost $5,000 for the year. This penalizes machines now owned with a cost that cannot be saved (since there is assumed no trade-in value). This cost should be removed.

Also, there should be charged in the schedule of cost for the four B-type machines, not only 10 per cent depreciation on their assumed $56,000 total investment, but also interest, insurance, and property taxes on this additional investment. A more relevant comparison is thus the one shown below:

	Keep 5 A's	*Buy* 4 B's
Direct labor	$ 32,000	$ 28,000
Direct materials	40,000	36,000
Variable indirect	20,000	24,000
Fixed indirect	12,000	12,000
	$104,000	$100,000
Less sunk-cost	5,000	
	$ 99,000	$100,000
Add interest, insurance and property taxes on additional investment (10%)		5,600
Total	$ 99,000	$105,600

It should also be noted that the effect of income taxes needs to be considered, both with regard to the savings or extra costs, and the obsolescence write-off, also if new machines are acquired. It should also be observed that the depreciation charge on the new machine is minimal and should probably be higher for this situation.

A word may be necessary as to the charge for interest, insurance and property taxes. It may be objected that these should be based on average rather than total investment. The reason for showing them as a percentage of total investment is that the superiority of the new machines is being tested on the basis of the first year of operation, i.e., in comparison with the current-year outlook for the machines now in service. To base investment charges on average investment is to assume too much about the problematical future. The advantage in the new equipment — if there is one — should be obvious in the initial year and it should be sufficient to cover the investment charge for that year.

CONCLUSION

These are not all of the situations that could be described. All of the problems of tailor-making cost data have not been presented here. What I have tried to do is to make it clear that the use to be made of cost data governs their content and that cost data must be tested for relevance before they can be relied upon in management decision-making.

Cost accountants must not only be aware of these distorting influences in the data with which they work but must also be willing and able to analyze data in whatever patterns may be necessary to get proper perspective and to present the basic information that management needs. It is not enough to present all of the data, leaving the interpretations to the readers of reports. The responsibility of the cost accountant is to learn the uses that are to be made of his cost data, and to make certain that the data are used as they should be, and to see that relevant and irrelevant data are handled properly, so that management may rely on the figures for what they purport to be — bases for decision.

The acceptance and discharge of this responsibility does not involve any shift in principles, abandonment of extant methods or other disturbances. Rather, such an approach to the cost accountant's job will develop a more essential and fruitful relationship between managers who need information about their business and the cost accountants who can supply such information. By this means cost accountants can assume a rightfully deserved place in the productive efforts of industry. They can establish themselves as contributors to the attainment of progress.

17

Toward Probabilistic Profit Budgets

WILLIAM L. FERRARA and JACK C. HAYYA*

Three Methods for the Construction of
Probabilistic Profit and Loss Statements

Practical techniques have recently been developed for business applications of probability concepts so that they can be easily integrated with profit planning. This paper shows how some of these techniques can be used in the construction of probabilistic profit budgets, i.e., budgets that display expected values and a probability interval for every item.

Related Studies and Literature

The accounting literature does not specify how probabilistic profit budgets are constructed. A 1960 study on profit planning by executives, for example, makes no mention of probabilistic approaches to profit budgets.[1]

The 1966 *Statement of Basic Accounting Theory*, encourages accountants to adopt probabilistic financial statements, but does not offer any guidelines.[2] Byrne, *et al*, offer similar encouragement when they state that decision-tree and network concepts ". . . may be a better way of utilizing the double-entry principle — at least when probability distributions are to be compounded for such purposes as . . . projection of profit-and-loss statement categories along with related balance-sheet and flow-of-funds analysis."[3]

* From *Management Accounting* (October 1970) , pp. 23-28. Reprinted by permission of the Managing Editor. The authors are indebted to Joseph Mackovjak (now with General Electric) who provided simulation expertise and other valuable assistance.

1 Leon E. Hay, "Planning for Profits—How Some Executives Are Doing It," *The Accounting Review*, April 1960, pp. 233-37.
2 *A Statement of Basic Accounting Theory*, American Accounting Association, 1966, pp. 38, 59, and 65.
3 R. Byrne, A. Charnes, W. W. Cooper, and K. Kortanek, "Some New Approaches to Risk," *The Accounting Review*, January 1968, p. 33.

Magee,[4] Hertz,[5] and Jaedicke and Robichek[6] focus on issues related to probabilistic profit budgets. Magee develops a detailed decision-tree in calculating the expected net present value of alternative capital investments. Hertz also deals with capital investments, but uses computer simulation to derive expected discounted return on investment and a probability distribution which expresses the variability of expected return on investment. Jaedicke and Robichek handle uncertainty in cost-volume-profit analysis by assuming that uncertainty is in the form of a normal probability distribution.

Coughlan,[7] Hespos and Strassman,[8] Springer, Herlihy, Mall and Beggs[9] offer, in ascending order, some of the more detailed approaches to preparing probabilistic financial statements.

Coughlan uses discrete probability distributions to calculate expected net receipts. His treatment of probability intervals, however, is incomplete.

Hespos and Strassman, like some afore-mentioned authors deal with investment decisions. They expand the treatment of risk analysis in decision-trees by substituting continuous distributions for the discrete probabilities at the chance event nodes.

Springer, Herlihy, Mall and Beggs use an analytic technique and Monte Carlo to estimate probability intervals for net profit. In this respect, their work is similar to ours.

The intent of this paper is to integrate three probabilistic techniques suggested in the literature with profit budgets. The PERT-like and probability-tree approaches used here emphasize most likely and mean values as well as measures of variability for each item in the income statement. Monte Carlo is used to simulate probability intervals for complex distributions that are too difficult to treat analytically.

The Typical Profit Budget

Let us assume that the profit budget in a single-product company is as shown in Exhibit 1. The direct-costing format of Exhibit 1 facilitates the use of breakeven and cost-volume-profit analysis. Fixed costs are classified into managed and committed costs. Managed fixed costs are those costs

[4] John F. Magee, "How to Use Decision Trees in Capital Investment," *Harvard Business Review*, September-October 1964, pp. 79-96.

[5] David B. Hertz, "Risk Analysis in Capital Investment," *Harvard Business Review*, January-February, 1964, pp. 95-106, and "Investment Policies that Pay Off," *Harvard Business Review*, January-February 1968, pp. 96-108.

[6] R. K. Jaedicke and A. A. Robichek, "Cost-Volume-Profit Analysis Under Conditions of Uncertainty," *The Accounting Review*, October 1964, pp. 914-26.

[7] John W. Coughlan, "Profit and Probability," *Advanced Management Journal*, April 1968, pp. 53-69.

[8] Richard F. Hespos and Paul A. Strassman, "Stochastic Decision Trees for the Analysis of Investment Decisions," *Management Science*, August 1956, pp. 244-59.

[9] Clifford H. Springer, Robert E. Herlihy, Robert T. Mall, and Robert I. Beggs, *Probabilistic Models*, Richard D. Irwin, Inc., Homewood, Ill., 1968: Of particular relevance are Chapters 4 and 5.

which can be modified in the short run. Committed fixed costs are those which cannot be modified in the short run. The distinction between variable, managed and committed costs in this model is not only useful, it is particularly appropriate (as will become clear) in the preparation of probabilistic budgets.

The segregation of fixed costs into managed and committed fixed costs gives rise to the "short run margin." This margin is the contribution to earnings for which managers can be held accountable in a given budget period. The short-run margin further shows that committed costs are an obstacle which must be hurdled before a net profit is realized.

The weakness of Exhibit 1, and other models like it, is that they give no indication of the potential variability of the various estimates used. It is clear that the items in the budget are subjective estimates of most likely values, i.e., estimates of what is most probable in terms of revenues, costs and profits. The function of probabilistic profit budgets is to extend such models to indicate the variability of each budget item.

Exhibit 1

Profit Budget for Year Ending June 197X

Sales (100,000 units @ $10)		$1,000,000
Variable costs		
Manufacturing ($5 per unit)	$500,000	
Marketing ($.50 per unit)	50,000	550,000
Marginal contribution		$ 450,000
Managed fixed costs		
Manufacturing	$ 20,000	
Marketing	10,000	
Administrative	40,000	70,000
Short-run margin		$ 380,000
Committed fixed costs		
Manufacturing	$180,000	
Marketing	40,000	
Administrative	60,000	280,000
Net income before tax		$ 100,000
Tax — 50%		50,000
Net income after tax		$ 50,000

Optimistic, Pessimistic and Most Likely Values

Consider first the "three-level" estimates referred to as optimistic, pessimistic and most likely values. Such a "three-level" profit budget can be easily prepared, as shown in Exhibit 2.

It is evident that the three-level estimates of Exhibit 2 are more informative than the most likely one of Exhibit 1. For example, Exhibit

2 shows that net income after tax may be as low as $13,500 or as high as $78,500. The lone use of the most likely estimate of $50,000, as in Exhibit 1, can therefore be misleading.

Exhibit 2*

Profit Budget for Year Ending June 197X

	Pessimistic	Most Likely	Optimistic
Sales ($10 per unit)	$800,000	$1,000,000	$1,100,000
Variable Costs			
Manufacturing	408,000	500,000	528,000
Marketing ($.50 per unit)	40,000	50,000	55,000
Marginal contribution	$352,000	$ 450,000	$ 517,000
Managed fixed costs			
Manufacturing	10,000	20,000	30,000
Marketing	10,000	10,000	10,000
Administrative	25,000	40,000	40,000
Short-run margin	$307,000	$ 380,000	$ 437,000
Committed fixed costs			
Manufacturing	180,000	180,000	180,000
Marketing	40,000	40,000	40,000
Administrative	60,000	60,000	60,000
Net income before tax	$ 27,000	$ 100,000	$ 157,000
Tax − 50%	13,500	50,000	78,500
Net income after tax	$ 13,500	$ 50,000	$ 78,500

From the data of Exhibit 2, one can calculate means and standard deviations for sales, variable costs, and marginal contribution by using the PERT formulas[10] or through probability-tree analysis. If we are to use the PERT formulas, the person who is providing the estimates must be made aware that a most likely estimate is a mode rather than a mean, and that the pessimistic and optimistic estimates are assumed to be six standard deviations apart.

Probability-Tree Analysis: General

A more useful method for the preparation of probabilistic profit budgets

* The data are based on Exhibit 1 with optimistic, most likely, and pessimistic values for sales volume and variable costs being 110,000, 100,000, 80,000 and $4.80, $5.00, $5.10, respectively. Unit variable costs are assumed to vary inversely with volume. Committed costs and unit variable marketing cost are assumed to be certain; some managed costs are modified to reflect changing volume levels.

[10] The PERT formulas for the standard deviation (σ) and the mean (μ) are:

$$\sigma = \frac{b - a}{6} \qquad\qquad \mu = \frac{1}{3}[2m + \frac{1}{2}(a + b)]$$

Where "b" is the optimistic estimate, "a" is the pessimistic estimate and "m" is the most likely estimate.

is probability-tree analysis.[11] Probability-tree analysis is a generalization of the PERT method.

In using probability-tree analysis, probability estimates must be made for every level of volume and variable manufacturing cost considered. Thus, in our case, probabilities are assigned to each of the three sales and variable manufacturing cost levels as indicated in Exhibit 3. The probabilities (the p's and q's) assigned to each level are usually applicable to ranges whose mid-points are used in the calculations.

The budget variables under consideration in Exhibit 3 are sales, variable manufacturing cost, variable marketing cost, managed costs, committed costs, and net income after tax. The nine combinations in the Exhibit result by considering the three sales estimates to be independent of the three variable manufacturing cost estimates.[12]

In Exhibit 3 variable marketing costs, managed costs and committed costs are assumed to be non-probabilistic. The Exhibit shows net income after tax (NIAT) for each of the nine combinations and the expected value (the average or mean value) of NIAT.

The expected value of NIAT in Exhibit 3 $[\Sigma (NIAT) JP]$ is $44,710. On the other hand, the corresponding result for Exhibit 2 as calculated by use of the PERT formula for the mean turns out to be $48,666. The two results differ because they are based on two different models.

Probability-Tree Analysis and Profit Budgets

In Exhibit 4 the expected value (μ) and the standard deviation (σ) of every item in the income statement is presented. The normal distribution and probability intervals[13] of $\pm 2\sigma$ or $\pm 3\sigma$ from the mean cannot be used here since the probability distributions under consideration are not normal. They are discrete probability functions, i.e., functions where the random variable must assume distinct values.

It may be preferable to use the coefficient of variation rather than a probability interval in describing variability for discrete probability distributions of the type shown in Exhibits 3 and 4. The coefficient of variation is the percentage relationship between the standard deviation and the mean. The calculated values of this coefficient are presented in Exhibit 4 for each item in the income statement.

The coefficient of variation is a useful tool for planning and control purposes. From the point of view of planning, the coefficient of variation predicts the potential variability of budgeted items. A high coefficient of variation, for example, indicates that an outcome (e.g.,

11 The probability-tree analysis used in this study differs from formal decision-tree analysis in that all nodes in the probability-tree are chance event nodes.
12 Exhibits 2 and 3 represent different models. The model of Exhibit 2 assumes that volume and variable manufacturing costs are inversely related. The model of Exhibit 3 assumes them to be independent.
13 Referred to as confidence intervals when the parameter to be estimated is not known.

Exhibit 3

Three-Level Diagram of Basic Problem Including Expected Values

Volume (price = $10)	Variable Manufacturing Cost	Variable Marketing Cost	Managed Costs	Committed Costs	Net Income After Tax-50% (NIAT)	Joint* Probability (JP)	Combination	JP × NIAT
80,000 p = .3	q = .2 $5.10	$0.50	$45,000	$280,000	$13,500	0.06	1	$ 810
	q = .6 $5.00	$0.50	$45,000	$280,000	$17,500	0.18	2	3,150
	q = .2 $4.80	$0.50	$45,000	$280,000	$25,500	0.06	3	1,530
100,000 p = .5	q = .2 $5.10	$0.50	$70,000	$280,000	$45,000	0.10	4	4,500
	q = .6 $5.00	$0.50	$70,000	$280,000	$50,000	0.30	5	15,000
	q = .2 $4.80	$0.50	$70,000	$280,000	$60,000	0.10	6	6,000
110,000 p = .2	q = .2 $5.10	$0.50	$80,000	$280,000	$62,000	0.04	7	2,480
	q = .6 $5.00	$0.50	$80,000	$280,000	$67,500	0.12	8	8,100
	q = .2 $4.80	$0.50	$80,000	$280,000	$78,500	0.04	9	3,140
					Expected Value of Net Income after Tax			$44,710

* Joint probabilities are calculated by multiplying the probabilities on the path (the succession of branches) moving toward each outcome.

actual sales) has relatively large variations about the budgeted value. From the point of view of control, differences between budgeted and actual outcomes are understood more meaningfully when they are related to the coefficient of variation.

Exhibit 5 summarizes Exhibit 4 in the format of an income statement. The three columns provide the mean, the standard deviation and the coefficient of variation.

An alternative format is presented in Exhibit 6, which displays the 100 per cent and the 90 per cent probability intervals (or ranges) for the budget items. As the terms imply, the 100 per cent probability interval includes all the elements in the distribution, whereas a 90 per cent probability interval excludes 5 per cent in each of the two tails of the distribution. Probability intervals are obtained from Exhibit 4 by inspection as explained below.

Clearly the highest and lowest possible values for an item would contain a 100 per cent probability interval. This can be obtained readily from Exhibit 4. The 90 per cent range, on the other hand, is arbitrarily chosen in this instance because it fits the distribution of the nine possible values for each item shown in Exhibit 4. The highest value for each item has a probability of 0.04, while the lowest value for each item has a probability of 0.06. Thus the 90 per cent range is determined by excluding the highest and lowest values for each item (with the exception of sales). By definition, the 90 per cent probability interval as it has been presented here is slightly off center.

The probabilistic income statements of Exhibits 5 and 6 provide more information than the three-level format of Exhibit 2. The improvement results from attaching probabilities to sales and unit variable manufacturing cost. The choice of any of these formats, however, depends on managerial needs and preferences.

A Model with Continuous Distribution

Thus far we have considered two general approaches to preparing probabilistic income statements, i.e., the three-level and the probability-tree approaches. We now consider the construction of a probabilistic income statement for a model with continuous probability distributions.

Description of the Model. The assumptions of the model are listed in Exhibit 7. Note that basic data (e.g., price, mean volume, or mean-unit variable manufacturing cost) similar to the previous illustrations are adopted. Again the model is for a single-product firm. The main variables (volume and unit variable manufacturing cost) are normally distributed and statistically independent with known means and standard deviations. A relevant range for volume $(80,000 \leq Q \leq 120,000)$, but not for unit variable manufacturing cost, is assumed. In addition, two costs are functions of volume. These are managed manufacturing cost and managed administrative cost. The former has a linear and the latter a quadratic relationship with volume. The other costs, and also unit price, are constant.

Exhibit 4

Calculation of Expected Values, Standard Deviations and Coefficient of Variation for All Income Statement Items

Dollars in Thousands

Combination	1	2	3	4	5	6	7	8	9
Joint Probability	.06	.18	.06	.10	.30	.10	.04	.12	.04
Sales	$800	$800	$800	$1,000	$1,000	$1,000	$1,100	$1,100	$1,100
Variable Costs:									
Manufacturing	408	400	384	510	500	480	561	550	528
Marketing	40	40	40	50	50	50	55	55	55
Marginal contribution	352	360	376	440	450	470	484	495	517
Managed Costs:									
Manufacturing	10	10	10	20	20	20	30	30	30
Marketing	10	10	10	10	10	10	10	10	10
Administrative	25	25	25	40	40	40	40	40	40
Short-run margin	307	315	331	370	380	400	404	415	437
Committed costs	280	280	280	280	280	280	280	280	280
Net income before tax	$ 27	$ 35	$ 51	$ 90	$ 100	$ 120	$ 124	$ 135	$ 157
Tax @ 50%	13.5	17.5	25.5	45	50	60	62	67.5	78.5
Net income after tax	$ 13.5	$ 17.5	$ 25.5	$ 45	$ 50	$ 60	$ 62	$ 67.5	$ 78.5

In Dollars

	Expected value*	σ^2***	σ	Coefficient of Variation***
Sales	$960,000	$12,400,000,000	$111,400	11.6%
Variable Costs:				
Manufacturing	478,080	3,164,913,600	56,300	11.8%
Marketing	48,000	31,000,000	5,560	11.6%
Marginal Contribution	433,920	2,623,033,600	51,200	11.8%
Managed Costs				
Manufacturing	19,000	49,000,000	7,000	36.8%
Marketing	10,000	0	0	—
Administrative	35,500	47,250,000	6,870	19.4%
Short-run margin	369,420	1,462,363,600	38,250	10.4%
Committed costs	280,000	0	0	—
Net income before tax	89,420	1,462,363,600	38,240	42.8%
Tax @ 50%	44,710	365,590,900	19,120	42.8%
Net income after tax	44,710	365,590,900	19,120	42.8%

* $\Sigma \, x_1 \rho \,(x_1)$ where the x_1 are the values of each combination and the $\rho \,(x_1)$ are the joint probabilities assigned to each x_1.

** $\Sigma \, [x_1^2 \, \rho \,(x_1)] - \mu^2$ where μ is the expected value (mean).

*** $\dfrac{\Gamma}{\mu}$, the % that Γ is of the mean.

Exhibit 5

Profit Budget for Year Ending June 197X

	Expected Value	Standard Deviation	Coefficient of Variation
Sales	$960,000	$111,400	11.6%
Variable costs			
Manufacturing	478,080	56,000	11.8
Marketing	48,000	5,560	11.6
Marginal contribution	$433,920	51,220	11.8
Managed fixed costs			
Manufacturing	19,000	7,000	36.8
Marketing	10,000	0	0
Administrative	35,500	6,870	19.4
Short-run margin	$369,420	38,240	10.4
Committed fixed costs			
Manufacturing	180,000	0	0
Marketing	40,000	0	0
Administrative	60,000	0	0
Net income before tax	$ 89,420	38,240	42.8
Tax—50%	44,710	19,120	42.8
Net income after tax	$ 44,710	19,120	42.8

The model presented may not be representative of the typical firm. Nevertheless, it is useful, for gaining insight into the construction of probabilistic profit budgets.

Difficulties associated with the construction of probability intervals when the probability distributions are not readily identifiable. To estimate a 95 per cent probability interval for the various budget items, we must know how these items are distributed.[14] If these items are normally distributed, or if they belong to distributions that are tabulated, it would be a simple matter to obtain the desired distribution limits. However, in spite of the simplifying assumptions of our model, difficulties associated with identifying the proper distributions occur.

These difficulties increase as one progresses from the top to the bottom of the income statement. This is especially true with regard to the "short-run margin" and the "net income before and after tax" since these items are functions of a product of two normal variables, a linear function of a normal variable and a quadratic function of a normal variable.[15] Without knowing the specific or approximate distribution of

[14] The probability interval could be set at whatever level desired if 95 per cent is considered inappropriate.

[15] The Short-Run Margin, $SRM = 60,700 + Q\ (8.75 - v) - .64\,(10^{-5})Q^2$, where Q is the volume, v is the unit variable manufacturing cost, and Q and v are independently and normally distributed. Net income before and after tax is of the same form.

Exhibit 6

Profit Budget for Year Ending June 197X

	Expected Value	100% Range		90% Range	
Sales	$960,000	$800,000	– $1,100,000	not applicable	
Variable costs					
Manufacturing	478,080	384,000	– 561,000	400,000	– 550,000
Marketing	48,000	40,000	– 55,000	40,000	– 55,000
Marginal contribution	$433,920	352,000	– 517,000	360,000	– 495,000
Managed fixed costs					
Manufacturing	19,000	10,000	– 30,000	10,000	– 30,000
Marketing	10,000				
Administrative	35,500	25,000	– 40,000	25,000	– 40,000
Short-run margin	$369,420	307,000	– 307,000	315,000	– 415,000
Committed fixed costs					
Manufacturing	180,000		–		–
Marketing	40,000		–		–
Administrative	60,000		–		–
Net income before tax	$ 89,420	27,000	– 157,000	35,000	– 135,000
Tax – 50%	44,710	13,500	– 78,500	17,500	– 67,500
Net income after tax	$ 44,710	13,500	– 78,500	17,500	– 67,500

these functions one cannot hope to obtain a probability interval for the items under consideration.

The distribution of these functions can be derived with involved numerical and mathematical techniques. By using simulation, however, we can more easily derive such probability intervals.

Probabilistic Intervals Through Simulation

The model described in Exhibit 7 was simulated by computer and the mean and a 95 per cent probability interval for each budget item was determined. The result is the profit budget of Exhibit 8.

The simulation program involved 1000 iterations; for in this type of problem, experience indicated that 1000 iterations yield a reasonable approximation to the theoretical distribution.[16] We have partially verified this in our case as test runs of 3000 iterations did not produce significantly different results.

Exhibit 7

Assumed One-Product Company Model

1. Volume (Q) is normally distributed with estimated mean, $\mu_Q = 100,000$ units, standard deviation, $\sigma_Q = 10,000$ units, and relevant range 80,000 $\leq Q \leq 120,000$.

2. Sales price is constant at $10 per unit.

3. Unit variable manufacturing cost (v) is normally distributed with estimated mean, $\mu_v = \$5.00$ and standard deviation, $\sigma_v = \$0.20$.

4. Volume (Q) and unit variable manufacturing cost (v) are statistically independent.

5. Managed manufacturing cost (Cm mfg) has the following linear relationship with volume (Q):

$$Cm \ mfg = \$20,000 + \frac{1}{2}(Q - 100,000),$$

within a relevant range: 80,000 $\leq Q \leq 120,000$.

6. Managed administrative cost (Cm ad) has the following quadratic relationship with volume (Q):

$$Cm \ ad = -\$40,000 + 0.25 \ Q + 0.64 \ (10^{-5} \ Q^2)$$

within a relevant range: 80,000 $\leq Q \leq 120,000$.

7. All other costs are constant: managed marketing ($10,000), committed manufacturing ($180,000), committed marketing ($40,000), committed administrative ($60,000), and variable marketing ($0.50 per unit).

[16] Additional information concerning how many iterations are appropriate in this type of problem is available in:

R. W. Conway, "Some Tactical Problems in Digital Simulation," *Management Science,* October 1963, p. 49.

Daniel Teichroew, "A History of Distribution Sampling Prior to the Era of the Computer and its Relevance to Simulation," *Journal of the American Statistical Association,* March 1965, pp. 27-49.

Exhibit 8

Profit Budget for Year Ending June 197X

	Expected Value	95% Probability Interval*	
Sales	$1,002,146	$807,746 −	$1,195,900
Variable costs			
Manufacturing	500,452	406,370 −	600,546
Marketing	50,123	40,387 −	59,795
Marginal contribution	$ 451,571	366,022 −	548,412
Managed fixed costs			
Manufacturing	20,111	10,387 −	29,795
Marketing	10,000**	−	
Administrative	49,937	20,825 −	70,049
Short-run margin	$ 371,523	314,057 −	433,914
Committed fixed costs			
Manufacturing	180,000**	−	
Marketing	40,000**	−	
Administrative	60,000**	−	
Net income before tax	$ 91,523	34,057 −	153,914
Tax − 50%	45,762	15,682 −	75,870
Net income after tax	$ 45,761	15,682 −	75,870

Summary and Conclusions

This paper presents three methods for the construction of probabilistic profit and loss statements: the three-level, the probability-tree and the continuous distribution approaches.

The paper begins with a typical profit and loss statement which displays most likely values. Valuable information, however, is added to budgeted profit and loss statements if every item in those statements displays a mean and a probability interval. The mean is an expected value — what the value of the item would be on the average if we are afforded a large number of trials. The probability interval, on the other hand, tells us that a stated percentage of the distribution of a budget item falls within a given range. Thus the probability interval serves as a measure of variability for the budget item. Other indices of variability suggested are, of course, the standard deviation and the coefficient of variation.

In models with continuous distributions, it is recommended that Monte Carlo simulation be used where the probability distributions in question are difficult to handle analytically. One thousand iterations usually yield an accurate approximation of the desired distributions.

* Determined by dropping the upper and lower $2\frac{1}{2}$ per cent of the 1000 iterations.

** Costs which are constant do not have a probability interval since they are considered "certain".

18

An Application of Curvilinear Break-even Analysis

HORACE R. GIVENS*

Curvilinear break-even analysis is made more meaningful to the student if the analytical and mathematical procedures used can be related to a simulated real world situation. To do this it is necessary to ascertain the cost and revenue data of a non-linear character, and then to derive cost and revenue equations that will form the basis of the mathematical analysis. Such an analysis was presented by Professor Travis P. Goggans in his article "Break-even Analysis with Curvilinear Functions" in the October 1965 *Accounting Review.*

The purpose of this paper is to illustrate the derivation of such equations and their subsequent use. To do this we will assume the following cost and revenue observations:

Unit Volume	Total Revenue	Total Cost
5	$ 6	$ 5
10	12	7
15	17	10
20	21	14
5	8	7
10	14	9
15	19	12
20	23	16

A useful first step in determining the cost and revenue equations is to plot the data on a scattergraph. This has been done in Illustration I for the cost data. Through examination of this scattergraph we may estimate the shape of the best line to fit this data. In order to obtain an equation for such a line we are required to use a statistical technique such as the least squares method. In Illustration I the data closely approximate a parabolic curve. Obviously, the data in this example have been highly stylized in order that the procedure not be obscured by unnecessary complexity in the computations. (More irregular data would be more difficult to fit, but similar procedures could be used.)

* From *The Accounting Review* (January 1966), pp. 141-43. Reprinted by permission of the American Accounting Association.

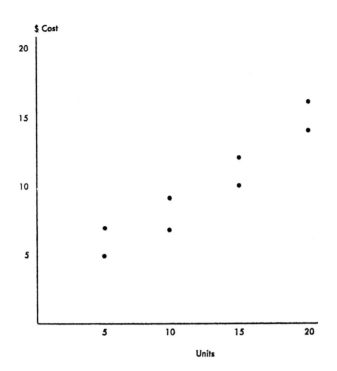

Illustration I   Scattergraph

Assuming a parabolic case we would use the parabolic normal equations:

$$a\,(N) \;+\; b\,(Sx) \;+\; c\,(Sx^2) \;=\; S\,(y)$$
$$a\,(Sx) \;+\; b\,(Sx^2) \;+\; c\,(Sx^3) \;=\; S\,(xy)$$
$$a\,(Sx^2) \;+\; b\,(Sx^3) \;+\; c\,(Sx^4) \;=\; S\,(x^2y)$$

in which, for our example:

$x=$Any volume observation

$y=$Any dollar observation (cost or revenue)

$Sx=$Sum of the volume observations

$Sy=$Sum of the dollar observations

$N=$Number of joint cost or revenue and volume observations

Solving these three equations will result in the determination of one equation in three unknowns of the general form

$$y \;=\; a \;+\; bx \;+\; cx^2$$

that is the best-fitting equation for the data used. Inserting our cost and volume observations in these normal equations and solving for the single equation, we obtain the following cost equation:

$$y = 5 + .1x + .02x^2$$

A similar procedure may be used to determine the revenue equation. In this example, plotting the revenue data on a scattergraph reveals that it too is of parabolic character. Using the parabolic normal equations once again, we can ascertain the best-fitting equation:

$$y = 1.5x - .02x^2$$

(As may be expected the coefficient of the constant (a) is zero in the revenue equation due to the fact that the revenue line must intersect the ordinate at the origin, the equation having no value for $x=0$.)

Using this revenue equation in conjunction with the cost equation determined earlier, it is possible for us to compute the break-even points by setting the two equations equal and solving for the required level of volume. Thus:

$$1.5x - .02x^2 = 5 + .1x + .02x^2$$

Then,

$$0 = 5 - 1.4x + .04x^2$$

Solving this quadratic yields:

$$x = 4.037 \quad \text{and} \quad 30.963$$

The break-even levels of operation would be at these points.

The third stage involves the determination of the point of maximum profit. Economic theory tells us that this point will be reached when the marginal revenue is equal to the marginal cost. Since our cost and revenue functions are curved, the marginal cost and marginal revenue change constantly as volume changes. Therefore, within the profit area there will be a period of increasing profit as volume increases. In this area, the marginal revenue exceeds the marginal cost, and the slope of the cost line will be less than the slope of the revenue line. (See Illustration II.) At higher volume levels profits will decrease as volume increases. In this area the marginal cost exceeds the marginal revenue, and the slope of the revenue line is less than the slope of the cost line. Clearly, there must be some point at which the slopes of the revenue and cost lines are equal, and this must be the point of maximum profit. To determine this point it is necessary that we take the first derivative of each of the functions, set them equal, and solve for the required volume. The derivative of the revenue equation is:

$$1.5 - .04x$$

The derivative of the cost equation is:

$$.1 + .04x$$

Then,

$$1.5 - .04x = .1 + .04x$$

Solving for x we find the required volume level to be 17.5 units. We may test this result by evaluating the basic cost and revenue equa-

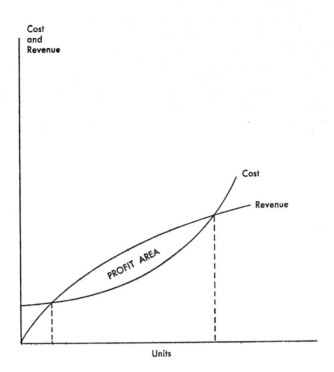

Illustration II   Curved Cost and Revenue Functions

tions for this volume, a higher volume and a lower volume. By our reasoning, both higher and lower volumes must yield lower profits if our answer is correct. The following will be found by performing this evaluation:

Volume	*Profit*
17.0	$7.24
17.5	7.25
18.0	7.24

We may assume our answer to be correct.

Concluding Note

A benefit often obtained by the writer in presenting such an example to students is that those whose mathematical background is weak often gain a greater insight into the concept of the derivative and its applications to real world situations through the connection drawn between the derivative and the marginal revenue and marginal cost concepts.

Caution should be exercised, however, in discussing the results of any mathematical analysis involving cost and revenue data. The complexity of the mathematical process often tends to imply a greater precision than actually exists. No accounting (or mathematical) results can be better than the raw data used. If that data has been determined wholly or in part by subjective judgments as may be the case with cost and revenue information, and further, if some form of averaging has been done, as in the use of normal equations, the results are by no means invalidated. Nevertheless, the possible qualifications must be kept in mind.

19

Profit Centers, Transfer Prices and Mysticism

M. C. WELLS*

Two recent articles[1] attack the myth that profit centers and transfer prices can help in inducing managers of semi-autonomous divisions of companies to work in the best interests of the firm as a whole, and in controlling what they do. Both discard fictitious transfer prices and propose instead that divisions be charged the marginal or incremental costs of a contemplated action. They also suggest that a system of budgets should be used to control the actions of managers, and that managers are unlikely to be induced to work towards organizational objectives by any other means.

It is not suggested that profit centers and transfer prices are of no use where divisions are autonomous and trade freely in the market place. In that case, where a company *KNOWN TRASFER PRICE* can be logically broken down by type of business instead of functional activity (manufacturing, marketing, and so forth), a profit-center system is appropriate. And, when appropriate it has [amongst others] the following advantages:

> The manager is motivated to maximize the return on his investment, and thus contribute to the profit goals of the company. (In other words, his goals are consistent with those of the company.)

> A profit-center manager can be evaluated on the basis of his profit performance.[2]

We will contend that, while incremental costs may be proper data to be used when allocating company resources, there is *no* situation, in the circumstances described, in which *any* form of transfer price is useful or meaningful. This view is reinforced by the conclusion that if profit centers are to be eliminated as proposed by Goetz, or amended as pro-

* From *Abacus*, Vol. 4, No. 2 (December 1968), pp. 174-81. Reprinted by permission of the Editor.

1 Bruce D. Henderson and John Dearden, "New System for Divisional Control," *Harvard Business Review* (September-October 1966), p. 144; and Billy Goetz, "Relevant Transfer Prices," *The Accounting Review* (July 1967), p. 435.
2 John Dearden, "Computers: No Impact on Divisional Control," *Harvard Business Review* (January-February 1967), p. 100.

posed by Henderson and Dearden,[3] then *all* forms of transfer prices must be dealt with in the same way.

TRANSFER PRICES

Transfer prices have been described as: "the net value per unit that records the transaction for the purposes of operating statements,"[4] the "pricing [of] the goods and services that are exchanged between . . . divisions within the firm,"[5] "the intra-company charges at which goods or services are 'sold' by one organizational unit to another in the same company" (Goetz). There are differences of terminology in these descriptions — the value of a transaction, the price of an exchange, and the charge for a sale. And subtle differences in the terms used can easily lead to confusion. But there is a central idea common to these descriptions. It is the representation in monetary terms of a movement of goods from, or the rendering of a service by, one division or department to another within the same company. The monetary amounts proposed vary from cost or cost-plus through market or negotiated prices to marginal or incremental costs. Yet the proposals are all in respect of a change within the company.

By means of a "reasonably believable specific case," Goetz illustrates his contention that "relevancy and goal congruence demand that incremental costs be used as transfer prices." The incremental costs of a proposed activity are found by "budgeting the present mix, budgeting the contemplated mix, and subtracting the total of the second budget from the total of the first." The example involves four divisions, *A, B, C* and *D. D* hires a computer from a manufacturer for $4,000 per week, plus $50 per hour for each hour in excess of 40 per week. Divisions *A, B* and *C* have the following jobs done on the computer: *A*, 15 jobs of one hour each; *B*, one job of 15 hours; and *C*, 2 jobs of six hours each. A total of 42 hours' usage at a cost to the company of $4,100.

Assuming that all these jobs are at present being done on the computer, the transfer price for each division is the saving in cost from discontinuing any one job or package of jobs. Accordingly "Division *D* should charge Division *A* $50 for each of Division *A's* 15 jobs, or $100 for any package of two or more (or even all 15) of these jobs . . . Division *B* $100 for its one 15-hour job, and Division *C* $100 for each of its two jobs, or for a package of the two." In each case the proposed

---

[3] Henderson and Dearden propose that the divisional contribution be the mainstay of the control system. They reject the conventional concept of profit when they dismiss return on investment as a valid control device. The difference of approach is that Henderson and Dearden's "contribution" requires the assumption of revenue for each division, whereas it is here suggested that nothing is achieved by pricing inter-divisional transfers.

[4] J. Dean, "Decentralization and Intracompany Pricing," *Harvard Business Review* (July-August 1955), p. 66.

[5] J. Hirshleifer, "On the Economics of Transfer Pricing," *Journal of Business* (July 1956), p. 172.

charge is the reduction in the weekly hire of the computer which would result from discontinuing the job or jobs concerned.[6]

Marginal Cost Variations

	Div. A Hrs.	Div. B Hrs.	Div. C Hrs.	Total Usage Hrs.	Total Cost $	Difference Between Present and Contemplated Mix $
Present usage:	15	15	12	42	4100	—
Contemplated usage:	14	15	12	41	4050	50
	13	15	12	40	4000	100
	12	15	12	39	4000	100
	15	0	12	37	4000	100
	15	15	6	36	4000	100
	15	15	0	30	4000	100

On the further assumption that identical services are available outside the company for $120 per hour, it is also shown that transfer prices derived from market prices or traditional cost accounting procedures may encourage managers "to make decisions inimical to the welfare of the company."[7]

This example leads one to conclude that, in the circumstances described, anticipated incremental costs may be useful and valid data when deciding whether to have a job done outside the company or on the company's own computer. They cannot, however, be described as "the unique correct transfer price here, and everywhere in intra-company transfers." In this case, the assumptions are unusually restrictive — no allowance is made for progressive changes and, as Goetz points out in a different context, the transfer price to one division may be changed by the unilateral decision of another division. That is, the proposed transfer price to Division A is $50 per one-hour job; but if two jobs are discontinued, the incremental saving from subsequently discontinuing a third job is zero. Does the transfer price to Division A then become zero? Assuming no further jobs are available, will it remain zero? Is the manager acting in the best interests of the firm if he discontinues two jobs so that he can obtain the other 13 for nothing? Similarly, when one

[6] The transfer prices are shown in the last column of the table.
[7] See, for example, p. 437. The charge to Division C, at market prices will be $1,440 for 12 hours' usage. If Division C's two jobs are worth $650 and $300 respectively to the firm, it will pay Division C to discontinue both. In that event, the company will discontinue jobs worth $950, and will save only $100 in computer hire cost (see footnote 6). Similar argument is used in respect of traditional cost accounting methods. The argument is not disputed.

division withdraws 2 hours of usage, does the transfer price to the other divisions also fall progressively to zero? Can it be $100 for Division B in one period, $50 the next, and perhaps zero the next, depending on the actions of Divisions A or C? These questions are not answered by Goetz, but a positive answer is implied by his example.

Increasing use of services is also dealt with. It is assumed that the computer is acquired when the weekly load has accumulated to 30 hours' usage. The weekly hire cost is then $4,000, or $133.3 per hour. This is presumably the transfer price for that first package of jobs. A further 10 hours of usage can now be added at no incremental cost, and accordingly, no charge to the other divisions, until 40 hours' usage per week is reached. From then until 168 hours' usage per week is reached, the incremental cost is $50 per hour. If the value of the jobs warrants it, a second computer will then be acquired at an incremental cost of $2,000,[8] and this cost will be shared by the package of jobs put on it at that time. Now, depending upon when it happens to be discovered, the transfer price for a one-hour job may be either $133 per hour, $0, $50, or some other amount as a part of the package of jobs which incurs the incremental cost of $2,000. If this is the case, the transfer price is in no way related to the benefit to the firm of having the job done, nor does it assist in allocating company resources. It is simply a function of the order in which jobs are discovered.

There are two further questions which may be raised: Which divisions should have access to company resources, and why is it necessary to charge divisions for the use of those resources?

Divisional Allocations. The proposed charges are inequitable as between divisions. For a packaged deal, Division C is charged $100 for 12 hours' usage while Divisions A and B are charged the same amount for 15 hours' usage. On an individual job basis Division A is charged at the rate of $50 per hour while Divisions B and C are charged $6.6 (15 hours for $100) and $16.6 (6 hours for $100) respectively. In the absence of any special features, such charges are unlikely to lead to harmony between divisional managers. Yet if the company is to make the best use of its resources, then they should be allocated in order, according to the extent that the anticipated increment to costs of using the resources are exceeded by the anticipated benefits. This is the same problem as that encountered in investment decisions generally. Its solution requires the determination of a "shadow price," the maximum amount a firm might be expected to pay for a resource in any given circumstance. It represents the "economic value per unit of scarce resource" — the extent to which expected incremental benefits exceed expected incremental costs for the firm as a whole.[9]

---

[8] $4,000 weekly hire for the new computer minus $2,000 saved by transferring 40 hours of overtime from the first to the second computer.

[9] D. W. Miller and M. K. Starr, *Executive Decisions and Operations Research* (Prentice-Hall, Englewood Cliffs, 1960), p. 404. See also W. Beranek, *Analysis for Financial Decisions,* (Irwin, Homewood, 1963), pp. 91-92. I am grateful to Mr. G. McNally of the University of Canterbury, New Zealand, for bringing this point to my attention. He does not necessarily agree with any other views expressed.

Both Hirshleifer[10] and Henderson and Dearden (p. 149) have pointed out that sub-optimal decisions may result if the likely effects of a contemplated action are not assessed for the firm as a whole. And, even if the alternative with the highest shadow price is not adopted because of some special or non-quantifiable factors, the shadow price is still relevant to the decision as an indication of the opportunity cost to the firm of the course of action adopted. But it must be stressed, this does not require that divisions be subsequently charged for the use of those resources. Neither has it anything to do with managerial evaluation. The actions of managers are controlled and evaluated *after* the resources have been allocated. They relate to the use actually made of those resources, and the costs incurred in employing them. In both cases, an anticipated result of action is compared with an actual result. In neither case is this facilitated by transfer prices.

Divisional Evaluation. Goetz states that his proposals imply that financial responsibilities centers, or profit centers, "have no validity, are worse than useless, wherever one organizational subdivision does work for another; that divisional managers cannot be evaluated in terms of 'profits' made by their division." Similarly, Henderson and Dearden state: "It is our conviction that R.O.I. for divisional performance evaluation can be so misleading that it is destructive" (p. 144). If these suggestions are correct, if profit centers are not helpful for these purposes, then what relevance have transfer prices of any sort? If it is not intended to calculate a "profit," why is there a need to charge divisional managers at all for the use of company resources?

The example referred to above, which is given under the heading "Decisions to Make, Buy, Change, or Discontinue," demonstrates that incremental costs are appropriate here. But they have nothing to do with transfer prices. The decisions referred to all involve parties that are *external* to the firm and, under the proposed system, no transfer price is charged unless there is a transaction with an outside party which gives rise to an incremental cost. Yet according to the descriptions of transfer prices given earlier, they are only in respect of an *internal* movement of goods and services. They are a necessary requirement of profit centers. The whole purpose of transfer pricing is to enable a divisional "profit" to be determined. If profit centers are dismissed as having "no validity," and as being "worse than useless," then surely transfer prices must be dismissed in like terms!

It is widely recognized that the evaluation of divisional managers requires a clear definition of their individual responsibilities.[11] Managers can only be held responsible for the use of those factors over which they

10 J. Hirshleifer, "Economics of the Divisionalized Firm," *Journal of Business* (April 1957), pp. 96-108. The examples demonstrate the dangers of unilateral decisions by divisional managers where the firm manufactures or markets competing rather than complementary products.

11 See, for example, C. T. Horngren, *Cost Accounting, A Managerial Emphasis* (Prentice-Hall, Englewood Cliffs, 1967), p. 266. Horngren quotes from John A. Higgins, "Responsibility Accounting," *The Arthur Andersen Chronicle* (April 1952).

exercise control. This requires that it be possible to trace each item of cost to the manager responsible for incurring it. Transfer prices do not satisfy this test. They are necessarily imposed (except under Dean's proposals where they would be negotiated); and the internal profit measures which their use makes possible suffer from the well-known problems of arbitrary allocations of overhead, or the difficulties of defining an investment base.

Financial responsibility centers are not the same as profit centers. The former imply responsibility for certain identifiable items of a financial nature. The latter are defined by Dean in terms of the responsibility of divisional managers for economic performance, taking the "basic goal" as profits.[12] This definition incorporates two distinct attributes from which may be derived two different, but operationally meaningful, concepts. These are responsibility centers, where a given level of management can be held responsible for certain operations, costs, etc.; and profit centers where, in addition to these, the "basic goal is profits." But divisional profits can only be measured if the division is an autonomous economic entity and it does not contribute goods or services to other divisions of the company, nor draw goods, services, capital or knowledge from them. If these conditions are not satisfied, some allocation of either or both costs and revenues will have to be made before the "profit" can be determined. This conflicts with the concept of traceability. It prevents the evaluation of the manager's discharge of his responsibilities.

"PROPERLY CONCEIVED SYSTEM OF BUDGETARY CONTROL"

For the purposes of controlling the use of a firm's resources, and of evaluating the performance of divisional managers, it has been suggested that a system of budgetary control based upon responsibility centers will provide the necessary data. It can also be used, it is said, to induce managers to work towards the achievement of company goals (Goetz). Henderson and Dearden have developed a three-tier system for these purposes, comprising a contribution budget, a fixed- and managed-cost budget, and a capital budget. This system provides a satisfactory method of guiding and controlling divisional managers; and because the budgets are linked, it also provides for an overall assessment of plans and intentions. But in both cases the authors propose the abolition of profit centers while retaining transfer prices. This conflict seems to stem from the view that budgets are necessarily in monetary terms and that, to be included in a division budget, any item must be expressed in monetary terms.[13] This is a conventional view. It is also an unnecessary restraint to impose on a budgetary system.

12 Dean, "Decentralization and Intracompany Pricing," p. 67.
13 Goetz accepts the usefulness of quantitative budgets, and suggests that they provide "a less debatable measure of efficiency than dollar cost, at least when the latter is contaminated by doubtful allocations or transfer prices." That being so, why not dismiss the need for transfer prices entirely?

Usually, a divisional manager will have no control over, nor any interest in, the costs previously incurred in obtaining or producing the goods transferred to his division. His concern is with the costs of further treatment of the goods. The receiving manager should therefore account for the quantity of goods received, and the costs incurred subsequently in his division. The despatching manager will have previously accounted for his costs in a similar manner. Performance may then be judged by comparing processing costs incurred with expected processing costs; the quantities processed with the quantities expected to be processed in a given time; and the general costs of each department with the expected general costs. Processes and departments may be judged to be economical or efficient without recourse to a profit test.

Budgets prepared in this way, incorporating quantities and monetary amounts, each in its proper place, are related directly to the things under the control of divisional managers. They also remove the need for any form of transfer pricing in internal reporting.

EXTERNAL REPORTING

There may be some situations in which divisional transfers seem to be required to be expressed in monetary terms. These are reporting to external parties, and the calculation of income tax liability. In both cases, goods transferred from one division to another are usually valued at "cost or market." This has the appearance of transfer pricing. However, the object is not divisional evaluation, but the determination of the results and position of the firm as a whole.

If the proposals of Goetz and of Henderson and Dearden are adopted, the internal records of the firm will be of little help in the preparation of external reports, and they may be confusing. But if quantitative budgets and traceable costs are used, the same inputs will serve both internal and external reporting requirements. Only a two-way classification of costs is required — as to responsibility centers and as to products.

If some of the recent suggestions on external reporting were to be adopted, the need to express transfers in monetary terms would disappear entirely.[14] If replacement prices or current exit prices were used to value inventories, then only quantities of inventories at each stage of production would need to be recorded. The monetary amount of inventories on hand would be obtained by multiplying those quantities by the relevant prices. Also, the costs of constructing or acquiring fixed assets would be irrelevant for these purposes. The monetary amount for external reporting would be the asset's current price.

14 See, for example, G. J. Staubus, *A Theory of Accounting for Investors* (University of California Press, Berkeley and Los Angeles, 1961); R. T. Sprouse and M. Moonitz, *A Tentative Set of Broad Accounting Principles for Business Enterprises* (A.I.C.P.A., 1962) ; R. J. Chambers, *Accounting Evaluation and Economic Behavior* (Prentice-Hall, Englewood Cliffs, 1960).

CONCLUSION

A good deal of accounting, as currently practised, has a mystical quality. Depreciation methods, inventory valuations, arbitrary distinctions between capital and revenue, overhead allocations, and joint product costing are examples of accounting procedures that fall into this category. So also do profit centers and transfer prices. Revenue which is not revenue, transfer prices which are not prices, and profit centers which do not earn a profit, are mystical inventions. They are fictions which cannot serve as a basis for action.

It is here contended that the notion of transfer prices is a corollary of the notion of profit centers. If, as has been suggested, the notion of profit centers is unnecessary, the need for any form of transfer price is also eliminated. The usefulness of incremental costs and revenues for certain decisions is not denied. In the example quoted, decisions of the "make, buy, or discontinue" variety were considered. For investment decisions generally, incremental costs, or shadow prices, are relevant. But such choices do not require the use of transfer prices. Three descriptions of these were quoted. They all referred to an internal exchange of goods and services, and not to a transaction which involved parties external to the firm.

We noted that Goetz dismisses the concept of profit centers and responsibility centers, and, with Henderson and Dearden, proposes instead a system of budgetary control. We distinguished profit centers from responsibility centers and concluded that the proposed system of budgetary control requires only the latter. It does not follow, as Henderson and Dearden suggest, that goods being transferred from one responsibility center to another need be charged at their marginal cost. Only the quantity of goods transferred need be recorded. Divisional and other managers are "charged" only with costs which are incurred on their initiative. Costs can then be compared with budgeted figures for the purposes of evaluating managers and inducing them to work towards the general goals of the firm.

The conventional needs for external reporting were considered. Costs must be traced for external reporting to products, as they are for internal reporting to responsibility centers. But we noted that the adoption of recent proposals for external reporting might remove the need for product costing and thus, also, the need for the pricing of transfers. But the arguments for and against these proposals are beyond the scope of this paper.

IV
Performance Evaluation

The use of management accounting techniques in performance
appraisal has drawn considerable attention in the last decade or
more from behavioral scientists and what may be called behavioral
accountants. The articles in Section I by Buckley and McKenna, and
Caplan, give a general indication of the thrust of debate. This section
takes a closer look at some evaluation techniques employed by
accountants (profit budgets; responsibility accounting, which is a
form of budgets; return-on-investment concepts; and human resource
accounting) and the criticisms which have been raised about each.
Not surprisingly, most authors are advising us to use each accounting
technique with care. Stronger pieces of advice than this about
behavioral effects of accounting techniques are seldom seen. Humans are
complex, and this fact presents an ambiguous situation to accountants
and other information providers. Behavioral effects do not just go
away when one immerses oneself in complex standard cost arithmetic.
Yet, some management accounting material devotes a disproportionate
amount of space to arithmetic.

"What Kind of Management Control Do You Need?" provides
several case illustrations of a prime theme of performance appraisal:
"Profit should be used as a measure of financial responsibility
only when it is possible to calculate it in such a way that a
manager's "profit" increases as the result of actions for which he is
responsible and which he has taken in the best interests of the
company." The article is especially strong in showing relationships
between several concepts of financial responsibility (such as variations
of return on investment) and special needs of different organizations.

"Responsibility Accounting" is an edited version of a paper

published over twenty years ago. It shows how modifications in accounting systems designed for external reporting, and some other evaluations, can be made to obtain information for performance appraisal. The piece is solely a description of how the original concept would function. The material is included here to explain in detail how the technique operates, and how it is connected to other management accounting procedures.

"Control and Freedom in a Decentralized Company" gives a broader perspective to a form of responsibility accounting. The article is as strong in its case illustrations as in its review of relationships between accounting and other functions of a business. Undesirable behavioral consequences are bound to arise if an accounting technique designed for one structure is superimposed on a quite different organizational structure. Both Villers and Vancil make this point forcefully.

"Dysfunctional Consequences of Performance Measurements" examines research studies pertaining to the use of single, multiple and composite measures of performance and concludes that all three "quantitative performance measurements . . . are seen to have undesirable consequences for over-all organizational performance." Thus, no matter whether responsibility accounting, flexible budgets, return on investment analysis and so forth are used alone, or two or three are employed, or some composite of accounting and non-accounting measures are used, unwanted side effects can occur.

"Budgeting and Employee Behavior: A Rejoinder to a 'Reply'" was reprinted in the first edition of this book and is the third article in a series which appeared in the *Journal of Business* in October 1962 and April 1964. Some of the comments in this third piece are difficult to understand when isolated from the previous articles. Yet it is still possible to obtain a reasonable grasp of the complexity of one behavioral issue: possible effects on morale from allowing employee participation in the setting of budgets which may later be used to evaluate their performance.

"The Asset Value of the Human Organization" and "Where 'Human Resources Accounting' Stands Today" review many approaches to the technique of accounting for human assets. The former article sets out several conceptual methods of measuring human assets as well as the evolution of the subject, whereas the latter summarizes some practical applications. Like many techniques included in textbooks, human asset accounting has not been adopted widely in practice. Practitioners probably have isolated few benefits to the technique at this stage in its development and see many costs of implementation. Several academics and a few practitioners are currently investigating facets of the concept and interesting developments should occur in the future. Once again, the technique must be tailored to the organization; and, many companies likely have little present need for human resources accounting.

20

What Kind of Management
Control Do You Need?

RICHARD F. VANCIL*

Before designing measures of the financial
responsibility of managers, consider the strategy
and structure of the company. A good method
of measuring a manager's financial contribution
to a company must meet two criteria. It
must seem fair to the manager, and it must
reward him for working for the benefit of the
whole company, not just his department or
division. Although simple in theory, these
criteria become difficult to meet in practice.
The characteristics of the business may lead
managers to work at cross-purposes; moreover,
the strategy of a business should have a profound
effect on the kinds of decisions made. In this
article the requirements of designing effective
management control systems are examined
in both simple and complex organizations.
Pointing to realities with which businessmen
are familiar, the author seeks to guide executives
in weighing the advantages and disadvantages
of functional forms of organization, product
division forms, and the so-called matrix concept
of organization. He points out that profit
centers are by no means a universal answer,
however appealing they may be in principle
to business leaders.

TYPES OF FINANCIAL RESPONSIBILITY

The principal types of financial responsibility can be classified as follows:

Standard cost centers are exemplified by a production department
in a factory. The standard quantities of direct labor and materials

* From *Harvard Business Review* (March-April 1973), pp. 75-86. © 1973 by the
President and Fellows of Harvard College; all rights reserved.

239

required for each unit of output are specified. The foreman's objective is to minimize the variance between actual costs and standard costs. He also is usually responsible for a flexible overhead expense budget, and his objective, again, is to minimize the variance between budgeted and actual costs.

Revenue centers are best illustrated by a sales department where the manager does not have authority to lower prices in order to increase volume. The resources at his disposal are reflected in his expense budget. The sales manager's objective is to spend no more than the budgeted amounts and to produce the maximum amount of sales revenue.

Discretionary expense centers include most administrative departments. There is no practical way to establish the relationship between inputs and outputs. Management can only use its best judgment to set the budget, and the department manager's objective is to spend the budgeted amount to produce the best (though still unmeasurable) quality of service that he possibly can.

Profit centers, the focus of this article, are units, such as a product division, where the manager is responsible for the best combination of costs and revenues. His objective is to maximize the bottom line, the profit that results from his decisions. A great many variations on this theme can be achieved by defining "profit" as including only those elements of cost and revenue for which the manager is responsible. Thus a sales manager who is allowed to set prices may be responsible for gross profit (actual revenue less standard direct manufacturing costs). Profit for a product-line marketing manager, on the other hand, might reflect deductions for budgeted factory overhead and actual sales promotion expenses.

Investment centers are units where the manager is responsible also for the magnitude of assets employed. He makes trade-offs between current profits and investments to increase future profits. Stating the manager's objective as maximizing his return on investment or his residual income (profit after a charge for the use of capital) helps him to appraise the desirability of new investments.

PROFIT CENTERS

Profit centers are a major tool for management control in large industrial corporations. They possess important advantages:

1. Profitability is a simple way to analyze and monitor the effectiveness of a segment of a complex business. For example, a product division competes in the marketplace against several other companies in its industry, and also competes among other divisions in its company for an allocation of corporate resources for its future growth. Relative profitability in both types of competition is a useful decision criterion for top management.

2. Profit responsibility is a powerful motivator of men. Managers

understand what profit is all about, and aggressive managers welcome the opportunity to have their abilities measured by the only real entrepreneurial yardstick.

Simple and powerful, profit centers sound like a panacea, the answer to a top manager's prayer. No wonder the concept has been so widely adopted. However, as with many a miracle drug, all too often the side effects of the medicine may be worse than the illness it was intended to cure.

There is an excellent body of literature on the problems that arise in implementing the profit center concept.[1] The question I shall discuss is a more basic one: *When* should profit centers be used? More precisely, what executives below the president of a corporation (who clearly is responsible for profits) should be held responsible for the profits from segments of the business?

Parts of this discussion will come as no surprise to corporate presidents or to their controllers. I shall stress the relevance of corporate strategy and organization structure to profit center systems — an approach that may seem obvious to such executives. But I cannot find a discussion of these considerations in the literature, and thus I am led to believe that a concise statement of the conventional wisdom may be worthwhile.

CHOICE OF FINANCIAL GOALS

The cornerstone of every management control system is the concept of responsibility accounting. The basic idea is simple: each manager in a company has responsibility for a part of the total activity. The accounting system should be designed so that it yields a measurement of the financial effects of the activities that a manager is responsible for. This measurement can be stated in the form of a financial objective for each manager. Specifying that objective helps in delegating authority; a manager knows that the "right" decision is the course of action that moves him down the path toward his financial objective.

But this system does not go far enough. No single measurement, no matter how carefully constructed, can accurately reflect how well a manager had done his job. Part of the failure is simply due to the fact that corporations — and their managers — have multiple objectives. For instance, there is the matter of corporate social responsibility. Good performance toward that goal, even if measurable, cannot be added to the profit equation. Another major inadequacy of a single financial measurement is that it reflects performance during a particular time period, ignoring the effects that current actions may have on future performance. Every manager must make trade-offs between conflicting short-term and long-term needs; examples range all the way from the

---

1 See, in particular, John Dearden, "Appraising Profit Center Managers," HBR May-June 1968, p. 80; "Bonus Formula for Division Heads" (with William S. Edgerly), HBR September-October 1965, p. 83; "The Case Against ROI Control," HBR May-June 1969, p. 124; "Limits on Decentralized Profit Responsibility," HBR July-August 1962, p. 81; and "Mirage of Profit Decentralization," HBR November-December 1962, p. 140.

shop foreman who defers preventive maintenance in order to increase this month's output, but at the expense of a major breakdown next month, to the division manager who cuts his R&D budget in order to improve the year's profits but loses or delays the opportunity to introduce a profitable new product three years from now.

Despite these flaws, oversimplified financial measurements are almost universally used. The reason is not their value in evaluating a manager's performance — the faults noted are too obvious and important to ignore — but their effect on future performance. Specifying a financial objective can help a manager to think realistically about the tough decisions he must make, even if the objective does not always point the way to the right decision.

The selection of the right financial objective for each manager, therefore, can have an important effect on how he does his job. Although the range of *possible* objectives is very great, the financially measurable results of any manager's activities can usually be classified into one of the five categories of responsibility centers described at the beginning of this article. As indicated, financial responsibility is simplest in the case of standard cost centers, most complex in the case of investment centers.

How should management measure the financial results achieved? It is not enough simply to say that a particular product division is a profit center; decisions are also required that specify how the profit is to be calculated, focusing in particular on how transfer prices shall be set and how the costs of services received from other organization units shall be charged against the division. Similarly, while the basic concept of an investment center is simple, it is difficult to decide which assets to include in the investment base and how they shall be valued. Therefore, although there may be only five types of financial responsibility centers, there are many methods of financial measurement that can be used for specific organizations.

Criteria for Selection

Figuring out the best way to define and measure the financial performance for each manager is the corporate controller's most challenging — and analytically demanding — task. Two types of considerations affect each choice. The first is the strategy of the company: its broad objectives, the nature of the industries in which it operates, and the niche it seeks to carve for itself in each industry on the basis of its distinctive competence. The second is the organization structure of the company — the way the total task is divided among the managers to permit delegation of authority and specialization of effort.

The controller must have a thorough knowledge of his company's strategy and organization structure. He draws on this knowledge to apply two criteria for deciding which measure of financial responsibility to use for each organization unit and how it should be calculated:

1. *Fairness* — Each manager must believe that the summary financial measurement used to report on his performance is appropriate.

This means he must see all of the signals he receives about his job as consistent with each other. Moreover, he must believe that the measurement encompasses all the factors he can control and excludes those over which he has no control. And he must be convinced the measurement is calculated in such a way that a "good" decision on his part will be reflected as such by the financial measurement. The "fairness" of a financial measurement is not a fact; it is a perception through the eyes of the manager to whom it applies.

2. *Goal congruence* — The most difficult compromises that must be made in designing a management control system have to do with varying goals.[2] When a manager is assigned a financial objective for his activities and a fair measurement of performance is determined, ideally he should be able to pursue his objective without concern for whether or not his actions are in the best interests of the corporation. But in reality, as we know, that ideal is not easy to attain. The controller, designing a management control system with a corporatewide perspective, must ensure that managers are not working at cross-purposes. He must select objectives and measurements in such a way that a good decision by any manager is also a good decision for the corporation as a whole.

For the controller, applying these two criteria simultaneously means that he must combine the points of view of both the individual manager and the corporation. That becomes progressively more difficult as the complexity of the organization structure and the business increases. In the balance of this article I shall discuss the use of the two criteria, dealing first with relatively simple organization structures and then with more complex ones.

USE IN SIMPLE STRUCTURES

Discussing the design of a management control system for "simple" organizations is not a theoretical or academic exercise. Some small businesses have simple organization structures, and even the largest corporations progressively sub-divide the management tasks to the point where an individual manager is responsible for a single functional activity. Functional units are the organizational building blocks in the most complex corporations.

What varieties of control systems are possible and feasible in simple organizations? When are the criteria of fairness and goal congruence satisfied? How does a company's strategy affect the choice of a system?

Practical Alternatives

The simplified organization chart shown in *Exhibit I* is typical of a

2 For the original statement of this problem, see Robert N. Anthony, *Planning and Control Systems: A Framework for Analysis* (Boston: Division of Research, Harvard Business School, 1965).

great many companies or parts of companies. The structure of the organization is simple in two respects:

1. There are only two levels of line managers in the hierarchy (the "general manager" might be thought of as the president of a small company).

2. The subordinate managers each have responsibility for a functional activity, which implies a rather natural distribution of tasks and authority between them.

Exhibit I

Functionally Organized Business

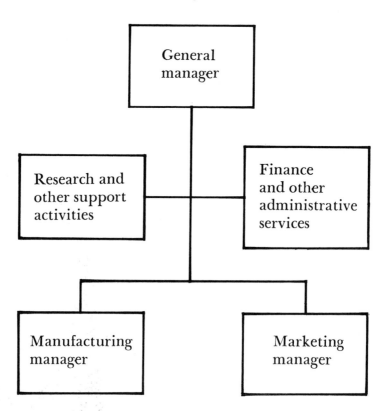

The business also requires some administrative and support activities, but the choice of financial measurements for these organizational units is less complex and will not be discussed here.

Selecting an appropriate financial measurement for this president's performance is not really a problem. He is responsible for the entire business, its profits, and the investment required. The financial responsibility of his two principal subordinates, however, is not so easily determined. The manufacturing manager, responsible for all production operations in the plant, could be charged with the responsibility of running either a standard cost center or a profit center. And the marketing manager, responsible for all sales and promotion activities, could be treated as the head either of a revenue center or of a profit center. With just two functional units, and two alternatives available for each, there are still four alternatives for the design of a management control system for this business:

Alternative	*Manufacturing*	*Marketing*
1.	Standard cost center	Revenue center
2.	Standard cost center	Profit center
3.	Profit center	Revenue center
4.	Profit center	Profit center

These four alternatives are not simply theoretical possibilities; each may be appropriate under different circumstances. The critical circumstances concern the nature of the key decisions to be made and the way decision-making authority is delegated in the organization.

As for the decisions, most of them involve choices in allocating resources. There are questions of *purpose* (e.g., whether incremental marketing expenditures should be used for advertising or for hiring more salesmen) and of *timing* (e.g., when a piece of production equipment should be replaced). In an ideal world, an all-wise and all-knowing president could make every decision, and his decision would always be "right" in the sense that it is the best course of action for the company at the time even though it may turn out to be wrong as future events unfold. The problem is that no president can make all the decisions and that, as he delegates power to subordinates, he runs the risk they will make decisions that are different from those he would make.

Effective decision making in a functionally organized business is hampered by the fact that no subordinate has the same broad perspective of the business that the president or general manager has. Many decisions, and almost all the important ones, affect more than one function in the business. They are seen differently by managers according to the functions they manage. One possible response to this problem is not to delegate authority for important decisions below the level of general manager. Another approach is to broaden the perspective of the functional manager by delegating such authority to him and then holding him responsible for the profitability of his decisions.

The implications of the second approach can best be seen by examining a series of examples. I shall describe a company situation for each of the four design alternatives mentioned.

1. No profit centers: Company A manufacturers and distributes fertilizer. It buys chemicals, minerals, and other components from large suppliers and mixes them in various combinations to produce a limited variety of standard fertilizers with specified chemical properties. These are sold to farmers in bulk. Because the quality is specified and subject to verification by chemical analysis, all producers sell at the same price and offer identical volume discounts. Transportation costs are a major factor, and Company A thus enjoys a relative advantage in its local market. Its salesmen call on purchasing agents for large corporate farms and on distributors that sell to smaller farmers. Most orders are placed well in advance of the growing season, so the mixing plant is busy several months of the year, but there is still a large seasonal peak in both marketing and manufacturing.

Prices tend to fluctuate with the cost of the primary chemical components. The results is that an efficient fertilizer producer tends to earn about the same profit, as a percentage of the sales dollar, on each of the products in his line.

In this company the mission of the marketing manager is to sell as much fertilizer as he can. He has no control over product design or pricing, and promotional activities other than direct selling efforts are ineffective. His primary concern is with the effective use of his salesmen's time and with the development and maintenance of good customer relations. His stated objective is to produce as much revenue as he can with the number of salesmen currently authorized. In technical terms he is a "revenue center." He is also responsible for the expense budget for his activities.

The mission of the manufacturing manager, on the other hand, is to produce fertilizer in the required quantities as efficiently as possible. The work force is only semiskilled, and his primary concern is to ensure that they are properly trained and well supervised and that material wastage is held to a minimum. He is a "standard cost center," financially responsible for meeting the standard direct cost of each unit produced and for controlling overhead expenses against a variable budget reflecting the volume of throughput.

The president of Company A is the only man financially responsible for the profit of the company. There are a limited number of key, cross-functional decisions to be made, and he makes them. One concerns the size of the sales force; another concerns the acquisition of equipment to increase the capacity or reduce the labor costs in the mixing plant. Both of these are what are called "capacity decisions." While the evaluation of alternatives for either decision is not easy, it can be handled as well or better by the president than by either of his two subordinates.

2. Marketing profit centers: Company B produces a line of branded consumer toiletries. The products are heavily advertised and made available to consumers in drugstores, supermarkets, and other retail outlets throughout the country. The marketplace is in continual turmoil as competitors jockey for consumer attention through price promotions, premium offers, and "new" formulas and "secret" ingredients announced through both media advertising and point-of-purchase promotion. The company's field sales force is small; salesmen call on distributors and purchasing agents for large retail chains. The product itself is simple to manufacture, but consistently reliable quality is considered important to maintain customer goodwill.

Marketing is where the action is in Company B. The marketing manager is responsible for profitability, which is defined as sales revenue less standard direct manufacturing costs and all marketing costs. The president of the company is very interested in the marketing function and devotes much of his time to it. At the same time, he realizes that there are a myriad of marketing decisions to be made, many of them requiring specialized knowledge of local markets and detailed current information on competitors' actions. Therefore, he needs to delegate considerable authority to the marketing manager.

The manufacturing manager, like his counterpart in Company A, is a standard cost center, responsible for standard direct costs and a variable overhead budget.

3. Production profit centers: Company C produces a line of specialty metal products sold as semifinished components, primarily to manufacturers of high-style lighting fixtures. The company has only a few dozen customers, four of which account for over 50 per cent of the sales volume. The business is price competitive, Company C's equipment is not unique, and other manufacturers are frequently asked to bid against Company C on prospective contracts. Company C is renowned, however, for its technical skills in solving difficult manufacturing problems. Even on relatively routine contracts, the company is sometimes able to charge a slightly higher price because of its consistently high quality and its responsiveness in meeting its customers' "emergency" delivery requirements.

Price quotations on each contract are prepared by an estimator in the plant. The field sales force calls on old customers and prospective new ones, maintaining and developing relationships and soliciting opportunities to bid for their business.

Manufacturing is the name of the game at Company C. The manufacturing manager is responsible for profit, defined as the contribution to overhead after subtracting all direct manufacturing costs. He keeps himself informed of the backlog of orders and personally reviews all bids over a nominal amount, estimating the price to quote in view of his desire for the business and his assessment of the customer's loyalty. He is also responsible for meeting his variable overhead budget.

As for the marketing manager, he is a revenue center, like his counterpart in Company A. He endeavors to use his sales force as effectively as possible to turn up attractive bidding opportunities on which the company can compete successfully.

4. Multiple profit centers: Company D is a partly integrated oil refining and marketing organization. The company's refinery purchases crude oil and refines it into gasoline, kerosene, and other products. The company also operates a regional chain of service stations, advertising its brand of gasoline to consumers. The company's strategy is to be less than self-sufficient in producing enough gasoline to meet its retail requirements. Thus the refinery is usually able to operate at capacity, and gasoline is purchased from other refiners as required.

Both the manufacturing (refinery) manager and the marketing manager are responsible for *part* of the profits earned by Company D. The refinery manager sells his gasoline to the marketing department at the same price charged by other refiners; the profit on the refinery is an important measure of the efficiency of his operations. The marketing manager, much like his counterpart in Company B, is also a profit center; he attempts to find the optimum balance and mix of marketing expenditures that will be most profitable for the company.

In this kind of situation, therefore, the president needs to delegate considerable decision-making power to not one but two subordinates. With respect to each he acts in the way described for companies B and C.

The foregoing examples, simple as they are, show how difficult it is to generalize on the question of whether or not a functional manager should be held responsible for profit. The first, most obvious, statement is that the decision turns on the nature of the business. The tangible differences between businesses and the unique tasks they imply for management must be reflected in the management control system. The challenge for the controller is to synthesize the characteristics of the business and select a financial objective for each manager that (1) motivates him to achieve the company's objectives, and (2) minimizes unnecessary conflict between managers.

However, the characteristics of a business are not the sole determinants of financial responsibility. In fact, they are not the most important ones. This brings us to the next point: the implications of corporate strategy.

Crucial Role of Strategy

As an illustration, let us consider the situation of a franchised automobile dealership called Connelly Autos, Inc. The company sells new and used cars and auto repair services. Connelly's organization structure is simple; under the president there are two marketing managers, one for new cars and one for used cars, and a service department manager.

In this case, and in retail distribution businesses generally, it is easy to see the advantages of holding a sales manager responsible for the profits of his department. Moreover, suppose a customer with a certain amount of money to spend is undecided about a stripped-down new car or a more expensive model that is a year or two old. If Connelly's two sales managers compete for this customer's business, the result is probably that the customer is better served, in the sense that he has more information about the relative advantages of his two major alternatives and can ultimately make a choice that satisfies him better.

Also, the dealership is probably better off as a result of the competition. There are many other new car and used car dealers, so if the company itself offers both choices in a manner that is as competitive as the two departments would be if they were in separate dealerships, it stands a better chance of getting a customer's business no matter which car he chooses to drive.

The difficult problem is designing a management control system for Connelly's service department manager. What is his financial responsibility? How should Connelly measure his performance in financial terms? The service department is not simply another sales department, delivering retail repair services to customers. It is also a "manufacturing" department producing service for the two automobile sales departments; it prepares new cars for delivery and services them during the warranty period, and it repairs and reconditions used cars to be sold at retail.

The real question becomes: What does Connelly want his service department manager to do? Here are several possible answers:

☐ Run the service department as though it were an independent auto repair shop. With this mission, the service department manager would be responsible for profits and should probably sell his services to the new and used car departments at the regular retail price, or perhaps with a slight "dealer" discount.

☐ Employ the capacity of the shop to the fullest, using renovation work on used cars as a way of absorbing slack capacity. With this mission, repair services should probably be sold to the used car manager at standard direct costs. The used car manager would buy cars needing repair work, at wholesale auctions if necessary, thus providing all the volume the service department could handle. The service department would be essentially a standard cost center, and the profit on retail repairs would be de-emphasized.

☐ Run the shop in such a way as to maximize customer goodwill, attempting to build a reputation that will yield regular, repeat customers for new cars. Under these circumstances, it would be very difficult to calculate a financial measurement that would appropriately reflect the performance of the service department manager. He should not be held responsible for profits, nor should he be expected to run close to capacity if he is to be responsive to customer emergencies. The shop should probably be treated as a standard cost center, but without emphasis being placed on financial performance.

Finding an answer: Thus the answer to the question of what the service department manager should do turns on Connelly's strategy for his dealership. The three alternatives outlined really characterize three different strategies. The first envisions a "balanced" dealership, the second has a strong used-car focus, and the third emphasizes new car sales.

Not all automobile dealers pursue the same strategy, nor should they. Local competitive conditions are a major factor in selecting a strategy, and the quality and type of resources available to Connelly are also critical factors in his choice. (Resources include the location of the dealership, the capital available for investment in new and used car inventories, and the competence and aggressiveness of Connelly's three subordinates.) Finally, the strategy Connelly selects will affect his image in the community as a businessman and a citizen, and his personal aspirations concerning the size and reputation of the business also have a bearing on the problem.[3]

There are thousands of automobile dealers in the United States, and they appear to be identical in terms of the characteristics of their business. Managers adopt different strategies, however, in order to differentiate their business from that of their competitors. The controller, designing a management control system, must understand both the nature of the business and the strategy being pursued if he is to create a set of financial measurements that will motivate functional managers to contribute to the achievement of company objectives. This task is not easy even in simple, functional organizations; it is more difficult still in complex organizations.

USE IN COMPLEX STRUCTURES

As a business grows and the magnitude of the management task increases, its organization structure tends to become more complex. Products come to be manufactured in more than one location and sold in more than one market; new models and lines may be added. Such multiplant, multimarket, multiproduct corporations typically have a multitier organization structure consisting of three or more layers of managers. Naturally, the management control system becomes more complex, too.

Part A of *Exhibit II* is an organization chart for a complex, functionally organized business (it may have started as the company shown in *Exhibit I*). As long as the business continues to be functionally organized, much of the discussion in the preceding section about the design of a management control system is applicable.

But an important difference should be noted. In the simple organization shown in *Exhibit I,* top management has very little choice about how to divide the functional tasks among subordinates. In many situations of the type shown in Part A of *Exhibit II,* however, reorganization along the lines shown in Part B of the same exhibit may be feasible and appropriate. In such cases, what pros and cons should be considered in deciding whether to adopt the product division approach? Except in cases where that approach seems a "natural" (for example, a conglomerate that has grown through the acquisition of independent businesses), the answer depends largely on how much management wants to maximize efficiency and on how much it wants to maximize responsiveness to markets. Let us consider this trade-off in some detail.

---

[3] For a more complete discussion of all the factors influencing the formulation of strategy, see Kenneth R. Andrews, *The Concept of Corporate Strategy* (Homewood, Illinois: Dow Jones–Irwin, Inc., 1971).

Turn to Product Divisions?

Product divisions are almost always treated as profit or investment centers. The responsibility of the division manager is usually broad enough so that he can conceive of his division as though it were an independent company. In addition, the scope and substance of his task and the objective he is to strive for may be delineated clearly. In such circumstances, the task of designing a management control system for the functional subordinates of the division manager is precisely the same as that discussed earlier; the division manager is really the general manager shown in *Exhibit I.*

Now, what can functional organizations do that product divisions cannot? Functional organizations have the potential of great efficiency. The efficiency of an activity can frequently be measured in terms of the quantity of inputs required to yield one unit of output. For a great many activities, efficiency increases as the size of the activity grows — at least, up to some point where there are no further "economies of scale" to be realized. The reason that efficiency increases is that large-scale operations permit the utilization of increasingly specialized inputs. For instance, a general-purpose machine tool and a skilled operator may be able to produce 100 parts per hour; but a specially designed piece of equipment might produce 1,000 parts per hour and require no operator at all. Also, specialization of workers can yield economies of scale, as the learning curve of production workers demonstrates.

The arguments, then, in favor of retaining the organization structure shown in Part A of *Exhibit II* might run as follows. While it is technically feasible to equip each plant so that it turns out one of the three products of the company, it would be a great waste to do so. Manufacturing costs would be much lower if each plant specialized in certain aspects of the manufacturing process, doing only a limited number of functions on all three products. Further, the quality of manufacturing supervision and technical services, such as engineering and quality control, is better when those activities are centralized under one manufacturing manager. Scattering such activities across three product divisions would both lower the quality of the personnel that could be afforded and reduce the efficiency of their services. Similar arguments might be made about the efficiency of the marketing organization.

What advantages are unique to product divisions? They hold out the promise of more *effective* management than is the case with functional organizations. (One way of contrasting effectiveness with efficiency is to say that efficiency means doing something right and effectiveness means doing the right something.) The benefits are harder to document or quantify, but the potential for improvement exists both in strategy formulation and in tactical decision making.

In a strategic sense, it is easier for a product division than a functional organization to focus on the needs of its customers, rather than on simply manufacturing or selling the current line of products. The division manager can develop a strategy for his particular business,

**Exhibit II
Complex Organizations**

A. Functional type

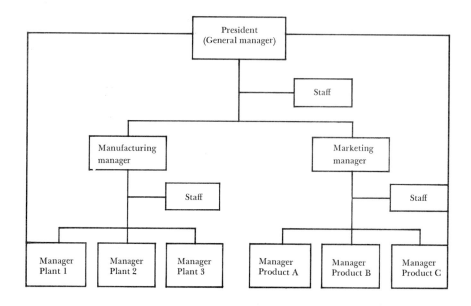

finding a competitive niche for it that may be different from the strategy being pursued by other division managers with different product lines. Tactically, a product division can also be more responsive to current customer needs. The division manager has the authority to change the production schedule in response to the request of an important customer; in a functional organization, by contrast, such a request must "go through channels," which may be ponderous and time-consuming.

Finally, it can be argued that product divisions are an excellent training ground for young managers, fostering entrepreneurship and increasing the number of centers of initiative in a corporation.

A business organization must be both efficient and effective if it is to survive, be profitable, and grow. The fundamental choice in organizational design is not an either-or question, but one of achieving the best possible balance between the benefits from economies of scale and those from strategic and tactical responsiveness.[4] One approach that is being used increasingly in a variety of settings is the matrix form of organization.

---

[4] For an excellent treatise on the complex factors that must be considered in making a basic change in organization structure, see Alfred D. Chandler, Jr., *Strategy and Structure: Chapters in the History of the American Industrial Enterprise* (Cambridge: The M.I.T. Press, 1962).

B. Multidivision type

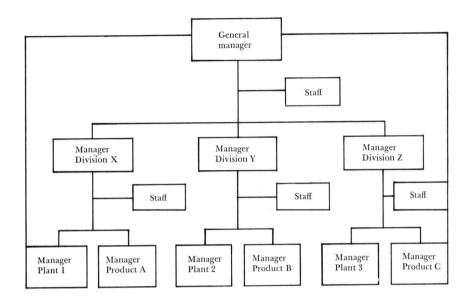

Adopt the Matrix Form?

This relatively new form of organization apparently was developed first in the aerospace industry nearly three decades ago. Companies in that industry had massive capacity, both human and physical, for the design and manufacture of weapons systems, and they were organized according to functional specialties. At any one moment, such a company might have had several large contracts in its shop, each at various stages of completion and each drawing on the various functional departments to a greater or lesser extent.

In these cases, management's focus was on the efficient use of each department's capacity; this meant that inadequate attention was devoted to cost and schedule performance on each contract. The solution was to establish a new set of project managers, one for each contract, and to superimpose them across the existing functional hierarchy. A project manager's responsibility was to coordinate the inputs from each department in such a way that contractual performance requirements would be fulfilled.

Although matrix organizations, in a formal sense, are not widely used in industry, the concept has several attractive features. It holds the promise of both efficiency *and* effectiveness. Functional specialization is retained, thus permitting the efficiencies of economies of scale. But at the same time that program or product managers are viewed as the users of

Exhibit III
Concept of a Matrix Organization

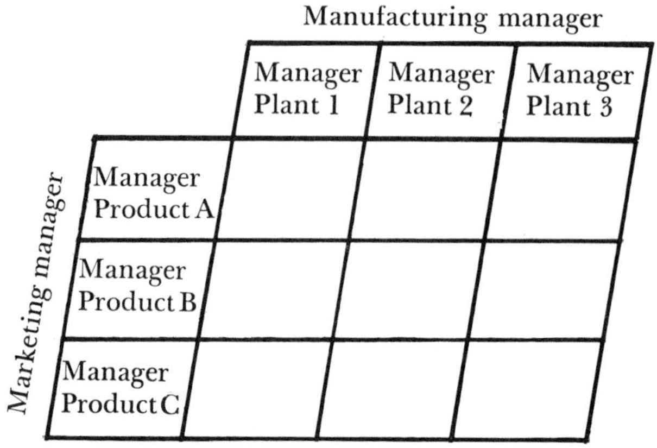

Manufacturing manager

functional skills, they are also charged with producing a result that is competitively attractive to the customer and profitable for the company.

A matrix organization is essentially a functional organization. The six third-level managers in Part A of *Exhibit II* appear in *Exhibit III* and could still report to their respective functional superiors. However, there is an important difference: the relationships between the six managers are much more explicit in *Exhibit III*.

The matrix form of organization may be appropriate when much interaction between the functions is necessary or desirable. It can be particularly useful when one function (such as marketing) is concerned with planning for the effective combination of resources, while another function (such as manufacturing) is concerned with acquiring resources and using them efficiently. These two tasks obviously must be integrated and coordinated continuously. The matrix organization is intended to describe the interrelationships between the manufacturing and market-ing functions and, without dismantling the old hierarchy, to legitimatize and encourage direct contact between the two parties concerned with any interlocking tasks or "cell" in the matrix. The matrix design does not really represent a structural change; it is simply a more realistic, com-prehensive description of organizational relationships.

From the point of view of the designer of a management control system, a matrix organization poses no special problems and may offer an opportunity for a unique type of control system. Selecting the appro-priate financial measurement for each functional manager may require nothing more, in some circumstances, than an application of the type of analysis described earlier. But management may need to go a step further if the nature of the business and its strategy are more complex than in those examples previously cited.

Problems in responsibility: In some businesses, both the marketing and the manufacturing functions may be highly interdependent and responsible for activities which have major effects on profits. How can the managers of the two functions be held jointly responsible!

One way is to hold each man responsible for a portion of the profits of the company, using a transfer price to permit a calculation of that profit. The determination of transfer prices in highly interdependent situations may be difficult, but it may be worth the trouble in order to motivate each manager properly.

Another approach is to use the matrix form of organization as an acknowledgment of the interdependence, and to hold each functional manager responsible for the entire profit of the business. This approach requires "double counting" of each profit dollar. In terms of *Exhibit III,* the manufacturing manager would be responsible for profit, defined as sales revenues less all manufacturing costs and all direct marketing expenses, for all products manufactured in the three plants. Each plant manager might have a similar responsibility for his plant. The sum of the defined profits for the three plants would be the total contribution to corporate overhead and net profit. Each product manager would also be responsible for profits, defined in the same way, for the products in his line. The sum of the profits for the three product managers would be the same as the total profit of the three plants.

Such a management control system may seem confusing at first, but it can be effective. The intent of double counting the profit is to make clear to all managers involved that they must work together in order to achieve their own individual objective. A profitable action which requires cooperation does not reflect to the credit of only one party, nor does it require a fictitious division of the profit between them. Both men benefit. Thus Plant Manager 1 would work with all three product managers, trying to find ways to use the facilities at his disposal in order to yield the highest profit for his plan. And Product Manager A would work with all three plant managers, attempting to utilize their resources in such a way as to maximize the profitability of his product line.

An intended effect of such a system is a certain amount of tension in the organization—an atmosphere of constructive conflict in which the managers in one function know they are working toward the same goal and must compete among themselves to cooperate with managers from the other functional area. Such conflict, if handled sensitively by a sophisticated top manager, can break down some of the parochialism of a purely functional organization without splintering it into less efficient product divisions.

Because of these potential advantages, we may see increasing use of the matrix concept in companies where functional interdependence is high and the rewards from functional specialization are too great to ignore.

CONCLUSION

Responsibility for the design of a management control system rests inescapably on top management. For one thing, it is top management that decides on the strategy and organization structure of a business. For another, the control system is a major tool for implementing those decisions effectively. The controller, as a member of the top management team, has an important role to play because the design of a control system is too complex a task for the chief executive to undertake without the benefit of staff support.

The president and his controller, joint designers of the management control system, face a great many choices as they try to decide (a) the type of financial objective to be specified for each organizational unit, and (b) how to calculate that measurement. There is a natural bias among corporate executives in favor of responsibility for profit. Profit is a powerful measurement; it provides a clear objective, is easily understood, and is a good motivator of such men. But not all managers are responsible for profits in any meaningful sense of that term. Creating a set of profit centers may cause more problems than it is worth.

Profit should be used as a measure of financial responsibility only when it is possible to calculate it in such a way that a manager's "profit" increases as the result of actions for which he is responsible and which he has taken in the best interests of the company.

21

Responsibility Accounting

JOHN A. HIGGINS*

The subject of this article, I venture to predict, is one of which we shall hear considerably more in the next decade. The topic sounds as if it would be of primary interest to controllers and not treasurers, but that is not so. Actually, responsibility accounting is assuming greater importance with a wider range of management groups, and it is because of this that I believe it will be of interest to many persons concerned with operating problems at various administrative levels.

This modern approach to financial accounting appears to adapt itself particularly well to illustration by use of charts. This new approach to accounting and reporting is the development of an accounting system designed to control expenditures by directly relating the reporting of expenditures to the individuals in the company organization who are responsible for their control. This system results in the preparation of accounting statements for all levels of management, designed primarily so that they can be effectively used by the operating people as a tool in controlling their operations and their costs. It is a system which emphasizes information that is useful to the operating management and de-emphasizes the accounting and bookkeeping aspects that clutter up so many of our accounting and financial statements today. It should be of interest to all treasurers because it makes possible the operation of a good budget system which is a necessary adjunct of a good cash forecast, and I know that fiscal officers are all concerned with good cash forecasting. It is generally agreed that a cash forecast is no better than the underlying budgets on which it is based. If the underlying budgets have no substance, then neither has the cash forecast. To go one step further in the progression, no budget system is fully effective unless it is built around one basic premise or philosophy, and that is that budgets and responsible individuals must be synonymous. By synonymous I mean that each responsible individual in an organization must feel that the budget is *his* budget and not something forced upon him which he might feel is unrealistic and unworkable, and unless the responsible individual does feel that it *is* *his* budget, he will only make a superficial attempt to live within it or use the information as a means of controlling his operations.

Now if one will accept this philosophy in his approach to budget-

* From *The Arthur Andersen Chronicle* (April 1952). Reprinted by permission of Arthur Andersen & Co.

ing, one more step must be taken to complete the picture. One must put the reporting of expenditures (cost accounting) in phase with the budget performance responsibility, which is another way of saying that expenditures must be reported on the basis of where they were incurred and *who* had responsibility for them. Hence comes the term responsibility accounting or reporting. In effect, the system personalizes the accounting statements by saying, "Joe, this is what you originally budgeted and this is how you performed for the period with actual operations as compared against your budget." By definition it is a system of accounting which is tailored to an organization so that costs are accumulated and reported by levels of responsibility within the organization. Each supervisory area in the organization is charged *only* with the cost for which it is responsible and over which it has control.

There are three major objectives of cost accounting in manufacturing companies: (1) cost control; (2) product cost; and (3) inventory pricing. The cost systems of most companies meet the last two objectives, but for the most part fall on their faces when it comes to the objective of real cost control. Practically all of them have systems that emphasize the development of product cost rather than emphasizing the controlling of costs at the centers where the costs are incurred. Under responsibility accounting it is possible to meet all three of these objectives by first summarizing cost on the basis of "who did it" and then reshuffling the deck, so to speak, or blending the costs to arrive at product cost and cost for inventory pricing. In effect, what we are doing is putting the emphasis on the objective of cost control for the purposes of management reports but also arriving at the normal cost statements—but on a greatly deemphasized basis.

As mentioned, I have prepared a series of charts to illustrate a system of responsibility accounting and have chosen a typical manufacturing company to make my points. Our hypothetical company has been named the ABC Manufacturing Company and is a multiproduct metal manufacturer with annual sales of approximately $4,000,000 and some 300 employees. I have chosen the multiproduct metal manufacturing plant to illustrate a general application to manufacturers using a standard cost system, although it could be applied to job costs. These general procedures, with suitable modifications, have also been applied to manufacturers using process cost accounting and also to public utilities. The theory of responsibility accounting in public utilities has been accepted rather widely throughout the utility industry. A number of commercial and manufacturing companies are presently operating under a responsibility accounting system and I believe that most of the progressive companies in the country will have adopted such a system by the end of the 50s. Inasmuch as the backbone of any responsibility accounting system is the organization chart of the company, I will first use an illustration showing an organization chart of the imaginary ABC Manufacturing Company.

Chart 1

This organization chart shows a president and general manager of a single company. It could, of course, apply to a general manager of a reasonably autonomous plant or a division of a company. Three vice presidents are indicated to head up the basic divisions of a normal manufacturing business organization, production, sales and finance. In addition to these three vice presidents, there is a chief engineer and a personnel manager reporting directly to the president and general manager. It is assumed that the vice president in charge of production has a general superintendent who is responsible for seven productive departments, each in charge of an individual foreman. Also indicated are typical service departments responsible directly to the vice president in charge of production.

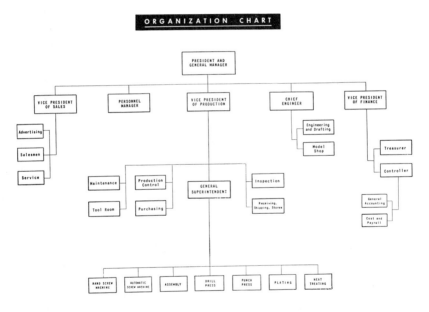

Chart 1

Chart 2

This is the same chart blocked out to illustrate that segment of the organization around which I have built these illustrated reports. The flow of responsibility starts with the foreman in charge of the drill press department and proceeds us through the general superintendent to the vice president in charge of production and finally to the president and general manager. Obviously, I could have chosen any other segment of the organization to illustrate the build-up of responsibility of reports.

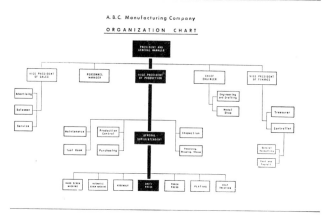

Chart 2

Chart 3

You will notice that on this chart I have separately set out that segment of the organization around which has been built these illustrative responsibility statements. The four levels of responsibility in the organization have been indicated and numbered. Of course, in a practical application there could be more or less than these four levels, depending on the complexity of the company organization. This chart will serve two purposes:

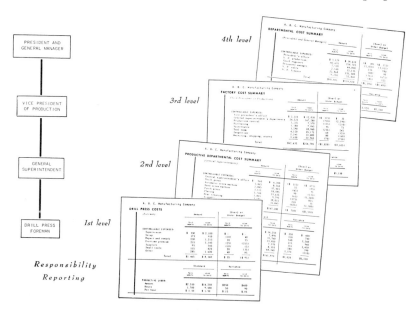

Chart 3

(1) It tends to emphasize the parallel relationship of the levels of responsibility and the reports which are directed at each of the levels; and (2) it will serve as an anchor chart in this article because one will constantly refer back to this chart as each of the reports is discussed through the various levels of responsibility.

Chart 4

The first statement to be discussed is the statement prepared for the first level of supervision which in this case is the foreman in charge of the drill press department.

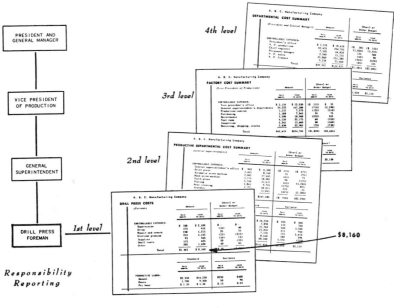

Chart 4

Chart 5

This responsibility report is for the foreman of the drill press department. The top section of the report consists of a listing of certain controllable expenses for which the foreman is to be held fully responsible. These costs have been previously budgeted by the foreman and now the budgeted costs are being compared with the actual costs. It will be noticed that these controllable expenses do not represent the full burden of the department. They are confined to the expenses for which the management holds the foreman completely and directly responsible. Naturally, they will vary between different organizations. Classification of these expenses is often a standard classification for all productive departments or even for all factory departments, but this is not necessary to the pro-

A. B. C. Manufacturing Company

DRILL PRESS COSTS

(Foreman)	Amount		(Over) or Under Budget	
	THIS MONTH	YEAR TO DATE	THIS MONTH	YEAR TO DATE
CONTROLLABLE EXPENSES—				
Supervision	$ 350	$ 2,100	$ -	$ -
Setup	175	910	(10)	40
Repair and rework	230	1,215	20	35
Overtime premium	215	1,145	(25)	(215)
Supplies	95	545	(10)	(5)
Small tools	115	625	20	(35)
Other	285	1,620	40	85
Total	$1,465	$ 8,160	$ 35	($ 95)

	Standard		Variance	
	THIS MONTH	YEAR TO DATE	THIS MONTH	YEAR TO DATE
PRODUCTIVE LABOR—				
Amount	$2,550	$14,250	$250	$400
Hours	1,700	9,500	50	90
Per hour	$ 1.50	$ 1.50	$.15	$.05

Chart 5

cedures being illustrated. This classification can be flexible so that each foreman can have reported to him his expenses in the detail and by the classification that he feels is most useful to him for controlling his own expenses. It is very important that the foreman be made to feel that he can have the breakdown of his costs made in any way that he feels will aid him in controlling and budgeting these costs. On the lower portion of this report appears the productive labor in hours and amount at standard with the variances from standard being shown. Productive labor is shown on this report because the foreman is responsible for the efficiency of the productive labor even though he is not responsible for establishing the budget of productive labor. Naturally these variances from standard can be detailed in whatever manner may be practical under the circumstances. If a job cost system were used, of course, there would be no variances and the labor reported would be actual only with perhaps a comparison to budget. It will be noticed that all through these illustrations, as I build up from the lower level to the top level of responsibility, productive labor is carried along with the controllable expenses on the theory that again each of the areas is responsible entirely for the controllable expenses but in the case of productive labor is responsible for the efficiency of that labor and, therefore, should be shown on a statement directed at each responsibility level. If one will take note of the total of the controllable costs for the drill press department, I will proceed back to our anchor chart and from these proceed to the No. 2 level of recording.

Chart 6

On this chart one sees that the totals for the drill press department have been carried forward into a report for the general superintendent who is designated as the second level of reporting or responsibility. Now proceed to the report directed at the general superintendent.

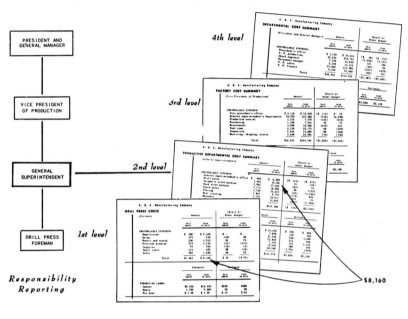

Chart 6

Chart 7

Here one sees the total amount of $8,160 representing the total controllable costs for the month for the drill press department. Likewise it will be noted that controllable cost totals have been carried forward for the other productive departments for which the general superintendent is held responsible. Also one sees listed, under summarized controllable expenses, the cost of the general superintendent's own office, and it is also supported by a detailed statement which is not shown here. The general superintendent can have, and probably will want, statements for each of the foremen responsible to him. In the bottom section of the report, the productive labor for which the general superintendent is responsible has been summarized by areas of responsibility, the drill press department being one of those areas. Take particular note of the total amount of controllable expenses for which the general superintendent is held responsible, then proceed back to our anchor chart and from there go on to the No. 3 level of reporting.

A. B. C. Manufacturing Company

PRODUCTIVE DEPARTMENTAL COST SUMMARY

(General Superintendent)	Amount		(Over) or Under Budget	
	THIS MONTH	YEAR TO DATE	THIS MONTH	YEAR TO DATE
CONTROLLABLE EXPENSES—				
General superintendent's office	$ 960	$ 6,300	($ 115)	($ 675)
Drill press	1,465	8,160	35	(95)
Automatic screw machine	2,845	17,445	(65)	75
Hand screw machine	3,115	18,085	90	(135)
Punch press	5,740	33,635	(65)	(1,240)
Plating	1,865	9,795	(175)	825
Heat treating	3,195	18,015	210	35
Assembly	5,340	35,845	(625)	(1,380)
Total	$24,525	$147,280	($ 710)	($2,590)

	Standard		Variance	
	THIS MONTH	YEAR TO DATE	THIS MONTH	YEAR TO DATE
PRODUCTIVE LABOR—				
Drill press	$ 2,550	$ 14,250	$ 250	$ 400
Automatic screw machine	1,310	7,890	110	740
Hand screw machine	5,240	31,760	540	1,560
Punch press	3,720	23,850	215	940
Plating	1,410	7,370	155	1,410
Heat treating	1,630	8,510	180	390
Assembly	11,260	68,340	1,570	(310)
Total	$27,120	$161,970	$3,020	$5,130

Chart 7

Chart 8

As shown by this anchor chart, one sees that the third level of reporting is the vice president in charge of production and that the total controllable costs under the general superintendent have been carried forward from the second level to form a part of the responsibility costs of the vice president in charge of production.

Chart 9

This report for the vice president in charge of production has been labeled "Factory Cost Summary." Here one sees that the total amount of controllable costs of the general superintendent has been carried forward as one of the areas of responsibility for which the vice president in charge of production is to be held responsible. These other areas of responsibility, mainly service departments, which report directly to the vice president would also be supported as was the general superintendent's statement by detailed statement of the costs of the respective areas. Again one sees that the cost of the vice president's own office is set forth in total and

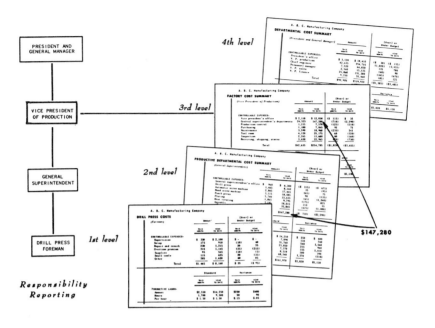

Chart 8

A. B. C. Manufacturing Company

FACTORY COST SUMMARY

(Vice President of Production)

		Amount		(Over) or Under Budget	
		THIS MONTH	YEAR TO DATE	THIS MONTH	YEAR TO DATE
CONTROLLABLE EXPENSES-					
Vice president's office		$ 2,110	$ 12,030	($ 115)	$ 35
General superintendent's departments		24,525	147,280	(710)	(2,590)
Production control		1,235	7,570	(125)	(210)
Purchasing		1,180	7,045	95	75
Maintenance		3,590	18,960	(235)	245
Tool room		4,120	25,175	60	(320)
Inspection		2,245	13,680	80	(160)
Receiving, shipping, stores		3,630	22,965	(70)	(730)
Total		$42,635	$254,705	($1,020)	($3,655)

		Standard		Variance	
		THIS MONTH	YEAR TO DATE	THIS MONTH	YEAR TO DATE
PRODUCTIVE LABOR		$27,120	$161,970	$3,020	$5,130

Chart 9

that when it is combined with the controllable costs of all the other areas of responsibility, one arrives at the total controllable costs for which the vice president is held accountable. The productive labor has also been carried forward directly from the previous report. Again I might add that this vice president may and probably will want to see the detailed statements supporting this summary.

Now take particular note of the total controllable expense for the third level of responsibility, so one can turn back to the anchor chart and from there go on to the No. 4 level of reporting.

Chart 10

Here it is evident that the fourth level of reporting is a summary of departmental controllable costs. This report is prepared for the president and the general manager of the company. Here one notes that the total controllable costs of $254,705 for which the vice president of production is held responsible, have been brought up to this top level as one of the major responsibility areas of the president and general manager.

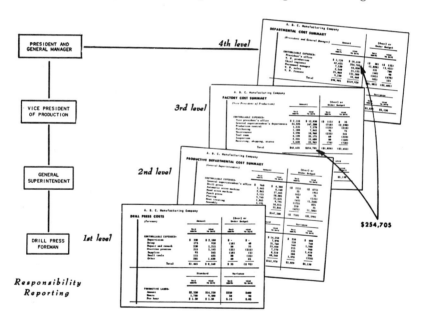

Chart 10

Chart 11

This statement, which summarizes controllable costs by responsible departments, is the responsibility report for the top level of management, the president and general manager of the company. This statement concisely summarizes for the top executives the performance of the entire company with respect to controllable costs by comparing actual against budget by responsibility areas. If the system of responsibility reporting has been correctly tailored, these side captions will relate directly to the original organization chart. Remember that the major areas were the president and general manager, vice president in charge of production, chief engineer, personnel manager, vice president in charge of sales, and vice president of finance. Also note that productive labor has again been carried forward from the previous statement as a separate item. Now in order that one may review this build-up of controllable costs by responsibilities, it is proper to review the chart on page 268.

A. B. C. Manufacturing Company

DEPARTMENTAL COST SUMMARY

(President and General Manager)	Amount		(Over) or Under Budget	
	THIS MONTH	YEAR TO DATE	THIS MONTH	YEAR TO DATE
CONTROLLABLE EXPENSES—				
President's office	$ 3,120	$ 18,410	($ 30)	($ 155)
V. P. production	42,635	254,705	(1,020)	(3,655)
Chief engineer	7,520	44,830	135	780
Personnel manager	2,540	15,135	(40)	90
V. P. sales	25,860	151,380	(345)	(670)
V. P. finance	9,230	55,460	(85)	125
Total	$90,905	$539,920	($1,385)	($3,485)

	Standard		Variance	
	THIS MONTH	YEAR TO DATE	THIS MONTH	YEAR TO DATE
PRODUCTIVE LABOR	$27,120	$161,970	$3,020	$5,130

Chart 11

Chart 12

This chart sets forth the complete build-up of controllable costs from the lowest level, which was the drill press department, up to the highest or top level of reporting. To review this build-up in detail, it will be recalled that we started with a statement prepared for the drill press department which set forth all of the controllable costs of operating the drill press department and compared these costs as originally budgeted with actual, showing the over and under budget in each case. The total controllable costs of the drill press department were then carried forward into a statement for the general superintendent. When the total cost of the drill press department was combined with the costs of the other areas for which the general superintendent had responsibility, including the costs of running his own office, one arrived at the total controllable costs for which the general superintendent was responsible. The total cost of the second level of responsibility was then carried forward in total as one of the areas of responsibility in the third level, which in this case was the vice president in charge of production. Again when this total was combined with the cost of the other areas for which the vice president was responsible, including the cost of operating his own office, one arrived at the total costs of the third level of responsibility. The total of this third

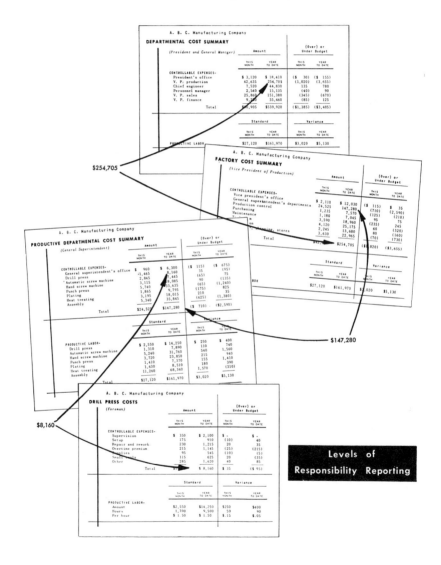

Chart 12

level was then carried forward as one of the departments in the top level summary where all expenses of the company were summarized by departments responsible for the incurrence of the costs. The productive labor in each of these areas has been shown and carried forward from one level to the other. This build-up is not particularly complicated. It is basically simple, and one does not have to be an accountant to understand it. I should like to emphasize that what has been done here is simply to have placed reporting of costs in phase with the responsibility for the incurrence of the costs. To say it another way, cost reporting has been put in phase with budgeting.

Up to this point, I have been dealing only with the reporting of costs by responsibility and have paid no attention to the accounting that is subsequently going to have to be recognized in order to arrive at conventional accounting statements. I must now translate and blend these costs so as to arrive at cost of production, cost of sales, selling expenses and other classifications of cost that must be obtained for purposes of a conventional profit and loss statement.

Chart 13

This is a statement labeled "Translation of Departmental Cost to Product Cost." One will recall that the first figure here, $90,905, is the total of the controllable costs set forth on the departmental responsibility cost sum-

A. B. C. Manufacturing Company

TRANSLATION OF DEPARTMENTAL COSTS TO PRODUCT COST

	THIS MONTH	YEAR TO DATE
EXPENSES-		
Departmental controllable expense	$ 90,905	$ 539,920
Expenses not charged to departments-		
Depreciation	7,520	44,840
Taxes - Real estate and personal property	2,130	12,780
Insurance	1,090	6,530
Total expense	$101,645	$ 604,070
PRODUCTIVE PAYROLL	30,140	167,100
MATERIAL PURCHASED	185,965	1,056,325
Total costs incurred	$317,750	$1,827,495
DISPOSITION OF ABOVE COSTS-		
Standard cost of sales	$248,140	$1,415,905
Cost variations	14,890	46,490
Inventory increase or (decrease)	10,430	105,760
Selling expenses	27,950	171,740
General and administrative expenses	14,945	83,080
Costs capitalized	1,395	4,520
Total costs distributed	$317,750	$1,827,495

Chart 13

mary. Now to this total are added expenses not charged to departments. These are expenses that cannot be defined as being a "Controllable Cost" and, therefore, have not been assigned to a responsibility of a particular area in the organization. For examples of these costs I have used depreciation, taxes and insurance and have now arrived at a total expense of $101,645. The productive payroll is now added. This is the total of the standard labor of $27,120 shown on the departmental responsibility cost summary plus the variance from standard of $3,020. The cost of raw material was not included in the responsibility statements because no one department is responsible for the cost; it is in much the same category as taxes and insurance. The result is now total cost incurred for the period.

·   ·   ·   ·   ·   ·   ·   ·   ·   ·   ·   ·

In closing this discussion, I would like to summarize the major points. Responsibility accounting does not involve a drastic change in accounting theory or principles. It is for the most part a change in emphasis from product cost to the cost control aspects of accounting wherein the statements to management emphasize the control of costs by reporting and summarizing them on the basis of "who did it" before they are adjusted and blended for product cost purposes to obtain the conventional financial statements. To say it another way, it is a system which emphasizes the information that is useful to operating management and de-emphasizes the accounting and bookkeeping aspects that clutter up so many of our financial statements today.

22

Control and Freedom in a Decentralized Company

RAYMOND VILLERS*

> . . . Control is not by itself a hindrance to individual freedom. Rather, control is in fact a prerequisite to decentralization, and without decentralization there can be no real freedom.

Industrial management today faces a strange dilemma. Half a century of experience has shown conclusively that planning and control are the basic requirements of economical manufacturing. But a decade or so of intensive research in human relations shows with equal conclusiveness that our large organizations and our methods of planning and control are, more often than not, antagonistic to good human relations, so essential to the successful management of an industrial enterprise. Reliable studies indicate that our methods of planning and control may even tend to deprive the members of our industrial organizations of one of man's basic needs—a sense of purposeful and worthwhile accomplishment.[1]

PRACTICAL PROBLEM

Planning and control are nevertheless as necessary today as ever; large organizations are here to stay—and will continue to develop further. The practical problem, therefore, "is that of building large organizations and of retaining, at the same time, the quality and strength of small, well-integrated work groups."[2] How can this be done?

An increasing number of companies are endeavoring to find the answer in a policy of decentralization of decision-making; that is, they are trying to spread the responsibility for final decisions. The methods followed in implementing this policy vary greatly from one company to another. Some companies have decentralized along geographical lines,

* From *Harvard Business Review* (March-April 1954), pp. 89-96. © 1954 by the President and Fellows of Harvard College; all rights reserved.
1 See, for instance, Chris Argyris, "The Impact of Budgets on People," *Harvard Business Review* (January-February 1953), p. 97.
2 Burleigh B. Gardner and David G. Moore, *Human Relations in Industry* (Chicago: Richard D. Irwin, Inc., 1950), p. 402.

others by products manufactured, others by management functions, and so on; sometimes these various factors are combined.

In every case, however, certain functions or activities are kept centralized. At General Motors, for instance, the divisions are decentralized both geographically and by products, but the financial and legal functions have remained centralized. At Koppers, where decentralization is also the general rule, the purchasing function is centralized for most products. And in many other companies the personnel function has remained centralized.

Regardless of the specific approach used, all companies face the same two major obstacles to success in their efforts:

1. The difficulty of decentralizing down to a sufficiently small unit. (The decentralized unit of a large corporation is generally of substantial size, often including many plants and several thousand employees. There is little or no decentralization *within* such a unit.)

2. The difficulty of controlling the decentralized unit. (Simplified controls, such as those based essentially on the well-known criterion of "return on investment," often prove to be deceptive and can be applied successfully only to decentralized units of substantial size.)

USEFUL CONCEPT

It is the purpose of this article to describe the concept of centralized planning and control associated with decentralized authority and responsibility which management can use to overcome these obstacles. This concept reconciles the organization's need for coordinated action with the legitimate aspirations of individuals; and it is applicable to large, small, and medium-size companies alike. Although it is comparatively new, it has gained increasing acceptance in recent years, no doubt due in large part to the results it has secured.

After a brief description of its basic features, three case studies will show how it works in the hands of executives who are under pressure to solve everyday business problems. This will give us a realistic idea of the difficulties and the benefits which can be expected when the concept is applied.

Four Essential Features

There are four essential features of the concept of centralized planning and control in conjunction with decentralized authority and responsibility:

Management must functionalize planning and control, centralizing it in a separate department.

Management must make a precise determination of the lines of authority and responsibility.

Management must define clearly the methods by which the various division and department heads can participate in planning.

Management must develop methods of control which are adapted to the need of coordinated action in a decentralized organization.

Now let us examine these points in a little more detail.

Centralized Control

In the process of planning and controlling the complex activities of such specialized departments and functions as purchasing, marketing, engineering, personnel, accounting, and so on, modern management has developed techniques which have themselves become so complex that they have to be handled by specialists. When this need is recognized, general managment retains the full responsibility for high policy decisions, for giving directives, for rewarding or penalizing; but the technical activities involved in planning and control are entrusted to a specialized department. Some companies call it the "control department," others the "administrative controls department," and still others merely extend the regular duties of the controller's office to include the new function.

Although the details vary greatly among individual companies, a planning and control department usually has these general functions:

1. It collects the data necessary to general management at the time decisions of high policy are being made — sales estimates, marketing policy, size of inventory, level of employment, financing needs, and so on.

2. It translates high policy decisions into specific assignments. The department heads who receive such assignments are given an opportunity to express their views and may under specified conditions request a change in the scope or the timing of the assignments.

3. It compares the quantity, quality, timing, and costs of actual performance with the specifications in the assignment, and prepares managerial reports based on the comparison. The reports are addressed to the department which has received and accepted the assignment, as well as to executives at higher levels of management who are responsible for coordinating action in the organization. Under this centralized approach, in turn, such reports can be kept together in an up-to-date "control book."

Lines of Authority

The translation of high policy into specific assignments for departments or individuals obviously means that someone must make decisions with respect to lines of authority and responsibility. The planning and control department is *not* responsible for decisions of this sort. Rather, they should be made by the top operating executives in the form of permanent operating procedures for the whole organization.

Much has been said about the dangers of specialization. The reader is no doubt familiar with the picture often presented of the conditions prevailing in the average modern plant where no member of management supervises a wide variety of jobs but instead each is restricted to a narrow field of activity. Instead of being left alone with a crew of men as in the "good old times" (which incidentally were not very pleasant times in terms of human relations), the modern foreman sees his activity limited by many specialists — the engineer, the inspector, the personnel director, and so forth. He tends to feel like a small cog in a big wheel.

To some extent this picture is true. Supervisors do often feel frustrated in this way. But in another respect it is misleading. The popular assumption about the cause of the dissatisfaction is not justified. It is not specialization so much as the *lack of communication* that causes supervisors to feel the way they do.

Moreover, it is futile to try to solve the problem by turning the clock back. Specialization is the unavoidable consequence of our industrial civilization. It will get us nowhere to be nostalgic; rather, we must think in terms of constructive adjustment to the needs of today's industrial life. Most certainly we should not ignore the human problem, but we should consider it in the light of the requirements of modern industry.

In sum, we do not need to be afraid of drawing lines of authority and responsibility to meet the needs of specialization if at the same time we keep the lines of communication between the various functions wide open. Then each specialist can visualize in its proper perspective the part he plays in the whole organization, even though his field of authority and responsibility is clearly and, if need be, narrowly defined. Instead of feeling like a cog in a wheel, he can feel like a member of a team — a specialized but eminently useful member.

Participation in Planning

The specialist's feelings of being part of a team are reinforced if he is called upon to participate in the planning of his activities and is given complete independence of action within his field of specialization. These purposes are served and encouraged within the framework of planning and control when the following principles are observed:

1. The planning and control department acts as a service department only. It does not issue orders, but simply translates general decisions into specific assignments. It does not tell each department *how* a certain goal should be reached but defines *what* should be accomplished and *when* it should be done, in order to implement decisions of policy made at a high management level.

2. These specific assignments are initially *proposals.* In actual practice they take the form, for example, of a schedule of material requirements addressed to the purchasing department, or of a schedule of production of finished items addressed to the plant superintendent, or of a schedule of preparation of blueprints for tools addressed to the manager of the tooling department.

Each department manager who receives such an assignment has the privilege of declining it for any valid reason, such as that the time allowed is too short or the quality is unobtainable. If the department concerned cannot agree with planning and control on a substitute assignment, the matter is referred to a higher level of management as in the case of any controversy between departments in a well-managed organization.

3. To expedite matters and avoid unnecessary meetings, it has been found advantageous to establish the general rule that if the department head who receives the assignment raises no objections to it within a given period, say three or four days, he becomes fully responsible for the performance. At the same time he and his associates are free to choose their own ways and means as long as the goal assigned is reached at the right time, at the right cost, and in accordance with the terms of the assignment or standard specifications.

Methods of Control

The risk involved in the foregoing practices is obvious. A department or an individual is entrusted with a given assignment and left alone in accordance with the principle of decentralization of authority and responsibility. That is fine if he succeeds, but what happens if he fails? Obviously, this is a crucial question.

A partial answer is that the members of the organization should be given the proper training and should have opportunities to develop their ability to handle responsibility. If they can judge wisely what assignments they can fulfill and what they cannot, failures to perform will be rare. Furthermore, they can be asked to give a warning as soon as they have a serious reason to doubt that they will be able to perform as expected. Through this procedure the damaging consequences of an eventual failure can be minimized.

Nevertheless, it is a fact that failure will occur from time to time. A policy of decentralization of authority, based on the concept that individuals may be entrusted with the full responsibility for certain assignments, is acceptable only if the risk entailed by failure is not of excessive magnitude. It is essential, therefore, for control to be exercised at such frequent intervals as is necessary to prevent excessive damage in the case of a failure to perform. This means that there is a limit to how far decentralization can go. To illustrate:

If new tools are required for a certain production run six months hence, the assignment issued to the tool engineer might be broken down into these five stages:

1. Preliminary report and proposed design
2. Cost estimate
3. Blueprint and ordering of materials
4. Test run
5. Delivery of tools to tool room

The planning and control department assigns a deadline to *each* of these steps, using the final deadline set up by top management for a guide, and allowing for a certain safety cushion in the timing. If a delay occurs in the test runs, for instance, it is reported immediately. Proper managerial action by a higher authority can be taken in time to prevent the whole production program from being jeopardized because tools are not available.

Finally, it is in some cases possible and desirable to evaluate in dollars and cents the consequences of a failure to perform. If, for instance, an undue delay occurs in the delivery of materials, the cost of this delay, in terms of dollars of direct labor representing the time lost in the plant, may be recorded in a special report which reflects the responsibility of the purchasing agent in the matter.

THREE CASE STUDIES

Now let us turn to three actual cases[3] which illustrate, in narrative form, some of the difficulties and advantages of applying the concept of planning and control associated with decentralized authority and responsibility.

Plant Superintendent

This is the case of a plant superintendent in a plant employing over 700 workers.

Prior to the creation of a planning and control department, the organization of planning was very much neglected. The plant superintendent was accustomed to regulating production on the basis of orders received by the company from its customers and of indications given to him in an informal way by the sales department. He would request the services of the maintenance department when needed; his assistant would keep an eye on the materials in the warehouse; he would anticipate his needs in personnel in time of seasonal peaks and give instructions for future hiring to the personnel department; and so forth. While he complained about being forced into such an exhausting activity, and while he was sincere in his complaint, he actually found it gratifying in many respects.

Then a planning and control department was established. He learned that in the future this department would tell him what items should be produced and when, and that no longer would he have responsibility for materials, tools, personnel, and so on. Instead, he would merely have to requisition from the warehouse; tools would be ready for use the day an item was scheduled for production; and personnel needs would be anticipated on the basis of future production programs without requiring his intervention. Quite naturally, he felt as if he had been demoted.

It soon became apparent that his area of authority had in fact decreased; to this extent his first reactions were confirmed. Granted, his

[3] Adapted from the author's book, *The Dynamics of Industrial Management* (New York: Funk & Wagnalls Company, 1954).

authority was more clearly defined. But he was no longer negotiating with the sales department about a rush order, or with the tooling department about urgent requirements, or with the purchasing department about needed materials. He was told what to produce and when.

Yet if his authority had decreased in *surface,* it had increased in *depth.* He soon noticed that, within his own field of responsibility, he had more stature as a manager than before. No one at a higher level would suggest to him that he should, for instance, instruct his foremen to watch more carefully the quality of production or the productivity of their workers — subjects which had in the past been a frequent source of controversy between him and his vice president. He was shown the results obtained in his plant in more detail than he had ever known in terms of cost, rejects, sales returns, absenteeism, turnover, and so on; but this was information rather than interference, for it was left to him to improve the situation, as needed, in his own way.

In turn, he learned to apply similar principles in his relationships with his foremen; and, thanks to the planning and control department, he had more data with which to control their performance objectively.

After about a year this plant superintendent came to the conclusion that he had gained in independence of action and that his real responsibility had increased. He concentrated willingly and with sincere satisfaction on his newly defined assignment. In retrospect, that things turned out this way seems to be due in large part to two factors, which experience indicates are essential to the successful centralization of planning and decentralization of responsibility:

1. Centralized planning was limited to a service activity; it did not operate as an order-issuing agency.

2. Informal relationships developed between specialized functions — e.g., between the plant superintendent and the head of the tooling department — which made it possible for them to work together despite the fact that neither had authority over the other.

Purchasing Agent

In this case (all names disguised), Richards was the purchasing agent in a highly centralized company, the Rigid Corporation. The president of the company was in the habit of checking every move of his executives. He would call Richards at any time of the day, and sometimes in the evening at his home: "Have you written to the supplier about that problem we discussed this morning?" Or, "Don't write; go and see him." Or, "Don't tell him this; rather, take it from that angle. . . ." He would also make remarks implying that his executives were not punctual, such as, "I called you half an hour ago, but you had not yet arrived."

Richards' salary was good and his job secure, but after ten years he finally decided that the situation was hopeless, and he quit at the first opportunity. He went to the Hart Manufacturing Company as purchasing agent. His predecessor there had been transferred prior to his arrival and was not available to instruct him about the details of his new job.

The Hart Manufacturing Company had been reorganized two years before. A planning and control department had been created, and a policy of decentralization of authority had been adopted. Having served as an advisor to the company, the writer was asked to initiate Richards. The initiation went much as follows:

From what you tell me, I would say that you will find that the methods of management at the Hart Manufacturing Company are almost exactly the opposite of those you have used to at the Rigid Corporation. You will find that no one here will check how you are doing your job.

Ralph, whom you met this morning, is the head of the planning and control department. He will tell you what materials are needed for production and when. Every six months he will give you a general purchasing program and you will place the orders. You get the specifications from the engineering department. You select the suppliers yourself. You decide yourself about what prices you want to pay.

You will find that for most materials used we have standard prices. The variance between the price you pay and the standards are carefully followed up by Ralph's department and reported both to you and to your vice president, who keeps in touch with the market and will step in if he feels that the prices you are paying are too high. Incidentally, if you find a way of getting lower prices, he will step in, too — to congratulate you.

But, in any case, he will step in *after* you, under your own responsibility, have placed the purchase order, not before — unless you turn to him for advice, which you may do at any time. In some exceptional cases, he may take the initiative; but you will find this a very rare occurrence.

For planning purposes the weeks of the year are designated by consecutive numbers. Every week you will receive a release schedule which will tell you what materials, on order but not yet delivered, are needed for production during each of the following eight weeks. As you know, we are short of materials. [This was a few months after the outbreak of the war in Korea.] This release schedule is therefore a very important matter. Check it carefully when you receive it. If you do not call Ralph within a few days after you have received it, you are considered as having accepted it.

It then becomes your responsibility to supply the materials on time. Any delay will disrupt production. The cost of the disruption will be evaluated by the planning and control department and will be charged against your department.

At this point, Richards asked two questions and received the following answers:

Question: You know how suppliers are. They may say "yes"

and yet they don't deliver. They may just say "perhaps." What do you want me to tell Ralph, when I receive his release schedule, in a situation where I am 50-50 sure?

Answer: Your position is fully appreciated. But you must realize that, in the whole organization, you are *the one* who is in the best position to evaluate the situation, Now, someone has to take responsibility. As you know, a plant cannot have a "perhaps" production schedule or "perhaps" tools on hand or a "perhaps" machine setup. It has to be "yes" or "no." Sometimes we will be disappointed. Everyone agrees that it can happen that you will say "yes," and yet the material will not be there on time. But that doesn't lessen your responsibility.

The real issue is how often it will occur and what the damage will be. At the end of the year, two accounts will tell the whole story. The price-variance account will show how active you have been in getting good prices. The time-lost account will show how reliable your deliveries to the production department have been.

In addition, of course, we expect that your materials will be up to specifications — and that you will not systematically protect yourself by refusing to accept Ralph's release schedules.

Question: What do I do if I think that I cannot get the material in time?

Answer: You call Ralph and tell him so. Nine times out of ten, even more often that that, you will settle the matter between yourselves by changing the production schedule. Your release schedules are issued weekly for an eight-week period. As a rule, this gives you at least four weeks' advance notice, inasmuch as we avoid changing the coming four weeks unless it is absolutely necessary. Now, if you and Ralph cannot see eye to eye, the matter will have to be referred to the executive committee, but you will find that Ralph is pretty good at solving problems.

By the way, let me make this clear to you. Ralph is no more your boss than you are his. If the foreman of the tool room needs to purchase anything, you know that he is not permitted to go and buy it outside. He must send *you* a requisition. Now, this does not make you his boss. You are the head of a service department, available to service him. Ralph is the head of another service department. The release schedule he sends you is a service he renders to you and to the whole organization. It is important for you to understand the spirit in which his department functions.

You will find that the control you submitted to is very detailed, but it is objective. You receive an assignment. You may accept it or reject it. But if you accept, you must perform. There is no excuse for a failure — no argument, either. If you fail, the damage is evaluated. We all make mistakes. The important point is to avoid making too many mistakes and also to understand fully that this extensive control is the necessary balance to the great freedom of action you are being given.

No one will ask you at what time you arrive in your office, why you did not show up last Thursday, or whether you have neglected to write to this or that supplier. You are your own boss as far as your function is concerned.

Failure and Resentment. About three months elapsed. Richards was delighted. A new life had started for him. He felt like himself again — no fears, a real feeling of independence. He worked harder than ever, but he worked really for himself.

During Week No. 24 he was advised that Part No. 1234 — a critical part — would be needed for assembly on Tuesday morning, Week No. 32. He found that the regular supplier could not deliver. He called every-where, finally found a supplier in the Middle West, and accepted the commitment.

He followed up by mail. Yes, the supplier assured him, the part would be ready. The matter was so important that on Thursday of Week No. 31 he checked by phone. Yes, the shipment had left on time. Richards was reassured and did not check further. But on Tuesday of Week No. 32 the part was not in the warehouse. Inquiry revealed that the shipment had been misdirected by the railroad company and was still in Chicago.

The writer was asked to "arbitrate" the case and decided that the time lost in the plant should be charged to the purchasing department. Certainly the plant manager could not be asked to underwrite a loss due to failure of delivery over which he had no supervision.

Richards listened attentively and smiled politely as the decision was explained. But obviously he felt that an injustice had been com-mitted; he was bitterly disappointed. He said that he thought he had done all he possibly could. It did no good to remind him that he had performed very well in the past and would certainly perform well again in the future.

From that point on Richards' attitude was changed.

New Understanding. Some time later, while teaching his course in industrial engineering at Columbia University, the writer was describing to his students the advantages of centralizing planning and control in conjunction with decentralizing authority and responsibility. In all fair-ness to the students, he felt they should be told that at least in one specific case the plan had not worked well. He invited Richards to come as a guest lecturer and present the other side of the picture. Here is what happened:

Class time was 9.00 a.m. Shortly before, Richards entered the writer's office. He was smiling and looking forward to the chance to let off steam. "Don't hesitate to tell them how you feel," he was told. "Don't beat around the bush."

Richards smiled; he certainly would take full advantage of the opportunity. He said he would tell them that he liked the idea in general, but that you should not go too far with it. Suddenly he stopped talking and looked worried.

"May I use your phone to place a long-distance call to the office?" he asked. "I just forgot to tell them I would not be in today."

It was the writer's turn to smile. "I should like to ask you one question. In your previous job, at the Rigid Corporation, would you have forgotten to tell them that you were not coming?"

"Certainly not," he said. "I would have requested permission three weeks in advance, and most probably the permission would have been refused."

The suggestion was made: "Why don't you tell that to the class, too?"

Richards' face changed. He was obviously thinking deeply. "Oh," he said, "I think I see the point."

The session in class was rather different from what had been expected. The students were surprised to hear a guest lecturer who, contrary to their expectation, was not at all critical of the concept they were studying!

Plant Variance

In a certain organization, objections were being made to a report which the planning and control department was putting out.

This report was a weekly analysis of the variance between the actual direct labor payroll in the assembly department and what the payroll would have been if all goods had been produced at standard cost. The planning and control department was in charge of assigning to each department concerned the responsibility for a portion of the variance. The maintenance department would be responsible for breakdown, the purchasing department for lack of material, the sales department for rush orders, the plant management for time lost, and so on. Virtually the whole variance could thus be accounted for.

The cost of this report was considered excessive by some executives. It required, at that time, almost the whole attention of two clerks and about eight hours of IBM equipment. For a certain period, the report was issued without bringing any return; and some executives remarked sarcastically, "What is the use of knowing where we are losing money if we lose it anyway?"

After a few months, however, their attitude changed. The first beneficial effect of the report was that it eliminated a source of friction that had for years cast a shadow over the relationships between sales and production, namely, requests for rush orders. It is the rare executive who is not familiar with this kind of problem:

The sales department requests a rush production. The plant scheduler argues that it will disrupt his production and cost a substantial though not clearly determined amount of money. The answer coming from sales is: "Do you want to take the responsibility of losing the X

Company as a customer?" Of course the production scheduler does not want to take such a responsibility, and he gives up, but not before a heavy exchange of arguments and the accumulation of a substantial backlog of ill feeling.

Analysis of the payroll in the assembly department, determining the costs involved in getting out rush orders, eliminated the cause for argument. Henceforth, any rush order was accepted with a smile by the production schedulers, who made sure that the extra cost would be duly recorded and charged to the sales department — "no questions asked." As a result, the tension created by rush orders disappeared completely; and, somehow, the number of rush orders requested by the sales department was progressively reduced to an insignificant level.

Even more spectacular was the virtually total elimination of a "plant variance" of almost $1,000 a week. Everyone in the organization knew that the labor expense in the assembly department was much higher than the standard; but the causes were so numerous and their relative impact so undetermined that every executive or supervisor was sincerely convinced that he was *not* the one who could help. But when the head of the assembly department was shown that $1,000 a week was attributable to time lost in his department, he realized that this was really his responsibility. So he reorganized entirely his procedures of job assignment and made it a point every week to study the payroll analysis report at a meeting he held with his foremen.

After six months the plant variance had virtually disappeared. The savings resulting from that factor alone more than compensated for the cost of the whole analysis.

CONCLUSION

As the foregoing cases indicate, neither specialization nor control presents insurmountable obstacles to the free development of human personality in our modern industrial organizations. It is true that specialization narrows the *area* of responsibility of each executive, but it does not necessarily lessen the *depth* of his authority. Within his field, he may have more responsibility and leeway than his predecessors of earlier years. Much the same applies to control. Contrary to a widespread prejudice, born of the many abuses that have been committed in the past, control is not by itself a hindrance to individual freedom. Rather, control is in fact a prerequisite to decentralization, and without decentralization there can be no real freedom.

The high-ranking executive who is responsible for the operations of large sections of an industrial organization and who is not in a position to make use of effective controls, tends to be tyrannical because he is worried. He will give much greater independence to his subordinates if he knows that their mistakes will be detected before any irreparable damage results. That is a key function of the concept described in this

article — centralized planning and control in conjunction with decen-⌉
tralized authority and responsibility.

This concept is not, however, a substitute for good management. It
is only a tool of management. Like any other tool, it may be misused;
and precisely because it is effective, it may become dangerous. It may
become an instrument of oppression if excessive emphasis is placed on
"control"; or it may become the source of serious disruptions if, on the
contrary, "decentralization" is overemphasized.

At the same time, experience shows that this concept, if applied
with skill and moderation, provides a solution to the strange dilemma in
which industrial management finds itself today. Management can use the
concept to reconcile the technical necessity for planning and control with
the pressing need for good human relations in industry.

23

Dysfunctional Consequences of Performance Measurements

V. F. RIDGWAY*

There is today a strong tendency to state numerically as many as possible of the variables with which management must deal. The mounting interest in and application of tools such as operations research, linear programming, and statistical decision-making, all of which require quantifiable variables, foster the idea that if progress toward goals can be measured, efforts and resources can be more rationally managed. This has led to the development of quantitative performance measurements for all levels within organizations, up to and including measurements of the performance of a division manager with profit responsibility in a decentralized company. Measurements at lower levels in the organization may be in terms of amount of work, quality of work, time required, and so on.

Quantitative measures of performance are tools, and are undoubtedly useful. But research indicates that indiscriminate use and undue confidence and reliance in them result from insufficient knowledge of the full effects and consequences. Judicious use of a tool requires awareness of possible side effects and reactions. Otherwise, indiscriminate use may result in side effects and reactions outweighing the benefits, as was the case when penicillin was first hailed as a wonder drug. The cure is sometimes worse than the disease.

It seems worthwhile to review the current scattered knowledge of the dysfunctional consequences resulting from the imposition of a system of performance measurements. For the purpose of analyzing the impact of performance measurements upon job performance, we can consider separately single, multiple, and composite criteria. Single criteria occur when only one quantity is measured and observed, such as total output or profit. Multiple criteria occur when several quantities are measured simultaneously, such as output, quality, cost, safety, waste, and so forth. Composite criteria occur when the separate quantities are weighted in some fashion and then added or averaged.

SINGLE CRITERIA

A single criterion of performance was in use in a public employment

* From *Administrative Science Quarterly* (September 1956), pp. 240-47. Reprinted by permission of the Managing Editor.

agency studied by Peter M. Blau.[1] The agency's responsibility was "to serve workers seeking employment and employers seeking workers." Employment interviewers were appraised by the number of interviews they conducted. Thus the interviewer was motivated to complete as many interviews as he could, but not to spend adequate time in locating jobs for the clients. The organization's goal of placing clients in jobs was not given primary consideration because the measurement device applied to only one aspect of the activity.

Blau reports another case in a federal law enforcement agency which investigated business establishments. Here he found that work schedules were distorted by the imposition of a quota of eight cases per month for each investigator. Toward the end of the month an investigator who found himself short of the eight cases would pick easy, fast cases to finish that month and save the lengthier cases till the following month. Priority of the cases for investigation was based on length of the case rather than urgency, as standards of impartiality would require. This is one of many instances in which the existence of an "accounting period" adversely affects the overall goal accomplishment of the organization.

Chris Argyris also reports this tendency to use easy jobs as fillers toward the end of a period in order to meet a quota.[2] In this case, a factory supervisor reported that they "feed the machines all the easy orders" toward the end of the month, rather than finish them in the sequence in which they were received. Such a practice may lead to undue delay of the delivery of some customers' orders, perhaps the most profitable orders.

David Granick's study of Soviet management reveals how the attention and glory that accrue to a plant manager when he can set a new monthly production record in one month leads to the neglect of repairs and maintenance, so that in ensuing months there will be a distinct drop in production.[3] Similarly, the output of an entire plant may be allowed to fall off in order to create conditions under which one worker can make a production record, when the importance of such a record is considered greater than overall plant production.

Joseph S. Berliner's report on Soviet business administration points out sharply how the accounting period has an adverse effect upon management decisions.[4] The use of monthly production quotas causes "storming" at the end of the month to reach the quota. Repairs and maintenance are postponed until the following month, so that production lags in the early part of the month, and storming must again be resorted to in the following month. This has impact upon the rate of production for suppliers and customers who are forced into a fluctuating rate of operations with its attendant losses and wastes.

1 Peter M. Blau, *The Dynamics of Bureaucracy* (Chicago, Ill.: U. of Chicago Pr., 1955).
2 Chris Argyris, *The Impact of Budgets on People* (Ithaca, N.Y.: Cornell U., 1952).
3 David Granick, *Management of the Industrial Firm in the U.S.S.R.* (New York: Columbia U. Pr., 1954).
4 Joseph S. Berliner, "A Problem in Soviet Business Management," *Administrative Science Quarterly,* 1 (1956), pp. 86-101.

Standard costs as a criterion of performance are a frequent source of dissatisfaction in manufacturing plants.[5] The "lumpiness" of indirect charges that are allocated to the plants or divisions (indirect charges being unequal from month to month), variations in quality and cost of raw materials, or other factors beyond the control of the operating manager, coupled with inaccuracies and errors in the apportionment of indirect charges, cause distrust of the standards. A typical reaction of operating executives in such cases seems to be to seek explanations and justifications. Consequently, considerable time and energy is expended in discussion and debate about the correctness of charges. Only "wooden money" savings accrue when charges are shifted to other accounts and there is no increase in company profits. It should be pointed out, however, that having charges applied to the proper departments may have the advantage of more correctly directing attention to problem areas.

Granick discusses two measures of the success of the Soviet firm which have been considered and rejected as overall measures by Soviet industrial leaders and economists.[6] The first, cost-reduction per unit of product, is considered inadequate because it does not provide a basis for evaluating new products. Further, variations in amount of production affect the cost-reduction index because of the finer division of overhead costs, quality changes, and assortment. The second overall measure of a firm's performance, profitability, has been rejected as the basic criterion on the grounds that it is affected in the short run by factors outside the control of management, such as shortages of supplies. Profitability as a measure of success led to a reduction in experimental work and deemphasized the importance of production quantity, quality, and assortment. Neither cost-reduction nor profitability was acceptable alone; each was only a partial index. The Soviets had concluded by 1940 that no single measure of success of a firm is adequate in itself and that there is no substitute for genuine analysis of all the elements entering into a firm's work.

Difficulties with single criteria have been observed in operations research, where one of the principal sources of difficulty is considered to be the choice of proper criteria for performance measurement.[7] The difficulty of translating the several alternatives into their full effect upon the organization's goal forces the operations researcher to settle for a criterion more manageable than profit maximization, but less appropriate. The efficiency of a subgroup of the organization may be improved in terms of some plausible test, yet the organization's efficiency in terms of its major goal may be decreased.

In all the studies mentioned above, the inadequacy of a single measure of performance is evident. Whether this is a measure of an

[5] H. A. Simon, H. Guetzkow, G. Kozmetsky, G. Tyndall, *Centralization vs. Decentralization in Organizing the Controller's Department* (New York, 1954).

[6] Granick, *op. cit.*

[7] Charles Hitch and Roland McKean, "Suboptimization in Operations Problems" in J. F. McCloskey and Flora F. Trefethen (eds.), *Operations Research for Management* (Baltimore, Md., 1954).

employee at the working level, or a measure of management, attention is directed away from the overall goal. The existence of a measure of performance motivates individuals to effort, but the effort may be wasted, as in seeking "wooden money" savings, or may be detrimental to the organization's goal, as in rushing through interviews, delaying repairs, and rejecting profitable opportunities.

MULTIPLE MEASUREMENTS

Recognition of the inadequacies of a single measure of success or performance leads organizations to develop several criteria. It is felt then that all aspects of the job will receive adequate attention and emphasis so that efforts of individuals will not be distorted.

A realization in the employment office studied by Blau that job referrals and placements were also important led eventually to their inclusion in measuring the performance of the interviewers.[8] Merely counting the number of referrals and placements had led to wholesale indiscriminate referrals, which did not accomplish the employment agency's screening function. Therefore, to stress the qualitative aspects of the interviewer's job, several ratios (of referrals to interviews, placements to interviews, and placements to referrals) were devised. Altogether there were eight quantities that were counted or calculated for each interviewer. This increase in quantity and complexity of performance measurements was felt necessary to give emphasis to all aspects of the interviewer's job.

Granick relates that no single criterion was universally adopted in appraising Soviet management.[9] Some managers were acclaimed for satisfying production quotas while violating labor laws. Others were removed from office for violating quality and assortment plans while fulfilling production quotas. Apparently there is a ranking of importance of these multiple criteria. In a typical interfirm competition the judges were provided with a long list of indexes. These included production of finished goods in the planned assortment, an even flow of production as between ten-day periods and as between months, planned mastery of new types of products, improvement in product quality and reduction in waste, economy of materials through improved design and changing of technological processes, fulfillment of labor productivity tasks and lowering of unit cost, keeping within the established wage fund, and increase in the number of worker suggestions for improvements in work methods and conditions and their adoption into operation. But no indication of how these indexes should be weighted was given. The preeminence of such indexes as quantity, quality, assortment of production, and remaining within the firm's allotment of materials and fuels brought some order into the otherwise chaotic picture. The presence of "campaigns" and "priorities" stressing one or more factors also has aided Soviet manage-

8 Blau, *op. cit.*
9 Granick, *op. cit.*

ment in deciding which elements of its work are at the moment most important.

Without a single overall composite measure of success, however, there is no way of determining whether the temporarily increased effort on the "campaign" criteria of the month represents new effort or merely effort shifted from other criteria. And the intangibility of some of these indexes makes it impossible to judge whether there has been decreased effort on other aspects. Hence even in a campaign period the relative emphases may become so unbalanced as to mitigate or defeat the purpose of the campaign.

The Soviet manager is working then under several measurements and the relative influence or emphasis attached to any one measurement varies from firm to firm and from month to month. Profits and production are used, among other measurements, and these two may lead to contradictory managerial decisions. Granick hypothesizes that some managers have refused complicated orders that were difficult to produce because it would mean failure to produce the planned quantities. Acceptance of these orders would have been very profitable, but of the two criteria, production quantity took precedence.

Numerous American writers in the field of management have stressed the importance of multiple criteria in evaluating performance of management. Peter Drucker, for example, lists market standing, innovation, productivity, physical and financial resources, profitability, manager performance and development, worker performance and attitude, and public responsibility.[10] This list includes many of the same items as the list used by Soviet management.

The consensus at a round-table discussion of business and professional men[11] was that although return on investment is important, additional criteria are essential for an adequate appraisal of operating departments. These other criteria are fairly well summed up in Drucker's list above.

Thus we see that the need for multiple criteria is recognized and that they are employed at different levels of the organization — lower levels as in the employment agency, higher levels as considered by Granick and Drucker. At all levels these multiple measurements or criteria are intended to focus attention on the many facets of a particular job.

The use of multiple criteria assumes that the individual will commit his or the organization's efforts, attention, and resources in greater measure to those activities which promise to contribute the greatest improvement to over-all performance. There must then exist a theoretical condition under which an additional unit of effort or resources would yield equally desirable results in over-all performance, whether applied to production, quality, research, safety, public relations,

10 Peter F. Drucker, *The Practice of Management* (New York: Harper & Row, 1954).
11 William H. Newman and James P. Logan, *Management of Expanding Enterprises* (New York: Columbia U. Pr., 1955).

or any of the other suggested areas. This would be the condition of "balanced stress on objectives" to which Drucker refers.

Without a single over-all composite measure of performance, the individual is forced to rely upon his judgment as to whether increased effort on one criterion improves over-all performance, or whether there may be a reduction in performance on some other criterion which will outweigh the increase in the first. This is quite possible, for in any immediate situation many of these objectives may be contradictory to each other.

COMPOSITES

To adequately balance the stress on the contradictory objectives or criteria by which performance of a particular individual or organization is appraised, there must be an implied or explicit weighting of these criteria. When such a weighting system is available, it is an easy task to combine the measures of the various subgoals into a composite score for over-all performance.

Such a composite is used by the American Institute of Management in evaluating and ranking the managements of corporations, hospitals, and other organizations.[12] These ratings are accomplished by attaching a numerical grade to each of several criteria, such as economic function, corporate structure, production efficiency, and the like. Each criterion has an optimum rating, and the score on each for any particular organization is added to obtain a total score. Although there may be disagreement on the validity of the weighting system employed, the rating given on any particular category, the categories themselves, or the methods of estimating scores in the A.I.M. management audit, this system is an example of the type of over-all performance measurement which might be developed. Were such a system of ratings employed by an organization and found acceptable by management, it presumably would serve as a guide to obtaining a balanced stress on objectives.

A composite measure of performance was employed in Air Force wings as reported by K. C. Wagner.[13] A complex rating scheme covering a wide range of activities was used. When the organizations were put under pressure to raise their composite score without proportionate increases in the organization's means of achieving them, there were observable unanticipated consequences in the squadrons. Under a system of multiple criteria, pressure to increase performance on one criterion might be relieved by a slackening of effort toward other criteria. But with a composite criterion this does not seem as likely to occur. In Wagner's report individuals were subjected to tension, role and value conflicts, and reduced morale; air crews suffered from intercrew antagonism,

12 *Manual of Excellent Managements* (New York, 1955).
13 Kenneth C. Wagner, "Latent Functions of an Executive Control: A Sociological Analysis of a Social System Under Stress," *Research Previews*, Vol. 2 (Chapel Hill: Institute for Research in Social Science, March, 1954), mimeo.

apathy, and reduced morale; organization and power structures underwent changes; communications distortions and blockages occurred; integration decreased; culture patterns changed; and norms were violated. Some of these consequences may be desirable, some undesirable. The net result, however, might easily be less effective over-all performance.

These consequences were observable in a situation where goals were increased without a corresponding increase in means, which seems to be a common situation. Berliner refers to the "ratchet principle" wherein an increase in performance becomes the new standard, and the standard is thus continually raised. Recognition of the operation of the "rachet principle" by workers was documented by F. J. Roethlisberger and William J. Dickson.[14] There was a tacit agreement among the workers not to exceed the quota, for fear that the job would then be rerated. Deliberate restriction of output is not an uncommon occurrence.

Although the experiences reported with the use of composite measures of performance are rather skimpy, there is still a clear indication that their use may have adverse consequences for the over-all performance of the organization.

CONCLUSION

Quantitative performance measurements — whether single, multiple, or composite — are seen to have undesirable consequences for over-all organizational performance. The complexity of large organizations requires better knowledge of organizational behavior for managers to make best use of the personnel available to them. Even where performance measures are instituted purely for purposes of information, they are probably interpreted as definitions of the important aspects of that job or activity and hence have important implications for the motivation of behavior. The motivational and behavioral consequences of performance measurements are inadequately understood. Further research in this area is necessary for a better understanding of how behavior may be oriented toward optimum accomplishment of the organization's goals.

[14] F. J. Roethlisberger and William J. Dickson, *Management and the Worker* (Cambridge, Mass: Harvard U. Pr., 1939).

24

Budgeting and Employee Behavior:
A Rejoinder to a "Reply"

SELWYN W. BECKER and DAVID GREEN, JR.*

In our "Budgeting and Employee Behavior" we made two statements:
(1) a reiteration of McGregor's fundamental reservation that "participation is not a panacea"; and (2) the assertion that "participation is *not*
a single-value variable but rather a concept encompassing several explicit
variables." Stedry agrees with the substance of these statements and
attributes to us the notion that these statements are the "fundamentals"
of our argument. He states: "It is not clear how, reasoning from these
fundamentals, they arrive at a set of conclusions."[1] Stedry not only is
unclear about the reasoning which leads to our conclusions, he also is
unclear about what constitutes the fundamentals of an argument.

We stated an interest in exploring "the *belief* that increased participation can lead to better morale and increased initiative."[2] Having
noted that such belief is inconsistent with the literature (we, too, knew
about the results of the French, Israel, and Ås study), we stated our
reservation and hypothesized that participation was not a panacea because
it was not a simple variable but a complex of variables summarized under
at least two concepts, process and content. An understanding of these
concepts, we felt, would allow us to specify the conditions under which
participation could produce beneficial results.

The fundamentals of our position and the reasoning which led us
to our conclusions are as follows:

Given that participation is an interaction through which individuals become involved in managerial decisions which affect them —
the essence of "process" and "content,"

If greater interaction leads to greater group cohesiveness, and
If group cohesiveness and induction to produce at either a higher
or lower rate are positively correlated,[3]

* From the *Journal of Business,* Vol. 37, No. 2 (April 1964), pp. 203-5. Reprinted from
the *Journal of Business* by permission of the University of Chicago Press. Copyright
1964 by the University of Chicago.
1 "Budgeting and Employee Behavior: A Reply," *Journal of Business* (January 1964),
p. 195.
2 "Budgeting and Employee Behavior," *Journal of Business* (October 1962), p. 394.
3 In his conclusion Stedry compares a statement made by Schacter *et al.* with one we
made. His citation from Schacter *et al.* was: "In summary, the data indicate no necessary relationship between cohesiveness and high productivity . . . whether or not

Then the process of participation can be used to induce either higher or lower production.

If participation, at an upper level, generates positive attitudes on the part of the participating supervisors,

Then individual supervisors (each being a member of a cohesive subgroup) will attempt to induce those group and individual aspirations at the subgroup level which lead to higher rather than lower production.

If aspirations for high levels of performance are induced,

Then higher levels of performance will ensue,

If expectations of reward or punishment associated with the achieved level of performance are validated on the basis of knowledge of that achievement,

Then communication of results can affect subsequent levels of aspiration and subsequent performance.

Therefore, as we implied in our first paper, a successful participation budget increases group cohesiveness and induces positive attitudes, and

Therefore, as we made explicit in our first paper, a successful participation budget does two things: (1) it induces proper motivation and acceptance of specific goals, and (2) it validates expectations to associating reward or punishment with performance. These lead to new aspirations and motivations that set the state for the next participation budget,[4] the very conclusion to which Stedry objects. Let us examine each of the *"if-then"* statements and evaluate Stedry's remarks in terms of their relevance to the issues.

The first section of Stedry's review of the "relevant" (his adjective) literature, leadership style, and productivity is concerned primarily with worker reaction to foreman behavior and attitude. This section of the literature review is irrelevant to our intended argument for two reasons: (1) it pertains to none of the "if-then" clauses; and (2) our argument was restricted to supervisory personnel above first line to minimize member and reference-group differences. We tried to make this restriction clear in discussing the effects of knowledge of results when

---

highly cohesive groups are more likely to develop standards of high production is a separate question," etc. We would like to fill in the ellipsis: "Group members will accept induction either to increase or decrease production." Schacter *et al.* also state: "The relations between cohesiveness and productivity are as follows: Communications calling for increased production result in no significant differences between the high and low cohesive groups. There are differences, however, when the notes urge a reduction in production. In this "slow-down" condition, subjects in high cohesive groups decrease continuously from induction period to induction period. Scores for both periods are significantly below the base line level of production at better than the 1% level of confidence" (S. Schacter, N. Ellertson, D. McBride, and D. Gregory, "An Experimental Study of Cohesiveness and Productivity," *Human Relations* 1951, No. 4, pp. 229-38).

4 Becker and Green, *op. cit.,* p. 238.

we stated, "If he is not informed of the results of the comparison he cannot know whether his striving for a particular level was worthwhile or not. Nor can he, in turn, pass on the word to *his subordinates* in whom he induced specific levels of aspiration."[5] We also stated, "The participating *supervisors* bring to the new participation situation. . . ."[6] However, we are vulnerable on the clarity of this distinction and our failure to include first line supervisors.

In the second section, Stedry is concerned with the relation between morale and productivity. He cites literature to support the conclusion that morale and productivity are not perfectly correlated. He is, of course, absolutely correct. In our argument we demonstrated that cohesiveness was almost synonymous with the usual use of the term, morale. One of our "if-then" clauses is that high cohesiveness (high morale) leads either to higher or lower production. Thus we have no disagreement with this section of Stedry's review.

In the third segment Stedry discusses participation and our implication that as long as participants participate the effects will be beneficial. He cites the French, Israel, and As study and then comes up with the conclusion that "the non-universality of the participation hypothesis of improved productivity should be clear."[7] Is this not merely a non-alliterative restatement of the phrase, "Participation is not a panacea"? In this section Stedry also cites evidence that those who view participation as legitimate increase their productivity under participative supervision and decrease it where it was not viewed as legitimate. This is relevant to our "if-then" clause that only when the content of participation produces positive attitudes will higher rather than lower levels of aspiration be induced, followed, in turn, by higher rather than lower production.

The view that participation is not a legitimate managerial tool, that it is used only for manipulative purposes, would preclude the adoption of positive attitudes subsequent to participation, thus increasing the likelihood that lower rather than higher levels of aspiration would be adopted. It cannot be guaranteed that those who view it as legitimate will automatically adopt positive attitudes. Should personality clashes or other unfavorable (to the group) content result from participation, few positive attitudes will develop and group cohesiveness will remain low. This part of Stedry's review is not contradictory to our argument and is complementary to one of the "if-then" clauses.

The fourth and final segment is devoted to aspiration levels and performance. We assumed that higher levels of aspiration lead to higher goal attainment (higher productivity) and cited two studies in support of the assertion. We also noted, in passing, that we were not citing Stedry in support of his assumption even though he stated,

> The group of high budget subjects who received their budgets prior to setting their aspiration levels performed better than any

5 *Ibid.*, p. 237.
6 *Ibid.*, p. 238.
7 Stedry, p. 246.

other group, whereas the "high" budget group who set their aspirations before receiving the budget were the lowest performance of any group.

> An hypothesis which might satisfactorily explain this phenomenon is as follows: The high performing group formed its aspirations with the high budget levels in mind, while the low performing group rejected the high budget after forming aspirations with relation to their last performance.[8]

In effect, he hypothesizes that the low performers rejected a higher level of aspiration, otherwise they might have performed at a higher level. This conjecture was necessary because the data were equivocal regarding this relationship. We also question the efficacy of allowing subjects to select a goal; then, after telling them their goal should be higher than the one selected, ask what they *hope* to achieve and take that response as the goal for which they are striving — the one which should bring feelings of success if reached and feelings of failure if not reached. This section of his review relates to our questioning the method he used in measuring level of aspiration but is not relevant to the central argument or to any of the "if-then" clauses.

To sum up, where Stedry has not presented irrelevancies, he twice has agreed with or cited data in support of our arguments. Nor has he offered an alternative to our conclusions. We might better have entitled this "A Rejoinder to a 'Non-reply'."

---

[8] *Budget Control and Cost Behavior* (Englewood Cliffs, N.J.: Prentice-Hall, Inc., 1960), pp. 89-90.

25

The Asset Value of the Human Organization

MICHAEL H. GILBERT*

> Human Asset Accounting: vital for improved
> resource allocation and management practices.

There is considerable evidence that the value of a business as a going concern is much greater than the value of its tangible assets. Evidence of the magnitude of the investment in non-physical assets of a business organization is provided by the prices companies pay for firms they acquire. Usually the market price of a company's common stock is significantly larger than the shareholder's equity because market forces take into consideration the totality of the firm's resources and income-producing assets. These valuable assets, not reflected in the balance sheet, include such things as customer goodwill, patents and land whose value is in excess of book value, and the human organization.

The value of human assets was recognized by accountants as far back as 1932, when the *Accountants' Handbook* suggested that the origin of goodwill was certain values arising from the personal qualities and technical skills of owners, managers, and employees.[1] In present accounting practice we find organization costs and some prepaid expenses being treated as assets because of their future economic benefits, which is the basis of the human asset concept.

In human asset accounting we are concerned with developing and attaching explicit dollar values to a firm's human organization. . . .[2] The question remains: Is human asset accounting a feasible and practical concept?

Limitations of Current Accounting Practice

Many executives say that people constitute the most priceless asset of business, yet current accounting practices neither measure nor report their value. This exclusion handicaps all levels of management through inadequate and often inaccurate information. Measures which ignore the

* From *Management Accounting* (July 1970), pp. 25-28. Reprinted by permission of the National Association of Accountants.

1 W. A. Paton, ed., *The Accountant's Handbook*, The Ronald Press Co., 1932), p. 793.
2 Rensis Likert, *The Human Organization* (New York: McGraw-Hill Book Co., 1967), p. 148.

key personnel factor of an organization are likely to lead the manager to non-optimal decisions.

The problem arises from the traditional accounting view of assets. This view emphasizes assets as "things" of value "owned" which give worth to the firm as a going concern. Both the proprietary and entity theories of accounting insist that items must be owned to qualify as assets. Labor, as an economic factor of production, is not considered an asset.[3]

This preoccupation with physically owned evidence often results in the expensing of outlays that should be treated as assets. Thus, expenditures for investment in humans are usually expensed, although, in an economic sense such expenditures represent benefits to the firm.

By treating these expenditures as expenses, a key part of the investment base is ignored. Using an incorrect investment base yields an incorrect rate of return on investment. Under the general assumption that funds within the economy seek the highest rates of return, this situation causes an imperfect allocation of resources within the economy.

By not keeping accurate, quantitative control over valuable human assets, current accounting practices also do not protect these assets from poor management within the firm. The omission of a large percentage of the income producing assets from the balance sheet encourages decisions which yield short-range gains at substantial long-range costs.

Without human asset accounting a "pressure artist" may be able to achieve high earnings over a few years while causing unmeasured deterioration of the loyalties, favorable attitudes, and motivations of the personnel. The liquidation of these psychological variables will be reflected in reduced earnings in the future.[4]

Basis for Human Asset Accounting

The justification for assigning asset status to human resources is based on the economic concept that an asset is capable of providing some future service in money or some future service convertible into money. Thus, economists equate assets, resources, expected future services, and factors of production — which clearly justifies human resources being considered as assets.

A broader basis for human asset accounting is found in the need for bringing together the fields of accounting and management. Accounting must shed its narrow view of historical values and fixed relationships among variables, and must expand to provide the information needed by management. In order to develop a more dynamic management accounting system there must be a recognition of behavioral science concepts which will bring to management's attention the importance of the firm's investment in its human assets.[5]

[3] Roger H. Hermanson, *Accounting for Human Assets*, Occasional Paper #14, Bureau of Mines & Economic Resources, Graduate School of Business, Michigan State University, East Lansing, Mich., 1964, p. 3.
[4] Rensis Likert, *Op. cit.*, p. 114.
[5] Edwin H. Caplan, "Behavioral Assumptions of Management Accounting," *The Accounting Review*, XLI, July 1966, p. 509.

Methods to Determine the Value of Human Assets

Several authors have proposed procedures for developing explicit values for human resources within the firm.

Capitalization of salary. Hekimian and Jones[6] felt that an acceptable way would be to capitalize a man's salary to find his value. However, this approach is limited in usefulness because of the lack of a direct relationship between salary and an employee's value to the firm. Personnel receiving the same salary rarely contribute the same value to the firm.

Another problem is reflected in the choice of the discount rate to use for the capitalization of the salary, and over what time period the present value of the stream of salary payments should be calculated. Also, what salary should actually be used? There will most likely be increases in the salary over the years, yet the size and timing of these would be unknown.

Acquisition costs. Another method is to determine the acquisition costs of the human assets. To find the original dollar value of an employee would require collecting or imputing the costs involved in recruiting, hiring, and training him. Although some estimates would have to be made under this approach, it is theoretically possible to establish dollar values, and this method is compatible with the standard accounting treatment of assets.[7]

This approach faces problems because the value of a man may easily change during his employment, causing an inaccurate return on investment figure. Furthermore, if humans are regarded as assets, should their cost be allocated to future periods through a form of "depreciation"? A good question concerns the tax deductibility of any depreciation of human assets. Would the federal government provide a tax benefit through human asset depreciation?

Start-up costs. Likert proposes a more inclusive approach by measuring start-up costs. This measurement uses original costs of hiring and training personnel, but also takes into consideration the synergistic component of costs and time required for members of the firm to establish effective cooperative working relationships.[8] While this viewpoint correctly identifies an investment in time for developing these working relationships, it is more difficult to measure and quantify such an investment.

Replacement costs. Another method is to value humans at the estimated cost to the firm of replacing them with others of equivalent talents and experience. The replacement cost concept has the advantage of adjusting

---

[6] James S. Hekimian and Curtis H. Jones, "Put People on Your Balance Sheet," *Harvard Business Review*, January-February 1967, p. 107.
[7] R. Lee Brummet *et al*, "Human Resource Management—A Challenge for Accountants," *The Accounting Review*, April 1968, p. 219.
[8] Rensis Likert, *Op. cit.*, p. 147.

the human value to price trends in the economy, thereby providing a more realistic value in inflationary times.[9] However, this approach is not consistent with current accounting means of valuing assets, and would keep the value of human assets from being comparable with other assets in the firm.

Competitive bidding method. An interesting approach using the economic concept of opportunity cost has been proposed by Professors Hekimian and Jones. The value of an asset is determined by the opportunity cost of the asset, which is its maximum value in an alternative use. This value is established by competitive bidding within the firm, with investment center managers bidding for scarce employees in the marketplace of the company. A human asset will have a value only when it is a scarce resource; that is, when its employment in one division denies it to another division. The investment center with the highest bid would win the human resource and include the price in its investment base. The competitive bidding process provides an optimal allocation of personnel within the firm and a quantitative base for planning and developing the human assets of the firm.

Although this approach is based on the theoretically sound law of supply and demand, it makes serious omissions of certain asset values. Employees of the type that can be hired readily from the outside are not regarded as scarce recources and are not subject to a bid, or able to be part of the asset base of an investment center.

This concept also ignores the current value of ordinary personnel and emphasizes those with special capabilities which are in great demand. Even the potential future services of non-scarce employees are not considered under this alternative, and this exposes the narrow viewpoint of not expecting or planning for growth or improvement in the value of certain employees. This situation would tend to perpetuate, at least for some employees, the traditional mechanical viewpoint of human motivation, which is contrary to the objective of improving the management of human resources. Also, would this not lead to increased shifting of personnel within the firm, thereby disrupting work in progress, and possibly affecting employees' security and inter-personal relationships?

Economic value methods. Another major approach to the evaluation of human assets is to calculate their economic value. This concept is based on the view that differences in present and future earnings of two similar firms in the same business are due to differences in their human organization.[10]

Brummet, Flamholtz, and Pyle suggest a general approach for estimating the contribution of human resources to the total economic value of the firm. Future earnings must be forecast and then discounted

[9] Hekimian and Jones, *Op. cit.*, pp. 107-10.
[10] Rensis Likert, *Op. cit.*, p. 148.

to find their present value. A portion of the present value is then allocated to human resources based on their relative contribution.[11]

Present value method. Professor Hermanson proposes a more sophisticated approach for determining the economic value of the human assets. First, the future wage payments over the next five years are determined and then discounted at the rate of return on owned assets in the economy for the most recent year. This yields the present value of the future five years of wage payments. The next step is to calculate the firm's efficiency ratio, which is a measure of the firm's rate of return in relation to the average rate of return for the industry. The formula is based on earnings performance over the past five years, but weights recent years more heavily in order to emphasize the present efficiency of the firm. The final step is to multiply the present value of the future wage payments by the firm's efficiency ratio, which yields the present value of the future services of the firm's human assets.[12]

The major benefit of the Hermanson system would be in a more efficient allocation of resources within the economy because investors would be encouraged to provide additional funds to firms earning a high rate of return on their assets. Thus, the cost of capital to these firms would be lowered.[13] Those firms with inefficient handling of human resources would face increasing costs of capital, thereby discouraging the further addition of assets to the investment base but leading to increased efforts to improve the efficiency of the present assets.

In this proposal a closer relationship between financial statements is achieved because the measurement of valuable income-producing human assets is standardized, thus providing greater comparability of financial statements and more accurate information for investors.

Hermanson believes that the accounting profession may finally be ready to move toward a basis of recording assets that reflects their actual value, and that the recording of human resources at their fair value should aid in the rejuvenation of the position statement. The proposal also provides the financial analyst a starting point for the analysis of the total assets of the firm and a more accurate estimation of the firm's value.

A major drawback to the Hermanson method is that it proposes a dynamic change for accounting practice and it must be accepted across-the-board by the accounting profession if it is to function as intended. A single firm using it alone will add to the value of its asset base, thereby causing a decrease in its return on investment relative to other firms. Funds will then tend to flow to less efficient organizations, thereby destroying the incentive for more efficient allocation of resources. Full acceptance is also required to realize the benefits of greater accuracy and comparability in financial statements.

11 R. Lee Brummet *et al.*, *Op. cit.*, p. 220.
12 Roger H. Hermanson, *Op. cit.*, p. 17.
13 *Ibid.*, p. 36.

Goodwill method. Another economic valuation method is to translate a company's earnings in excess of the industry average into goodwill. This goodwill is then allocated to human resources in terms of the ratio of human assets to total assets.[14] While theoretically feasible, this theory assumes the asset ratio to be "given," and does not explain how one is to initially value the human assets within the firm and derive the asset ratio.

Hermanson also proposes an unpurchased goodwill method in which earnings in excess of the industry average are capitalized and allocated to the organization's human resources. This is a desirable method because it uses only past objectively verifiable net income figures in the calculation.[15] However, this approach faces the problem of determining the proper capitalization rate to use.

Both goodwill methods assume that human assets add value to the firm only when earnings exceed the industry average, which is a questionable hypothesis. It does not recognize differences in the size, quality, and efficiency of owned assets which can produce divergences in earnings.

Behavioral variables method. Professor Likert has proposed, as reported by Brummet,[16] a human asset accounting procedure whereby periodic measurements are made of the key causal and intervening variables for the corporation as a whole, or for each profit center or unit for which productivity, costs, waste, and earnings can be computed. Statistical analysis of variations in leadership styles, technical proficiency levels, supervisory levels, and organization structure (causal variables), and the resulting changes in subordinate attitudes, motivations, and behavior (intervening variables) can establish relationships among such variables. If a meaningful relationship is established between changes in causal variables which result in changes in the intervening variables, and these produce changes in end result variables such as productivity, innovation, and manpower development, then trends in earnings can be predicted.

Then, according to Likert,[17] the forecast of predicted earnings would be discounted to find the present value of the human resources for the profit center, small unit, or total corporation.

This proposal would be particularly desirable because it not only produces an explicit dollar value, as achieved by the Hermanson method, but it directs management's attention to the key human variables of an organization. The system would reveal whether the human organization was increasing, remaining unchanged, or decreasing in value, and would show trends in vital elements such as employee loyalty and motivation.

For the firm developing such a system a great deal of data and time will be required before the relationships are fully established and

14 R. Lee Brummet *et al, Op. cit.,* p. 219.
15 Roger H. Hermanson, *Op. cit.,* p. 8.
16 R. Lee Brummet *et al, Op. cit.,* p. 221.
17 Rensis Likert, *Op. cit.,* p. 150.

the current dollar value of human assets are computed continuously. As with other concepts, the Likert method also must somehow determine the appropriate capitalization rate.

Signs of Acceptance

From the point of view of the firm and the total economy, human asset accounting is a feasible and useful concept. The accounting profession is moving toward the acceptance of a basis for recording both physical and human assets at their true values, and there is some evidence to support this. A recent development is the legal precedent set by tax courts that in certain defense contracts return on investment might take into account in the investment base the prior expense of gathering together certain kinds of engineering talent. Utilities have also begun investigating the possibilities of including human assets in their rate base and the value of the sales force of an insurance company has been calculated by the economic value method of discounting future earnings attributable to the sales force.[18]

It seems that a gradual shift is taking place, and that eventually a system such as that proposed by Dr. Hermanson could become part of accounting practice throughout industry. In the meantime, the Likert method can be initiated in individual firms and provide benefits through improved management consideration of human variables. If a firm attempts to apply Likert's approach, it should achieve immediate benefits by focusing management's attention on the relationships among the causal, intervening, and end result variables.

Studies of measurements for causal and intervening variables are currently being made at The Institute of Social Research, University of Michigan. Researchers Brummet, Flamholtz and Pyle are presently engaged in a joint effort with members of the R. G. Barry Corporation of Columbus, Ohio in what is believed to be the first operational human resource accounting system.[19]

The Employee's Point of View

The feasibility and benefits of human asset accounting from the employee's point of view are certainly questionable. The effect on an employee's attitudes, motivations, and other feelings from having a specific value established for him are not known. It is easy to imagine employees repulsed by such a concept, for it has been traditionally unacceptable to society. Organized labor is probably powerful enough to stop such a movement if it wished. On the other hand, one could argue that by having his value recognized, a person would be motivated to better himself and increase his worth.

18 R. Lee Brummet *et al, Op. cit.*, pp. 218 and 219.
19 R. Lee Brummet, Eric G. Flamholtz and William C. Pyle, "Human Resource Accounting: A Tool to Increase Managerial Effectiveness," *Management Accounting*, August 1969, p. 12.

Conclusion

Proponents of human asset accounting present a strong theoretical argument for giving asset status to human resources and listing these in the balance sheet at dollar values. The use of such a system would aid decision making by providing more accurate information to management and investors. More meaningful information will provide a better estimate of the value of the firm and its return on investment, which will lead to a more efficient allocation of resources within the economy.

26

Where "Human Resource Accounting" Stands Today

MARVIN WEISS*

Reports
1. Internal
2. External

> Many articles have appeared recently on the subject of human resource accounting (HRA). While most have focused on the internal applications of this new — some would say radically new — method of accounting, little has been said about the pros and cons of HRA in external (public) financial statements. This article summarizes some actual and potential uses of HRA not only internally *and* externally, but also from the viewpoint of conventional accounting practice.
>
> THE EDITORS
> (of Administrative Management)

Human resource accounting had its origins in the work of Rensis Likert, former director of the Institute for Social Research. Writing in *New Patterns of Management* and *The Human Organization,* Likert was concerned with the shortcomings of conventional financial controls, which emphasized end-result variables, such as profits, costs, and output, while ignoring the intervening variables of employee morale, attitude, and perception.

While management might achieve short-run profits by concentrating on end results and ignoring the intervening variables, Likert argued that it was improvement in the intervening variables that would promote higher profits in the long run. Furthermore, existing financial structures focused on end results, rewarding job-centered management. Employee-centered management was penalized. In addition, favorable morale built up over a period of time might be affected adversely by a job-centered manager who, by lowering morale, "wasted" human assets.

Likert went on to suggest that this waste should be reflected by a charge in a manager's P&L statement, and that a credit to measure an

* From *Administrative Management* (November 1972), pp. 43-48. Republished with permission from *Administrative Management,* copyright © 1972 by Geyer-McAllister Publications, Inc., New York.

increase in human resources be added to the extent that morale improved during the period.

To explore further the accounting aspects of HRA, Likert invited an accounting educator, R. Lee Brummet, and his colleagues Eric Flamholtz and William C. Pyle, to help set up an HRA system at R. G. Barry Corp., fashion accessories manufacturer. Barry has released HRA information in its financial statements since 1969. Its reporting system departs from original outlay cost accounting by using a replacement cost approach to establish an initial HRA balance, and then adding to this a combination of outlay costs and company development "standard" costs.

Others have proposed alternative means for HRA, ranging from replacement cost through Likert's proposal that the balance be determined directly through changes in morale and attitude over time. Between these extremes have been proposals for direct capitalization of future salary payments, and the use of bidding or opportunity cost systems. Actually, HRA is only one example of an effort being made to extend conventional accounting, another being the measurement of ecology-related expenses as a social investment.

Conventional financial accounting practice frowns upon the capitalization of internally generated intangibles such as HRA. However, for internal reporting to management, there are no limitations on HRA, and it may be that it has a more immediate application here than for external reporting to shareholders.

Banks, for example, have become heavily involved in training programs for their own staff, as well as in social impact programs such as the retraining of veterans and inner-city youth. This involvement, together with persistent pressure on reported earnings, has forced a re-examination of the policy of treating such costs as expenses in the period incurred. While the day is not close when HRA could be shown on a bank's external balance sheet, banks and other organizations are considering the inclusion of such items on divisional financial statements used as the basis for measuring managerial performance.

One multi-unit bank is currently considering the entry of a charge in the internal P&L statement of a division manager to reflect the loss suffered through the turnover of a trained staff member. Another bank is considering the development of a comprehensive system to handle HRA, in which the cost of training a particular category of employee would be deferred as an asset and so carried on the divisional financial statement. Upon turnover of an employee, the asset would be written off as a lump sum charge in the period of termination. This bank is also considering the gradual amortization of that asset over the employee's career, but is uncertain as to the appropriate rate.

There are situations in which companies have considered moving to a new location, and have called in a consultant to advise them on the number of executives who would leave rather than move, as well as the cost of re-establishing the organization in the new location. HRA could provide, through the formal internal accounting system, a means by which management could continually evaluate various alternatives, incuding the decision to relocate. Here unamortized HRA balances could be compared with the potential cost of personnel replacement, although unamortized historical costs might not be relevant for this comparison.

A number of other alternatives can also be examined — for instance, to grant a salary increase, or to refuse and risk having to hire a replacement, or the question of hiring an experienced manager, or training a junior staff member for the spot.

By far, the most intriguing application of HRA involves determining the rate-of-return on investment in projects that until now were not ranked with conventional productive investments. For example, the cost of paving an employee parking lot may be considered a necessity and not ranked. However, if turnover can be reduced by putting in the lot, the resultant cost savings in not retraining new people can be quantified in dollar terms. Then, these savings, over a suitable period of time, can be discounted and compared with the outlay for the lot, using conventional techniques. Perhaps the ROI on the project is not "O," as has been commonly assumed. This investment may prove to be more productive than the alternatives proposed.

HRA in External Reporting

Under conventional financial accounting, the capitalization of employee development expenditure is unacceptable practice. Nevertheless, if HRA is restricted to internal reporting only, shareholders and others will be deprived of information that may be the key factor in estimating future earnings potential.

Shareholders and financial analysts should be concerned if, in a labor-intensive company, the firm is experiencing above-normal turnover of personnel. The problems of replacement and re-training costs will become evident in future financial statements. If HRA expenditures were capitalized, then excess amortization of that balance over current deferral of such expenditures would indicate that the human organization was being dissipated.

In sizing up a company for possible investment, analysts consider managerial talent an important factor. If that is so, then why shouldn't some quantification of this be on the balance sheet?

R. G. Barry's initial determination of human assets in January, 1968, showed a net book value of $528,300. In its first pro-forma statement at the end of 1969, this had grown to $986,094. In the HRA-based income statement, $173,569 has been added back to reflect the fact that the deferrals of expense to the HRA account exceeded the amortization of prior capitalized balances. This indicated that the net investment in human resource investment grew during the year by the amount indicated. After provision of an assumed 50 per cent tax rate, net income under HRA was increased by 50 per cent of the before-tax addition.

For the non-accountant, it should be explained that the company obviously deducted HRA expenditures for income tax purposes as incurred. Under existing tax regulations, it appears that even if the company wanted to capitalize for tax purposes as well — which would be unlikely — deduction of amortization in a future year would not be permitted.

Accordingly, since the company received a tax benefit which it did not yet claim on its books, 50 per cent of the asset balance has been offset by a deferred tax liability. This reflects the fact that amortization of HRA in future periods would be non-deductible, since such costs had been deducted in the period of incurrence. The remaining 50 per cent flows through as an add-back to retained earnings.

In 1970, the asset balance in HRA fell by $43,900, because amorti-

"THE TOTAL CONCEPT"

R. G. Barry Corporation and Subsidiaries
Pro-Forma
(Financial and Human Resource Accounting)

Balance Sheet	1970 Conventional and Human Resource	1970 Conventional Only	1969 Conventional and Human Resource	1969 Conventional Only
Assets				
Total Current Assets	$10,944,693	$10,944,693	$10,003,628	$10,003,628
Net Property, Plant and Equipment	1,682,357	1,682,357	1,770,717	1,770,717
Excess of Purchase Price of Subsidiaries over Net Assets Acquired	1,188,704	1,188,704	1,188,704	1,188,704
Net Investments in Human Resources	942,194	—	986,094	—
Other Assets	166,417	166,417	106,783	106,783
	$14,924,365	$13,982,171	$14,055,926	$13,069,832
Liabilities and Stockholders' Equity				
Total Current Liabilities	$ 3,651,573	$ 3,651,573	$ 5,715,708	$ 5,715,708
Long Term Debt, Excluding Current Installments	2,179,000	2,179,000	1,935,500	1,935,500
Deferred Compensation	77,491	77,491	62,380	62,380
Deferred Federal Income Taxes as a Result of Appropriation for Human Resources	471,097	—	493,047	—
Stockholders' Equity:				
Capital Stock	1,087,211	1,087,211	879,116	879,116
Additional Capital in Excess of Par Value	3,951,843	3,951,843	1,736,253	1,736,253
Retained Earnings:				
Financial	3,035,053	3,035,053	2,740,875	2,740,875
Appropriation for Human Resources	471,097	—	493,047	—
Total Stockholders' Equity	8,545,204	8,074,107	5,849,291	5,356,244
	$14,924,365	$13,982,171	$14,055,926	$13,069,832

Statement of Income	1970 Conventional and Human Resource	1970 Conventional Only	1969 Conventional and Human Resource	1969 Conventional Only
Net sales	$28,164,181	$28,164,181	$25,310,588	$25,310,588
Cost of sales	18,252,181	18,252,181	16,275,876	16,275,876
Gross profit	9,912,000	9,912,000	9,034,712	9,034,712
Selling, general and administrative expenses	7,546,118	7,546,118	6,737,313	6,737,313
Operating income	2,365,882	2,365,882	2,297,399	2,297,399
Other deductions, net	250,412	250,412	953,117	953,117
Income before Federal income taxes	2,115,470	2,115,470	1,344,222	1,344,222
Human Resource expenses applicable to future periods	(43,900)	—	173,569	—
Adjusted income before Federal income taxes	2,071,570	2,115,470	1,517,791	1,344,222
Federal income taxes	1,008,050	1,030,000	730,785	644,000
Net income	$ 1,063,520	$ 1,085,470	$ 787,006	$ 700,222

HRA System at R. G. Barry Corp. was established under the guidance of Rensis Likert, former director of the Institute for Social Research, together with R. Lee Brummet and his colleagues Eric Flamholtz and William C. Pyle. Barry's reporting system utilizes a replacement cost approach to establish an initial HRA balance. Combined outlay costs and developed "standard" costs were then added. Reduction in HRA expenditures led to a 1970 net income that was lower than conventional net income.

zation exceeded new investment deferral by this amount. Accordingly, HRA net income is lower than conventional net income in 1970.

The importance of HRA in external reporting to shareholders is highlighted by the comparisons in the HRA account from 1969 to 1970. The Barry "shareholder letter" in the 1970 annual report supports the observation that could be made from the pro-forma statements, that Barry did indeed cut back in employee development and training outlays during that period.

Critics of HRA in external reporting charge that deferral of employee development expenditures is a sham that would result in higher current earnings. In the Barry case, a reduction in HRA expenditures led to a 1970 net income that was *lower* than conventional net income.

The initial HRA system covered 95 managerial people. In 1971, the system was expanded to include clerical and factory personnel, adding $481,370 to the HRA balance. In addition, deferral exceeded amortization of prior costs by $137,000, so that 1971 HRA net income was higher than conventional net income.

HRA expenditures at Barry were classified in six categories: recruitment costs, hiring costs, formal training, on-the-job training, familiarization, and development. Within the six, consideration was given to salary, non-salary, and "opportunity" costs incurred in each of the categories. Opportunity costs include the revenue foregone by possible alternative uses of management personnel while engaged in training and development. At present, Barry is only capitalizing salary and non-salary costs in the HRA account.

The use of "replacement investment," as opposed to actual original outlay cost, may explain why HRA information had to be presented in pro-forma rather than primary statements. Furthermore, while recruiting, hiring, and formal training costs are easy to measure, the remaining three costs are more difficult. But they reflect the increasing worth of the individual as he grows within the organization.

Measurement in the latter three categories *is* too subjective to be accepted in external financial reports. However, even if attention is focused on the first three categories, which can be measured with reasonable objectivity, the capitalization of such costs on an original outlay (historical cost) basis would be more meaningful than is the existing treatment of immediate expense. Considering the more sophisticated training and recruitment programs in larger companies, there would appear to be a substantial understatement of assets under conventional financial reporting.

While HRA measurement of an original cost basis may only represent a small portion of the true worth of "human assets," further refinement, for external purposes, would have to wait for modification of overall accounting measurement procedure. In the interim, the HRA system could generate dual measurements, namely historical cost-based information for external reporting, and replacement or current-cost information for internal use.

How Others Used HRA

☐ *The Milwaukee Braves case.* When the Milwaukee Braves' franchise was shifted from Boston in 1962, the club implemented an HRA reporting system for its investment in player contracts and for player development and recruiting expenditures. Milwaukee's HRA predated Barry's by more than six years. The club's balances were presented in formal financial statements that had been audited and accepted without comment by a major CPA firm.

Milwaukee capitalized the cost of player contracts acquired from the prior owner of the club, and the subsequent farm club, scouting, and recruitment operations of the new team. Player development costs were amortized at a 12.5 per cent rate, contract costs at 10 per cent. This treatment was in effect from 1962 to 1966, at which time the Braves, now in Atlanta, reverted to an expense-as-incurred basis for player development costs, which was the common practice, but continued to capitalize player contract costs. In 1967, IRS Revenue Procedure 67-379 mandated the capitalization, for tax purposes only, of contract and rookie bonus costs for all teams.

In the 1963 shareholder's letter, the team president justified HRA by noting that Milwaukee was considered a leader in the area of future-team development, by having invested more than $900,000 in 1963 alone. The letter said such expenditure was comparable to expenditures by other industries for research and development, which are commonly capitalized. Furthermore, Milwaukee's policy was to maintain a fixed base investment in player personnel, with amortization of existing player investments offset by deferral of costs of training new players. In practice, this policy didn't work and in 1964 the asset balance fell by $119,172.

☐ *The EDS case.* The 1970 annual report of Electronic Data Systems (EDS) contains a deferred charge on the company balance sheet for the cost of training engineers in their systems engineer development program (SED). This amount is being amortized over a two-year period to expense, with an immediate write-off if a trainee leaves EDS during that period. The firm amortizes such costs on a reverse sum-of-the-digits basis, under the assumption that, as the employee becomes more experienced over time, he also becomes more productive. Amortizing such costs should thus be on an increasing-charge basis.

☐ *The Flying Tiger case.* Most airlines make a heavy investment in the training of flight crews and ground personnel, and the compensation paid to pilots reflects in part the level of training and the importance of this group to revenue production.

Many lines have a policy of deferring and amortizing training costs, but these are usually lumped into a deferred charge amortized over the life of the equipment in question, rather than over the life of employees.

One airline, however, Flying Tiger Inc., has separated its "training costs applicable to aircraft" into a separate account. Integration costs of equipment other than training are also deferred, but in a separate account. In 1969, Flying Tiger converted to an expense as incurred basis for training costs, in keeping with similar policies adopted by other major air carriers.

Pros, Cons of External HRA

There can be little argument that HRA could provide vital information for managerial decision-making through the internal reporting system. While many companies are now considering the use of such internal systems, significant data are being omitted from conventional external financial statements, and such omission seems contrary to basic accounting principles.

The position of the Accounting Principles Board (the rule-making body for the American Institute of Certified Public Accountants) with regard to the expensing of internally generated intangibles is clear-cut, and the EDS case violates this mandate. (The Milwaukee action preceded APB's pronouncement.)

The following, from a letter by the chief financial officer of a major utility, summarizes the reaction of many financial officers toward HRA —

> In checking with our outside auditors . . . [and] a member of [our] Accounting Executive Committee, I can find no serious interest in this subject nor any evidence that any regulatory commission has given serious consideration to including personnel acquisition and integration costs in the rate base. In fact, none of us recall seeing this subject covered in any accounting literature we have seen in recent years. While the personnel of a company may constitute valuable "assets" in terms of placing an appropriate value on a going concern, we must keep in mind that this asset is highly mobile and does not have the characteristics of assets which are customarily recorded on the books of a company. Certainly, we cannot state that such an "asset" is owned by the company. As I see it, these are continuing costs which are properly charged to current expenses rather than capitalized.

Aside from the comment on the lack of HRA literature, which is certainly not the case, the following points *are* made in the above quotation:

☐ *Requirement for future benefit.* If turnover rates are high, and employees are highly mobile, then there is no future benefit to accrue as an asset. The doctrine of conservatism dictates that where the period of future benefit is uncertain, the charge in question should be expensed rather than capitalized. (In practice, some high-flying companies have violated this doctrine consistently, capitalizing everything possible to show the highest possible earnings during periods in which capital was being raised. Nevertheless, the doctrine is one of the basic tenets of conventional accounting practice.)

☐ *Ownership status.* HRA expenditures are not owned in the conventional sense of the word. This argument suggests that assets must be legally owned to be recorded as such, and it also suggests that employees might resent their treatment as "assets," as though they were on a par with plant and equipment.

☐ *Roll-over.* It is implied in the above statement that even if HRA expenditures were capitalized, the rate of amortization and rate of deferral would coincide, so that the effect on net income would be the same under conventional treatment or HRA. Thus, while items comprising the asset balance would change, the asset total would remain constant. The Milwaukee Braves planned their policy on this basis, but as we have seen, it did not work in practice.

In addition to these "con" arguments, others cited recently include the possibility of reported-earnings manipulation, and the inability to amortize the asset balance on a rational basis once it has been established.

An editorial writer in *Barron's* had a field day with EDS when he noted a statement deferring training costs. The impact was to increase earnings per share about .02 cents, but nevertheless, the possibility that EDS and other companies would choose to follow this treatment raised the eyebrows of the financial establishment. Nevertheless, in terms of future earnings potential, one must consider whether it is right to understate income now and overstate it in the future under the conventional treatment of employee development costs.

Arguments for Capitalization

☐ *Amortization period.* The question of future benefit and the period of amortization are related. Based on past experience with regard to turnover, companies have a fair idea of how long the average employee is likely to remain. Pension programs, after all, are based on a rational system for accruing pension expense over the expected service life of the employee. If actuarial calculations have been made for this purpose. they could also be used to amortize charges incurred for employee development.

Under IRS 67-379, ball clubs are required to establish amortization periods that parallel the service-life expectancy of the player for amortization of contract acquisition costs. In practice, clubs have adopted uniform rates ranging from two to five years. If such procedures are accepted by IRS, they should be accepted in general accounting as well.

It should be noted that HRA proponents have not suggested that *all* employee development costs be capitalized. Clearly, certain costs are in an expense category, and should remain as such in HRA. In the EDS case, for example, only SED costs were capitalized, with the key factor being that this training program lasted beyond one year. Training programs of shorter duration were expensed in the year of training.

In addition, two writers have suggested a distinction between specific and general training. Blaine and Stanbury* contend that from an economic viewpoint, under conditions of perfect competition firms ordinarily would not provide general training. They might provide specific training, viewing it as an investment in "human capital" which increases worker productivity.

In the real world, firms apparently do invest in general training programs, such as college tuition reimbursement, even though they are not necessarily under competitive pressure to do so. Since under most of these programs an employee is free to leave at any time, such expenditures probably could not be construed as assets, and should not be capitalized. EDS, on the other hand, takes the position that its SED program is so highly specialized that the training could not be carried over to another employer, and that future benefit would attach to the company, assuming the employee remained.

Likert's broader view of HRA as encompassing any morale-building expenditure probably would call for capitalization of general-type expenditures. Accountants can rightly argue that the future benefit of such expenditures is uncertain, and the charges do not warrant asset status.

☐ *Employee mobility and ownership status.* While the roll-over argument made above may be valid under certain circumstances, it is generally agreed that the basis for accounting should be the individual changes in the HRA account, even if the impact on the income statement would be nil because amortization and deferral rates coincide. This policy has been established in dealing with income-tax allocations, and with pension fund liability accounts. HRA treatment would be no different.

With regard to ownership, it is recognized that certain types of assets need not be "owned" in the conventional sense to be treated as assets. The capitalization of rental payments under long-term leases is an example of asset treatment where the item is not owned in the legal sense. Furthermore, the notion that employees would resent treatment as "assets" is probably the weakest argument against HRA, since the implementation of such a system would be accompanied by a general upgrading of management practices and employee morale.

☐ *The matching concept.* The arguments of conservatism and of possible manipulation of earnings have ignored the more fundamental concept of accrual accounting, namely the matching of revenue and expense in the proper period. While individual HRA expenditures may be small, the aggregate amounts are large enough to warrant serious consideration of the misstatement of income resulting from the charging of employee development expenditures to current expense, while these expenditures clearly produce future benefits that will clearly last beyond the current period. More significant, these expenditures are made for employees who are still in the process of learning their functions, and may

* Blaine, E., and Stanbury, W. T., "Accounting for Human Capital," *Canadian Chartered Accountant*, January, 1971, pp. 67-72.

not be revenue-producers in the year of their training. Yet their training, and related salary costs, are being matched with current revenue, which they did not help produce.

In future periods, when these employees become productive, net income is overstated. This is the excess earning capacity that eventually winds up as "goodwill," because of failure to treat these expenditures properly in the period when originally incurred.

HRA and Mergers

There has been ample consideration in the literature of the problems surrounding the creation of "goodwill" when companies merge, where the merger is treated as a purchase and not a pooling-of-interests. Goodwill is the amount that accounts for the difference between the fair value of assets acquired and the amount of cash or cash equivalents given up in a merger transaction. While IRS and some accountants believe that goodwill has an indefinite life, in the absence of evidence to the contrary, APB has mandated the amortization of goodwill over a period of no longer than forty years.

While APB opinion 17 specifically indicates that internally generated intangibles, such as HRA, should be expensed, APB 16 recognizes and discusses the treatment of goodwill. Some accountants see a basic inconsistency here, in that internally generated intangibles are expensed, while intangibles in the form of goodwill can be capitalized.

IRS views goodwill per se as having an unlimited life, and says the expense resulting from its mandatory amortization is not deductible for tax purposes. However, if the IRS would agree to the partial allocation of goodwill to an HRA account, it could then be argued that due to natural factors, this account has a very definite limited life, and amortization of *this* amount should be allowed for tax purposes. IRS' general view, however, seems to be that management talent is a revolving asset, and that as experienced managers grow older, they are replaced by younger ones in the normal course of business. This is the roll-over, or revolving account argument, cited in the quotation above.

Existing HRA literature deals with alternative methods of valuing human resources, but does not consider the reasons firms are not adopting HRA in external financial reports.

While HRA methods may be conceptually more sound than conventional ones, the fact remains that present accounting practice is based on original historical cost. If HRA is to appear in external reports, it must conform to the imperfections that exist in conventional practice.

The capitalization of actual outlay cost, while not going "all the way," would certainly contribute to the generation of financial statements that provide greater information as to the true worth of a company.

Despite APB's position, large CPA firms have established research groups to explore applications of HRA, and further work is scheduled by members of the Brummet team to measure the understatement of assets under conventional practice, and the omission from the balance sheet of what may be the most important asset of all.

A "Human Resource" Bibliography

Blaine, E., and Stanbury, W. T., "Accounting for Human Capital," *Canadian Chartered Accountant* (January, 1971)

Brummet. R. L., Flamholtz, E. G., and Pyle, William C., "Human Resource Accounting: A Tool to Increase Managerial Effectiveness," *Management Accounting* (August, 1969), pp. 12-15

Brummet, R. L., Flamholtz, E. G., and Pyle, W. C., "Human Resource Measurement—A Challenge for Accountants," *The Accounting Review* (April, 1968), pp. 217-224

Brummet, R. Lee, Flamholtz, Eric, and Pyle, W. C., (ED.) *Human Resource Accounting* (Foundation for Research on Human Behavior, Ann Arbor, Mich., 1969)

Cullather, James L., "The Missing Asset: Human Capital," *Mississippi Valley Journal of Business and Economics* (Spring 1967), pp. 72-73

Eggers, H.C., "The Evaluation of Human Assets," *Management Accounting* (November, 1971), pp. 28-30

Elias, Nabil, "Some Aspects of Human Resource Accounting, *Cost and Management* (November-December, 1971), pp. 38-43

Hekimian, James S., and Jones, Curtis H., "Put People on Your Balance Sheet," *Harvard Business Review* (Jan.-Feb. 1967), pp. 106-113

Lev, Baruch, and Schwartz, Aba, "On the Use of the Economic Concept of Human Capital in Financial Statements," *The Accounting Review* (January, 1971), pp. 103-112

Likert, Rensis, *The Human Organization: Its Management and Value,* (New York, McGraw Hill, 1967)

Likert, Rensis, *New Patterns of Management* (New York, McGraw-Hill, 1961)

Norton, H. S., and Hiker, B. F., "Public Utility Concept and Human Capital," *Public Utilities Fortnightly,* (April 11, 1968), pp. 15-20

Paine, Frank T., "Human Resource Accounting—The Current State of the Question," *The Federal Accountant,* (June, 1970), pp. 57-69

"People Are Capital Investments At R. G. Barry Corp.," *Management Accounting* (November, 1971), pp. 53-55

V

Pricing, Output and Investment Decisions

Exhibit III-1, (p. 143) listed several management evaluations and management accounting techniques which may aid each evaluation. This section takes a closer look at pricing, output and investment decisions beyond that provided in Section III. The articles in this section are either expansions of subjects given brief treatment in most introductory/intermediate textbooks, or thought-provoking pieces.

"Management's Pricing Decision" continues a main theme of this collection of readings: attempting to show which management accounting techniques assist which management evaluations. In a sense, pricing/output decisions could be short- or long-run, involving a price leader or a price follower. Naturally, many other variations of these four exist. Generally speaking different accounting techniques are needed to combine with nonaccounting information for each decision; the price follower, for example, must decide whether to produce or not at the price others have set, and might even have to consider liquidating the entire business — a disinvestment decision. This article describes a few simple pricing decisions by bringing in accounting techniques and thereby indicates a potential role for accounting. Note, however, that the article is merely an introduction to a complex matter.

"Product Contribution Analysis for Multi-Product Pricing" provides greater insight into pricing decisions. The author brings several accounting techniques together in his analysis: contribution margin, profit-volume comparisons, discounted cash flows, earnings per share effects and return on investment. Of special interest is the recognition given to different management goals: ". . . management's objectives will dictate which ranking is most significant. That is, if the short-run objective is to raise revenue, the revenue ranking will be important. If the management wishes to increase earnings per share, however, the contribution ranking would be more significant." To some the sacrificing of profit in favor of revenue may seem strange, but different short-term objectives must be stressed at different times to balance longer term objectives. See also the discussion of "satisficing" in the articles by Buckley and McKenna, and Caplan.

"Use of Sensitivity Analysis in Capital Budgeting" explains how "to calculate in advance what effect errors in estimation would have on the estimated rates of return (on investment) and thus to determine the significance of such errors." Concepts such as sensitivity analysis and simulation can be very helpful in assessing risk in investment decisions. The former is often useful as a less costly device than the latter in indicating which estimates should be made with extra care.

"Anyone for Widgets?" employs a light style in assessing the place of standard costs in pricing, overall performance appraisal, and inventory valuation for external reporting purposes. The author strongly argues that "cost-plus-profit" approaches to pricing in all but cost-plus contract situations are inappropriate. Note carefully that he seems to be using the concept of performance efficiency in a sense different than that employed by advocates of responsibility accounting. Also observe the remarks about the effect that tax laws and external reporting "principles" can have on management accounting information and its usefulness for specific decisions.

"Cost-Volume-Profit Analysis Under Conditions of Uncertainty" explains how to incorporate risk and uncertainty into an accounting technique helpful in output and investment decisions. ("The best alternative cannot be chosen without some statement of the firm's attitude toward risk. However, given a certain attitude, the proper choice should be facilitated by using probability information. . . .") This article is another example of how statistics and mathematics can make traditional management accounting techniques stronger aids to management.

27

Management's Pricing Decision

JOHN C. LERE*

> Both absorption costing and direct costing
> schools have their advocates. But, as this article
> shows, what is appropriate for one firm or
> industry may be wholly inappropriate for
> another —

An accountant called upon to provide information to assist the management of a firm in its pricing decision will probably react by computing
some type of cost figure. Numerous "cost" figures have been proposed
at different times as solutions to the "cost for pricing purposes" problem.
Faced with many potential candidates for a cost to give management for
use in pricing and convincing arguments in favor of each, the accountant
may throw up his hands in dismay, use a coin to make the decision for
him, or perhaps use his "favorite" cost figure, whatever that favorite cost
figure may be.

One approach to solving the accountant's dilemma is for him to
further analyze the decision management must make. The decision to be
made may be one of two basic types: 1) What price should we charge
for our product? 2) Should we accept a price offered for our product?

The actual decision a firm faces makes a difference in the most
suitable "cost" to use in the pricing decision. The remainder of this
article expands the idea of different costs for different pricing decisions.
Although only two costing methods, absorption and direct, are used in the
article, the analysis could be extended to other costing methods.

Initially, ways of using each costing method in pricing are presented. Then, four different types of firms are described in order to
determine the actual decision being made and a suggested "cost" to assist
the decision maker.

Two exhibits help to explain how absorption costing and direct
costing might be used in product pricing.

One must start with a basic set of data from which to work. Two
similar firms will be used in the exhibits. AB Company uses absorption

* From *Management Advisor* (September-October 1971), pp. 39-42. Reprinted by permission of *Management Advisor*. Copyright © 1971 by the American Institute of Certified Public Accountants.

costing. DIR Company chooses to use direct costing. To facilitate comparison, the same basic data will be used in both of the examples.

Basic Data

Past experience of AB Co. and DIR Co. has shown that each unit that they produce requires two and one-half units of raw material and three hours of direct labor. In addition, they have determined that the average purchasing price for raw material is $2.00 per unit and that the average wage rate they pay is $2.50 an hour. The company must also decide upon a measure of business activity with which to associate cost for purposes of allocating variable overhead. Any indicator of the level of activity at which AB Co. and DIR Co. are operating could have been selected, e.g., machine hours operated or units produced. Both companies have chosen to use direct labor hours. Studies by their engineering departments have indicated that those elements of overhead which can be classified as variable are incurred at the rate of $1.00 per direct labor hour.

Several additional facts are necessary to permit use of absorption costing. Some measure of activity must be chosen for use in allocating fixed overhead to units of production. Since it has already been indicated that variable overhead incurrence is related to the number of direct labor hours worked, direct labor hours will also be assumed to be a suitable basis for fixed overhead allocation in order to simplify the example. Again, any indicator of the level of activity at which AB Co. is operating could have been chosen. Once an activity base is selected, it is next necessary to estimate the expected amount of activity for a given period of time. Also, the fixed overhead which the company expects to incur during the same period of time must be predicted. One year will be used in this example. The base chosen depends on the operations of the particular firm. During the period of one year, AB Co. expects to work 200,000 direct labor hours and expects to incur $300,000 of fixed overhead. When absorption costing is used in the pricing decision, some method of converting production cost into price is customarily provided. A markup rate of 50 per cent of total manufacturing cost will be used, but numerous other possibilities exist. With this information available, it is now possible to begin computation of an absorption costing price.

Exhibit I, below, shows the computation of an absorption cost price for the AB Co.'s product.

Briefly, computing a price for the AB Co. product under absorption costing involves seven steps. First, raw material usage for one unit of finished product is multiplied by the average cost of a unit of raw material. Second, labor usage in producing one finished unit is multiplied by the average wage rate. In the third step, the same labor usage figure is used and multiplied by the variable overhead rate in order to determine the amount of variable overhead to assign to a finished unit. The fourth step in Exhibit I involves the same labor usage figure. This time, however, the figure is multiplied times the fixed overhead rate (computed by dividing the fixed overhead expected for the period of time by the

Exhibit I

AB Co. Product Price: Absorption Costing

Unit Cost of Manufacturing

Direct Material	(2½ units x $2.00/unit)	$5.00
Direct Labor	(3 hours x $2.50/hour)	7.50
Variable Overhead	(3 hours x $1.00/hour)	3.00
Fixed Overhead	(3 hours x [$300,000/200,000 hours])	4.50
	Total Unit Manufacturing Cost	$20.00
Markup ($20.00 x 50%)		10.00
Unit Selling Price		$30.00

expected number of labor hours to be worked during the same length of time). Direct material cost per unit, direct labor cost per unit, unit variable overhead cost, and unit fixed overhead cost are totaled in the fifth step to determine unit manufacturing cost. For the AB Co. product, the sixth step involves multiplication of the markup rate times the unit production cost. The final step is the addition of manufacturing cost and the markup to determine price.

In using direct costing to assist DIR Co.'s management in its pricing decision, one might take a different approach. Since the basis of direct costing is that fixed costs are not unit costs, the only cost elements to be used are ones which vary in total amount with the level of activity. Therefore, one might compute variable unit cost in much the same manner as was used above for the unit cost of manufacturing under absorption costing, except that fixed overhead is omitted. In addition to the variable manufacturing costs, one should also include variable selling and administrative expenses in the variable unit cost figure. For purposes of the example, the variable selling and administrative expenses are assumed to amount to $2.50 a unit. (See Exhibit II, below.)

The total variable unit cost, $18.00 in this case, is the significant figure for use in DIR Company's pricing decision. DIR Co. can use this figure to evaluate a price offered to it or a price determined by some other means. For example, the marketing division may suggest this as a successful price for a new product. In this example, price determined independently is assumed to be $29.00. If the bid price is greater than total variable unit cost, each unit the firm sells will reduce a net loss or increase net income by the contribution margin, which is the difference between price and total variable unit cost. (This assumes that the firm need not increase facilities to produce the product being evaluated.) If no other alternatives are available for use of the firm's facilities, the firm would be advised to sell the product in the short run. During the short

Exhibit II

DIR Co. Product Price: Direct Costing

Unit Variable Manufacturing Costs:

Direct Material	(2½ units x $2.00/unit)	$5.00
Direct Labor	(3 hours x $2.50/hour)	7.50
Variable Overhead (3 hours x $1.00/hour)		3.00
Total Variable Manufacturing Costs per Unit		**$15.50**
Variable Selling & Administrative Costs per Unit		2.50
Total Variable Unit Costs		**$18.00**
Contribution Margin ($29.00-$18.00)		11.00
Price, obtained independently		**$29.00**

run, the firm will be unable to reduce productive capacity and hence a major element of fixed overhead, depreciation. Therefore, accepting any price greater than total variable unit cost under the circumstances will maximize short-run income or minimize short-run loss.

The two pricing exhibits point out the basic difference in approaching the pricing decision. Absorption costing results in the setting of a price and direct costing results in determining whether a firm should accept a price. In other words, absorption costing is more appropriate when a firm's pricing decision takes the form: What price should we charge for our product? On the other hand, direct costing appears more useful when a firm's pricing question is: Should we accept a price offered for or suggested for our product?

Determining the Pricing Decision

Consideration of several industry examples may illustrate some of the different pricing decisions faced by firms. Four firm types will be discussed. The types are a) a seller of a uniform product on an open market, b) a novelty item firm, c) a price leader, d) a price follower. . . . . .

Looking first at the firm selling a uniform product on an open market, one may observe that this firm has an economic environment that closely approximates what the economists call "perfect competition." By definition, a firm in perfect competition has no control over price. Price is determined in a market where the aggregate buyers and sellers interact to yield a price. Then the seller must decide if he will accept the price or not. Accepting the price will enable the firm to sell as many units of its product as it wishes at the market price. Not accepting the price means that the firm sells none of its product and probably will not produce any units of the product. If the firm has no reasonable alternative ways to use its capacity, then it faces a net loss equal to its fixed costs, because it cannot reduce them in the short run. This firm is faced with the decision of accepting a price or rejecting a price. Therefore, the firm will probably find direct costing a more useful aid in the pricing decision than absorption costing.

Place for Direct Costing

Although one may be unable to find firms in a situation exactly like that described above, one may still find the analysis useful. To the extent that a firm must accept a price determined in the market place, direct costing better answers the question than does absorption costing.

The second type of firm definitely doesn't face the market-place-determined price because usually no market exists for its product. The novelty firm develops a product like the "hula hoop" or "super ball" or "frisbee." It must then, in effect, establish a market place for its novelty item. One might reason that the novelty firm management is definitely faced with a decision of what price to charge for its product. Management of this novelty firm has, however, found that a price recommended by marketing researchers is more realistic for its economic environment than a price developed by accountants. The management of the firm is faced with the need to evaluate the price presented by the marketing experts. The evaluation determines whether or not the novelty item is produced.

The evaluation presumably is based on the acceptability of the price recommended. In other words, should we accept the suggested price or not? This decision is clearly one of the type for which information provided using direct costing will be more useful.

A few introductory comments might help to make discussion of the last two types of firms clearer. Many industries today seem to be guided by a firm called a "price leader." The price leader's function is to set a price which other firms in the industry will voluntarily follow.[1] An increase in the price leader's price serves as a signal to the other producers that costs have increased to such a level that prices must be increased to protect the level of profits.[2] Since the leader's position is one existing only because of the voluntary acceptance of his price by others in the industry, one is faced with two different types of decision. One decision must be made by the price leader, the other by the price follower.

Looking first at the price leader, one can see that he must set a price. That firms do have the ability to set a price and make it stick is well documented.[3] The question is, then, what type of pricing decision must be made. Since the price leader is concerned with a price to protect profits, he is required to decide what price to set, not whether to accept a price. He would be served better by absorption costing in making the decision as it yields a price.

1 Chamberlin, Neil W., *The Firm: Micro Economic Planning and Action*, (New York: McGraw-Hill Book Co., Inc., 1962), p. 366.
2 *Ibid.*, p. 365.
3 Galbraith, John Kenneth, *The New Industrial State* (Boston: Houghton-Mifflin Company, 1967), pp. 48-49.

This solves the problem of the price leader. A decision is also faced by the "price follower."

Presumably he need not set a price. He need only review a price change made by the leader in his industry and decide whether to follow or not. His decision, should he "accept" a price "offered" for his product, is of a form better solved using direct costing.

In these last two cases, one can see that not only are firms in different types of industries faced with different decisions, but even firms in the same industry may be required to answer different questions.

The Decision

Although some accountants may find explicit answers to pricing problems they face in this article, they are misguided if they attempt to fit all pricing decisions into the four "cubbyholes" reviewed above. Each firm has a slightly different economic environment and different factors influencing the price. Just as there is no example of the economist's "perfect competition," there also are no one or two pricing decisions all firms face. As accountants we should be aware of this. When management asks for financial information to aid in the pricing decision, we should stifle the urge to bring out our favorite absorption costing figures, or direct costing figures, or marginal costing figures, until we have answered for ourselves the question: What is management's pricing decision?

28

Product Contribution Analysis for Multi-Product Pricing

WILLIAM S. KALLIMANIS*

Pricing in a multi-product firm can mean the difference between profit and loss. Yet, there is no agreement as to how prices should be set. Prices may be set on a cost plus a percentage markup, or what the market will pay, or what the industry leader will set as a price. All these and myriads of possible combinations fail to get into the heart of the problem of providing management with relevant data regarding a pricing decision. Nor do they show management the economic consequences of a pricing decision.

Price is influenced by the supply, quality, state-of-the-art, usefulness of the product and competition, whether we consider identical or substitute products. The price is also influenced by its stage in its life cycle. In this paper I propose to deal with the problem of pricing products on the basis of contribution, within competition and production constraints, and with the proper consideration of income flow over the estimated life cycle of the product.

The product life cycle, although its length will vary by product and industry, consists of the following stages: development, introduction, growth, maturity, decline and phase-out. For pricing decision purposes it is also important to recognize management's objectives during any given stage.

During the *product introduction* period, for example, one might use either a saturation or skimming price. Price reduction will be necessary to discourage competition or to meet it during the *growth* stage. Finally, when the product reaches *maturity* the price can be further reduced by passing along manufacturing savings to customers during the *decline* phase while preparing to bow out of the market or to start a new cycle with its replacement.

GENERAL ANALYSIS

What has briefly been described in the previous paragraph is known as marketing strategy. Marketing strategy and pricing policy, however, can be rather meaningless without reliable quantitative measures on which

* From *Management Accounting* (July 1968), pp. 3-11. Reprinted by permission of the National Association of Accountants.

to base decisions. To measure the consequences of any marketing strategy it is necessary to anticipate prices, demand, and variable costs at several desirable volume levels. These data are used to calculate gross contribution at each level projected, both for the new and for the old products being replaced.

Assume, for example, the general contribution statement for a company's sales mix to be as follows:

Contribution Analysis
12-31-67

	(*$ millions*)	%
Net sales	40	100
Variable cost	24	60
Contribution (*Gross. fig*)	16	40
Period costs	8	20
Taxable income	8	20
Tax at 50%	4	10
Net income	4	10

The most significant item in this statement is the 40 per cent contribution. This means that with our present prices and sales mix, every time a $1.00 sale is made, the company has 40 cents remaining for payment of its period costs and contribution to profit.

Although the general contribution statement is useful, it cannot be used for management decisions because it does not show product contribution or the specifics of sales mix. We may prepare a more useful form to reveal contribution by individual product as in Exhibit 1. This statement reveals a wide range of percentage contribution rates among products:

Product	Contribution %
A	40%
B	45
C	35
D	70
E	65
F	30
G	50
H	21
Overall	40%

Exhibit 1 Comparative Contribution Statement ($Millions)

	Total		PRODUCTS A		B		C		D	
	Amount	%	Amount	%	Amount	%	Amount	%	Amount	%
Sales	$40.00	100	$24.00	100	$1.00	100	$1.40	100	$ .60	100
Variable Cost	24.00	60	14.40	60	.55	55	.91	65	.18	30
Contribution	$16.00	40	$ 9.60	40	$ .45	45	$ .49	35	$ .42	70

	PRODUCTS E		F		G		H	
	Amount	%	Amount	%	Amount	%	Amount	%
Sales	$2.00	100	$3.00	100	$4.00	100	$4.00	100
Variable Cost	.70	35	2.10	70	2.00	50	3.16	79
Contribution	$1.30	65	$ .90	30	$2.00	50	$ .84	21

A more meaningful way of comparing the revenue and contribution of products is to rank them according to the dollar magnitude of individual products:

Rank According to Magnitude of Revenue

Product	Revenue		Percentage		
	Each	Cum.	Each	Cum.	Rank
A	$24.00	—	60.0	—	1
G	4.00	$28.00	10.0	70.0	2
H	4.00	32.00	10.0	80.0	3
F	3.00	35.00	7.5	87.5	4
E	2.00	37.00	5.0	92.5	5
C	1.40	38.40	3.5	96.0	6
B	1.00	39.40	2.5	98.5	7
D	.60	40.00	1.5	100.00	8
Total	$40.00		100.00		

Rank According to Magnitude of Contribution

Product	Contribution Each	Contribution Cum.	Percentage Each	Percentage Cum.	Rank	%
A	$ 9.60	—	60.0	—	1	60
G	2.00	$11.60	12.5	72.5	2 ⎫	
E	1.30	12.90	8.2	80.7	3	
F	.90	13.80	5.5	86.2	4	
H	.84	14.64	5.3	91.5	5 ⎬ 40	
C	.49	15.13	3.1	94.6	6	
B	.45	15.58	2.8	87.4	7	
D	.42	16.00	2.6	100.0	8 ⎭	
Total	$16.00		100.00			100%

We can now prepare a comparative ranking schedule:

Product	Rank Contribution	Rank Revenue
A	1	1
G	2	2
E	3	4
F	4	3
H	5	2
C	6	5
B	7	6
D	8	7

Note that Product H ranks No. 2 in sales revenue but falls to No. 5 in dollar contribution toward period costs and profit.

The management's objectives will dictate which ranking is most significant. That is, if the short-term objective is to raise revenue, the revenue ranking will be important. If the management wishes to increase earnings per share, however, the contribution ranking would be more significant. In either case, the reliance on one at the sacrifice of the other would be detrimental to the firm.

Another point is also significantly illustrated by this analysis. We note that Product A contributes 60 per cent and the other seven products contribute only 40 per cent of the total dollars contributed. Consequently the decisions one must make regarding Product A could and will vary greatly from those made about products B through H:

Product	Contribution	
A		60%
G	12.5 ⎱	
E	8.2	
F	5.5	
H	5.3 ⎬ 40%	
C	3.1	
B	2.8	
D	2.6 ⎰	
Total	100%	

Recognizing the heavy dependence on Product A, the management will attempt to control its manufacturing costs and to maintain volume at highest contribution level while planning to systematically phase out and replace it.

Management can now strategically plan and influence the cost, price and volume, as well as mix structure of the remaining seven products in order to improve contribution and, consequently, profit. Simulation methods may here be helpful.

PRICE VOLUME CONTRIBUTION SIMULATION

Let us assume that the relevant prices are $40, $38 and $42, and that the variable cost per unit remains unchanged within this range of prices and demand. Question: Which of these alternatives is most desirable from the economic point of view?

Before this question can be answered, we would need to simulate a separate income statement for each price; then compare their contribution flows and present values in the following manner:

1. Simulate contribution for each price:

A. Unit price $40:

	Unit Price		Demand by Year					
			1	2	3	4	5	Total
Volume (units)			8,000	10,000	13,000	8,000	5,000	44,000
	Amount	%						
Sales	$40	100	$320K	$400K	$520K	$320K	$200K	$1,760K
Variable cost	24	60	192	240	312	192	120	1,056
Contribution	$16	40	$128	$160	$208	$128	$ 80	$ 704

B. Unit price $38:

	Unit Price		Demand by Year					
Volume (units)			*1* 12,000	*2* 13,000	*3* 10,000	*4* 8,000	*5* 5,000	*Total* 48,000
	Amount	*%*						
Sales	$38	100	$456K	$494K	$380K	$304K	$190K	$1,824K
Variable cost	24	63	288	312	240	192	120	1,152
Contribution	$14	37	$168	$182	$140	$112	$ 70	$ 672

C. Unit price $42:

	Unit Price		Demand by Year					
Volume (units)			*1* 6,000	*2* 8,000	*3* 10,000	*4* 8,000	*5* 6,000	*Total* 38,000
	Amount	*%*						
Sales	$42	100	$252K	$336K	$420K	$336K	$252K	$1,596K
Variable cost	24	55	144	192	240	192	144	912
Contribution	$18	45	$108	$144	$180	$144	$108	$ 684

2. Recap of the contribution flows:

	Contribution by Price / Year			Difference over Index Price	
	Index Price	Alternative Prices			
	$40	$38	$42		
Year	(1)	(2)	(3)	*4 (1-2)*	*5 (1-3)*
1	$128K	$168K	$108K	($40)	$20
2	160	182	144	(22)	16
3	208	140	180	60	20
4	128	112	144	16	(16)
5	80	70	108	10	(28)
Total	$704	$672	$684	$24K	$12K
Volume (Units)	44,000	48,000	38,000	(4,000)	6,000

At the $38 price, in order to maintain the contribution flow of the desired index, the company should sell 1,500 $\left(\dfrac{\$24K}{\$16} \text{ contribution/unit}\right)$ more units, or a total of 45,500. At the $42 price, the company must sell 750 $\left(\dfrac{\$12K}{\$16} \text{ contribution unit}\right)$ more units, or a total of 44,750 to recover the difference in contribution flow.

3. Present value of contribution flow:

Although a recap of contribution is useful, the analysis is far from being complete because the flows under each price have different patterns over the life cycle of the product, hence different present values. For example, at the $40 price the contribution peaks out during the third year; at the $38 price the contribution begins high, peaks during the second year, then goes down. Finally, at the $42 price the flow starts out slow, peaks out during the third year, then levels off.

For long-range planning purposes then, we should convert to estimated current value as illustrated in Exhibit 2. Question: Which of these alternatives is most desirable? To answer this question we need to ask two other questions: (a) Which of the three volumes can best fit in the projected production load? and (b) Which of the contribution flows has the greatest present value?

Exhibit 2   Contribution Flows by Year and Price

Year	Present Value Factors 15%	$40 Index Price Amount	P.V. Amt.	$38 Amount	P.V. Amt.	$42 Amount	P.V. Amt.
	1	*2*	*3 (1x2)*	*4*	*5 (1x4)*	*6*	*7 (1x6)*
1	.870	$128K	$111K	$168K	$146K	$108K	$ 94K
2	.756	160	121	182	138	144	109
3	.658	208	137	140	92	180	118
4	.572	128	73	112	64	144	82
5	.497	80	40	70	35	108	54
Total		$704K		$672K		$684K	
			$482K		$475K		$457

If the answer to the question (a) is: the company cannot accommodate larger production loads without increasing the cost (manpower and equipment), the choice would then be the $42 price. The sales force should devote additional effort to selling the additional units needed to recover the contribution difference between the index price and the decision price. This concentration of sales effort should be made early in the product life cycle, in order to bring the present value of the contribution in line with that of the index price.

If production is not a critical problem (capacity is adequate to facilitate a slight increase in production load), the $40 index price is the most favorable alternative. This is shown by the fact that present value of the contribution flows is largest at $482,000. On the other hand, if production capacity is not a problem and the objective is to penetrate the market, the best alternative would be the $38 price, which has a present value contribution flow of $475,000. This is only $7,000 less than the maximum present value at the $40 price. Management should also try to increase sales by the number of units necessary to recover the difference in present value of contribution flow.

OPERATIONAL AND STRATEGIC ANALYSES

So far the discussion has centered around one product. In the remainder of this paper the group of reports presented deal with the evaluation of the economic consequences of a pricing decision for multiple products. These reports have been grouped in two categories:

1. Operational analysis.
2. Strategic planning.

Operational analysis refers to an analysis of the present potential, such as unit, product and product line contribution.

Unit Contribution Analysis is the master file, in which all relevant data pertaining to a product are kept. This master file is used to extend units sold or forecast, to arrive at product contribution data. (See Exhibit 3 opposite.)

Product contribution analysis is a list of products sold, ranked according to the dollar magnitude of their contribution. From this report a marketing manager can readily see that there are a myriad of other analyses which can be designed to measure salesman, region and customer contribution performance. We are not here concerned with these added possibilities for analysis. Exhibit 4, however, shows the significance that the information can take when presented in a combined revenue and contribution schedule.

The management planning committee, having the standard file of relevant product information, the actual history of sales and the product contribution can now think in terms of how to develop pricing strategy. To aid the committee in this task, two additional reports are needed: (1) product life cycle analysis and (2) strategic analysis.

Product life cycle analysis is intended to give the management planning committee a complete history of relevant facts about the product, such as prices, quantity sold, revenues and contribution, from the date of product introduction to date of decision. (See Exhibit 5 on page 332.)

Strategic analysis. The management committee, having the basic data on a product master file, knowing the current contribution picture and product life cycle, can then consider the consequences of possible price changes on the profitability of the company. The purpose of strategic analysis is to provide management with a measurement of economic consequences for each given price decision or strategy (Exhibit 6, page 333).

Using the original pricing structure, it is anticipated that Product A's sales will increase by 20 per cent and that the remainder will have a 10 per cent gain. The revenue to be generated from the additional sales is $6,400,000 (forecast $46,400,000 − $40,000,000 last year's sales) and the contribution will be increased $2,560,000 (forecast $18,560,000 − $16,000,000 last year).

Exhibit 3. Unit Contribution Analysis (Standard File)

Product	Price	Std. Hrs.	Material Amt.	% Total Var. Cost	Labor Amt.	% Total Var. Cost	Var. Burd. Amt.	% Total Var. Cost	Total Amount	Unit Contribution Amount	% of Price
D	$60.0								$18.0	$42.0	70%
E	20.0								7.0	13.0	65
A	40.0								24.0	16.0	60
G	40.0								20.0	20.0	50
B	10.0								5.5	4.5	45
C	14.0								9.1	4.9	35
F	30.0								21.0	9.0	30
H	40.0								31.6	8.4	21

Exhibit 4.

Products	Revenue	Variable Costs	Margin	Contribution Amount	Contribution % of Total	Accum. %	Rank	Revenue % of Total	Rank
A	$24.00	$14.40	40%	$ 9.60	60.0	—	1	60.0	1
G	4.00	2.00	50	2.00	12.5	72.5	2	10.0	3
E	2.00	.70	65	1.30	8.2	80.7	3	5.0	5
F	3.00	2.10	30	.90	5.5	86.2	4	7.5	4
H	4.00	3.16	21	.84	5.3	91.5	5	10.0	2
C	1.40	.91	35	.49	3.1	94.6	6	3.5	6
B	1.00	.55	45	.45	2.8	97.4	7	2.5	7
D	.60	.18	70	.42	2.6	100.0	8	1.5	8
Total	$40.00	$24.00	40%	$16.00	100.0			100.0	

Exhibit 5. Product Life Cycle Analysis

Product	Date	Month	Day	Price	Quantities Volume Each	Cum.	% Each	Cum.	Revenue Amount 000's Each	Cum.	% Each	Cum.	Variable Cost Amount 000's Each	Cum.	Contribution Amount Each	Cum.	Each	Cum.
Z	June 65	1		$50	1,000	—	1.17	—	$ 50	$ —	1.30	—	$ 30	$ —	$ 20	$ —	1.56	—
		2			1,200	2,200	1.41	2.58	60	110	1.56	2.86	36	66	24	44	1.87	3.43
		3			1,500	3,700	1.76	4.34	75	185	1.95	4.81	45	111	30	74	2.34	5.77
		4			2,000	5,700	2.34	6.68	100	285	2.60	7.41	60	171	40	114	3.12	8.89
		5			3,000	8,700	3.52	10.20	150	435	3.90	11.31	90	261	60	174	4.67	13.56
		16			4,800	55,300	5.63	64.84	216	2648	5.62	68.69	144	1659	72	989	5.61	77.02
		17			4,400	59,700	5.16	70.00	198	2846	5.15	74.04	132	1791	66	1055	5.14	82.16
	Jan 67	18		40	3,600	63,300	4.22	74.22	162	3008	4.22	78.26	108	1899	54	1109	4.21	86.37
		19			3,900	67,200	4.57	78.79	156	3164	4.06	82.32	117	2016	39	1148	3.04	89.41
		20			3,700	70,900	4.34	83.13	148	3312	3.85	86.17	111	2127	37	1185	2.88	92.29
		21			3,000	73,900	3.52	86.65	120	3432	3.12	89.29	90	2217	30	1215	2.34	94.63
		22			2,400	76,300	2.81	89.46	96	3528	2.50	91.79	72	2289	24	1239	1.87	96.50
		23		35	1,800	78,100	2.11	91.57	72	3600	1.87	93.66	54	2343	18	1257	1.40	97.90
		24			2,000	80,100	2.34	93.91	70	3670	1.82	95.48	60	2403	10	1267	.78	98.68
		26			1,500	81,600	1.76	95.67	53	3723	1.39	96.86	45	2448	8	1275	.62	99.30
		27			1,000	82,600	1.17	96.84	35	3758	.91	97.77	30	2478	5	1280	.39	99.69
		28		30	500	83,100	.59	97.43	18	3776	.49	98.26	15	2493	3	1283	.23	99.92
		29			200	83,300	.23	97.46	7	3783	.18	98.44	6	2499	1	1284	.08	100.00
		30			2,000	85,300	2.34	100.00	60	3843	1.56	100.00	60	2559	—	1284	—	100.00
		Total			85,300		100.0%		$3,843.		100.0%		$2,559.		$1,284.		100%

Exhibit 6. Strategic Analysis

Forecast at Present Prices I

Product	Price	Anticipated Volume	Amount Revenue	Variable Cost	Anticipated Contribution Amount	% of Total Contribution	Cumulative Percent	Rank
A	$40.00	72,000	$28,800K	$17,280K	$11,520	62.08	—	1
G	40.0	110,000	4,400	2,200	2,200	11.85	73.93	2
E	20.0	110,000	2,200	770	1,430	7.70	81.63	3
F	30.0	110,000	3,300	2,310	990	5.33	86.96	4
H	40.0	110,000	4,400	3,476	924	4.98	91.94	5
C	14.0	110,000	1,540	1,001	539	2.90	94.84	6
B	10.0	110,000	1,100	605	495	2.67	97.51	7
D	60.0	11,000	600	198	462	2.49	100.00	8
Total		743,000	$46,400K	$27,840	$18,560	100.00		

Exhibit 7. Strategic Analysis

Product	Revised Price	Anticipated Volume	Anticipated Revenue	Contribution Amount	% of Total Contribution	Cumulative Percent	Revised Rank	Prior Rank
A	$40	72,000	$28,800	$11,520	59.94	—	1	1
G	42	100,000	4,200	2,200	11.45	71.39	2	2
E	20	110,000	2,200	1,430	7.44	78.83	3	3
F	34	105,000	4,200	1,365	7.10	85.93	4	4
H	38	130,000	4,940	1,092	5.68	91.61	5	5
C	14	100,000	1,680	588	3.06	94.67	6	6
B	10	130,000	1,300	585	3.04	97.71	7	7
D	60	10,500	630	441	2.29	100.00	8	8
Total		757,500	$47,950	$19,221	100.0			

Question: What would happen if the management committee decided to change prices as indicated by Strategy Y below?

Strategy "Y" Change Price—Primary Effects

Product to be Changed	Current Price	Proposed Price	Change in Vol.	Change in Rev.	Change in Contribution
F	$30	34	− 5,000	$900K	+$375
H	40	38	+20,000	+540	+ 168
G	40	42	−10,000	−200	-0-
			5,000	$1,240K	$543

It is anticipated, that by increasing the price of Product F to $34 instead of $30, Product G to $42 instead of $40, and dropping Product H's price to $38 instead of $40, the company will gain $543,000 in contribution. In addition to these primary effects, there will also be secondary consequences:

Secondary Volume Effects (Gained and Lost Contributions)

Products with Secondary Qty. Changes	Price	Change in Volume	Change in Revenue	Change in Contribution
C	$14.0	+10,000	$140K	$49K
B	10.0	+20,000	200	90
D	60.0	− 500	− 30	−21
		29,500	$310	+$118

The result of the secondary consequences is favorable. That is, the net results will further increase contribution (by $118,000). The next step is to combine the changes and prepare a revised forecast of contribution (Exhibit 7, page 333).

Looking at the revised forecast, one can see a summary of the economic consequences of Strategy Y. That is, the volume will go up by 145,000 units, the revenue will increase $1,550,000 and the contribution will be raised by $660,000. This technique is repeated for as many feasible strategies as possible and then summarized according to management objectives and in order of magnitude of:

1. Liquidity

2. Earnings per share

3. Manufacturing output (compared to physical constraints)

4. Maximize revenue

   5. Maximize contribution
   6. Maximize profit
   7. Return on investment (net present value)
      a. % return on gross sales
      b. % return on net sales
      c. % return on capitalization
      d. % return on assets employed

SUMMARY

What is really significant in a pricing decision is neither cost nor price but rather the present value of the contribution that the product makes toward the recovery of period costs and profit over each product's life cycle. The simulation of price-cost-volume-contribution by life cycle yields consequences which can be anticipated and used in strategic planning geared toward achieving a specific corporate objective.

29

Use of Sensitivity Analysis in Capital Budgeting

WILLIAM C. HOUSE*

> Any investment always involves an estimate
> of the expected rate of return. But no one can
> guarantee that the estimate will be correct.
> What a company can do, however, is calculate
> the possible degree of error in its estimate
> and weigh this against the alternative uses
> of its capital.

The anticipated rate of return on investment is one of the principal criteria used by corporate managements in deciding whether to accept or reject a proposed capital expenditure. Like any forecast, however, the rate of return estimate may prove to be inaccurate.

Estimates of rates of return are based on forecasts of such elements as sales volumes, selling prices, product purchase or production prices, operating expenses, capital investment outlays, and project economic lives. Any or all of these forecasts may be erroneous, and the result may be an actual rate of return that falls far below what has been anticipated.

Thus, management needs some method for determining the likelihood and amount of such errors before making a final decision to accept or reject a given proposal. It is sometimes possible to develop probability distribution curves that indicate the likelihood of occurrence of specific rates of return for individual projects. If enough information is available about the outcomes of similar past proposals, then management can make its choice on the basis of expected values (i.e. the values with the highest probability of occurrence) derived from a probability distribution of rates of return. In many cases, however, capital investment proposals represent unique events for which there is little or no relevant past experience. Then expected values cannot be determined objectively, and the likelihood of errors cannot be predicted.

It is always possible, however, to calculate in advance what effect errors in estimation would have on the estimated rates of return and thus to determine the significance of such errors. The appropriate

* From *Management Services* (September-October), pp. 37-40. Reprinted by permission of the Editor.

technique to use is that of sensitivity analysis. Its application, illustrated by means of a case example, is explained in this article.

Analysis of the sensitivity to error of rates of return is the process of determining whether small changes in various estimates cause significant changes in estimated rates of return. If management finds that a 5 or 10 per cent error in forecasting a certain estimate (e.g., production costs) will cause the estimated rate of return for a given project to decline below the estimated rate of return for a competing project or below a prescribed minimum figure, it will probably decide to investigate more thoroughly the likelihood of changes in production costs before making a final decision to accept or reject the project under consideration. On the other hand, if management discovers that a relatively large error (e.g., 25 or 30 per cent) must occur in forecasting production costs before the estimated rate of return is affected significantly, then further efforts to reduce errors in forecasting production costs may not be deemed economically justifiable.

Even when estimated rates of return are sensitive to errors in certain estimates (i.e., a small change in an estimate causes a significant change in the estimated rates of return), management may not always be able to reduce significantly either the likelihood or the impact of estimating errors. However, knowing the conditions of sensitivity puts management in a better position to decide if the risks are large enough to cause the rejection of investment proposals under consideration.

MEASUREMENT

The sensitivity of estimated rates of return to errors in estimates cannot be measured precisely for several reasons. First, management must base its analysis of the relationships among the variables which affect the rates of return on past experience; these relationships, however, may not hold completely true in the future. Second, in its examination of the sensitivity of rates of return to errors in estimating individual variables, management may have to ignore the fact that a change in one estimate (e.g., sales volume) may cause changes in another estimate (e.g., operating expenses) because such cause and effect relationships are difficult to measure. Third, autocorrelation[1] may exist between two or more estimates for a given variable, distorting what appears to be the sensitivity of estimated rates of return to errors in estimation.

Thus, lack of actual data on how one estimate will vary if another is altered may make it difficult for management to determine the precise effects of errors of estimation on estimated rates of return. However, management does not need to know precisely the sensitivity of estimated

---

[1] Autocorrelation is, to a certain extent, the dependence of the estimated value of a variable in one year on the value of that variable in a previous year. Thus, a 5 per cent change in selling prices in one year may actually cause a change of more or less than 5 per cent in selling prices the next year. (See Michael J. Brennan, *Preface to Econometrics*, (Cincinnati, Ohio: Southwestern Publishing Co., 1960), p. 348.)

rates of return to errors in estimation. If the relative differences in the effects of errors in estimating various elements can be determined, management will be able to identify the estimates that deserve further attention. Selection of estimates to investigate more thoroughly can be made on the basis of whether or not the sensitivity of estimated rates of return to errors in any given estimate is significant.

SIGNIFICANCE

How can management determine whether a significant degree of sensitivity of rates of return to errors in estimation exists if sensitivity cannot be measured precisely? Two major guidelines are helpful. First, a stated degree (e.g., 10 per cent) of error in an estimate must cause the estimated rate of return for a proposal to decline below that for a competing proposal or some prescribed minimum figure. Second, the stated degree of change in the estimate being considered must be within a range of error (e.g., 10 per cent) considered to be feasible, based on management's past experience or its subjective evaluations. When both these conditions are met, the sensitivity of rates of return to errors in estimation can be said to be significant.

If the sensitivity of a measure of return to errors in a given estimate is significant (i.e., a stated degree of error in the estimate would cause management to reverse its decision to accept a given proposal), what can management do? It should examine such estimates more thoroughly or collect more information in an effort to reduce errors in forecasting and the likelihood of making the wrong choice.[2] It may need to recalculate the estimates of rates of return on the basis of new underlying data, perhaps using discounted measures of return.

The changes that occur in estimated rates of return when the basic estimates are changed are difficult to compare for two reasons. If the estimated rates of return for the different projects vary widely, the same amount of change in estimated rates of return for any two given proposals may not have the same significance for both proposals. If both simple and discounted rates of return with different original values are calculated for each proposal, the changes in these values caused by any particular error in estimation may not be comparable. To solve these problems, the sensitivity of estimated rates of return to errors in estimation can be measured in terms of the percentage increase or decrease from base-case values for rates of return resulting from errors of a given size.

More valid comparisons of the sensitivity of different estimated rates of return to errors in the estimates for the same project or of the

[2] An incorrect decision is one that management could have avoided if more complete information about the future had been available. It may be possible for management to reduce its uncertainty about expected values of estimates by applying managerial resources to the task of improving its accuracy in forecasting. This, in turn, would decrease the likelihood of management's selecting projects which would have been rejected if more complete information had been available.

same rates of return for different projects can be made by stating the change in the estimated rates of return as a function of a percentage deviation from the original estimated values. This approach surmounts many of the difficulties ordinarily encountered in comparing rates of return for projects of different sizes and/or different measures of return when base-case values are different.

CASE EXAMPLE

The following case example illustrates some of the significant aspects of the application of sensitivity analysis applied to a capital investment decision. The table on this page shows the discounted cash flow rate of return for an oil company manufacturing project based on original estimates or base-case assumptions. The effects of 10 per cent changes in various estimates used to compute the discounted cash flow rate of return are also shown. It can be seen that 10 per cent errors in certain estimates (sales prices and raw materials costs, for example) are much more significant than errors in other estimates in terms of their effect on the discounted cash flow rate of return.

Sensitivity Analysis of a Manufacturing Project

	Discounted Cash Flow Rates of Return[1]			
Likely Maximum Error in Given Estimate	*Base-Case*	*Base-Case Revised*	*Increase (Decrease)*	*Percentage[2] Change*
10% decrease in estimated sales prices	12.0%	4.7%	(7.3)%	60.8%
10% decrease in estimated sales volume	12.0%	10.1%	(1.9)%	15.8%
10% increase in estimated low material cost	12.0%	7.4%	(4.6)%	38.3%
10% increase in estimated processing cost	12.0%	11.6%	(0.4)%	3.3%
10% increase in estimated overhead/maintenance cost	12.0%	11.4%	(0.6)%	5.0%
10% increase in capital investment	12.0%	11.2%	(0.8)%	6.7%

[1]Based on an estimated economic life of 20 years
[2]Calculated by dividing the increase or decrease in the discounted cash flow from the base-case figure by the base-case discounted cash flow rate of return

Let us assume further that the management of the oil company in question has established a cutoff rate of return of 8 per cent for all manufacturing projects. The base-case discounted cash flow rate of return for this proposal is 12 per cent, well above the cutoff rate. If the base-case estimates are used to compute the discounted cash flow rate of return, the project will probably be accepted.

However, a 10 per cent decrease in sales prices or a 10 per cent increase in raw material cost will cause the discounted cash flow rate of return to decline below the cutoff rate of 8 per cent. Therefore, an investment decision based on the discounted cash flow rate of return in this case is sufficiently sensitive to errors in estimates of sales prices and raw materials costs to justify further investigation of the accuracy of such estimates before accepting the proposal in question. Errors of 10 per cent in the remaining four estimates do not cause the discounted cash flow rate of return to decline to or below the cutoff point. Therefore, further investigation of the accuracy of these estimates is not required.

If there are no formal cutoff points in effect, the percentage changes that occur in the discounted cash flow rate of return when various estimates are altered by a fixed percentage can be used as a gauge of the significance of such errors. In the case cited, a 10 per cent decrease in estimated sales prices causes a 60.8 per cent decrease in the discounted cash flow rate of return (from the base-case figure) and a 10 per cent increase in raw materials cost causes the discounted cash flow rate of return to decline 38.3 per cent. A 10 per cent decrease in sales volume causes the discounted cash flow rate of return to decline by 15.8 per cent. Errors of 10 per cent in processing cost, overhead/maintenance cost, and capital investment cause the discounted cash flow rate to decline by 7 per cent or less.

These results indicate that a decision to invest in this project (on the basis of the discounted cash flow rate of return) is very sensitive to errors in estimates of sales prices and of raw materials costs and moderately sensitive to errors in estimates of processing cost, overhead/maintenance costs, and capital investment. Assuming that management cannot investigate the accuracy of all estimates more thoroughly, it would seem advisable to concentrate on the most significant estimates (i.e., sales prices, raw material costs, and possibly sales volume).

Some would argue that much of the same information as that shown here can be obtained using conventional breakeven analysis. However, the use of a discounted measure of return within the sensitivity analysis framework offers several important advantages. First, it permits cash flows to be related to invested capital; this cannot be done easily with breakeven analysis, and the productivity of capital may be impossible to portray in a meaningful manner. Second, it gives consideration to the time value of money while breakeven analysis does not. Finally, breakeven analysis is based on the assumption that the variables being considered are linearly related. In actual practice this may not be true. The sensitivity analysis approach does not require a strictly linear relationship among the variables being considered.

IMPLICATIONS FOR MANAGEMENT

Determining, among a selected group of estimates, those in which errors have the most significant impact on measures of return and identifying cases in which calculation of discounted rates of return gives significantly different results from calculation of simple measures of return could be extremely helpful to management. It would indicate which estimates must be forecast more precisely than others if a correct investment decision is to be made and when the use of a discounted rate of return is economically justifiable. Such information will aid management in allocating scarce managerial resources such as time, money, and effort to the process of measuring and reducing or eliminating the risks involved in capital budgeting.

The amount of information sensitivity analysis can convey to management is limited. The approach outlined here would not permit management to draw precise conclusions about possible combinations of errors in estimating significant variables and the resultant effects on estimated rates of return. Nor would it indicate what effect a change in one estimate might have on another estimate. Despite these drawbacks, information about the effects of errors in estimation on the choice of capital investments may be significant for management since it will often indicate where the greatest risks in making investments lie.

Fortunately, determinations of the sensitivity of rates of return to errors in estimates need not be precise to be useful to management. If the relative difference between the effects of error in various estimates on rates of return is known, management will often be able to determine which estimates deserve more attention than others and in what cases the use of discounted as opposed to simple rates of return is economically justified.

30

Anyone for Widgets?

HOWARD C. GREER*

> "The standard cost employed for price-figuring,
> for inventory valuation and for efficiency
> measurement should be the smallest outlay
> conceivable under the best imaginable
> conditions — the shining target at which every
> arrow should be aimed."

The Waxahatchie Widget Company was started a couple of years ago by an acquaintance of mine who lives down our street a little way. In true neighborly spirit, the proprietor, knowing my background, decided to sponge off me for some free professional advice (easy thing to do — I'm not too busy, always flattered when someone seeks my counsel).

"Starting a little manufacturing business," he confided modestly one autumn afternoon, when we were seated side by side at a high school football game that wasn't very exciting. "Thought maybe you could tell me what I need in the way of a cost system."

The facts were simple. He had rented a small shop building, and installed two widget-making machines, each with a capacity of 500 widgets an hour. Operating 40 hours a week, for 50 weeks in a year, a machine could turn out one million widgets. Labor and material costs would run ten cents per widget. Other factory expenses were expected to total about $300,000 a year.

"That's an easy one," I told him. "Running at capacity, your plant can make two million widgets a year, at a total cost of $500,000. That's 25 cents each. How much can you sell them for?"

He wasn't sure — thought he should estimate his cost, then add a percentage for overhead and profit, see what he'd have to charge for them. I shook my head in irritation.

"Come now," I protested. "That's the worst way in the world to establish a selling price. Question is, what are widgets *worth?*" When he looked puzzled, I went on impatiently: "What can a buyer afford to pay for a widget? What's its value to him — materially, commercially, psycho-

* From *The Journal of Accountancy* (April 1966), pp. 41-49. Reprinted by permission of the Editor. Copyright 1966 by the American Institute of Certified Public Accountants, Inc.

logically? That isn't necessarily a function of its cost — it may be much more, or much less, depending on a lot of things."

When he continued to frown uncertainly, I prodded some more.

"Anything similar on the market now?"

"Helox makes one something like it that sells for 35 cents."

"Good," I said. "Try 35 cents for yours. At that price you'll have ten cents per unit for overhead and profit, total $200,000 a year, *if* you can run full blast and sell the entire output."

He looked uncomfortable. He said he probably couldn't do that well, not in the first year, anyhow. And his unit cost per widget was sure to be higher than 25 cents.

"Correction," I told him cheerfully. "You may *spend more money* than that, but it won't be for the widgets; it'll be for owning a plant you're not operating at capacity. In other words, any excess expenditure, over 25 cents per widget, will not be a production cost; it will be an outlay for idle machine time. Expenditures like that add no real value to your product; they're just unabsorbed burden, which is an operating expense, not a product cost element."

He looked really mystified now. "What's unabsorbed burden?" he asked, feebly.

"Absorbing" the "Burden"

"It's like this," I explained. "In owning those two machines you are, in effect, buying yourself 4,000 hours of potential machine time, for a total of $300,000. That's $75 for one machine-hour, in which you can turn out 500 widgets. That figures out at 15 cents each. Thus you 'absorb' factory expense at that rate. Operation at full capacity will 'absorb' the entire 'burden.' Operation at a lesser rate will leave part of the burden 'unabsorbed.' Call it 'idle machine expense,' if you like; whatever you call it, recognize it as a *loss,* not an outlay that makes your product any more valuable, to you or anyone else."

"All the accountants treat it that way?"

"Unfortunately, no," I conceded promptly. "A lot of them will tell you to use so-called *actual* cost in your figuring and price-setting. They'll claim you've got to recover all your expenses in your price, no matter how excessive those expenses may be. They say that the *standard* cost should be the expectable *average* cost, or the cost attainable under *normal* operating conditions ('normal' presumably being 'typical' past experience, good, bad or indifferent as it may have been)."

"That's bad?" my listener inquired, with challenge in his tone. "I've always been told it was dangerous to base prices on costs attainable only under *ideal* conditions, which may never be actually experienced. That's what ruins the market," he added, piously, "people trying to steal business by selling below cost." He'd obviously been absorbing some good old fundamentalist hellfire-and-damnation cost-price indoctrination from some source.

I wasn't having any, so I said, "Do you want advice, or are you just trying to promote an argument? I give advice free; if I have to argue, I charge for my time.

"Here's my advice, based on long experience and careful study. Set your price at what the traffic will bear; that is, at whatever figure will get you enough orders to keep those machines busy. And don't louse up your bookkeeping with any elaborate computed *expectable* costs or *average* costs or *normal* costs or any other artificial and meaningless derivatives of arithmetical accounting procedures. They won't disclose a single useful piece of financial information, or lead you to a single sound business decision."

"You think my cost-plus-profit approach to pricing is wrong, then?" he asked dubiously.

"Completely," I insisted. "Pricing comes first, costing second. Find out what you can safely charge for your product, then under what conditions you can keep your costs within that available price. Start thinking about how much money you can make, at any given price level, if you can operate at capacity, with maximum efficiency and minimum waste of material, labor and machine time.

"Next, find out, at the end of each period, how far you missed (and may go on missing) the minimum operating cost you know is attainable under ideal conditions. Then determine in what respects your expenses are too high (variance over standard). Then concentrate on what can be done to eliminate, or reduce, such variances (overexpenditures) in your future operations." I paused, having run out of breath.

He stared at me meditatively. "You make it sound easy," he began.

"So who said it was easy?" I countered, indignantly. "It's damn difficult, for almost everyone. But I'll tell you this: If you don't have the *ideal* constantly and clearly before you, and don't regularly measure and explain your failures to attain it, you'll never come close to getting the most out of your business. Content yourself with being *normal,* and you'll wind up normally unsuccessful."

Over the next few months I saw my friend only once in a while, never more than briefly. On one occasion he mentioned that they'd got the factory running satisfactorily, that they'd priced the widgets at 40 cents, and were developing some business. It was a year later that we first had an opportunity for a more extended discussion.

I asked him how things were going. He said they'd completed their first fiscal year, had sustained a small loss, but were optimistic about the future.

"How much business you do?" I queried. "Let's see: If I remember, you said your plant could turn out a couple million units in a year's time. You make that many?"

"Lord no," he said. "Takes a while to get started, plantwise and marketwise, too. We hit about a million total production. Not bad for a beginning!"

"Sell 'em all?" I inquired (I had a feeling he hadn't).

"Shipped 600,000 units," he declared firmly, inviting congratulation.

"H-mm," I said, pulling out a pencil and an old laundry bill with some blank space on the back of it. "By my figuring, that would put you pretty deep in the red." I made marks on the paper, while he glowered at me. After a moment, I read him the results.

"Sales of 600,000 units at a standard margin of 15 cents each (40-cent selling price minus 25-cent standard cost) would give you a gross margin *at standard* of $90,000. Producing at only half capacity, you'd be on the hooks for around $150,000 of unabsorbed burden, leaving you a $60,000 loss at that stage. Then you must have had some selling and administrative expense; how much?"

"About $30,000," he muttered.

"Deficit of $90,000 for the year," I concluded. "That the way you figure it?"

"Not at all!" he declaimed indignantly. "Not over a third that much — just about the amount of the overhead expense, in fact —." He glared at me. I looked skeptical.

Year-End Inventory

"My auditors worked up the figures," he explained. "Had 'em in because the bank insisted." He paused. "Conn, Ventional & Co., CPAs — You know them, I'm sure."

"Very highly respected firm," I agreed. "What did they tell you?"

"Said that if a million units cost $400,000 to make, that was 40 cents a piece; since that was the average selling price, it gave us a break-even at the gross margin line, and our loss would be only the amount of the general overhead expenses. About $30,000, as I told you. Not too bad."

"H-m-m," I said again. "In other words they valued the ending inventory at 40 cents (average manufacturing cost), despite the fact that the selling price is only 40 cents —."

"Oh, no," he interrupted. "We've raised the selling price; it's going up to 50 cents next week."

"Wait a minute!" I said. "Though you sold only a third of your potential output last year at a 40-cent price, and have competition at a 35-cent figure, you're now going to try a 50-cent tag and hope to increase your volume at that level?"

"The auditors said we'd have to!" he responded, a little sulkily. "They pointed out that with the factory cost running 40 cents we can't possibly make any money unless we get at least 50 cents for the widgets." He looked challenging again. I reminded myself that C. V. & Co. were getting a fee, and I wasn't, which automatically made their opinion worth a lot more than mine, and why should I argue about it anyhow?

"Irrefutable logic!" was the most appropriate comment I could offer. He shot me a suspicious glance, but I contrived to look bland and concurring, and happily escaped any further contention.

Breaking Even

Another year went by before the subject came up again. We got hemmed into a corner at a neighborhood cocktail party; we had to discuss something, and my curiosity got the better of my judgment. I remarked that he must have completed his second fiscal year, and how had things come out?

"A little better," he said, but without notable enthusiasm. "We about broke even."

"Business picked up, eh?" I encouraged.

"Well, no, as a matter of fact it didn't," he rejoined. "Our sales were only 400,000 units, and we had to cut our factory production back to 800,000 units. Gave us quite a year-end inventory, but the results don't look too bad." He was obviously unhappy, worried.

I delved into my memory for the figures we'd discussed at our last meeting. A light begun to glimmer faintly in the background of my consciousness.

"Hold the phone!" I said. "I'll tell you how it went."

A Shortage of Working Capital

"A year ago," I told him, "you wound up with an inventory of 400,000 units, valued at 40 cents each. This past year you sold 400,000 units at 50 cents each. Using the time-honored first-in-first-out philosophy, you assumed it was the previous year's production you sold; hence your accounts show a gross margin of ten cents per unit, or $40,000 in all; this covered your S&A expense, and made your P&L account come out even at the end of the year."

He nodded confirmation. I pulled out my trusty pencil and paper.

"In this same period," I continued, "you produced 800,000 widgets, at a cost of — let me see: labor and materials, $80,000 — factory expenses, $300,000 (he interrupted to say they'd pared expenses down to $280,000, so I made the correction) — okay, total $360,000. That's 45 cents per unit for the new production —" I folded up the paper. "So you put the 800,000 new units into the year-end inventory at that figure, $360,000, and everything came out ginger-peachy." When he seemed not to share my enthusiasm, I asked what was wrong.

"Nothing, except we're fresh out of cash," he answered resentfully. "How come the accountants tell us we're making money — or at least not losing any — and still I'm constantly adding to my loan at the bank? I don't get it."

"That, my boy," I assured him, "is what is technically known as a shortage of working capital!"

"Don't kid about it," he begged. "This is serious."

I dropped my facetious manner and assured him I could understand his concern.

"What's next year look like?" I inquired. He brightened a little.

"Well, we've got a budget," he assured me. "The auditors helped me set it up. . . ."

"Starting with another price increase, no doubt, to justify the 45-cent cost you've got against your inventory —"

"That's right," he conceded. "The new price will be 60 cents. We're going to tell the trade we've got a *new improved* article. We expect to double our advertising appropriation, hire another salesman, offer prizes to clerks in dealers' stores —"

I interrupted him. (I'd heard this story before, too many times.)

"This actually a new-type widget you're offering?" I inquired.

"Well, no, not really," he confessed. "We're putting it in a larger package, and it will carry a picture of a bathing girl holding a widget —. We need a little sex appeal, our ad man says — and it will give us a talking point —"

"How many you think you can sell?" I asked.

"The quota is set at 800,000," he answered defiantly.

"The exact quantity now on hand," I noted. "What will your production be?"

"We'll have to cut back on it, the bank says; I'm figuring on about 600,000, but it depends on how the sales go —"

"Yes, and on how liberal the bank will be with further loans," I reminded him.

I got out the pencil and paper again. The figures were easy to assemble. "With sales of 800,000 units, at a margin of 15 cents each (60-cent price minus 45-cent inventory cost), you'll have $120,000 margin for overhead and profit; you can spend up to $80,000 for advertising, selling and general activities, and still come up with a $40,000 net income. Enough to erase your deficit, give you a little surplus."

"That's what the auditors said," he confirmed.

"And your inventory at the end of next year will be 600,000 units, having a production cost of $330,000 (55 cents each), and you'll value them in your balance sheet at that figure; then all you have to do is jack up the selling price to maybe 75 cents for the following year —."

"Aw, cut it out!" my friend protested. "I'm bleeding already; don't use sandpaper on me." He looked almost desperate. "Look, I haven't any claim on your sympathy, and even less on your time, but would you go over this with me in detail and show me just where I've gone wrong on this thing?"

"Sure," I answered, mollified by this appeal to my better nature. "Let me have a copy of the figures as you now have them set up; I'll study them a little, and give you my interpretation. If you think it will help you any —"

The results of my efforts are shown in the accompanying analysis, which I took over to his house next evening. I laid the sheet on the table before us, exposing only the figures in the first four columns, Sections I and II (page 348).

"Let's take a piece at a time," I suggested. "Here's a summary of

WAXAHATCHIE WIDGET COMPANY
Actual and Prospective Results—Years 1963-65
(all amounts in Ms—000 omitted)

Section		Company Results and Forecast				Greer Forecast	
		1963	1964	1965	Three Years	1965	Three Years
I	Quantities (units)						
	Beginning inventory	—	400	800	—	800	—
	Manufactured	1,000	800	600	2,400	400	2,200
	Total	1,000	1,200	1,400	2,400	1,200	2,200
	Sold	600	400	800	1,800	200	1,200
	Ending inventory	400	800	600	600	1,000	1,000
II	Manufacturing costs (company)						
	Materials and labor	$ 100	$ 80	$ 60		$ 40	
	Factory expense	300	280	270		260	
	Total	$ 400	$ 360	$ 330		$ 300	
	Manufacturing costs per unit						
	Materials and labor	$ .10	$ .10	$ .10		$ .10	
	Factory expense	.30	.35	.45		.65	
	Total	$ .40	$ .45	$ .55		$ .75	
	Results (company)						
	Sales revenue	$ 240	$ 200	$ 480	$ 920	$ 120	$ 560
	Cost of goods	240	160	360	760	90	490
	Gross margin	$ —	$ 40	$ 120	$ 160	$ 30	$ 70
	General expense	30	40	80	150	80	150
	Profit (loss)	$(30)	$ —	$ 40	$ 10	$(50)	$(80)
	Results per unit						
	Sales revenue	$ .40	$ .50	$ .60		$ .60	
	Cost of goods	.40	.40	.45		.45	
	Gross margin	$ —	$ .10	$ .15		$ .15	
	General expense	.05	.10	.10		.40	
	Profit (loss)	$(.05)	$ —	$ .05		$(.25)	
III	Manufacturing costs (Greer)						
	Total outlay	$ 400	$ 360	$ 330		$ 300	
	Product value-standard	250	200	150		100	
	Burden variance	$ 150	$ 160	$ 180		$ 200	
	Results (Greer)						
	Sales revenue	$ 240	$ 200	$ 480	$ 920	$ 120	$ 560
	Cost of goods—standard	150	100	200	450	50	300
	Margin—standard	$ 90	$ 100	$ 280	$ 470	$ 70	$ 260
	Burden variance	150	160	180	490	200	510
	Margin—actual	$(60)	$(60)	$ 100	$(20)	$(130)	$(250)
	General expense	30	40	80	150	80	150
	Profit (loss)	$(90)	$(100)	$ 20	$(170)	$(210)	$(400)
IV	Inventory value						
	Company accounts	$ 160	$ 360	$ 330		$ 570	
	Standard	100	200	150		250	
	Difference	$ 60	$ 160	$ 180		$ 320	

your results, per books, for the past two years, plus your forecast for the present year. As you told me, your books say you lost a little money in 1963, broke even in 1964, and expect a modest profit in 1965 — enough to give you a small surplus (accumulated earnings, the accountants call it nowadays) at the end of the year."

"Uh-huh," he agreed gloomily. "What's wrong with it? The auditors say the statements have been prepared in accordance with generally accepted accounting principles. That means they're okay, doesn't it?"

"Let's skip that issue for the moment," I told him hastily. "The calculations are in conventional form, if that's what they're saying. But they embody a philosophy that is basically fallacious, no matter how much support it has in textbooks or in practice.

It's like this," I continued. "First, your 1965 forecast is absurdly optimistic, but that isn't primary fallacy — you're merely projecting into the future the erroneous concepts of the past."

"Like what?" he protested. "Be explicit, huh?"

The Idle Widget Machine

"The basic philosophical weakness," I responded, "lies in the assumption that any money spent in the course of production activity constitutes a *cost of the goods produced.* In 1963, for example, you spent $400,000 making a million widgets, so they tell you the things cost 40 cents a piece."

"Well, didn't they?" he complained. "Why not?"

"Because," I explained. "Out of the $300,000 you spent for factory expense, only about half was spent on *making widgets;* the other half was spent on maintaining an idle widget machine, which *made nothing.* *Widget-making* actually got the benefit of maybe 2,000 hours of machine time (worth, on an expenditure basis, say, $150,000). *Making nothing* consumed the other 2,000 machine-hours; that time was wasted, unused, and its expense was a *loss,* not a *cost* of *anything.*"

"But the factory is all one facility," he objected, "including my standby equipment—You can't split it out that way—"

"You're going at it backward," I corrected him. "Try it the other way around. Actually, the only costs you can assign specifically and incontrovertibly to a single item of product are those charges (in this case materials and direct labour) which relate directly and exclusively to that one item. When you start applying *indirect* charges, like machine-time expense, to units of product, you're in the realm of theory. You have to start making assumptions—"

"So why not assume that *all* the expense incurred applies to *all* the product made," he interjected triumphantly. "What's wrong with that for an assumption?"

"It's unrealistic," I assured him confidently. "If a machine operated *one day,* and stood idle for the *next 364,* would you assess the *whole year's* machine-time expense against that one day's production?"

"But it's not like that," he started to object.

"And, extending the assumption," I went on, "if the machine continued idle throughout the *entire following year,* would all *that* expense also be part of the cost of that *one day's production?* And so on?"

"You're making it ridiculous," he protested.

"It is ridiculous all right," I fired back at him. "But I didn't *make* it so; it just *is.*"

He digested that for a moment or two. "All right, so what makes sense?" he asked finally.

Production and Waste

"Charge each unit of product with machine-time expense proportionate to the amount of machine time actually employed in making that unit of product, and only that much. In other words, you can properly 'absorb' in product cost the expense of actual machine-time usage, and nothing more. When the machine isn't working, it creates no value, and it's delusive to pretend in your accounts that it does. You've got to distinguish between *production* and *waste,* or your whole business philosophy goes to hell, and your profit with it."

"Are you arguing for what the accountants call 'direct costing'?" he inquired.

"Far from it," I assured him. "The direct costing advocates have a still different philosophy, and it's even nuttier than that of the conventional accountants."

He was shaking his head. "I'm confused—" he protested.

"So who isn't?" I retorted. Could I sort it out for him, he asked.

"Well maybe," I rejoined, not too hopefully. "It goes this way. In dealing with fixed (i.e., nonvariable) factory indirect expense, the conventional accountants say that *all* of it is part of product cost, while the direct costers say that *none* of it should be so treated."

"None of it?" he repeated. "If it isn't a product cost, what is it?"

"Point remains obscure," I acknowledged. "Apparently it's just an unallocable operating loss of some sort. A *period* cost, the boys call it. Sun goes down, you're out-of-pocket the amount of a day's outlay for insurance, property taxes, depreciation, supervision, *et al.* You spent the money, but it didn't do any good, create any value; it just ran down the drain. The direct-costers would say your widgets cost only ten cents each, since that's all you can trace specifically to individual product items—"

He looked incredulous, but chose to skip over that. "Repeat your contention again, will you?" he requested.

Cost and Loss

"It's not a *contention,*" I insisted. "It's a statement of fact. Fixed expense —machine-usage expense, for example—is a *cost* to the extent that the facilities are actually *employed* in *production* of *marketable goods;* it's a *loss* to the extent that facilities are *idle,* or are turning out *defective goods, scrap, waste,* and so on." I paused to let it sink in. "There are some fringe issues, of course, like how to estimate maximum potential output, how to deal with shutdowns for normal maintenance, things like that, but the principle is as I stated it."

"And we'll run off the track if we do violence to this sacred principle of yours?"

"You already have," I insisted. "Look at your figures for 1963. They told you that widgets cost 40 cents each, so you charged off the ones sold at that cost; then you inventoried the ones on hand at the same figure; then you put the price up to cover your excessive cost; then in 1964 you repeated and magnified the error by imputing a 45-cent cost to a big year-end inventory; now in 1965 you propose to aggravate the situation further by raising—"

"How would you have done it?" he demanded.

"Like this," I told him soberly, exposing the lower half of the analysis (Sections III, IV, page 348). "You won't be happy with this showing, but it's closer to the realities of the situation. A fair 'standard' cost for your widgets was 25 cents each (ten cents labor and material plus 15 cents absorbed burden), just as I told you it would be before you started up. Sales of 600,000 units at 40 cents each gave you a (properly calculated) earned gross margin of $90,000. Against this you had $150,000 of unabsorbed factory expense, plus $30,000 of general expense, for a loss of $90,000. The second year your sales volume was down a third in units, but down only $40,000 in money; with a higher selling price you racked up an actual increase in margin over a fair standard cost (it went up to $100,000), but your unabsorbed burden went up an equal amount (to $160,000), and your general expenses were higher, so you had a loss of $100,000 to add to the $90,000 deficit from 1963."

"It can't be!" he objected frantically. "How can there be that much difference?"

"It's in the inventory valuation, of course," I explained soberly. "Look at Section IV here, and you'll see where it shows up. Those 800,000 widgets you had on hand at the end of 1964, valued at a so-called *actual average cost* of 45 cents each, were in fact properly chargeable with no more than a *fair standard cost* of 25 cents each; the 20 cents difference, on 800,000 units, comes to $160,000. That's the exact difference between your book loss of $30,000 and my recomputed loss of $190,000."

"But that's not fair!" he objected. "Nobody's plant is busy 100 per cent of the time."

Would the Auditors Approve?

"Unproven, and probably untrue," I retorted. "Some plants even run overtime. Here's another slant on it. Let's suppose one of your two machines was located here, and the other in some distant place, like Arkadelphia, Arkansas, for example; then suppose you had made all the widgets here, incurring factory expense of, say, $160,000, and kept the Arkadelphia plant shut up tight for the entire year, with standby expenses of another $120,000. . . . " I paused to let it sink in. "Would you claim that the Arkadelphia expense should be added to your expense here, in arriving at your average widget cost? And would your auditors have approved it if you had?"

He got the point all right, but he wouldn't admit it, even to himself. He had to go back to his bankers, he said, and he couldn't very well give then my figures; he'd told them a different story, and now he was stuck with it. He was really low.

To cheer him up I pointed out that if he could sell widgets for 60 cents, he'd do well to buy 'em from Helox for 35 cents, shut his plant down, and get rich on the jobbing profit—maybe even get Helox to buy his plant, if they needed more capacity or would like to get rid of competition. He just gave me an indignant look, and I decided to make my departure before I affronted him further.

I don't know what his banker told him, but I later heard indirectly that he'd obtained some additional capital from a "friendly source" (a rich brother-in-law, to be exact). I consoled myself with a pious hope that they would both awake to the facts of life before going around on that carousel many more times.

*   *   *   *   *

Now you may think, gentle reader, that I made all this up, but if so you do me an injustice. What I have presented in the foregoing is a fictionalized, but essentially factual, account of the experience of a company with which I recently had a fairly close association, now terminated by mutual consent. For illustrative purposes, I have resorted to some minor exaggeration and oversimplification in presenting the calculations, and I have excluded some extraneous factors in the situation, but otherwise this account of the basic philosophical conflict involved is starkly realistic.

I emerged from this encounter bruised and somewhat chagrined; it's never pleasant to give sound advice and have it ignored, or to see people fail in well-meant endeavors that might have been successful. I grieved over my friend's disappointment (despite the fact that he's just made a killing in a big real estate deal, and needs widgets like I need another fifteen grandchildren).

Under such circumstances, I usually go back to my raspberry patch, which is quite a solace in times of sorrow. Fruit growing, however, presents a few problems of its own. It takes me 20 minutes to pick a pint of berries; the grocery will pay me only 50 cents for them; after deducting the cost of the box, and mileage to the store, this leaves me less than $1.50 an hour for my time; when they put the minimum wage up to that figure, I won't be able to pay myself that much, and I suppose I'll have to go out of the raspberry business, too.

But, since the California climate is pleasant, and my health is good, and I'm mellowing a little in my old age, I would probably have forgotten my irritation with my friend Wax (or, perhaps I should say, with his auditors, who were, in my opinion, primarily to blame for his fiasco), if I hadn't run head-on into the same problem just a few weeks later.

The Whole—More Than the Parts

The Q Company, a client of mine, was being taken over by the Z Company, a big outfit with which I also had some contacts. These folks were about to publish a consolidated income statement for a recently concluded fiscal year (one of these "pooling-of-interests" deals). The preliminary draft came my way, and I observed with considerable surprise that the combined net income figure was substantially greater than the sum of the two constituent net income figures which had been in my hands previously.

"Hmph," I remarked thoughtfully to the unclad young woman portrayed on the Playboy calendar which ornaments my desk. She continued to smile agreeably at me, but without offering any comment.

After a bit I phoned the Q Company finance officer, an old and valued friend.

"Ever hear of the whole being greater than the sum of its parts?" I asked him.

"I know just what you mean," he responded promptly. "Embarrassing, isn't it?"

"It would sure embarrass me," I informed him. "What happened?"

"Well, it's in the inventory, of course" (his unhappy sigh carried over the microwaves all the way from New York). "We've always used those fine tight standard costs you helped us set up years ago —"

"I well remember," I assured him, "how tough it was to get them adopted, and how enthusiastic all the plant managers were about them after they'd been used a while —"

"Still feel the same," he told me emphatically; "wouldn't change for anything. Our people are unanimous in saying that the strength of our business has been in hammering away at unfavorable cost variances, squeezing them down, then tightening the standards again. You know. But," he sighed again, "we're told that Big Daddy doesn't do it that way, so now we can't do it that way any more."

"What the hell!" I demanded furiously. "What difference does it make to Z Company?"

Operating Results

"Seems their auditors (auditors again!) insist that the only proper cost standard is one derived from *average actual experience* under *normal operating* conditions. . . ."

"Don't tell me," I interrupted, in disgust. "Q Company had an unfavorable cost variance last year; you initially wrote it off to P&L; then the auditors came in and made you reinstate the part of it they claimed was related to the closing inventory —"

"Little matter of a million-and-a-half iron dollars added to consolidated profit," he confirmed glumly, "which, frankly, I don't think we earned." I asked if he'd told his bosses so.

"Oh, yes, but they said there was a tax problem involved. Z has always used average costs, and the auditors say they're afraid their position will be jeopardized if a subsidiary deviates —"

"Taxes, schmaxes," I retorted, rudely. "When they tell you to do something stupid they always lay it onto IRS or SEC or FTC or some government agency or other. Income taxes should *never* be mixed into measurements of *operating results,* under *any* conditions, and it's dangerous to let your evaluation of management performance get fouled up by any of today's hocus-pocus on taxes."

"Matter of great concern to us here," he said seriously. "We know how to run this business and to make money at it, and we'll go on doing so if we can stick to sound costing principles, but if we get to adulterating our standards to reflect every freak change in the tax laws, I don't know where we'll wind up." He sounded depressed. I was, too.

"Nothing *you* can do, I suppose," he ventured, hesitantly, after a pause.

"If you mean go argue with the auditors, the answer is an emphatic *no*," I assured him. "What was it old John Sharp Williams, of Mississippi, said when he resigned from the United States Senate, years ago? 'I might as well be a hound-dog and bay the moon, as spend my days exhorting my colleagues here' — something like that. I know just how he felt."

"Well, you're lucky; you've retired," he said enviously.

"Why do you suppose I retired early? You'll be smart to do likewise."

"Don't just desert us," he pleaded. "You ought to try to help us out."

"Okay," I responded. "I'll write a letter to the American Institute of Certified Public Accountants about it."

He snorted. "They plainly don't think the subject is of much importance," he pointed out. "In that 469-page *Inventory of Generally Accepted Accounting Principles* this entire problem is casually dismissed in about three scattered sentences."

I reminded him that the subject is lucidly and competently discussed, at some length, in Kohler's *Dictionary for Accountants,* but that didn't cheer him greatly. "So who reads a dictionary?" he complained. "Takes something livelier than a definition to get people interested. Why don't you write an article about it for *The Journal of Accountancy*? They might even print it."

*   *   *   *   *

So I did, and here you have it (or as much of it as may have survived the blue pencil of an amused but scandalized editor and his "technical advisers"). I hope only that they have preserved, for your edification, a full expression of the two major concepts which this fable seeks to formulate.

1. The *cost* reflected in an inventory valuation, and in any price-cost margin computation, must be not more than the sum of those elements of outlay which constitute identifiable and measurable contributions to value-creation; namely, (a) expenditures for materials and services applicable specifically and exclusively to the production of the article concerned, plus (b) such portion of expenditures for ancillary mechanical and administrative activities and services as may be ascribable solely to the productive function involved, excluding costs of maintaining facilities and organization not fully and efficiently employed, along with all wastes and losses which are patently avoidable under optimum manufacturing conditions.

2. The *price* at which an article is offered for sale should be that which (a) reflects its potential use-value in the hands of the buyer, with due regard for its quality, reputation, attractiveness and availability, and (b) promises to generate a sufficient volume of business to ensure adequate utilization of those facilities which the producer may choose to (or be compelled to) employ in its production, with due regard for competitive pressures, alternative usage, etc.

With this important corollary:

The "standard" cost employed for price-figuring, for inventory valuation and for efficiency measurement should be the smallest outlay conceivable under the best imaginable conditions—the shining target at which every arrow should be aimed. Surprising how soon you can start hitting the bull's-eye if you never let it out of sight.

31

Cost-Volume-Profit Analysis Under Conditions of Uncertainty

ROBERT K. JAEDICKE and

ALEXANDER A. ROBICHEK*

Cost-volume-profit analysis is frequently used by management as a basis for choosing among alternatives. Such decisions as: (1) the sales volume required to attain a given level of profits, and (2) the most profitable combination of products to produce and sell are examples of decision problems where C-V-P analysis is useful. However, the fact that traditional C-V-P analysis does not include adjustments for risk and uncertainty may, in any given instance, severely limit its usefulness. Some of the limitations can be seen from the following example.

Assume that the firm is considering the introduction of two new products, either of which can be produced by using present facilities. Both products require an increase in annual fixed cost of the same amount, say $400,000. Each product has the same selling price and variable cost per unit, say $10 and $8 respectively, and each requires the same amount of capacity. Using these data, the breakeven point of either product is 200,000 units. C-V-P analysis helps to establish the breakeven volume of each product, but this analysis does not distinguish the relative desirability of the two products for at least two reasons.

The first piece of missing information is the *expected* sales volume of each product. Obviously, if the annual sales of A are expected to be 300,000 units and of B are expected to be 350,000 units, then B is clearly preferred to A so far as the sales expectation is concerned.

However, assume that the expected annual sales of each product is the same—say 300,000 units. Is it right to conclude that management should be indifferent as far as a choice between A and B is concerned? The answer is *no, unless* each sales expectation is certain. If both sales estimates are subject to uncertainty, the decision process will be improved if the relative risk associated with each product can somehow be brought into the analysis. The discussion which follows suggests some changes which might be made in traditional C-V-P analysis so as to make it a more useful tool in analyzing decision problems under uncertainty.

* From *The Accounting Review* (October 1964), pp. 917-26. Reprinted by permission of the American Accounting Association.

Some Probability Concepts Related to C-V-P Analysis

In the previous section, it was pointed out that the *expected* volume of the annual sales is an important decision variable. Some concepts of probability will be discussed using the example posed earlier.

The four fundamental relationships used in the example were: (1) the selling price per unit; (2) the variable cost per unit; (3) the total fixed cost; and (4) the expected sales volume of each product. In any given decision problem, all four of these factors can be uncertain. However, it may be that, *relative to* the expected sales quantity, the costs and selling prices are quite certain. That is, for analytical purposes, the decision maker may be justified in treating several factors as certainty equivalents. Such a procedure simplifies the analysis and will be followed here as a first approximation. In this section of the paper, sales volume will be treated as the only uncertain quantity. Later, all decision factors in the above example will be treated under conditions of uncertainty.

In the example, sales volume is treated as a *random variable*. A random variable can be thought of as an *unknown quantity*. In this case, the best decision hinges on the value of the random variable, sales volume of each product. One decision approach which allows for uncertainty is to estimate, for each random variable, the likelihood that the random variable will take on various possible values. Such an estimate is called a subjective probability distribution. The decision would then be made by choosing that course of action which has the highest *expected monetary value*. This approach is illustrated in Table I.

Table I. Probability Distribution for Products A and B

Events (Units Demanded)	Probability Distribution— (Product A)	Probability Distribution— (Product B)
50,000	—	.1
100,000	.1	.1
200,000	.2	.1
300,000	.4	.2
400,000	.2	.4
500,000	.1	.1
	1.00	1.00

The expected value of the random variables, sales demand for each product, is calculated by weighting the possible conditional values by their respective probabilities. In other words, the expected value is a weighted average. The calculation is given in Table II.

Based on an expected value approach, the firm should select

**Table II. Expected Value of Sales Demand
for Products A and B**

(1) Event	(2) P(A)	(1 ✕ 2)	(3) P(B)	(1 ✕ 3)
50,000	—	—	.1	5,000
100,000	.1	10,000	.1	10,000
200,000	.2	40,000	.1	20,000
300,000	.4	120,000	.2	60,000
400,000	.2	80,000	.4	160,000
500,000	.1	50,000	.1	50,000
	1.00		1.00	
Expected Value		300,000 units		305,000 units

product B rather than A. The expected profits of each possible action are as follows:

Product A:

$2 (300,000 units) −$400,000=$200,000

Product B:

$2 (305,000 units) −$400,000=$210,000.

Several observations are appropriate at this point. First, the respective probabilities for each product, used in Table I, add to 1.00. Furthermore, the possible demand levels (events) are assumed to be mutually exclusive and also exhaustive. That is, the listing is done in such a way that no two events can happen simultaneously and any events *not* listed are assumed to have a zero probability of occurring. Herein are three important (basic) concepts of probability analyses.

Secondly, the probability distributions may have been assigned by using demand data on similar products, or the weights may be purely subjective in the sense that there is no historical data available. Even if the probability distributions are entirely subjective, this approach still has merit. It allows the estimator to express his uncertainty about the sales estimate. An estimate of sales is necessary to make a decision. Hence, the question is *not* whether an estimate must be made, but simply a question of the best way to make and express the estimate.

Now, suppose that the expected value of sales for each product is 300,000, as shown in Table III. In this example, it is easy to see that the firm would *not* be indifferent between products A and B, even though the expected value of sales is 300,000 units in both cases. In the case of product A, for example, there is a .1 chance that sales will be only 100,000 units, and in that case, a loss of $200,000 would be incurred (i.e., $2 × 100,000 units − $400,000). On the other hand, there is a .3 chance that sales will be above 300,000 units and if this is the case, higher profits are possible with product A than with product B. Hence, the

Table III

Demand	P(A)	E.V.(A)	P(B)	E.V.(B)
100,000 units	.1	10,000	—	—
200,000 units	.2	40,000	—	—
300,000 units	.4	120,000	1.00	300,000
400,000 units	.2	80,000	—	—
500,000 units	.1	50,000	—	—
	1.00		1.00	
Expected Sales Demand		300,000		300,000

firm's attitude toward risk becomes important. The expected value (or the mean of the distribution) is important, but so is the "spread" in the distribution. Typically, the greater the "spread," the greater the risk involved. A quantitative measure of the spread is available in the form of the standard deviation of the distribution, and this concept and its application will be refined later in the paper.

The Normal Probability Distribution

The preceding examples were highly simplified and yet the calculations are relatively long and cumbersome. The possible sales volumes were few in number and the probability distribution was discrete, that is, a sales volume of 205,762 units was considered an impossible event. The use of a continuous probability distribution is desirable not only because the calculation will usually be simplified but because the distribution may also be a more realistic description of the uncertainty aspects of the situation. The normal probability distribution will be introduced and used in the following analysis which illustrates the methodology involved. This distribution, although widely used, is not appropriate in all situations. The appropriate distribution depends on the decision problem and should, of course, be selected accordingly.

The normal probability distribution is a smooth, symmetric, continuous, bell-shaped curve as shown in Figure 1. The area under the curve sums to 1. The curve reaches a maximum at the mean of the distribution and one-half the area lies on either side of the mean.

On the horizontal axis are plotted the values of the appropriate unknown quantity or random variable; in the examples used here, the unknown quantity is the sales for the coming periods.

A particular normal probability distribution can be completely determined if its mean and its standard deviation, σ, are known. The standard deviation is a measure of the dispersion of the distribution about its mean. The area under any normal distribution is 1, but one distribution may be "spread out" more than another distribution. For example, in Figure 2, both normal distributions have the same area

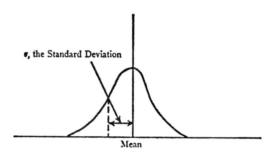

The Normal Probability Distribution

Figure 1

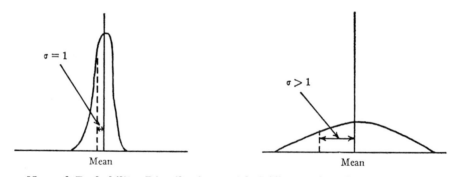

Normal Probability Distributions with Different Standard Deviations

Figure 2

and the same mean. However, in one case the σ is 1 and in the other case the σ is greater than 1. The larger the σ, the more spread out is the distribution. It should be noted that the standard deviation is not an area but is a measure of the dispersion of the individual observations about the mean of all the observations — it is a distance.

Since the normal probability distribution is continuous rather than discrete, the probability of an event cannot be read directly from the graph. The unknown quantity must be thought of as being in an interval. Assume, for example, that the mean sales for the coming period is estimated to be 10,000 units and the normal distribution appears as in Figure 3. Given Figure 3, certain probability statements can be made. For example:

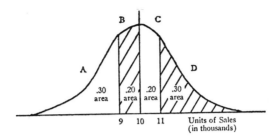

Figure 3

1. The probability of the actual sales being between 10,000 and 11,000 units is .20. This is shown by area C. Because of the symmetry of the curve, the probability of the sales being between 9,000 and 10,000 is also .20. This is shown by shaded area B. These probabilities can be given a frequency interpretation. That is, area C indicates that the actual sales will be between 10,000 and 11,000 units in about 20 per cent of the cases.

2. The probability of the actual sales being greater than 11,000 units is .30 as shown by area D.

3. The probability of the sales being greater than 9,000 units is .70, the sum of areas B, C, and D.

Given a specific normal distribution, it is possible to read probabilities of the type described above directly from a normal probability table.

Another important characteristic of any normal distribution is that approximately .50 of the area lies within ±.67 standard deviations of the mean; about .68 of the area lies within ±1.0 standard deviations of the mean; .95 of the area lies within ±1.96 standard deviations of the mean.

As was mentioned above, normal probabilities can be read from a normal probability table. A partial table of normal probabilities is given in Table IV. This table is the "right tail" of the distribution; that is, probabilities of the unknown quantity being greater than X standard deviation from the mean are given in the table. For example, the probability of the unknown quantity being greater than the mean plus .35σ is .3632. The distribution tabulated is a normal distribution with mean zero and standard deviation of 1. Such a distribution is known as a standard normal distribution. However, any normal distribution can be standardized and hence, with proper adjustment, Table IV will serve for any normal distribution.

For example, consider the earlier case where the mean of the distribution is 10,000 units. The distribution was constructed so that

Table IV. Area Under the Normal Probability Function

X	0.00	0.05
.1	.4602	.4404
.3	.3821	.3632
.5	.3085	.2912
.6	.2743	.2578
.7	.2420	.2266
.8	.2119	.1977
.9	.1841	.1711
1.0	.1587	.1469
1.1	.1357	.1251
1.5	.0668	.0606
2.0	.0228	.0202

the standard deviation is about 2,000 units.[1] To standardize the distribution, use the following formula, where X is the number of standard deviations from the mean:

$$X = \frac{\text{Actual Sales} - \text{Mean Sales}}{\text{Standard deviation of the distribution}}.$$

To calculate the probability of the sales being greater than 11,000 units, first standardize the distribution and then use the table.

$$X = \frac{11,000 - 10,000}{2,000} = .50 \text{ standard deviations.}$$

The probability of being greater than .50 standard deviations from the mean, according to Table IV, is .3085. This same approximate result is shown by Figure 3, that is, area D is .30.

The normal distribution used in C-V-P analysis. The normal distribution will now be used in a C-V-P analysis problem, assuming that sales quantity is a random variable. Assume that the per-unit selling price is $3,000, the fixed cost is $5,800,000, and the variable cost per unit is $1,750. Breakeven sales (in units) is calculated as follows:

$$S_B = \frac{\$5,800,000}{\$3,000 - \$1,750} = 4,640 \text{ units.}$$

Furthermore, suppose that the sales manager estimates that the mean expected sales volume is 5,000 units and that it is equally likely that actual sales will be greater or less than the mean of 5,000 units. Further-

[1] To see why this normal distribution has a standard deviation of 2,000 units, remember that the probability of sales being greater than 11,000 units is .30. Now examine Table IV, and it can be seen that the probability of a random variable being greater than .5 standard deviations from the mean is .3085. Hence, 1,000 units is about the same as $\frac{1}{2}$ standard deviations. So, 2,000 units is about 1 standard deviation.

more, assume that the sales manager feels that there is roughly a $\frac{2}{3}$ (i.e., .667) chance that the actual sales will be within 400 units of the mean. These subjective estimates can be expressed by using a normal distribution with mean $E(Q) = 5,000$ units and standard deviation $\sigma_q = 400$ units. The reason that σ_q is about 400 units is that, as mentioned earlier, about $\frac{2}{3}$ of the area under the normal curve (actually .68) lies within 1 standard deviation of the mean. The probability distribution is shown in Figure 4.

The horizontal axis of Figure 4 denotes sales quantity. The probability of an actual sales event taking place is given by the area under the probability distribution. For example, the probability that the sales quantity will exceed 4,640 units (the breakeven point) is the shaded area under the probability distribution (the probability of actual sales exceeding 4,640 units).

The probability distribution of Figure 4 can be superimposed on the profit portion of the traditional C-V-P; this is done in Figure 5. The values for price, fixed costs, and variable costs are presumed to be known with certainty. Expected profit is given by:

$$E(Z) = E(Q)(P\text{-}V) - F = \$450,000,$$

where

$$
\begin{aligned}
E(Z) &= \text{Expected Profit} \\
E(Q) &= \text{Expected Sales} \\
P &= \text{Price} \\
V &= \text{Variable Cost} \\
F &= \text{Fixed Cost.}
\end{aligned}
$$

The standard deviation of the profit (σ_z) is:

$$
\begin{aligned}
\sigma_z &= \sigma_q \times \$1,250 \text{ contribution per unit} \\
&= 400 \text{ units} \times \$1,250 = \$500,000.
\end{aligned}
$$

Since profits are directly related to the volume of sales, and since it is the level of profits which is often the concern of management, it may

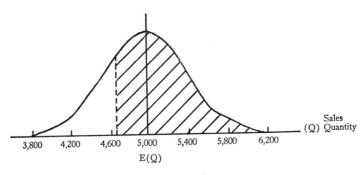

Figure 4

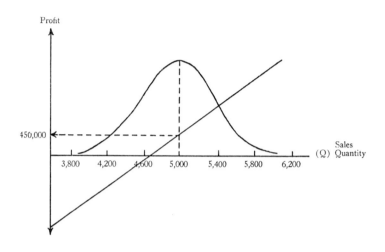

Figure 5

be desirable to separate the information in Figure 5 which relates to profit. Figure 6 is a graphical illustration of the relationship between profit level and the probability distribution of the profit level. A number of important relationships can now be obtained in probabilistic terms. Since the probability distribution of sales quantity is normal with a mean of 5,000 units and a standard deviation of 400 units, the probability distribution of profits will also be normal with a mean, as shown earlier, of $450,000 and a standard deviation of $500,000.

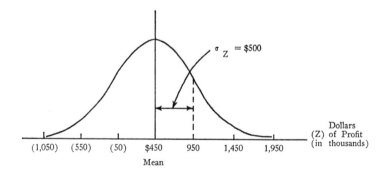

Figure 6

Using the probability distribution shown in Figure 6, the following probabilities can be calculated (using Table IV).

1. The probability of at least breaking even: This is the probability of profits being greater than zero and can be calculated by summing the area under the distribution to the right of zero profits. This probability can be calculated as $1 - $ (the probability of profits being less than zero). Since the distribution is symmetric, Table IV can be used to read left tail as well as right tail probabilities. Zero profits fall .9 standard deviations to the left of the mean

$$\left(\text{i.e.,} \quad \frac{\$450 - 0}{\$500} = .9 \right).$$

Hence, the probability of profits being less than zero is:

$$P \text{ (Profits} < .9\sigma \text{ from the mean)} = .184.$$

Therefore

$$P \text{ (Profits} > 0) = 1 - .184 = .816.$$

2. The probability of profits being greater than $200,000.

P (Profits > \$200,000)

$$= 1 - P\left(\text{Profits} < \frac{450 - 200}{500} \sigma \text{ from the mean} \right)$$

$$= 1 - P \text{ (Profits} < .5\sigma \text{ from the mean)}$$

$$= 1 - .3085 = .692.$$

3. The probability of the loss being greater than $300,000.
P (Loss > \$300,000)

$$= P \left(\text{Loss} > \frac{450 - (-300)}{500}, \text{ or } 1.5\sigma \text{ from the mean} \right).$$

$$P = .067.$$

The question of how the above information can be used now arises. The manager, in choosing between this product and other products or other lines of activity, can probably improve his decision by considering the risk involved. He knows that the breakeven sales is at a level of 4,640 units. He knows that the expected sales are 5,000 units which would yield a profit of $450,000. Surely, he would benefit from knowing that:

1. The probability of at least reaching breakeven sales is .816,

2. The probability of making at least $200,000 profit is .692,

3. The probability of making at least $450,000 profit is .50,

4. The probability of incurring losses, i.e., not achieving the breakeven sales volume, is (1.816, or .184),

5. The probability of incurring a $300,000 or greater loss is .067, etc.

If the manager is comparing this product with other products, probability analysis combined with C-V-P allows a comparison of the risk involved in each product, as well as a comparison of relative breakeven points and expected profits. Given the firm's attitude toward and willingness to assume risk (of losses as well as high profits), the decision of choosing among alternatives should be facilitated by the above analysis.

Several Relevant Factors Probabilistic

It is evident from the above discussion that profit, Z, is a function of the quantity of sales in units (Q); the unit selling price (P); the fixed cost (F); and the variable cost (V). Up to this point P, F, and V were considered only as given constants, so that profit was variable only as a function of changes in sales quantity. In the following discussion, P, F, and V will be treated in a manner similar to Q, i.e., as random variables whose probability distribution is known. Continuing the example from the preceding section, let

Variable	*Expectation (Mean)*	*Standard Deviation*
Sales Quantity (Q)	$E(Q') = 5{,}000$ units	$\sigma_Q' = 400$ units
Selling Price (P)	$E(P') = 3{,}000^2$	$\sigma_P' = \$50^2$
Fixed Costs (F)	$E(F') = \$5{,}800{,}000^2$	$\sigma_F' = \$100{,}000^2$
Variable Costs (V)	$E(V') = \$1{,}750^2$	$\sigma_V' = \$75^2$

For purposes of illustration, the random variables will be assumed to be independent, so that no correlation exists between events of the different random variables.[3] In this case, the expected profit $E(Z')$ and the related standard deviation $\sigma_{z'}$ can be calculated as follows:

$$E(Z') = E(Q')[E(P') - E(V')] - E(F')$$
$$= \$450{,}000.$$
$$\sigma_{z'}^4 = \$681{,}500.$$

Note that when factors other than sales are treated as random variables, the expected profit is still $450,000 as in the previous cases. However, the profit's risk as measured by the standard deviation is

[2] The mean and standard deviation for P, F, and V can be established by using the same method described earlier. That is, the sales manager may estimate a mean selling price of $3,000 per unit and, given the above information, he should feel that there is roughly a $\frac{2}{3}$ probability that the actual sales price per unit will be within $50 of this mean estimate.

[3] This assumption is made to facilitate computation in the example. Where correlation among variables is present the computational procedure must take into account the values of the respective covariances.

[4] For the case of independent variables given here, σ_Z' is the solution value in the equation:

$$\sigma_Z = \sqrt{[\sigma_Q^2(\sigma_P^2 + \sigma_V^2) + E(Q')^2(\sigma_V^2 + \sigma_V^2)} $$
$$+ [E(P') - E(V')]^2\sigma_Q^2 + \sigma_F^2]$$

increased from $500,000 to $681,500. The reason for this is that the variability in all of the components (i.e., sales price, cost, etc.) will add to the variability in the profit. Is this change in the standard deviation significant? The significance of the change is a value judgment based on a comparison of various probabilistic measures and on the firm's attitude toward risk. Using a normal distribution, Table V compares expected profits, standard deviations of profits, and select probabilistic measures for three hypothetical products.

In all three situations, the proposed products have the same breakeven quantity — 4,640 units. The first case is the first example discussed where sales quantity is the only random variable. The second case is the one just discussed, that is, all factors are probabilistic. In the third case, the assumed product has the same expected values for selling price, variable cost, fixed cost, and sales volume, but the standard deviations on each of these random variables have been increased to $\sigma_Q''=600$ (instead of 400 units); $\sigma_P''= \$125$ (instead of $50); $\sigma_F''=\$200,000$ (instead of $100,000); and $\sigma_V''=\$150$ (instead of 75).

Table V shows the relative "risk" involved in the three new products which have been proposed. The chances of at least breaking even are greatest with product 1. However, even though the standard deviation of the profit on product 3 is over twice that of product 1, the probability of breaking even on product 3 is only .17 lower than product 1. Likewise, the probability of earning at least $250,000 profit is higher for product 1 (which has the lowest σ) than for the other two products.

However, note that the probability of earning profits above the expected value of $450,000 (for each product) is *greater* for products 2 and 3 than for 1. If the firm is willing to assume some risk, the chances of high profits are improved with product 3, rather than with 2 and 1. To offset this, however, the chance of loss is also greatest with product

Table V. Comparison of Expected Profits, Standard Deviations of Profits, and Select Probabilistic Measures*

| | *Products* | | |
	(1)	*(2)*	*(3)*
Expected profit	$450,000	$450,000	$ 450,000
Standard deviation of profit	$500,000	$681,500	$1,253,000
The probability of:			
(a) at least breaking even	.816	.745	.641
(b) profit at least +$250,000	.655	.615	.564
(c) profit at least +$600,000	.382	.413	.456
(d) loss greater than $300,000	.067	.136	.274

* Note: The above probabilities, in some cases, cannot be read from Table IV. However, all probabilities come from a more complete version of Table IV.

3. This is to be expected, since product 3 has the highest standard deviation (variability) as far as profit is concerned.

The best alternative cannot be chosen without some statement of the firm's attitude toward risk. However, given a certain attitude, the proper choice should be facilitated by using probability information of the type given in Table V. As an example, suppose that the firm's position is such that any loss at all may have an adverse affect on its ability to stay in business. Some probability criteria can, perhaps, be established in order to screen proposals for new products. If, for example, the top management feels that any project which is acceptable must have no greater than a .30 probability of incurring a loss, then projects 1 or 2 would be acceptable but project 3 would not.

On the other hand, the firm's attitude toward risk may be such that the possibility of high profit is attractive, provided the probability of losses can be reasonably controlled. In this case, it may be possible to set a range within which acceptable projects must fall. For example, suppose that the firm is willing to accept projects where the probability of profits being greater than $600,000 is at least .40, provided that the probability of a loss being greater than $300,000 does not exceed .15. In this case, project 2 would be acceptable, but project 3 would not. Given statements of attitude toward risk of this nature, it seems that a probability dimension added to C-V-P analysis would be useful.

Summary and Conclusion

In many cases, the choice among alternatives is facilitated greatly by C-V-P analysis. However, traditional C-V-P analysis does not take account of the relative risk of various alternatives. The interaction of costs, selling prices and volume are important in summarizing the effect of various alternatives on the profits of the firm. The techniques discussed in this paper preserve the traditional analysis but also add another dimension — that is, risk is brought in as another important decision factor. The statement of probabilities with respect to various levels of profits and losses for each alternative should aid the decision maker once his attitude toward risk has been defined.

VI
Some Extensions

Many management accounting textbooks concentrate on a few types
of organizations — such as manufacturing concerns — when explaining
accounting techniques. Indeed, most financial and management
accounting educational material illustrates concepts in terms of
merchandising and manufacturing companies and ignores others, such
as: mining and oil exploration companies, real estate developers, mutual
funds, life insurance companies, trust companies and banks, franchisers
and a host of nonprofit institutions. An interesting speculation concerns
what effect this choice of a very few types of companies, for illustrating
accounting concepts, has on the later perspective of accounting
students and on their willingness to modify their views under different
conditions.

The accounting needs of managers of open-ended mutual
funds, for example, can be quite different from the needs of managers
of retail stores. Market prices of mutual fund common stock or mutual
fund units are generally based directly on balance sheet figures;
hence, some form of current "value" becomes essential input in compiling
financial statements. The so-called objectivity of historic cost becomes
a remote, secondary consideration in preparing balance sheets. In
summary, accounting techniques in this type of organization are
tailored to the specific needs of owners/managers.

This final section contains two pieces written by practitioners
on what might be labelled extensions of presentations found in typical
management accounting textbooks. The first reading shows how
program budgeting was applied in one nonprofit institution. The
article is a convenient one to refer to when critics object to types of
illustrations employed in the classroom, especially emphasis on

profit-seeking organizations. After reading some of the disasters reprinted earlier in this collection, we are certainly entitled to a success story.

"Social Accounting: Measuring the Unmeasurables?" considers the role of accounting in an age of changing personal values or beliefs. (". . . society faces monstrous problems which cannot be ignored. They will inevitably involve some sort of measurement — no matter how imprecise." "Decision makers must be permitted to measure the performance of their programmes against both the social and environmental criteria if they are to assess whether these funds are being used effectively.") The author acknowledges that measurement of social costs requires an interdisciplinary approach, but maintains that "accountants should be part of the team."

32

Program Budgeting Works in Nonprofit Institutions

RODERICK K. MACLEOD*

Cost accounting of professional services pinpoints sources and uses of funds, and facilitates decisions on money allocation. Professionals in nonprofit service organizations have long resisted the inauguration of cost accounting concepts (in many instances with good reason), but their resistance is breaking down in the face of supporters' demands for better controls over expenditure of the money, materials, and manpower they contribute. Often, however, the well-intentioned management and trustees of an institution do not know how to begin introducing cost accountability and program budgeting to their operation. In this article the author "walks" the reader through the establishment of a planning and accounting system which has resulted in much improved costing and planning at a once-drifting mental health clinic employing about 100 professionals. The same principles, he says, are applicable to other nonprofit professional activities.

A minor aspect of the honorable tradition of eleemosynary activity has been that you could not, and did not need to, account for the cost of services being provided. You could not because they were qualitative and intangible; you did not need to because funds were provided by gifts, grants, endowments, and so on. For the last several years this tradition has been called increasingly into question as the desire for cost information and accountability grows and as the control bases for cost accounting come more and more into focus. However, there has not been much recorded practical experience on which to judge the utility of cost accounting in institutional management.

* From the *Harvard Business Review* (September-October 1971), pp. 45-56. © 1971 by the President and Fellows of Harvard College; all rights reserved.

This article is a record of one such practical experience — broad enough to have general application but small enough to be fully described in a few pages. It is written for businessmen who, as trustees or directors of institutions, find themselves as frustrated as I was at the inability of some administrators to deal effectively with costs or even to keep track of what was happening financially. I hope it encourages them with the thought that it can be done.

Program cost accounting is in its third year of functioning at the South Shore Mental Health Center in Quincy, Massachusetts, a community agency with about 100 professional staff members. The agency derives its funds from a variety of sources for a variety of reasons, its professional staff is employed on a variety of terms, and there is no objective or numerical measure of the value of its diversified services. It therefore has most of the cost accounting problems of a nonprofit organization.

The first two of the following sections are written for those who are not familiar with either cost accounting or program budgeting. Both are essential to understanding the utility of program cost accounting. Anyone who knows these subjects should skip to the point in the article where I describe how we put them to use. It begins with the section, "Working in the dark."

COST ACCOUNTING

Defined as a body of techniques for associating costs with the purposes for which they are incurred, cost accounting was developed primarily for determining product costs in manufacturing processes. It is also used to determine the cost of services or activities.

"Nonprofit" Uses

In profit-making enterprises cost accounting is an essential aid to maximizing profits. While this incentive is not present in nonprofit institutions, cost accounting has at least these three other important purposes: efficiency and cost control, planning and allocating resources of people and funds, and "pricing" for cost reimbursement.

Efficiency & cost control: People often (some would say always) get careless about what they are doing, and if you are paying them, that means extra costs. If you know how much it costs to do something under optimum conditions and if you can measure the output of that something fairly accurately, then you can determine actual costs per unit of output and keep track of how efficiently the job is being done.

Of course, you have to be careful that cost saving is achieved without sacrificing quality of output. This is the reason why many institutions have felt that cost accounting is a bad influence. They say that the quality of service is too precious and fragile to be subjected to the pressure of cost accountability and to the drive for efficiency.

However, cost accounting can be used to set standards and to measure performance against them in a number of institutional activities without threatening the quality of service. Clerical and record-keeping operations, library services, nursing services, and storekeeping are examples of operations involving clearly defined results and enough labor to make worthwhile the effort of directing them efficiently.

Food service is another good example. A meal is either served and eaten, or it is not, and the size of portions and nutritional value can be measured and controlled. (Cost control and efficiency are accepted goals, even though it is recognized that pleasing the person who eats the meal is a highly qualitative and subjective thing.)

Another area which has received some attention, though not as much, is maintenance, including grounds keeping and housekeeping. Most maintenance activities can be quite clearly defined and the standard of quality made explicit. It is possible, for instance, to determine the optimum time for mowing a lawn, clearing a drain, making a bed, or repairing a boiler. For the most part, these estimates are used to schedule tasks and monitor performance, but they can easily be converted into dollar costs, when there is reason to do so.

So-called "efficiency experts" have earned a deservedly bad name in some quarters, and the feeling persists that work standards constitute another technological chain fettering the human spirit. Sensibly used, they need not be. It can be far more satisfying to work toward a well-defined and attainable goal than to work under the pressure of a never-ending backlog and an unknown and never-reached standard of excellence.

Furthermore, pride in one's work can be served better by the existence of standards authorizing the worker to call for help when a deviation appears, rather than obliging him to sink or swim. Standards should be a sensible way of organizing and carrying out tasks, not a means for applying pressure to reach unnatural levels of performance.

Resource allocation: A great deal of planning is done without cost accounting, and a great many institutions survive without planning. It is generally agreed, however, that careful planning and resource allocation are important elements of good management and that precise estimates of costs are necessary for careful planning.

Costs can often be gauged accurately enough for use in planning without going through the labor of accounting for actual costs. But there is no better way to verify the accuracy of estimates than to account for actual costs and then to compare them with the estimates.

While cost accounting has to be painstakingly accurate to be useful in measuring and controlling efficiency, a much wider range of imprecision is tolerable for planning purposes. A decision to expand a facility or to move in one direction rather than another will probably be affected by a 50 per cent change in the relevant costs, but seldom by a change of only 10 per cent or 20 per cent. This is why it is useful to cost professional services even though a legitimate respect for professional freedom of action requires acceptance of a substantial probability of inaccuracy.

Cost recovery pricing: The most compelling reason for undertaking the effort of cost accounting is the chance to get paid for what one does. In profit-making enterprises this incentive is obvious. In nonprofit institutions it is becoming obvious as they take on activities for which someone (usually the government) is willing to reimburse them. Medicare is one example. Another is the contract research work that many organizations undertake; cost accounting is at the heart of disputes over whether they are receiving adequate reimbursement.

When dollars change hands, accuracy is extremely important to both parties, but it is of a different order from that required for measuring efficiency. If they wish, the two parties to a cost reimbursement contract can agree on completely unrealistic or arbitrary definitions of cost. It is then necessary only to follow these agreements faithfully to obtain satisfactory reimbursement.

Usually, the simpler these agreements, the better, however much they may differ from principles of "real" cost determination. But continued use of unrealistic cost definitions ultimately makes the recipient of funds dependent on them and forces him to distort his actual experience to fit the reimbursement pattern.

Problems in Use

Associating costs with products or activities is simple enough conceptually, but in practice there are several problems for which there are no very satisfactory answers.

The most troublesome of these is what to do about costs that are common to several products or that do not vary with the amount produced. All the alternatives proposed or in use involve some means of prorating these overhead costs, joint costs, or fixed costs. The most common method is to relate these indirect costs to one or more of the direct costs, such as labor hours or labor dollars.

Whatever method is employed, users of cost data must keep in mind that the allocation is somewhat arbitrary. Troubles arise when they start thinking of these aggregates as "true" costs.

Another problem is caused by costs incurred at one point in time that underwrite activities and production over an extended period of time, such as expenditure for buildings and equipment. Plant costs are incurred before use in production, but other costs for which payment may be made in the distant future, such as employee pensions and deferred maintenance, must also be taken into account in determining the cost of current activities.

There are many theories concerning which of several methods of depreciation, amortization, or accrual is best and whether and how provisions for technological change and inflation should be made. As with overhead costs, however, all methods make somewhat arbitrary allocations.

Nonprofit institutions have traditionally ignored these capital costs, usually on the grounds that they were funded by gifts or grants. This tradition is being questioned increasingly as institutional managers try to compare costs of different activities and, particularly, as they find the government and others willing to pay for the "cost" of an activity, but demanding that the institution determine what the cost is.

Still another problem, one particularly troublesome to institutions, is determining what it is that you should compute the cost of. When you make widgets, it is easy enough to figure. In the service sector, providing meals and giving gamma globulin injections are clear-cut units of output. But it is not easy to define a satisfactory "production" unit for medical care, education, and many other kinds of social services.

There is a good deal of agonizing over this question, perhaps more than is necessary. It is useful to know the cost per patient-hour of medical treatment or the cost per student-hour of education, although they are not units of output. An hour of a doctor's care or of a professor's teaching is an input, not an output. The real output here is health or knowledge, and we do not yet know how to measure either well enough.

It is important for an organization to have accurate unit cost data for planning and evaluating the use of its resources. It is also important to be careful how the data are used for cost control. The real product could be seriously impaired by an attempt to minimize the cost per hour.

PROGRAM BUDGETING

Traditionally, budgeting in institutions has been a purely fiscal function divorced from social service planning. Customarily, about once a year the financial or accounting staff looked at the institution's expenses for heat, light, telephones, professional dues, and so on and guessed how much these might increase the next year. Sometimes the staff went so far as to ask the professionals what staff they expected to add or subtract, and at what change in cost. The result, the budget, was submitted to the board of trustees.

I wonder how many trustees have shared my experience of masking feelings of impotence and ignorance as I solemnly reviewed the lists of figures. From time to time I would ask why a figure differed from the corresponding one a year earlier.

If the income did not equal the outgo, I refused to approve the budget. But as soon as the budget was in balance, I approved it, without any real reason for knowing that the year could or should come out that way.

The process actually has worked quite well, and I do not mean to suggest that it be abandoned. After all, some sense of financial responsibility is better than none. And the trustees' review of the budget serves to remind dedicated professionals of the facts of life that they like to ignore in their pursuit of worthy social goals. Something better is available now, however.

The idea of program budgeting as an aid to planning the allocation of resources in a complex nonprofit organization is clear and very attractive. Actual practice, however, has been impeded by ignorance, caution, and preoccupation with technique.

Disciplined Thinking . . .

The principal conceptual innovation in program budgeting is disciplined thinking about what it is that an institution is producing. It follows logically that it is useful to budget the costs associated with those products and to evaluate the social benefits realized in relation to costs and alternative uses of funds and other resources.

Professionals have always thought to some degree about the programs they were engaged in, but usually without going so far as to associate costs with them. It is obvious, for example, that "patient hours" breaks down into diagnosis and prophylaxis as well as treatment and that a college's arts and sciences program includes instruction in physical sciences, social sciences, and the humanities. But professionals have generally thought it unnecessary or impossible to weigh the relative merits or costs of parts of such programs; so nobody tried. Current financial stringencies are making such "impossibilities" not only possible but also compelling.

Even rudimentary thinking about products brings useful insights. One notes that professors do not just teach students, they engage in research and consulting, they publish, they help other departments, they talk, they politick, and they join in community and social service activities. The levels of capital investment and nonprofessional support services can be seen to vary from one activity to another. The interdepartmental impact of new discipline can be glimpsed.

Sometimes, but not often, it is clear that results do not warrant the cost and that resources should be allocated elsewhere — such as converting a half-empty obstetrical ward into a geriatric ward.

In most allocation decisions, however, the relevant cost data and their relationship to the level of expected results are not at all clear. A factor even more critical to a decision is often overlooked: the implicit commitment to supply substantial additional resources in the future, as when a bequest for a new laboratory is gratefully accepted without the recipients' understanding the necessity for eventual expansion of all related and ancillary activities.

. . . & Organization

Program budgeting permits disciplined organization of the economic data relative to a decision involving the allocation of resources. Using it, one can gather costs by program, evaluate the impact of a program's expansion or contraction on directly and indirectly related costs, and estimate with some degree of confidence the program's future economic demands.

In its highest form, as developed and advertised by the Department of Defence, program budgeting also involves measuring and comparing the value of the output of various programs in terms of social utility. This is a dazzling concept, and we can look forward with great eagerness to the day when we can gauge the value of a heart surgery unit versus that of a better cancer treatment unit or the social utility of a degree in physics versus that of a comparable degree in psychology. Nobody can do it yet. But this fact should not detract from the great contribution program budgeting can make right now.

Program budgeting offers these aids to managers of service institutions:

☐ The conceptual discipline for defining what the institution is doing.

☐ The process of sorting out expenditures so as to identify the direct and allocated costs.

☐ The process of relating the various types of funding to the purposes for which they were intended and of identifying the uses to which unrestricted funds are being put.

☐ The means for estimating with confidence the cost consequences of expanding or contracting any program and the related impact on other programs and facilities.

☐ The means for examining the financial implications of a program over a span of time.

☐ The concept (and, sometime in the future, the means) of measuring the results of programs by some common denominator.

There are plenty of problems in employing program budgeting. Among them are getting professionals to submit to accountability, securing reliable data, defining programs sufficiently, and finding an adequate measure of output. The discovery that these matters can be dealt with fairly directly, and that it is worth doing, is the main message of this article.

WORKING IN THE DARK

The South Shore Mental Health Center began many years ago as a small children's clinic. When Dr. David Van Buskirk took over as director in 1967, it had expanded to the point where it was providing the nine communities in its area with substantially all kinds of mental health service except overnight and custodial treatment.

The services were carried out by about a hundred professionals under a bewildering and seemingly unlimited variety of individual arrangements. Some of them worked full time, but most of them had other jobs or private practices.

The principal source of funds was the Commonwealth of Mas-

sachusetts, which employed physicians, psychologists, nurses, social workers, and other professionals to work at the Center in civil service "blocks"
of time. The communities, represented by an association of citizens,
were responsible for securing the funds for facilities and administration
and, since the state salary scales were inadequate, for supplementing
the professional salaries. These funds were obtained primarily through
billing the communities served at a certain rate per patient-hour, and
secondarily from patient fees.

The Center also enjoyed an erratic flow of money from grants
and research contracts, principally through the National Institute of
Mental Health. Sometimes the grants were for additional work, and the
Center served merely as fiscal agent. Sometimes they were for participation in work that was the normal part of the Center's business, so that
the funds served in effect to relieve the communities of part of their
financial burden.

The Center also received money funded by groups or government
agencies for various programs. These included community education,
retarded children's schooling, a rehabilitation workshop, and several
training programs.

In spite of, or perhaps because of, the complexity of the Center's
operations and the funding of them, the agency's financial management
prior to 1967 was extraordinarily simple. A budget was prepared annually
in which each category of receipts and expenses was estimated and made
to balance. Toward the end of the year, the director and his assistant
adjusted their salaries (usually downward) to make the outgo equal
the income.

The board of trustees had only a general idea of the way in which
the Center's activities were funded and no idea at all of the important
relationships among the sources of funding. Through hindsight, it
appears probable that the administrators of the Center did not either.
They were exceptionally dedicated people; and they paid dearly for
their lack of financial acumen in the form of almost daily crises, over-
work, and low salaries.

Demand-Cost Squeeze

Dr. Van Buskirk's first months at the Center must have been a time of
great anxiety for him as he struggled to understand how things worked,
in the face of a nearly complete lack of information. He did manage to
put together figures on the number of hours given to patient diagnosis
and treatment.

To develop the "cost per patient hour," a statistic widely used in
the health profession, he divided the total operating cost by the number
of patient-hours. The result dismayed him. It showed that costs per
patient-hour were rising at a rate of about 25 per cent a year.

Because the funds provided by the state could be expected to
increase by no more than 10 per cent, if at all, the communities served
had to bear the rising costs alone. Since the nine communities had pre-

viously paid about one third of the total cost, the leverage effect was dramatic; the Center was faced with asking them to increase their appropriations to it by 65 per cent to 75 per cent. In a period of strong taxpayer resistance, that prospect was nearly intolerable.

The director recognized that an important reason for the soaring costs per patient-hour was the rapid expansion of other demands on the professional staff. The South Shore community was beginning to accept the long-held conviction among mental health professionals that early detection and prevention of emotional and mental problems is far better than is any amount of treatment. Instead of concentrating on seeing patients, the psychiatrists, psychologists, and social workers were beginning to spend more of their time with the front line of community social servants — school guidance counselors, teachers, police officers, court officers, and ministers.

The result was both a decline in the number of patient-hours needed for preliminary screening of applicants and an increase in the Center's total cost. Clearly, the cost per patient-hour was an inadequate and misleading statistic.

Dr. Van Buskirk had other incentives to innovate. He found that programs for which he was responsible were ballooning. The rehabilitation "sheltered workshop" project, for example, grew within a year from a small experiment to a well-established quarter-million-dollar operation, even before the board of trustees knew it existed.

Demands for new programs came from all directions and usually from persons with little interest or ability in helping to determine how they would be paid for. For example, the drug abuse problem, to which the suburban communities had awakened, began soaking up the time of the Center's professionals. "Hot line" and other counseling services were springing up all over the area, their founders assuming that the Center would take care of any and all treatment referrals.

Moreover, the professionals were asking controversial questions about the relative values of different activities. Should they give priority to services for adults or for children; to after-care and group services or to conventional doctor-patient treatment; to social services or to clinical services? There was no information available to aid the administration in evaluating any of these problems; the director was forced to make decisions solely on intuition and judgment.

DEVELOPING A SYSTEM

At about that time, a college senior came to the Center for three months as part of her work-study program. She had no accounting background or qualifications for the job Dr. Van Buskirk gave her, other than the average college student's ease with numbers and concepts. But before she left, she had helped the director install a program cost accounting system. Perhaps an important reason for this extraordinary accomplishment is that neither she nor the director was burdened with the professional accountant's knowledge of how difficult it is to set up a new system.

The first step was to define the programs that made up the Center's services. After much re-drafting of lists of functions, the director settled on five main categories subdivided into a total of 26 separate programs. These main areas were clinical services, community services, retardation and rehabilitation services, training, and research. As an example of the detail involved, clinical services included five programs: children's services, adult services, after-care services, disturbed children's nursery and kindergarten, and court-requested evaluations.

For the most part, the distinctions among programs were clear. The only important artificial separation involved the training function. As in most professional service activities, nearly everything that went on had important training elements, and the trainees contributed greatly to the Center's work. Dr. Van Buskirk decided arbitrarily that trainees' direct costs would be allocated to the programs in which they worked, while the cost of time spent by professionals and teachers in instruction and guidance would be charged to training.

Staff Time

The next step was to ask the professionals to report how their time during an average week was allocated among the 26 programs. A simple form was drawn up, listing the programs and asking for the individual's estimate of the percentage of time he devoted to every one that took more than 10 per cent of his time. Experience with this document inadvertently carried the project through three of the obstacles most commonly cited as rendering program cost accounting difficult, if not impossible:

1. It dispelled the notion that professionals simply will not hold still for rendering themselves accountable. This is no doubt the case when meticulous, detailed, and frequent reporting is required or when the ultimate value of the effort is not fully understood. However, spending fifteen minutes three or four times a year with a simple form is not overly demanding, especially when a respected superior has explained the importance of the results.

The value of top professional involvement in communicating the importance of the project cannot be overemphasized, and it is a likely reason for the success of this endeavor. The Center's professional head, not the nonprofessional administrators or accountants, initiated and carried out the project. He spent at least an hour with the professionals from each program, explaining what he hoped to achieve and discussing their own needs. The professionals were understandably more willing to give him their confidence and cooperation, and he, having a well-defined goal, was able to keep the project from getting bogged down in procedural details.

2. It taught us how to deal with inaccuracy and subjectivity in the initial time estimates. It is true that an annual or even quarterly estimate is unlikely to be very accurate, and it is also true that some of the staff might report their estimates of what ought to be happening, rather than what really is happening. We found these faults tolerable for two reasons.

First, other potential inaccuracies — e.g., those introduced by overhead allocation — require a generous tolerance for imprecision in the use of the results. Also, because the estimates of the programs' social utility are necessarily vague and subjective, no other factor entering into decisions about them, such as cost, need be measured with any great precision. I must again emphasize that even a rough idea of the cost of a program is so useful that arguments about precision are reduced to the level of quibbles.

Second, every program or activity has someone responsible for it, who watches it with great professional affection and jealousy. If he understands the value of the resulting information, he can be relied on to identify gross errors of omission and commission.

He can also be relied on to respond to the test of output. The head of a program may tolerate for one or two periods, but not indefinitely, a cost allocation disproportionate to results. The director made what amounted to a contract with each group of professionals to produce a given level and mix of services for a given level of cost, and as long as these were forthcoming and up to standard, he did not worry about the continued accuracy of the original time estimates.

3. Reporting in terms of percentages avoided problems arising from the use of other yardsticks. Accountants like to have reports prepared in precise units like hours or days, and the director had to resist the temptation to seek the orderliness inherent in using units one can measure, count, control, and balance out.

He was forced into the choice of percentages because at the Center there are too many varieties of part-time participation to permit any common denominator except "percentage of time devoted to Center activities." This choice avoided the often-heard complaint that professionals cannot report time because they do not work conventional hours. Whether a professional customarily works eighteen hours a day or four does not affect his percentage allocation.

From the time-allocation forms, the college student made the necessary calculations for assigning the appropriate fraction of each professional's salary to the programs he was engaged in. Some of the professionals were not on the Center's payroll at all because they were assigned to training or research projects by colleges and other organizations in the area. For each of these individuals, the director computed a salary equivalent that was recorded in a memorandum account as a source of funds from his particular organization. The corresponding "cost" was then allocated among the appropriate programs.

Income & Outgo

The Center's expenses were analyzed and segregated into those that related directly to programs and those that made up general administration and overhead. The total costs turned out to be 80 per cent program-oriented salaries, 11 per cent other direct costs, and 9 per cent general overhead (including administrative salaries).

Because none of the decisions to be made would hinge on a variation of cost as slight as 10 per cent, the overhead allocation problem was determined to be insignificant. Rather than trying to refine the process, the director simply allocated the 9 per cent of overhead costs to the 26 programs in proportion to their salary costs.

The director had a lot more trouble with allocating the portion of the Center's total cost (15 per cent) that related to the nine separate training programs. Is training an end product of the Center, or is it a necessary element in maintaining the levels of professional skill in the other programs? It is both, of course. Also, as I have noted, it is impossible to distinguish training from the service programs where the training takes place.

We decided to treat training first as a separate accountable endeavor and secondly as an integral part of the other service programs, following the principle that a substantial element of training is essential to a high level of professional service. Each training program was therefore either assigned to the service program where it took place or prorated among the several programs to which it related. The full cost of each training program was allocated without reduction for related grants received; the grants were considered part of the income directly relating to the service programs.

The remaining step was to figure out who was paying for each program. Money received for specific purposes was first assigned to the appropriate program: grants, stipends, the "equivalent salary" of contributed workers, fees received from patients and from agencies such as school boards — all went toward the programs for which they were received. Then the appropriate fraction of the state salary paid to the professionals who had indicated participation in these programs was identified and treated as a source of funds.

The difference between the total program cost and these identifiable funds had to be made up from the amounts billed to the communities served. One of the simpler examples, the finances for running the disturbed children's nursery and kindergarten, is presented in *Exhibit I.*

One other element of the new system required some thought: identifying units of service that would facilitate projections of the cost effect of a change in program. This was easy for conventional treatment services, where an interview with a patient almost invariably is scheduled to last an hour. In the school-type programs, such as the cerebral palsy nursery, we could use the traditional statistic, "full-time equivalent enrollee." The measurement of counseling and community service programs required more thought and, ultimately, presented us with another conceptual discovery.

It is a tradition in the medical profession that services are being

Exhibit I

Costs and sources of funds for
operating the disturbed children's nursery
and kindergarten

	Amount
Costs	
Professional salaries	$18,500
Direct costs	1,950
Overhead	2,200
Training, specifically identified	3,600
Total	$26,250
Sources of money	
Wheelock College training grant	$ 3,600
State salaries, specified	12,650
State salaries, unspecified	9,500
Total	$25,750
Community funds allocated by the Center	500
Total	$26,250

performed only when one is face-to-face with a patient. But in a community service program, a professional can spend hours preparing material; more hours in transit to and from a community; an hour, say, with a social agency there; and then still more hours writing down the results. If he reported only the one hour spent with the agency, the record of effort — and cost — actually invested would clearly be inaccurate.

From the community's point of view, however, the unit of output received from the Center is the single hour with the professional. There has to be a distinction between time spent for costing purposes and the unit of time used for output purposes. When both are used for planning purposes, one gets a clearer picture of why community service workers' case loads seem so light compared with those of clinical workers.

What is more important, when professionals can be persuaded to report on the basis of time invested in an activity rather than on the basis of interview output, the true costs begin to appear; and clinical services are relieved of the burden of carrying part of the cost of other programs.

SOLID RESULTS

At this writing, program costing is completing its third year of operation. Since the Center's activities roughly follow the pattern of the school year and since most of the professionals work according to a pattern of commitment that changes very little during a year, it probably is unnecessary to gather information and cost it out more often than once a year, but the director does it quarterly for verification purposes. Data on output are, of course, gathered currently and compared with the budget.

It takes more than two months to pull the cost data together, but not because of clerical or computational burdens. The time elapses because the process obliges the staff to discover, discuss, examine, define, and redirect. Inadvertent shifts of effort and focus are uncovered, as are activities that seem to be taking more time than they are worth. Once accepted by the professionals, the costing effort induces an element of planning that was absent before, and also foreign to many of them.

What You Pay For, You Get

The most dramatic result of the first crude program costing effort was also the most pragmatic: the Center started assessing users for the cost of the services they demanded. This was quite a contrast with the Center's early years, when the professionals were apologetic in seeking payment for its activities.

The approach to the town finance committees and city administrators used to be, "Please help us out with x thousands of dollars." Now the Center had the information to support this position: "Here is a list of services we have been asked to provide you and the amount that each will cost. Please authorize payment, or you'll have to get along without the service."

As everyone knows who is acquainted with methods of municipal government, it is never that simple. Getting acceptance of the change in approach necessitated much demonstration, explanation and cajoling. It was a delicate matter to explain to a community that, whereas in the past its financial support had been applied generally to the operation of the Center's programs, now these programs (many of them unfamiliar to, and typically not specifically demanded by, the community) were to be underwritten separately, or otherwise canceled.

In some cases the exigencies of politics required reversion to the time-honored procedure of raising charges per patient-hour. Nevertheless, the campaign to obtain payment for particular services rendered moved slowly ahead. The progress permitted the Center to hold the line on charges for long-established activities.

Sometimes we "found" costs that were reimbursable under one program buried in another. An example is the rehabilitation workshop, whose costs are reimbursed by a state agency. Program costing turned up about $35,000 worth of unrecognized professional and nonprofessional support which was being provided by persons at the Center not specifically identified with the workshop. And this discovery served to shift the burden of reimbursement from the communities to the state agency.

Cost Data in Planning

The next most important product of the cost accounting effort was the ability to examine the cost of new demands made on the Center. In earlier days, for example, the willing response of the agency's professionals to the awakening concern over drug addiction and related mental health problems would have included little thought for the consequences — an inundation of unanswered and unanswerable calls for help, diagnosis, and treatment. Now we have the information with which to sound the alarm about needed facilities and funding while interest in the service is at a peak.

Moreover, it is now possible to think and talk about relative costs in setting priorities. Priority setting remains highly subjective; the relative importance of various activities is more or less established by the director as he listens to the demands coming from various quarters and analyzes the interests and abilities of the people available. Having cost information available leads to considerations like these:

☐ We could double our work with the police departments if we were willing to give up 5 per cent of our children's clinical services.

☐ If we are asked to participate heavily in a drug abuse program, the resources for it cannot come from any of the programs funded by restricted money, and the nursery school and rehabilitation staffs are not qualified. So we would have to cut back on clinical or community services after determining which one would free the most money with the least loss to the communities.

☐ A suggestion that we join in a new community program on alcoholism must be rejected because we can foresee the amount of commitment that would be required if it were successful, and all our funds are committed to programs that seem to be more effective.

Spotlight on Funds Flows

A very important discovery was the interaction among the different kinds of funds. Before program costing and budgeting, the unrestricted money was "just used," and the forces affecting its use were unrecognized and uncontrolled. When available funds were related to the costs of programs we discovered such things as these:

☐ Receipt of restricted money pushes unrestricted money out of a program, making it available for other purposes.

☐ Loss of restricted money, even with a concurrent reduction in program, sucks up some unrestricted money, if for no other reason than the loss of contribution to overhead.

☐ The same service is often funded twice, thereby relieving the general demand on unrestricted funds. (For example, when a trainee — whose salary has been contributed — works on a project for which a grant was received, the portion of the grant money that otherwise would have been applied to his salary relieves the communities of part of their burden of providing the unrestricted funds for the Center.)

☐ Attractive service opportunities always receive "hidden funding" because they are supported by professionals who would otherwise be working on the programs for which they are being paid.

A case in point is the after-care program, which is 30 per cent supported by community funds and requires 10 per cent of the total community contribution. After-care is counseling and support of patients during their difficult period of adjustment after release from state mental hospitals.

Mental health professionals have long felt that an after-care program plays an extremely important part in a patient's cure, and, to the extent that he is completely rehabilitated, it is an important service to the community. However, no community has specifically contracted for an after-care program.

What, then, are the ethics of using funds appropriated for certain services to finance another service not on the list and perhaps not even known to the appropriating cities and towns? Yet if you do not do it this way, how do you get the chance to incubate new services?

There are several good answers to these questions, but the point is that you have to think of the questions before you can answer them. (In this case, we recognized "hidden funding" as a fact of life and articulated the policy that new program development is a recognized overhead cost, much like training.)

Wider Horizons

Program cost accounting has opened up some promising lines of thought that have yet to be explored. We wonder, for example, why treatment of adults seems to cost more per hour than does treatment of children, and work with school counselors more than work with courts and police. The director has not tackled these questions because he is not sure the statistics are right. The data base must grow and "season" for a while before it can be trusted to help answer such detailed questions.

Another set of interesting questions is raised by thinking about overhead costs and their relationship to programs. Perhaps most overhead items can be associated with specific programs when they are significant enough to warrant the trouble. The chief accountant and the chief engineer can make quite good estimates of where their staffs are spending their hours, and if necessary, they can require time reports so that costs can be accounted for by program.

But why should a fully funded program bear any of the costs of the accounts receivable department? Or why should the counseling program, carried out entirely off the premises, bear as much plant and maintenance cost as do those that use the plant?

Perhaps there is not really much true overhead in any institution; perhaps most of it is really part of unidentified additional programs or additions to particular programs. Consider the college admissions office, the development office, the alumni office, the news office, the placement office, and so on; are they overhead, or is each engaged in a purposeful program of its own?

These thoughts suggest the kinds of hard questions that can be asked about overhead on the basis of the program cost concept. What is causing the overhead cost? Is it worth it? Why do we need that overhead program? Is it paying for itself? Are we asking users to share the cost of doing something unnecessary or of something for a completely unrelated beneficiary?

On a more ambitious level, the director is thinking about freeing mental health services from the encumbrances of politics and civil service by contracting for specific outputs of service at a fixed price per unit of output. He needed accurate cost accounting before he could dare propose it.

In summary, all concerned are delighted with the results of program cost accounting. The professionals do not find it burdensome, and they know much they did not know before. The administrators and the trustees are beginning to feel they understand what is going on, and they move with more confidence, both in planning and in finding the funds.

CONCLUSION

The message is not that we have found program budgeting and accounting to be a good thing; everyone knows it is. My message is that *it can be done*. Here are my recommendations for institutional administrators and trustees:

☐ Insist on knowing what the institution's programs are and who is paying for them.

☐ Insist on analysis of the costs of proposed program changes.

☐ Insist that the reasons for proposed changes in expenditures be stated, and in terms of output of services.

☐ Insist on knowing what the institution is getting for its overhead.

If you insist on all of these things, it will take a program budgeting and accounting system (at least a rudimentary one) to give you the answers.

If you are persuasive or powerful enough to move the institution in this direction, one additional admonition is in order: keep it simple. Don't let the zeal of accountants and administrators for procedural order bog down the effort in mechanics.

Your reward will be the discovery that you can be in control of the institution you are responsible for, rather than the other way around.

33

Social Accounting: Measuring the Unmeasurables

GERALD H. B. ROSS*

Today's avalanche of social and environmental programmes are placing new demands on accountants. These programmes tackle society's major issues; they focus on pollution, crime, urban ghettos, drug addiction and so on, and while their costs are financial, their benefits are almost always expressed in terms of social progress.

The degree of social benefit we receive from our investment in these programmes can no longer be looked upon as an unmeasurable. While a social return is more difficult to measure than a financial return, we must ask ourselves how long we can afford to overlook the need for an accounting framework that embraces the social dimension. Decision makers must be permitted to measure the performance of their programmes against both the social and environmental criteria if they are to assess whether these funds are being used effectively.

For accountants, there is strong indication today that new kinds of accounting are required. These signs are becoming more evident with recent statements such as the following made by a bank president:

> We know we need the social cost budget as well as the conventional economic cost budget. We've taken the beginning step in asking our accountants to attempt to place detailed cost estimates on what management considers its major social responsibilities. We don't know how successful we will be, but we're certain some estimates are better than none. We're certain that they will enable us to make better business judgment and thereby avoid abrupt changes in significant programmes.[1]

Requests for such social accounting information will undoubtedly continue and will promote the extension of traditional accounting principles into new special areas. These principles can often find ready application to the problem of measurement in the social sciences.

The same concepts which accountants use in determining profits from operations, or return of capital investment, are equally applied in determining benefits received from costs incurred or

---

* From the *Canadian Chartered Accountant* (July 1971) pp. 46-54. Reprinted by permission of the Editor.
[1] A. W. Clawsen, President, Bank of America, "Notable & Quotable," *Journal of Accountancy,* (May 1971) , p. 84.

resources applied to social programmes. . . . Accounting as the discipline of measurement necessarily weaves like a thread through all social sciences.[2]

A variety of terms have been used to describe such applications of accounting; they include social accounting, socio-economic accounting, socio-environmental accounting, and so on. The formal titles do not matter; they all deal with the measurement and communication of information that relates to what people do. They are concerned with integrating the social and economic criteria in measuring the effectiveness of social programmes or assessing the social impact of environmental pollution. This is an accounting discipline that spans many skills and professions. It's an opportunity to improve the way we manage our society, not in the future, but right now when a large number of people are committed to it.

The accounting perspective has traditionally been oriented towards historical events — towards the recording of past transactions. With an eye on the past, accountants may perceive present opportunities as very distant prospects — almost as if they were being viewed through the wrong end of binoculars. Contemplation of these opportunities is then considered crystal ball gazing, and the present starts to look like the future.

By removing the binoculars and looking around, the depleted environment that has necessitated these new programmes becomes dramatically apparent. The tall buildings, congested streets, the worried faces and noxious atmosphere all come clearly into focus. It is hard to imagine what has happened to the more wholesome environment of only twenty years ago. The things that were once plentiful and taken for granted — large open spaces, abundant drinking water and invigorating air, etc. — are now scarce.

As well, many of these social or "non-proprietary" resources are no longer available for free consumption by all. Water resources, for example, constitute a basic raw material which is used up in the sense that it may not remain in its original state. It is polluted or destroyed at a cost to society at large — a social cost. The increasing scarcity of these and other resources means that they can no longer be indiscriminately consumed.

The competing demands for such resources require that they be allocated among users in some equitable manner. For "proprietary goods" — e.g. real estate, household goods, machinery, etc. — this task has traditionally been performed by the market mechanism. They are subject to ownership and, therefore, can be bought or sold. However, where society owns the resources — i.e. those that are "non-proprietary" — the market mechanisms are inadequate. Such resources as air and water do not belong to anyone in particular and cannot be marketed in the usual way.

2 David Linowes, "Social Responsibility of the Profession," *Journal of Accountancy,* (January 1971), p. 67.

Even proprietary resources may have certain characteristics which could be construed as belonging to the public. Timber, for example, can be cut and sold. However, trees produce certain social and environmental benefits which constitute part of the birthright of our nation. They produce oxygen, shelter animals, provide recreational areas, affect climate, prevent erosion and so on. These functions produce continuing benefits for the general public; but because the market mechanism usually reflects only the direct supply and demand for these resources, the interests of the second stage or indirect consumer — the public — may often be ignored.

This article will discuss the application of accounting concepts to social environmental problems. It will deal first with private corporations, government and crown corporations — their accountability to the public and the resulting implications for the accounting profession. It will then present examples of how social measurement techniques are applied.

NEW DIMENSIONS OF ACCOUNTABILITY

"Accountability" and "responsibility" go hand in hand. Corporate management, for example, is responsible to the shareholders to whom it must report. Management is thus "accountable" for its actions.

These traditional notions of accountability, however, are not easily applied to the social sphere. There is usually no obligation to report and, in many cases, there is no precedent. Furthermore, it is difficult to decide "to whom" to report and what should be reported on. New dimensions of accountability will have to be developed to accommodate these problems.

Private Corporations and the Unregistered Shareholders

Businesses are becoming increasingly vulnerable to the social feedback that results from their own actions. Public pressure is exerted on them through news media, consumer agencies, environmental groups, government agencies or by the public at large; such feedback is directed at corporations which are perceived as being socially irresponsible. In fact, this pressure is often translated into some form of remedial legislation. Dishonest advertising, desecration of natural recreation areas, faulty product design and unfair labour practices no longer escape the public eye.

The consumer and the public constitute perhaps a new class of shareholders who do not own the physical and financial assets of the company but have a stake in the social or non-proprietary resources like air and water which are often used as raw materials. Just as the traditional shareholders review the financial results, these other 'electorates' scrutinize the social operating results of the company.

There is a growing public awareness that business has created many of the central problems through its application of technology and its other private decision making. . . . At the same time people are realizing that for some problems, such as cleaning up pollution and providing jobs, business holds solutions in its own hands. Add to this the unanticipated role of television in amplifying this awareness . . . and people are goaded into action.[3]

This growing public awareness of our deteriorating environment has brought increased pressure to bear on the private sector to initiate and participate in social and environmental programmes. These include programmes for hiring the underprivileged, promoting community development, controlling pollution and so on. In fact, a number of corporations have recently implied that their primary objective is to serve society. Dividends to shareholders are possibly considered as an expense of the capital required to run the business. In a recent issue of *The Wall Street Journal* one company president put it this way:

> Maximum financial gain, the historical number one objective of American business, must in these times move into second place — whenever it conflicts with the well-being of society.[4]

These changing dimensions of the modern corporation may have a profound effect on accounting. Businesses are finding it increasingly profitable to recognize and account for social costs and benefits; this is especially the case with companies that directly feel the social feedback from their own operations. They are beginning to recognize that long-term profitability is only possible if corporations are socially responsible.

By the very nature of their operations, some industries are more exposed to this kind of feedback. Urban development, for example, is an industry which is particularly susceptible to public reaction — so much so that it can profoundly affect our ability to survive. Major downtown and urban renewal projects have a profound social impact on the surrounding community. Historically, however, urban development has occurred on a piecemeal basis. Patterns of urban growth have been the result of independent actions by many individual landowners and developers. The impact of the single proprietor was, of course, of only minor significance to the community — the single property owner has had very little control over the whole urban environment.

This is not the case today. Urban development is proceeding on a much larger scale and now involves the assembling of many individual parcels of land so as to build large, integrated complexes that combine offices, housing, shopping facilities, hotels and so on.

Developments of such magnitude have given rise to new and different social and environmental questions. They result invariably in high-density life-styles, and new landmarks on the urban landscape. When poorly designed, it is difficult to hide such monstrosities by a few shrubs or trees. Furthermore, these developments compound the problems

3 Hazel Henderson, "Should Business Tackle Society's Problems," *Harvard Business Review*, (July/August 1968), p. 80.
4 President of Gulf Oil Corporation in *The Wall Street Journal*, (March 22, 1971), p. 1.

of municipal servicing with regard to transportation access, police, fire protection and school facilities.

Fortunately, our local governments have the means to control or lessen the impact where the developers require the modification of certain municipal by-laws or the granting of other concessions, such as rezoning, to accommodate higher densities or multiple land use and, possibly, the relocation of streets and municipal utilities. Such concessions often result in extensive bargaining sessions where the developers try to justify their scheme to the planners and politicians — the latter, of course, are the custodians of the public interest. Most of these discussions focus on the socio-environmental impact of these projects. In fact, it is not uncommon for negotiations to involve public hearings at which the community may attempt to block such a development.

Certain forward-looking developers are now searching for better ways to evaluate the social impact of their projects in the hope of strengthening their position in the negotiations that are so critical to the success of their proposals.

Many major projects have been abandoned because of costly time delays or the complete breakdown of negotiations. These failures are often caused by lack of useful information and understanding in regard to the socio-environmental implications of the projects.

The availability of more appropriate methods of evaluation is equally important to municipalities since an unpopular development proposal may prove to be an economic and social white elephant. Quite naturally, municipalities are anxious to collect the increased tax revenues that are anticipated, and may pay only cursory attention to the social impact of the new development. Moreover, the prospect of immediate financial gain may be far outweighed by a consideration of the expenditures necessary to reduce the resulting social costs. For example, new transportation facilities may be required to relieve the increased congestion; changes in police and fire protection may be required, and thought must be given to parks and playgrounds to accommodate the need for open space. In such situations, a thorough and objective appreciation of the social impact would help make the negotiations more rational and beneficial to all parties.

Urban developers are only one of many private enterprises which can be seriously affected by social feedback from the public or their government representatives. The predicament of urban developers is particularly acute, since their projects are marketed on the basis of their favourable social impact. However, numerous other industries are equally concerned with the social dimensions of their actions. Today's public is better informed and better organized to express its collective opinion. Such expression includes extensive political lobbying, massive public demonstrations, and confrontation tactics by such groups as Nader's Raiders.

To stem the tide of public pressure as well as government intervention, corporations will have to exhibit considerable initiative:

A co-ordinated voluntary effort by business could limit the extent of government's intervention. Pending the development of long-range conservation programmes on a national scale, business organizations can initiate and sponsor industry-wide studies of pollution control and abatement, and they can contribute financial support to academic studies of conservation and environmental conditions.[5]

As companies become more aware of their social responsibilities, their obligations to shareholders and the community, they will require a form of social accounting information that satisfies their decision-making process as well as their external reporting and accountability.

Government—Reporting to the Taxpayers

The escalating role of government as an agent of social policy and as a major consumer in the economy has necessitated a new type of accountability to the tax-paying public. In fact, the rights of the taxpayer might be compared to those of the corporation shareholder: each is making a cash investment in the hopes of receiving a return. While the shareholder expects a monetary return, the taxpayer may receive part of his return in the form of social or intangible benefits. The latter involves primarily social or environmental improvement as translated into aesthetics, hygiene, security, etc. If the analogy is carried further, we might consider Parliament — our elected representatives — as the board of directors and government agencies or departments as on-going management. The responsibilities they have assumed require that appropriate forms of accountability be continually developed. This might be accomplished with a little ingenuity on the part of accountants.

> To plan, organize and supervise any group of people an information system is required. The information system of a business organization has been the responsibility of the accountant. This system requires measurement, communication and attestation of data. The members of the accounting profession are educated, trained and disciplined to execute these functions. With little fresh effort, the CPA can apply his expertise to improving the efficiency and controls of non-business, social institutions.[6]

The over-all progress of the nation is measured by one system of accounting and related information. While such figures as gross national product and national income are not intended to be a measure of our quality of life, they are supposed to reflect to some degree how the well-being of our nation has progressed. Unfortunately, however, our present system of national accounting does an inadequate job of reflecting the improvement or deterioration in our quality of life — more specifically, the social costs and benefits of economic growth. The accounts include

5 Edmund S. Boe, "Environmental Management: The Role of the CPA," *The Journal of Accountancy,* (November 1970) , p. 82.
6 David Linowes, *op. cit.,* p. 67.

the total income and expenditures for the nation, and as such fulfil a function similar to the financial statements of a private enterprise; but they summarize only the economic and financial aspects of the year's activities, and do not encompass the social effects. The benefits of capital appreciation or increased liabilities for such elements as congestion, smog, crime, health, declining outdoor recreational opportunities or others that directly relate to the quality of life are excluded. If we are to have an informative system of national accounting — one that gives us an adequate measure of progress — it must include these new factors.

If our society is to assess properly the effectiveness with which its government — the elected representatives — perform their job and fulfil their increasing responsibilities, it will require a vastly improved national accounting and reporting system.

Similarly, the social performance of individual government agencies and departments must be measured. A flood of socio-economic data — including price indices, the number of new housing starts, unemployment levels, and so on — is currently produced to help evaluate the exploding number of new social programmes. Unfortunately, however, this information is scattered and there are no uniform standards for measurement and reporting. The taxpayer, as a shareholder in the national economy, is entitled to information indicating the effectiveness of these various programmes. It is up to the accountant to work with other disciplines to provide that information.

Crown Corporations—The "Uncorporations"

A crown corporation is a hybrid — a cross between a government agency and a private corporation. While it may have specific social objectives, it usually attempts to retain a corporate organizational structure and image.

The responsibility of crown corporations to the public is more direct than that of private industries. Not only do they have explicit social objectives, but many enjoy special monopolies or other market advantages through government legislation. Because these special privileges are generally granted in the public interest, the success that crown corporations have in meeting their social objectives must be assessed for both internal and external reporting purposes.

The Cape Breton Development Corporation is an interesting example of a crown corporation established with social objectives in mind. The preamble to the Act of Incorporation notes the "substantial dependence of the people of Sydney and the surrounding area and of the economy of the Island of Cape Breton on the coal-mining operations", and it states that any phasing out of these operations must "take into account progress in providing employment outside the coal-producing industry and in broadening the base of the Island's economy." The Act further elaborates that the Federal and Provincial Governments, if shut-down or production cut-backs occur, should "reduce as far as possible any unemployment or economic hardship that can be expected to result."

The proposed Canada Development Corporation is possibly another example of a public enterprise which is expected to provide social as well as economic benefits. It is intended as a vehicle for retaining Canadian ownership of industry, as well as providing a greater segment of the public with the opportunity for equity participation in Canadian industry. These are both social and economic objectives. If the programmes initiated are to be evaluated in both social and financial terms, the corporate accounting framework will have to accommodate these two dimensions.

The explicit social objectives of many crown corporations make social accountability especially necessary. While private enterprise may be socially motivated because of self-interest — through the desire of long-term survival — the public enterprise has an explicit duty to fulfil its social responsibilities. Decision making must not be oriented towards financial profitability and the public interest. This has already been implicitly recognized and, in fact, government subsidies are often used to produce social benefits in face of financial losses. A case in point is the transportation field where unprofitable railway lines are subsidized in order to generate social benefits. However, objective measurements must be made if the social and economic benefits are to be properly weighed. New forms of accountability are already being developed, as illustrated in the Kootenay Lake fishing study described later in this article.

APPLICATIONS OF SOCIAL ACCOUNTING CONCEPTS

This section will present two examples of how accounting techniques can be applied to social problems. The first deals with an actual study involving social measurement of the recreational benefits of sports fishing; the second describes some of the accounting problems of recording and reporting pollution indices. These examples illustrate some accounting concepts and techniques that are applicable to these and many other social phenomena, and indicate that social accounting is not merely a textbook subject.

A Case Study Measuring Recreational Benefits

A study was commissioned to measure in monetary terms the social value of this recreational activity. A financial cost-benefit analysis indicated that the project should be built, but did not tell the whole story. The social benefits were thus quantified in an effort to correct this deficiency.

The study noted that there were two types of social benefits from sports fishing:

1. Benefits from external users. Fishermen from outside the region naturally spent money which stimulated the local economy. This component was measured using questionnaires on spending habits in conjunction with conventional economic multipliers. However, this was the simpler part of the analysis.

2. Benefits to local inhabitants. The measurement of the enjoyment of fishing on the part of local fishermen was performed by using the theory of indifference curves. This approach involved valuing the sports fishing by use of a questionnaire; it determined how much the fisherman would relate this dollar amount to the monetary costs and non-monetary benefits or enjoyment received from alternative recreational activities. Thus, a trade-off point from other recreational opportunities was identified; in this case, a family would have to be paid on the average $135 per annum to neutralize their desire for fishing.

This information enabled the social costs of the project to be presented. Intuitively, it was well known that fishing was beneficial; but the systematic measurement of this activity meant that it could be related to the financial cost-benefit analysis.

Accounting Problems with Indices

The peculiar problem with social indices, from the point of view of accountability, is that they usually describe complex and even abstract phenomena as a single figure. This presents much the same hazards as reporting the financial results of a large conglomerate in a single net income figure without disclosing further information on, for example, net income by type of industry, product line, etc. When activities must be summarized and presented with a small number of relevant figures, the accountants' skills can surely be of considerable use.

Let us for a moment delve into the complexities of a pollution index. Much as financial records are subject to differing interpretations, pollution indices can be manipulated to reflect a variety of conditions. The identification of relevant pollutants, the determination of maximum and permissible dosages, and the frequency and location of measurements, all can profoundly affect the index and how it is reported. These are, of course, interdisciplinary problems, but accountants should be part of the team. (Some of the accounting problems involved are indicated in the appendix to this article.)

An example of the kind of index reporting that can be misleading would occur when two major Canadian cities applied different bases for calculating their pollution indices — one using a measure of particular matter (dust, dirt and other light materials) and the other using a sulphur-dioxide index. The pollution index in one city might thus appear to be more favourable by virtue of its composition; but neither index would be wholly inaccurate, since each would measure significant pollution.

Pollution indices may be a common statistic of vital importance, but their use can present problems of "accountability." The questions of reliable measurement and consistent reporting become important if the information is to have sufficient credibility. The public is entitled to accurate pollution indices as a measure of effectiveness in dealing with this problem.

While the reporting of pollution counts normally relates to the present or the recent past, some forecasts of expected pollution levels might be very useful. Citizens who are particularly affected by pollution — for example, those with respiratory ailments — could be warned in advance to take some action to avoid the discomfort or danger of heavy air pollution. Furthermore, urban authorities could institute such preventive emergency measures as temporarily closing in advance the appropriate industrial plants or restricting automobile access to downtown areas.

These might be supplemented by "pollution maps" which would identify major sources of pollution in a particular metropolitan area. Such information would indicate to the public the major generators and recipients of pollution.

Pollution is by no means the only process that is subject to index measurement. A variety of social indices have become increasingly common and may soon seem to cover almost all aspects of the quality of life. Crime, traffic congestion, noise and other social phenomena all require objective measurement that is accompanied by adequate recording and reporting standards. The design of these standards is essential for the protection of the public. When the results of these measurements are reported, disclosure could usefully be made of the index components included, the basis of calculation — including what is meant by "permissible" and "danger" levels — and a comparison to indices of prior periods. This would help ensure that the interest of the public was safeguarded and that confidence would be placed in such information.

Accountants must take the initiative, however, if this kind of accounting is to develop. The public is largely unaware of the problems of reporting such significant social information. People inherently place faith in figures that are presented to them.

CONCLUSIONS

The social, economic and technological forces that are evident in North America and throughout the world are dictating the need for new kinds of roles for the major professions. Accountancy, as one of their number, must be prepared to help meet these challenges.

This article has touched on only a few of the social and environmental forces that give rise to new and different applications for accounting concepts. The flood of statistical data that has accompanied our growing number of social programmes will have to be converted into useful information if today's institutions are to effectively manage their social dimensions. The social costs and benefits will have to be properly assessed in the decision-making process.

Accountants have already confronted problems of measurement and valuation. In financial accounting there is a wide variety of cost and value concepts which are appropriate for different kinds of decisions. These include historical costs, liquidation values, replacement costs, appraisal values and so on. None of these can be considered a "true and correct" value, but each is appropriate for different decision making purposes. Accountants have long addressed themselves to the intricacies of these different valuations, and have designed criteria to indicate which is most informative in certain instances. For example, the liquidation value would not be used where the entity is a "going concern" — this would certainly be misleading!

In social accounting, similar kinds of problems are encountered. For example, the social equivalent of replacement cost might be the cost of rectifying a particular situation — e.g. restoring the environment. With a downtown development, it might involve the cost of providing green space or comparable access facility equivalent to that which previously existed. With urban renewal projects, it might include the cost of relocating displaced families. And with industrial pollution it might be the cost of installing pollution abatement equipment. The social equivalent of "market value" might be measured using indifference curves. In the Kootenay Lake study, the value of fishing was related to the enjoyment received from alternative pursuits and commodities.

The problems of measurement and valuation are a labyrinth to the unitiated. Accountants are already familiar with many of the pitfalls and cul-de-sacs, but they have been able to find their way through — at least in financial matters. They are in a position to pilot social scientists through the staggering complexities of social measurements. This will take some ingenuity and, above all, courage. The waters are as yet unchartered but there is a great deal that can be done using existing accounting concepts — as was mentioned in the case of pollution indices.

Social accounting will probably never be an exact science. However, society faces monstrous problems which cannot be ignored. They will inevitably involve some sort of measurement — no matter how imprecise. Yet we must not let the desire for precision become the blinders that will hide opportunities around us. As John Maynard Keynes warned of accountants: "It is better to be vaguely right than precisely wrong."

APPENDIX

Accounting Problems with Indices

1. What constitutes a pollutant?

While sulphur dioxide and carbon monoxide are two pollutants which are very much in the public eye, other substances which are less well understood may be equally injurious — e.g., lead from gasoline additives and asbestos from automotive mufflers. Should these be included in the indices? The accountant should ensure that disclosure is made of the designated pollutants that are included, as well as those excluded from the index and whether or not such omissions are material — i.e., would they make the index look more or less favourable.

2. What is a maximum permissible level of pollution?

Once again, this is a problem of the consistent application of criteria as established by qualified scientists. Should a maximum permissible dose have people dropping to their knees on the pavement? Should it constitute a life-span shortened by three years? Would ten years be more reasonable? The accountant has a vital role to play in ensuring that adequate criteria are established and that measurements are consistently reported against these criteria.

3. How should pollution be measured?

Once the pollutants and their permissible levels have been identified, the problem arises of how they should be measured. Is it more appropriate to take measurements from high buildings or from street corners where people are walking? Should they be taken downtown, in the suburbs or be some sort of average of the two? The accountant can be effective here in aiding scientists to establish an informative measurement of pollution levels — one that best reflects public exposure and communicates an honest measurement of the situation.

4. Which media should be used to present the indices and how frequently should they be produced?

Accountants have already turned their attention to the "relevance" of reporting periods and in the area of financial reporting generally have used the fiscal quarter and year end. With pollution, however, annual figures are probably not the most informative. Some possible reporting periods which might be relevant for different purposes include:

- *Hourly.* Peak-hour pollution indices are particularly important since a large segment of the population receives most of its exposure at these times. It is a particularly relevant index for those who must suffer through peak-hour traffic. Furthermore, the human organism can withstand inordinately high dosages for short periods. This means that there are different "permissible" and "danger" levels for short intervals than for longer periods.

- *Daily.* A reporting of the average pollution levels for the day is of use to citizens in deciding whether or not to go downtown shopping — or even to work. This is especially informative for those who have respiratory problems or are otherwise sensitive to pollution levels.

- *Monthly.* These are important as measures of progress for anti-pollution programmes. They are also useful for assessing seasonal variations in pollution levels. At certain times of the year, it may be necessary to have more stringent standards than at others.

- *Annual.* This information is extremely useful when examining long-term trends in pollution levels. While monthly figures indicate whether or not we are winning the "battles," the annual figures tell us whether or not we are winning the "war."

Questions

I INTRODUCTION AND OVERVIEW

RCA After the Bath

1-1 The author states that RCA shifted from an engineering emphasis to a product planning and marketing emphasis under Robert Sarnoff. What broad changes might be advisable in the company's accounting control system as a result of such a shift?

1-2 "At that moment RCA was in trouble, but few people knew it. Extraordinary profits from television obscured basic weaknesses. . . . Profits from the sale of color TV sets were about to hit a peak and slide down a long slope. . . ." (p. 8)

Required:
Which accounting techniques, if any, may have been helpful in focusing on the magnitude of the coming problem for RCA?

1-3 In order to offset declining profits in color TV, RCA made a sizeable investment in computers.

Required:
(a) What role might accounting have played in the decision, and in the monitoring of subsequent effects?
(b) According to the article how was the decision to enter computers made?

1-4 "RCA felt the impact more acutely than other companies because its liberal accounting and financial practices, which had lessened

losses in good years, exposed it to greater losses in the downturn."
(p. 12)

Required:

Explain the quotation.

1-5   "I hadn't seen what was happening. The group financial staff
hadn't seen it. The corporate financial staff hadn't seen it. The
outside accountants who were in our skivvies hadn't seen it. The
trouble was they were all used to seeing a cash sales business."
(p. 13)

Required:

What was happening? Why hadn't they seen it, and what could
have been done to improve insight?

1-6   "The increased payments, if they materialize, would lower the
amount of RCA's computer write-off, but they would not, under
the company's accounting system, increase reported earnings".
(p. 15)

Required:

Critically evaluate all parts of the quotation.

Harold Geneen's Moneymaking Machine Is Still Humming

2-1   The article refers to ITT's "unique" controller relationships under
which the chief financial officer in each operating unit reports to
ITT's controller but is also charged with keeping the chief
executive officer of the operating unit informed.

Required:

Outline the   strengths and weaknesses of the system in a divisionalized company.

2-2   ". . . not much earnings data has been available for the companies acquired, particularly after their disappearance into ITT."
(p. 20)

Required:

List the arguments in favor and against additional disclosure by
"divisions" from the viewpoint of stockholders.

2-3   ". . . there seems to be almost no one on Wall Street . . . who
does not believe the company is 'managing' or 'smoothing' its
earnings . . ." (p. 22)

Required:

Explain the term "smoothing" and explain the implications of
such a tactic for users of the resulting accounting information.

2-4   "Hartford's portfolio wealth has also been finding its way into
ITT's net income, though in a highly controversial way." (p. 25)

Required:

Explain the quotation and some implications.

Framework for Analysis

3-1   Anthony states that mistakes are made when generalizations valid for one subsystem of planning and control systems are applied to another subsystem.

Required:

Explain, and illustrate, Anthony's point.

3-2   List and explain some important characteristics of a management control system.

3-3   Distinguish among the following terms: strategic planning; management control; technical control.

Budgetary Control and Business Behaviour

4-1   The authors give some "guidelines . . . indicative of good budgeting practice." Are there any references in the ITT and RCA articles to good or bad "budgeting practice" as that term is used by Buckley and McKenna.

4-2   ". . . it is doubtful whether the concept of profit maximization is relevant to any but the most entrepreneurial of businesses." (p. 45)

Required:

Assume, for the sake of debate, that the quotation is a valid observation. What are the implications for management accountants? (i.e., are some management accounting techniques invalid in other than settings of profit maximization?)

4-3   ". . . performance is clearly of essence in giving salary and promotion rewards. But in making these assessments of how well managers have performed it may be wise to leave the budget outside the appraisal." (p. 65)

Required:

If, as the authors suggest, budgets can be potentially harmful in performance evaluation, of what use to management are they? What criteria should be employed in performance appraisal?

4-4   Briefly summarize the views of the authors on how employees react to budgets.

Behavioral Assumptions of Management Accounting

5-1   What are the principal differences between traditional and modern organizational behavior?

5-2   If businesses (through their participants) "satisfice" rather than "maximize", does this mean that many of the techniques of management accounting are worthless?

5-3   Explain what you think the principal objectives of management accounting are.

5-4   What are Caplan's main themes?

5-5   "If the modern organization theory model does ultimately prove to be a more realistic view of human behavior in business organizations, there is little doubt that the scope of management accounting theory and practice will need to be expanded and broadened." (p. 85)

Required:

What expansion and broadening would be necessary?

II   REPORTING ISSUES

A Shareholder's Perspective on External Accounting Reports

6-1   ". . . given human behaviour, the ground rules are set up improperly. . . ." ". . . this situation where management is in control, not only of the assets of the organization, but also of the system that reports their use or misuse of these assets is clearly unsatisfactory." (pp. 96, 95)

Required:

(a) What implications of the foregoing are identified by the author.

(b) What reporting systems other than the one noted by the author in the aforementioned quotation could be employed to overcome the "unsatisfactory" state.

6-2   "My hypothesis is that the auditor is just not sufficiently independent to overcome the power position of management." (p. 97)

Required:

Do you agree with the quotation?
Why?

6-3   " '. . . if you can imagine that in wrestling with the choice of depreciation methods the minds of those involved in the decision were ever troubled by the question of which approach resulted in the fairer presentation of performance, you have a more lively imagination than have I'." (p. 98)

Required:

To what extent is the difficulty mentioned in the quotation likely to be an important characteristic of management accounting procedures?

The Fine Print at Ampex

7-1 Compare and contrast the position taken by Ampex in its 1971 annual report with the accounting problems described in "RCA After the Bath".

7-2 "We asked ourselves: Are we just splitting hairs?" (p. 104)

Required:
(a) Do you agree with the conclusion reached by the author of the quotation?
Why?
(b) Would the problem described also likely occur in management accounting reporting systems?

7-3 "Judgment, we said to ourselves as we put down the telephone. Management's judgment". (p. 107)

Required:
Briefly outline the role of management's judgment in both financial and managerial accounting.

The Direct Costing Controversy—An Identification of Issues

8-1 "The abandonment of the historical cost basis would render direct costing just as obsolete as the alternative full costing."

Required:
Explain the quotation.

8-2 "Probably the most fundamental point of controversy between variable and full costing is the question of whether fixed manufacturing costs are costs of the product produced or of the period in which they are incurred."

Required:
Outline the arguments supporting each side of the controversy.

8-3 ". . . whether variable costing ever achieves general acceptance will depend primarily upon whether it comes to be regarded generally as useful in external reports (and, to be realistic, upon its acceptance for federal income tax reports also)."

Required:
What are the uses of variable costing to external groups?

Elements of Price Variation Accounting

9-1 Explain the significance of Chambers' definition of "financial state or position" to the method of measurement he advocates.

9-2 "If we ever have to work out our personal financial affairs . . . we all reckon . . . in terms of the selling prices of what we own."

Required:

Do you agree?

9-3 Summarize what Chambers has demonstrated in his series of "cases."

Continuously Contemporary Accounting

10-1 "We claim that a variety of accounting which we have called continuously contemporary accounting meets all these requirements as far as they can be met." (p. 129)

Required:

(a) List Chambers' "requirements" or "criteria."

(b) Do you agree with the quotation?

10-2 "If the resale price of a machine falls in a period through its use and obsolescence, the amount of the fall is the depreciation."

Required:

Critically evaluate the foregoing definition of depreciation.

10-3 "It is not the intention of the system to predict with a high degree of accuracy what would be obtained if any good were sold."

Required:

What *is* the intention of the system?

10-4 Why does Chambers introduce an element of price level restatements into his system?

III CORE ACCOUNTING TECHNIQUES AND MANAGEMENT EVALUATIONS

Management Misinformation Systems

11-1 According to the author what is the most important information deficiency which managers suffer from? What are the effects of this deficiency, and what does the author recommend to overcome the problem?

11-2 Do Ackoff and Vatter appear to be in substantial agreement on the relationship of the information provider (e.g., accountant or operations researcher) to the manager? Explain, and state whether or not you agree with the stated position of each author.

11-3 What are the five common "errors" made by designers of management information systems? Explain in detail.

The Chop Suey Caper

12-1 Speculate on why the author is "not all that fond of chop suey."

12-2 What reply would you give to Hobb's assertion that: "You cost men are supposed to know how to allocate costs."

12-3 Summarize the author's theme about the railroad cost controversy.

Matrix Theory and Cost Allocation

13-1 Explain the significance of the following quotation: " . . . processes of cost allocation and expense distribution . . . assume the validity of cost divisibility and recombination."

13-2 List some management accounting techniques described in your principal textbook which might be simplified by using mathematical procedures such as that illustrated in this article.

The Fable of the Accountant and the President

14-1 The Fable employs the term "contribution margin" in Act III. Do you agree with this usage?

14-2 Explain the trick mentioned in Act III.

14-3 What price should the Board set to sell off excess inventory? Explain your logic fully.

14-4 What is the moral of the story?

Cost Concepts for Control

15-1 Explain the author's reasoning underlying this statement: "We eventually concluded that an attempt to find objective means of differentiating among the various control systems in current use was not feasible. . . . "

15-2 Explain the significance of the following quotation to the conclusions reached in the article: " . . . not everyone is motivated identically by the same stimulus. That this is so is undeniable. Nevertheless, there must be some common patterns of human behavior that apply to large numbers of people."

15-3 In which respects would Anthony's views agree with those expressed by Vatter and Ackoff?

Tailor-making Cost Data for Specific Uses

16-1 " . . . in our zeal to get the one true and simple answer we frequently overlook the real nature of the problem." (p. 194)

Required:
Relate the above quotation to management accounting.

16-2 (a) Do you agree with all parts of the following quotation? "It is not enough to present all of the data, leaving the interpretations to the readers of the reports. The responsibility of the cost accountant is to learn the uses to be made of his cost data . . . and to see that relevant and irrelevant data are handled properly."

(b) Would Ackoff agree with all parts of the quotation in (a)?

16-3   To what extent would Vatter's main theme be appropriate in a financial accounting (external reporting) course?

Towards Probabilistic Profit Budgets

17-1   Briefly describe the three methods of constructing probabilistic profit budgets illustrated in the article.

17-2   What are the similarities and differences among fixed budgets, flexible budgets and probabilistic budgets?

17-3   Which management evaluations are likely to be aided by probabilistic budgets? Explain carefully, bringing relevant environmental conditions into your response.

An Application of Curvilinear Break-even Analysis

18-1   Why are there two break-even points in the situation illustrated?

18-2   Is it possible to have more than one point where the slope of the revenue curve equals the slope of the cost curve? If so, how might the point of maximum profit be ascertained?

Profit Centers, Transfer Prices and Mysticism

19-1   Summarize the author's theme as reflected in his comment: "A good deal of accounting, as currently practised, has a mystical quality."

19-2   According to the author, which management evaluations, as noted in Section I of this book, require the use of transfer prices when goods are switched between divisions of a decentralized company.

IV   PERFORMANCE EVALUATION

What Kind of Management Control Do You Need?

20-1   To what extent is ITT (see Article 2) following the author's control recommendations?

20-2   Explain the following quotation: "The matrix form of organization may be appropriate when much interaction between the functions is necessary or desirable." (p. 254)

20-3   Explain and illustrate this quotation: "The most difficult compromises that must be made in designing a management control system have to do with varying goals." (p. 243)

Responsibility Accounting

21-1 In which respects would the author agree with other writers such as Vancil, Anthony and Vatter?

21-2 Critically evaluate the following quotation: "There are three major objectives of cost accounting in manufacturing companies: (1) cost control; (2) product cost; and (3) inventory pricing."

21-3 Briefly illustrate and describe how "responsibility accounting" operates.

Control and Freedom in a Decentralized Company

22-1 Review several behavioral articles in this book (for example, Buckley and McKenna, Caplan, Ridgway, and Villers) and comment on the following quotation: " . . . a decade or so of intensive research in human relations shows with equal conclusiveness that our large organizations and our methods of planning and control are, more often than not, antagonistic to good human relations."

22-2 What control concept does the author advocate to help overcome the difficulty mentioned in the quotation in 22-1?

22-3 Discuss the meaning and significance of the following quotation: " . . . control is not by itself a hindrance to individual freedom. Rather, control is in fact a prerequisite to decentralization, and without decentralization there can be no real freedom."

22-4 Examine the facts about the Hart Manufacturing Company and Richards' problem with part 1234. Do you agree with the position taken by the arbitrator, Villers? Explain.

Dysfunctional Consequences of Performance Measurements

23-1 What might Anthony ("Cost Concepts for Control") say about Ridgway's comment that "Quantitative performance measurements — whether single, multiple, or composite — are seen to have undesirable consequences for over-all organizational performance"?

23-2 Distinguish among the terms single, multiple and composite, and explain why each measure might have undesired side effects.

Budgeting and Employee Behavior: A Rejoinder to a "Reply"

24-1 Summarize the authors' "if-then" clauses about the relationships between participation in setting budgets and better morale and increased initiative.

24-2   Compare the authors' views to the recommendations or conclusions listed in the article by Buckley and McKenna.

The Asset Value of the Human Organization

25-1   List some possible drawbacks to human asset accounting from the employee's point of view.

25-2   Briefly describe some methods of determining the "value" of human assets.

Where "Human Resources Accounting" Stands Today

26-1   List some arguments for and against human resources accounting in external financial statements. (In your response set out your view of the main purpose of external reporting.)

26-2   Critically evaluate the R. G. Barry Corporation approach to human resources accounting from the account given in the article.

26-3   Speculate on the (future) prospects for human resources accounting.

V   PRICING, OUTPUT AND INVESTMENT DECISIONS

Management's Pricing Decision

27-1   Compare and contrast the roles of direct costing and contribution margin analysis in pricing decisions.

27-2   Critically evaluate the following quotation: "Absorption costing results in the setting of a price, and direct costing results in determining whether a firm should accept a price."

27-3   Summarize the author's main themes.

Product Contribution Analysis for Multi-Product Pricing

28-1   Explain the following quotation concerning the role of accounting techniques in pricing decisions: "The product life cycle . . . consists of the following stages: development, introduction, growth, maturity, decline, and phase-out. For pricing decision purposes it is also important to recognize management's objectives during any given stage."

28-2   Explain this quotation: "What is really significant in a pricing decision is neither cost nor price but rather the present value of the contribution that the product makes toward the recovery of period costs and profit over each product's life cycle."

28-3   State the significance to management accountants of the following quotation: " . . . management's objectives will dictate which ranking is most significant. That is, if the short-run objective is to raise revenue, the revenue ranking will be important. If the management wishes to increase earnings per share, however, the contribution ranking would be more significant. In either case, the reliance on one at the sacrifice of the other would be detrimental to the firm."

Use of Sensitivity Analysis in Capital Budgeting

29-1   What are the benefits and limitations of sensitivity analysis in investment decisions?

29-2   Compare break-even analysis with sensitivity analysis as an aid in investment decisions.

Anyone for Widgets?

30-1   Compare and contrast the theme of this article with the themes of "The Fable of the Accountant and the President," "Management's Pricing Decision," and "The Direct Costing Controversy — An Identification of Issues."

30-2   In which respects would the author's views about "tight" standards draw criticism from the behavioral scientists and authors such as Villers and Higgins?

30-3   Do you agree with the authors' views on the "tightness" of standards? If so, for which decisions/evaluations mentioned in Exhibit III - I? (pp. 143-145)

Cost-Volume-Profit Analysis Under Conditions of Uncertainty

31-1   Of what importance is a firm's attitude to risk for output and investment decisions which are aided by cost-volume-profit techniques?

31-2   Discussions of cost-volume-profit analysis in most textbooks are usually accompanied by a long list of limitations or cautions to be borne in mind. What list of cautions should accompany the concepts illustrated in this article?

VI   SOME EXTENSIONS

Program Budgeting Works in Nonprofit Institutions

32-1   What is meant by the term "program budgeting", and in which evaluations may it be of help? (See Exhibit III - 1.)

32-2   Explain the latter part of the following quotation: "The most compelling reason for undertaking the effort of cost accounting is the chance to get paid for what one does. In profit-making enterprises this incentive is obvious. In nonprofit institutions it is becoming obvious. . . . "

32-3 Briefly describe how the program budgeting/costing system at the South Shore Mental Health Center "works."

32-4 Explain (and elaborate on) the following quotation from the article: "Program cost accounting has opened up some promising lines of thought that have yet to be explored."

Social Accounting: Measuring the Unmeasurables?

33-1 What role, if any, did accounting play in the Kootenay Lake fishing study?

33-2 What arguments does the author raise in favor of including accountants on a team which is concerned with measuring social costs?

33-3 Do you agree with the following comment by the author? "Accountants have long addressed themselves to the intricacies of these different valuations, and have designed criteria to indicate which is most informative in certain instances." (p. 398)